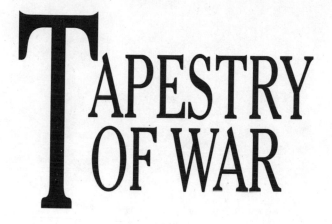

TAPESTRY OF WAR

TAPESTRY OF WAR

A PRIVATE VIEW OF CANADIANS
IN THE GREAT WAR

SANDRA GWYN

HarperCollins*Publishers*Ltd

First Edition

Canadian Cataloguing in Publication Data

Gwyn, Sandra
    Tapestry of war: a private view of Canadians in the Great War

ISBN 0-00-215787-X

1. Canada — History — 1914-1918.* 2. Canada — History — 1914-1918 — Biography.* 3. World War, 1914-1918 — Canada. 4. World War, 1914-1918 — Biography. 5. Canada — Biography. I. Title.

FC557.G89 1992   971.061'2   C92-094495-7
F1034.G89 1992

92 93 94 95 96 97 98 99 ❖ HC 9 8 7 6 5 4 3 2 1

This book is for Richard,
without whom it would never have happened.

Contents

Courcelette; Agar Adamson remarks on the first use of tanks; Adamson becomes commanding officer of the Patricias.

Acknowledgements

The fact that this book exists and was not consigned to the wastebasket approximately when I arrived at chapter eight and began to realize that in writing about the Great War I was venturing into territory for which nothing in my experience had prepared me, I owe to my husband Richard Gwyn. If the war itself has turned out to be the most important of all the characters, as one early reader of the manuscript remarked, this is because, time and again, Richard was there to set it in context for me and to bring his own understanding of the nature of warfare – some of it gleaned long ago at the Royal Military Academy, Sandhurst – to bear on the manuscript. His alchemy as in-house editor is manifest on nearly every page; for a number of important passages, setting the scene for the Somme and for Vimy and Passchendaele and the "Hundred Days," he really deserves a credit as co-author; so also for chapter eighteen, in some ways the single most important chapter in this book, in which the argument about Canada between Talbot Papineau and his cousin Henri Bourassa is explored with a rigour and a lucidity that I could not have achieved on my own. (Here, dare I say it, schooling by the Jesuits has not been unhandy.) It must also be said that during the five years I worked on this book, Richard himself was embarked on ventures outside his own earlier experience. As London-based columnist for the Toronto *Star*, he was reinventing himself as an analyst of international affairs, observing history rewriting itself as the Berlin Wall came down, Nelson Mandela was released from prison, and Desert Storm happened. Yet, coming back from his travels with great tales to tell, he never once raised an eyebrow to find the Great War still camped out in our London flat – books and papers overflowing into every room – and also in my own head to the point of obsession. Instead, with great good humour and energy he would turn his attention to unsnarling my latest problems and chivvying me out of my writer's blocks. This time, my love, it really *is* your turn; the dedication better expresses my thanks.

Many others helped in manifold ways. Pride of place goes to those who led me to some of the characters who appear here and helped make them come alive by lending me family papers. If there was a moment when *Tapestry of War* began to seem a feasible project – the difficulties of writing a book about the Canadian experience in the Great War while I myself was living in London were daunting – it came in the winter of 1987, when Anthony Adamson of Toronto, who had earlier been enormously helpful with the research for *The Private Capital*, provided me with, on long-term loan, a superbly organized set of typed copies of all the letters that his father, Agar Adamson, had written from the Front to his mother Mabel Cawthra Adamson. (The originals, and another set of typed copies, exist in the National Archives.) A year later, Anthony Adamson made me a gift of his marvellous family memoir, *Wasps in the Attic*, and, on a number of my flying visits to Toronto, amplified this with his exceptional memory. Later still, Adamson raided his attic for family photographs. He and his wife Augusta have once again been generous with their hospitality.

Diana Filer, recently retired as director of International Relations at CBC Headquarters in Ottawa, was another godparent. We first met in 1986 in London, when she was in charge of CBC's operations there; it was over dinner in a South Kensington restaurant that Diana mentioned casually that her mother, Grace MacPherson, had written diaries describing her experiences driving an ambulance in France. Before the evening was out, I was immersed in Grace's diaries and knew that she would be a character. It was also in London, at a New Year's Eve gathering ushering in 1988, that Professor Mel Watkins of the University of Toronto suggested that Harold Innis's wartime experiences might be of interest and arranged to lend me a copy of Alexander John Watson's outstanding doctoral thesis, *Marginal Man*. Later, Watkins kindly read my chapters about Innis and made a number of helpful suggestions. But my deepest thanks here go to John Watson himself, now executive director of CARE Canada in Ottawa, who has generously allowed me not only to quote extensively from *Marginal Man*, but to adopt as my own his central theme that the Great War was Innis's patron. I am grateful also to Hugh Innis for granting family permission to quote from his father's letters and diaries held at the University of Toronto Archives.

The list runs on and on, back and forth across the Atlantic. In England once again, Anthony Beckles Willson of Twickenham gave me Open Sesame to the diaries of his grandfather, Henry Beckles Willson, and provided his own gloss to this problematic figure. The playwright, Alfred Shaughnessy, kindly provided permission to use material from his memoir of his mother Sarah Shaughnessy. Over many delightful lunches and teas in her memento-filled house in St. John's Wood, Eileen Scott Morley, formerly of Ottawa (indeed, a cousin of the turn-of-the-century journalist Agnes Scott a.k.a. Amaryllis, whom some readers may recall from *The Private Capital*), reminisced about Ethel Chadwick and Blue Sea Lake and remembered a chance meeting with Agar Adamson in the late 1920s that gave me a particular insight into his fabled quality of charm.

I am also most grateful to John B. Claxton of Montreal for giving me permission to quote extensively from the unpublished memoir written by his father Brooke Claxton, and for reading my draft chapters about Claxton and correcting a number of errors. Equally, I am grateful to William Kilbourn, Professor of Humanities at York University, for sharing with me his insights into the character of Sir Max Aitken, later Lord Beaverbrook, for providing much useful material, and for reading early drafts of the chapters on Aitken and making a number of helpful suggestions.

The bulk of the research for this book was undertaken at a number of research institutions at home and abroad. At the National Archives in Ottawa, long since to me a second home, Jerry O'Brien, Brian Murphy and John Bell were particularly helpful, and, as always, the staff of the reading room were courteous and efficient. At the Canadian War Museum, Hugh Halliday, Curator of Posters and Photographs, guided me through the collection with gusto. In St. John's, Anne Hart, head of the Centre for Newfoundland Studies at Memorial University Library (also an accomplished literary sleuth as demonstrated by her intriguing studies of the life and times of Miss Jane Marple and Hercule Poirot), led me to a new and unexpected character by producing the leather-covered volume containing the letters of Owen Steele; she and the centre's archivist, Bert Riggs, were also helpful in providing photographs. I must also express my thanks to Dr. Graham Skanes, Dean of Continuing and Graduate Studies at Memorial, for bringing John Gallishaw's remarkable book, *Trenching at Gallipoli*, to my attention, and to Fred Hollingsworth of Memorial and Ed Coady of Ocean Pictures for arranging a private screening of the excellent documentary film, *Beaumont-Hamel: A Battle Remembered*.

In London, Terry Barringer, successor to the legendary Donald Simpson, as librarian at the Royal Commonwealth Society, helped me seek out much useful material. Ann House, librarian at Canada House, was equally welcoming. I must register my dismay, though, that both these research repositories have recently closed their doors: indeed the Royal Commonwealth Society Library has shut down permanently due to financial pressures, and its magnificent collection is being dispersed. At Canada House, the problem may be less acute, yet it is a matter for concern that this important source of information about Canada is currently unavailable to overseas researchers. Lastly in London, I would like to thank the staff of the House of Lords Record Office, in particular K. V. Bligh, assistant archivist, for helping me chart a course through the vast collection of Beaverbrook papers, and for granting me permission to quote a number of passages. At Oxford, I am grateful to Elizabeth Boardman, archivist at Brasenose College, for providing helpful information about Talbot Papineau's career there, along with copies of the college magazine, *The Brazen Nose,* describing British reaction to his open letter to Henri Bourassa, and containing a number of eulogies written after his death.

Special thanks go to Jacqueline DesBaillets of Montreal, formerly Jacqueline Papineau, who, although born too late to remember her Uncle Talbot, filled in several critical gaps in my knowledge of the Papineau family, and to Bill Lang, head of the Art Department at the Free Library of Philadelphia, for searching out information concerning the post-war life and career of Beatrice Fox Griffith.

I would also like to thank a number of friends and colleagues, either for having provided useful leads and nuggets of information, or for giving me constant encouragement. These include Robert Fulford, C. J. "Cy" Fox, Margaret Horsfield, Eric McLean, Brad Smith, David Silcox, Dianne Berlet, Helen O'Brien, and our friends and neighbours in London, Robin and Selina Walker. This list also includes my brothers Nicholas Fraser and Rory Harley, my sisters-in-law Jane Harley and Danielle Pavey, and, of course, my mother Ruth Harley, the bookworm.

Last but a long way from least. The best part of writing *Tapestry of War* was arriving at the final stages, and working with an exceptional group of people, most of whom were old friends from *The Private Capital*. Once again, my editor Ramsay Derry suggested all manner of ways in which the manuscript could be pruned, honed, and polished; once again, on the only substantive point over which we disagreed, he produced, at the very last moment, a lucid and elegant memo that convinced me he was right. I only wish I wrote more books more often, so that Ramsay could edit them and that the splendid Sarah Reid could copy-edit. Once again, John Lee has produced a design of distinction. To Nancy Colbert, formerly my agent and now my publisher at HarperCollins, I am grateful for great confidence and enthusiasm and infinite patience. The same applies to Linda McKnight, who, in a neat switching of roles, was once my publisher and is now my agent. I would also like to thank Iris Skeoch and Laura Krakowec of HarperCollins who have overseen the production of this book with skill, efficiency, and loving care.

One final debt remains to be discharged. This one is to the scores of authors, Canadian and otherwise, who have written about the Great War and whose insights have informed my own. Their contributions, if not identified directly in the text, are acknowledged in the source notes.

S.G.
Ottawa London Toronto
February 1987 – June 1992

Prologue:
These Years Were Their Lives

The year of this book's publication marks both the 125th anniversary of Canada's Confederation and the 75th anniversary of our victory at Vimy, mid-way through the Great War of 1914–18. I did not plan for this to happen: the work took me longer than I had anticipated. But the happenstance is fitting. Of those two rites of national passage, the latter matters far more, I've come to believe. Except as a pre-emption of a possible move northwards by the United States, the bonding together of the four colonies of British North America was of little consequence at Westminster and of no immediate consequence to the people of the new Dominion as they actually lived their lives.

Instead, it is the Great War that marks the real birth of Canada. Thrust for the first time upon the world's stage, we performed at all times creditably and often brilliantly – holding the line under gas attack at Second Ypres in 1915, capturing Vimy Ridge in 1917 and Passchendaele Ridge later the same year, performing in the vanguard in 1918 during the Hundred Days of the astonishing counter-attack that ended, abruptly, in the Armistice. As has been remarked many times, the effort of mobilizing and equipping a vast army modernized us, and our blood and our accomplishments transformed us from colony into nation. Prime Minister Borden's separate signature on the peace treaty of Versailles put the seal upon our new status; even without that symbolism, Canadians knew they had won it.

Remarked upon less often is the fact that the experiences Canadians underwent during the Great War cut the pattern for their society for roughly the next half-century. "Why is he dead? And why, when he is dead, do I remain alive? Why?" asks one of the characters in this book after watching a friend die from a random shellburst. Almost all who survived asked themselves that same, ultimate, question and then set out consciously to try to answer it by developing the kind of Canadian institutions and Canadian spirit that would serve as memorials to those who had fallen in foreign fields. The particular character who actually asked that question, Brooke Claxton, eventually found the answer he was looking for in public life, by becoming godfather to the Canada Council. Others would play the same role by setting up institutions such as the CBC and the Department of External Affairs. The best-known of the breed, Mike Pearson, transmuted his wartime experiences into a career as a peace-making diplomat, establishing an institutional and moral legacy that best defines contemporary Canada.

Nineteen ninety-two is also the seventy-fifth anniversary of the Conscription Crisis of 1917. If, while researching this book, there was any moment when I felt that the past had merged entirely into the present, it was when I was reading the extraordinary exchange of long letters, published in mid-1916, between Henri Bourassa, editor of *Le Devoir* and passionate *Canadien nationaliste,* and Captain Talbot Papineau, the fluently bilingual pan-Canadian nationalist, and realized that these could be republished today unchanged but for a few excisions and an updating of a few local references. We were divided before the war of course. But the chance existed then, as Papineau argued to Bourassa, to use the trial by ordeal we were undergoing, to "cement a foundation for a true Canadian nation." Instead, by tragic miscalculation and misunderstanding, we hardened ourselves into two solitudes.

So much for the Big Picture. This is a book about people. It recounts the Great War experiences of ten Canadians, three of them women, who left behind them in diaries and letters and personal memoirs an intimate and unguarded record of what they were doing and of what they were thinking and feeling *at the time*. These private chronicles have been amplified by other contemporary materials – newspapers, magazines, and so on – and by cullings from the many published histories and personal reminiscences of the war. The work itself is an exercise in social history, a companion piece to my first book, *The Private Capital: Ambition and Love in the Age of Macdonald and Laurier*, although not a direct sequel. Indeed, the first two characters to appear, the Ottawa belle Ethel Chadwick and the over-age soldier Agar Adamson, played minor roles in that book, and one reason I embarked upon this one was that I knew they both had far more to tell. If the exercise is successful, readers will think and feel and experience as those Canadians did three-quarters of a century ago. And if larger thoughts and might-have-beens occur in these pages, it is because my characters thought them, or sensed them, *at the time*.

The principal title, *Tapestry of War*, conveys the nature of the book. It is episodic and asymmetric, a weaving together of short and long strands. Some characters, like Ethel Chadwick and Agar Adamson, thread in and out of the narrative almost all the way through. Others, like Sir Max Aitken, better known to us as Lord Beaverbrook, or Harold Innis, then an artillery private, appear in only a couple of chapters, because they experienced the war briefly, or because they left behind comparatively little in the way of recorded experience. The settings shift constantly and cinematically, according to the movements of the characters; back and forth from the homefront in Ottawa to the trenches, to the great Canadian battles at Second Ypres, Vimy, and Passchendaele, to the headquarters and the hospitals behind the lines. The scene that reoccurs most frequently is London, where I happened to be living while putting all of this together, and which quickly became for me a city full of ghosts, the same *carpe diem* capital of wartime that it was for nearly all of my characters, as they swung their kitbags off the leave trains, or, in the case of the women, crossed the Atlantic to do war work, or to be close to husbands and sons and lovers.

These Years Were Their Lives, the title of this prologue, expresses the book's central theme. Those who experience war live during it more fully and more intensely than they ever did before, or ever will do again. Those who survive are never the same. Some emerge from it maimed, psychically or physically, others are broadened or deepened, their characters honed by the

spectrum of experiences – terror, boredom, exhilaration, camaraderie, the solitariness of command – that they have undergone.
Some, inevitably, capitalize upon the opportunities opened up by
the displacement of pre-war routines and hierarchies to advance
their careers – Beaverbrook is the prime example. What is true for
individuals is equally true for a country. Canada suffered terrible
losses during the Great War, but the country learned more and
matured faster during those years than at any other time in our
history.

In the course of the story, each individual character will introduce
himself or herself fully. It's enough to say here that they are all
prisms of history – to borrow a phrase from Barbara Tuchman –
and as happened also when I was writing *The Private Capital*, that
they became closer to me for a time than my own friends and
family. Ethel Chadwick, a young woman in her early thirties with
close links to the viceregal court at Rideau Hall, serves as principal guide to Ottawa in wartime, a hotbed of intrigue and rumour
where the Governor General, the Duke of Connaught, and the half-
mad Minister of Militia, Sam Hughes, virtually declared war upon
each other. Agar Adamson, next onto the stage, provides the
entry point to the war itself. At the age of forty-eight, he enlisted
as a captain in the Princess Patricia's Canadian Light Infantry, and
miraculously survived almost three years in the trenches, writing
letters almost daily to his wife, Mabel. She in turn had a war of her
own, initially travelling to London to be close to Agar, but then
founding a war charity, which led to her to spend much of her
time in Belgium, one of many Canadian women for whom the war
provided an opportunity for self-fulfilment, despite all its travail.
On a grander scale, Sir Max Aitken, as "Official Eyewitness" to the
troops in the field, established himself as a master propagandist
and in the process, discovered his genius for popular journalism.
Through Aitken, we meet the most bizarre character in the book,
the Canadian journalist and popular historian Beckles Willson,
who had a genius for getting himself into trouble, but also an
undeniable talent for astute observation.

Just as no one expected the war to last as long as it did, no
one anticipated its consequences. One of these was the first wave

of Canadian nationalism. Brooke Claxton, an artillery sergeant barely out of his teens, and a scion of Montreal's Anglo-Scottish ascendancy, was in the vanguard. Later, as a senior federal cabinet minister, he was the moving spirit behind the Massey Commission of the late 1940s that paved the way for the Canada Council. Then there was the Ontario farmboy Harold Innis, who served at Vimy. But for the war he would almost certainly have become a Baptist minister rather than Canada's first major economic scholar.

And there are the tantalizing, poignant might-have-beens. Handsome, charismatic, and the great-grandson of one of Quebec's greatest figures, Talbot Papineau is a Canadian tragic hero who might have stepped out of a novel. Indeed, as some readers will recognize, he appeared in semi-fictionalized form some years ago in *Willie*, Heather Robertson's *tour de force*. Ambitious and talented, Papineau possessed all the qualities needed to become Liberal leader and possibly prime minister, the natural successor to Wilfrid Laurier.

Others who appear to tell their tales are the young Vancouver secretary, Grace MacPherson, who drove ambulances in France for the British Red Cross, and the Newfoundlander, John Gallishaw, whose long-forgotten account of the fighting at Gallipoli is one of the first literary works to come out of the heat of battle. Gallishaw's compatriot in the Royal Newfoundland Regiment was Owen Steele. His letters home end abruptly on June 30, 1916, the day before he and the rest of his regiment went over the top at Beaumont-Hamel, the first day of the monstrous Battle of the Somme.

One last thought before moving ahead with the story. I am uneasily unaware that the book you are about to read contains a discordance. Of the principal characters, all but two survived the war. Among the others, only two, Ethel Chadwick and Agar Adamson became, in quite different ways, life-long war casualties. Quite a number – Beaverbrook by calculation; Innis, Claxton, and Grace MacPherson by circumstance – did well out of it. Yet the Great War cost us sixty thousand lives and tens of thousands more lives that were permanently blighted. If monumental in scale, it was the most monumentally stupid of all wars, achieving nothing more than to make certain another "great war" would succeed it.

In the descriptions of life and death in the trenches that appear in the following pages, above all in the personal accounts of two of the worst haemorrhages on the Western Front – Beaumont-Hamel and Passchendaele – is expressed the only truth about the Great War that ultimately matters, that it was a monstrous and futile Valley of Death, if also an extraordinarily heroic one. Yet the discord between the content of the war and the particular circumstances that many of my characters happened to encounter still troubles me.

Thus, as an epigraph to all that follows, let me quote some lines from a birthday poem for a fallen Canadian that I chanced upon during my research, but had no way of using because it was written neither by nor about any of the figures who appear in the book. The author was a professor of classics at McGill University named W. D. Woodhead, who was probably writing in memory of some former student. It is, I believe, the finest Canadian poem to have come out of the war, one that expresses far better than John McCrae's much more famous poem, *In Flanders Fields*, the aching reality of lives cut short and promise unfulfilled. While writing it, pain and sorrow fused into eloquence and Woodhead himself perhaps lived more intensely than in all the other years of his life.

Battle's grim dormitory this
And filled is every bed
And none may leave his place, or miss
The roll call of the dead.

Yet as I lie here silently
I think, if fate had willed,
Today I had been twenty-three
At twenty I was killed.

Oh you who love me, whom I love
Do not forget this day
Through all the years you are above
And I beneath the clay.

1
Up at Blue Sea Lake

*A month since I got here. Swam twice. North wind; wild
waves. Smelt bacon when I got up from my morning
plunge and I jolly well felt like it. Read* Paradise Lost;
*the north wind blew all day. Lovely little moon out, but
we sat indoors tonight . . .*
*. . . War is declared between Austria and Servia. Partly
the outcome, although there are other reasons, of the
assassination of the Austrian heir to the throne and his
wife by Servians.*

Ethel Chadwick. Diary entry; Monday, July 27, 1914

In the summer of 1914, Etheldreda Mary Chadwick was thirty-
two, a fashionable young Ottawa woman of literary bent who,
to her great chagrin, was still unmarried. She was keeping her
diary in a hard-backed grey exercise book stamped *Students Mss*,
of the same type that schoolchildren used for their essays. Years
later, when she was nearly ninety, almost the last one left of her
circle, she was never able to leaf through those light-hearted
entries without the stinging of tears. She remembered a vanished
Eden, a last golden idyll after which nothing would ever be as
innocent again.

At the time, of course, it was not like that at all. Up at Blue
Sea Lake, about seventy miles north of the capital in the Gatineau
Hills, it was a fairly typical holiday season, except that the
weather was exceptionally salubrious, and that Ethel's chronic
hay fever, thanks to a new treatment that she describes rather

alarmingly as "having my nostrils scarified," was troubling her much less than usual.

Then, as now, one of the best features of living in Ottawa was that it was so easy to get out of. The first two post-Confederation generations of local gentry had made their summer holidays as complicated as possible, trekking hundreds of sweaty, cindery miles in search of salt breezes, all the way to the lower St. Lawrence resorts of Murray Bay and Rivière du Loup, sometimes even as far as St. Andrews-by-the-Sea in New Brunswick. But just before the turn of the century, a new CPR railway spur, hugging the shores of the Gatineau River northwards into the Quebec wilderness, had opened up new and exciting possibilities. Blue Sea, the last frivolous stop before the train plunged on up to Maniwaki, into the real wilderness peopled mainly by lumberjacks, was (and is) one of the loveliest and most lustrous of all the lakes in the Gatineau country; more than twenty miles long, fringed with cedars and silver birches, framed by gentle, unintimidating mountains, dotted with islets and patches of waterlilies. The quality that makes Blue Sea special is the shimmering, Caribbean-like translucence of its waters. According to a legend recorded by Ethel, "it was named, it is said, by Indians, who, coming to bathe in the waters, which they believed had curative powers, considered that so large a body of water must surely be the sea."

By 1914, the shores of Blue Sea were dotted with summer places. Indeed, it shared only with Kingsmere – a swampy little lake so close to the city that it was almost suburban, Blue Sea people sniffed – the distinction of being considered a kind of unofficial summer capital. Those to be found there included Judge F. A. Anglin, soon to become Chief Justice of the Supreme Court of Canada; Colonel Percy Sherwood, chief of the Dominion Police, the security force of the day, which later merged with the North-West Mounted Police to become the Royal North-West Mounted Police and finally the RCMP; St. Denis LeMoine, Sergeant-at-Arms of the Senate, a seigneur from Quebec married into the McMahons, one of the great Ottawa Valley lumbering dynasties; Allan Keefer, one of a family of gifted civil engineers whose tenure in the capital could be traced all the way back to the days of Colonel By; and D'Arcy Scott, son of a senior cabinet minister to both Alexander Mackenzie and Wilfrid Laurier, Sir Richard Scott, without whose lobbying, back in the 1850s, Ottawa might never have become the capital at all.

Everyone at Blue Sea spoke of their "cottage" or their "cabin" or their "shack," but what they were really describing were big, comfortable, rambling houses, built of clapboard or shingle, designed for big families with plenty of servants and plenty of money – almost none of it taxable. All of these places had sweeping verandahs festooned with hammocks; massive fieldstone fireplaces; pantries equipped with enough knockabout china, usually of the Blue Willow pattern, to service entire regiments; so many bedrooms panelled in fragrant if slightly sticky cedar that they needed to be numbered. Down by the shore there were swimming docks with elaborate diving platforms and boathouses built right out over the water. Always, these contained a rowboat or two to which one-and-a-half- or two-horsepower Evinrude "kickers" could

Blue Sea Lake, in the Gatineau Hills north of Ottawa, *circa* 1910. By the eve of the war, its shores were dotted with summer places. The quality that still makes Blue Sea special is the shimmering, Caribbean-like translucence of its waters.

be attached, a Peterborough canoe, and perhaps an earlier one of birchbark, often as not a clinker-built, gaff-rigged dinghy for sailing, and occasionally a splendid "gasoline launch," made of Honduras mahogany or Burmese teak to which at least six coats of varnish had been lovingly applied and no less effort expended on shining up the brass fittings.

In one or another of these Blue Sea establishments, there was generally a numbered bedroom to spare for Ethel Chadwick, although, strictly speaking, as the daughter of an obscure and ill-paid House of Commons clerk, she could not claim one by right of entitlement. But, like many another girl in her position (Ethel would have winced at the description "shabby genteel," but she would not have disclaimed it), she'd long since cultivated the art of making herself agreeable: good at bridge, better than good at the flirtatious banter known as "chaffing," yet, unusual for her circle, ready to talk knowledgeably and entertainingly about literature if that were required. Besides, Ethel was exceptionally decorative, far more so now than she had been as a slightly chubby turn-of-the-century debutante, shy to the point of morbidity. A faded sepia snapshot taken that summer, in which she drips water all over a swimming dock and seems almost on the point of asking the viewer for a towel, evokes much of her own style and that of the period. The ludicrous bathing suit and long black stockings have rather missed the point, for these reveal rather than conceal the shapely figure and elegant legs of which she was inordinately vain. Ethel also had wonderful wavy black hair and an alabaster complexion. If her eyes were her constant despair, being smaller and less melting than fashion decreed and with a slight cast in one of them, they were set wide apart in a perfectly oval face.

That summer of 1914, Ethel was unusually lucky, for her customary Blue Sea fortnight had expanded to include all of July and the first half of August. The first few weeks she spent in a house called Silver Birches, "very high up, with rocks below slanting down to the lake," rented by her younger sister Rossie who, several years earlier, had married a man named Joe McDougal who was both rich and congenial. Towards the end of July, she moved on to Fairview Point, the most elaborate of all the summer places, and the home of the D'Arcy Scotts. This arrangement was even more to her liking, for Scott was one of the most amusing and attractive men in the capital, and between him and Ethel, to get a little ahead of the story, a delicious though innocent flirtation had been going on for years.

There were picnics, and canoe trips, and long solitary walks through the woods. On July 5 Ethel reports, "I startled some birds and animals by reciting *The Hound of Heaven* aloud." She spent hours in a deckchair or in a hammock, getting on with her summer reading programme, which, along with *Paradise Lost,* included *Medea* and *Oedipus the King* in the splendid new translations by the Oxford don, Gilbert Murray, and for light relief, a trifle by the popular novelist E. F. Benson called *Dodo the Second,* "a

Up at Blue Sea Lake, August 2, 1914. This snapshot from Ethel Chadwick's albums shows the last pre-war house party at Fairview Point. At lakes and seaside cottages all over the Dominion that hot midsummer weekend, others were taking similar pictures with their Kodaks. Ethel herself is on the extreme right, smiling out from under a large straw hat. Years later, she remembered a last golden idyll after which nothing would ever be as innocent again.

rather silly book," she confided to her diary, "trying to show the life of the smart, extremely modern girl." In the evenings on Blue Sea verandahs, someone always had a mandolin or an accordion to play for singsongs, "choruses" as they were called, all the old favourites like "My Little Canoe," "Sing Me to Sleep," and "Good-bye Summer"; at the Scotts, there was also a wind-up gramophone – a "talking machine," as Ethel describes it – so that the smart modern dances like the turkey trot and the swooping, risqué tango could be attempted, after the manner of Vernon and Irene Castle. Better still, from Ethel's point of view, was the scintillating quality of the conversation. Margaret Anglin, the Ottawa-born actress who'd gone on to fame and fortune on the New York stage, was visiting her brother, the judge, while the witty Dick Ritchie, an Ottawa lawyer and part-time poet and playwright, was visiting the Scotts. "We talked of many things," reports Ethel of a night when Anglin and Ritchie were obviously in top form. "Shaw and Wilde and the difference between them, and a great argument about Ibsen. It is nice to meet people who have been about or who read things intelligently enough to discuss them. It's rather rare."*

As always at Blue Sea, Ethel felt liberated, though that particular word would certainly not have occurred to her. Having a less-than-elastic wardrobe didn't matter; even for dinner, up at Blue Sea, an old middy blouse would suffice. Nor, since everyone at Blue Sea wore their hair down their backs in the manner of schoolgirls, tied back with a plain grosgrain ribbon, was there any need to spend hours fixing her coiffure in the current, modish style, flat on the crown and rolled round the sides, an effect far

---

* Margaret Anglin (1876–1958) was the daughter of Timothy B. Anglin, an early post-Confederation Speaker of the House of Commons. She achieved stardom in 1898, as Roxanne in *Cyrano de Bergerac*. By 1914, she had her own classical company, playing Shakespeare's Viola, Rosalind, and Cleopatra, and also Antigone, Medea, and Iphigenia. She retired from the stage in 1943.

J. A. (Dick) Ritchie is remembered for the lines carved in stone over the main entrance to the Parliament Buildings in Ottawa:

The wholesome Sea is at her gates,
Her gates both East and West,
Then is it strange that we should love
This Land, Our Land, the best?

more difficult to achieve than the pompadour of her girlhood, puffed out over an inelegant but convenient "rat."

She was, of course, as innocent as Eve. It would have shocked her beyond measure to know that within the literary circles she so much admired in England, people like Rupert Brooke and Virginia Woolf liked to describe themselves as the "New Pagans," and sometimes went swimming together in the nude. Yet Ethel was not at all unresponsive to the sensual pleasure of Blue Sea's translucent water rippling over bare skin. "I think I must have been a mermaid in my earlier incarnation," she exulted in mid-July, after "a lovely solitary dip au naturel (!) under a star-gleaming canopy of darkness." Nor did she care, or at least not very much, what people said when she and D'Arcy Scott, whose wife did not care for sailing, went off for hours alone in his dinghy, and the wilder the wind the better. "Judge Anglin is the limit," she reports in late July. "He said I ought not to wear a green sweater, when I went out sailing alone with a married man."

Ethel Chadwick at Blue Sea Lake, *circa* 1914. "I think I must have been a mermaid in my earlier incarnation," she wrote in her diary. The ludicrous bathing suit and long black stockings reveal rather than conceal the shapely figure and elegant legs of which she was proud.

Elsewhere throughout the Dominion, then just three years short of its fiftieth birthday, others were similarly enjoying the summer. Prime Minister Sir Robert Borden, still at that time generally referred to as "Premier," was golfing at Port Carling on Lake Muskoka: in white flannels and tweed cap he cut an estimable figure, but so far, three years into his stewardship, still impressed everyone as a rather colourless leader. Opposition Leader Sir Wilfrid Laurier, now seventy-two, a dozen years Borden's senior and no fan of physical exercise even in his green years, was doing as he'd done almost every year since the 1870s, sunning under the maples at his home in Arthabaska, in Quebec's Eastern Townships, watching his stout wife Zoë tend her beloved flowers. In those days, however, the Governor General was a much more newsworthy figure, and the present incumbent, Prince Arthur, Duke of Connaught, Queen Victoria's youngest and favourite son, was popping up everywhere. After three years in office, this was expected to be

his final season in Canada, and he was determined to bow out with appropriate fanfare. Having spent most of June in residence at the Citadel in Quebec, and having, as always, paid due respects to the skull of Montcalm at the Ursuline Convent, the Governor General embarked in early July on a three-week tour of the independent colony of Newfoundland. No sooner was he back from there than he set out on a farewell tour of the western provinces. On this journey, Connaught was accompanied by his Prussian-born duchess, Louise Margaret, and their glamorous twenty-eight-year-old younger daughter, Princess Patricia. The highlight was to be a fortnight's holiday at the Banff Springs Hotel.

But Connaught was first and foremost a bluff old soldier, a stickler for spit and polish, who was reputed to know every detail of every uniform in every British and Colonial regiment down to the last collar-button. Late in June, dressed in the full fig of a British field marshal, he'd presided over military manoeuvres at Camp Petawawa in the Ottawa Valley. These included a three-day mock battle in which ten thousand members of the Canadian militia were divided into the "white force" and the "brown force" and described by the Ottawa papers as "the nearest approach to real battle ever staged for men in training."

These ten thousand militiamen stood on guard for a nation with a population of about seven and a half million. Predominantly, Canada was an agricultural and rural society; most people lived either on farms or in sleepy little towns like Stephen Leacock's fictional Mariposa. Out on the Prairies, still quite frequently called by the old name "North-West Territories," for

(Opposite left)
Prime Minister Sir Robert Borden. The outbreak of war found him golfing at Port Carling on Lake Muskoka. This photograph was taken earlier that year by Lady Borden, on the grounds of Glensmere, his fine house in Ottawa.

(Opposite right)
Sir Wilfrid Laurier, Leader of the Opposition. By 1914 he was approaching his mid-seventies, but was as elegant as ever. This photograph was taken during a tour of western Canada a few years before the war.

Saskatchewan and Alberta had been provinces for less than a decade, it was customary for youngsters too small to help with the harvest to attend classes in the summer. At Wheat Heart Primary School, near Saskatoon, Saskatchewan, eighteen-year-old John George Diefenbaker, soon to enter his final year of arts at the University of Saskatchewan, was teaching nine- and ten-year-olds the rudiments of geography and history and grammar. A nervous and ambitious young man (perhaps already given to boasting about how, as a newspaper boy in the winter of 1910, he'd met Sir Wilfrid Laurier and had had a short conversation when the prime-ministerial train stopped at Saskatoon), Diefenbaker was probably using as a teaching tool either the Fourth Ontario Reader or a text closely modelled on it, for ever since the era of Egerton Ryerson, the great prophet of universal, moral, pro-British education, Upper Canada had set the tone for English-Canadian teaching. On the fly-leaf of this volume, beneath the Union Jack, appeared the motto, "One Flag, One Fleet, One Throne." It included two poems by Rudyard Kipling, Byron's "The Eve of Waterloo," "The Funeral of Wellington" by Tennyson, and for a touch of swashbuckle, Sir Francis Hastings Doyle's rousing setpiece, "The Private of the Buffs":

> Yes Honour calls! – with strength like steel
> He put the vision by;
> Let dusky Indians whine and kneel,
> An English lad must die.

However much Canadian lads thrilled to this kind of rhetoric, or to the *Boy's Own Annual* and the tales of G. A. Henty, they were shirkers when it came to that quintessential British educational instrument – cricket. Baseball was their game, imported from south of the border. In Chatham, deep in the rich rolling farm country of southwestern Ontario, Lester Bowles Pearson, a seventeen-year-old son of a Methodist manse, spent almost the entire summer with a glove on, and was good enough to dream about becoming a professional. Not yet nicknamed "Mike," Pearson was soon to enter his second year at Victoria College at the University of Toronto. There, the dean of his residence and one of his lecturers in history was twenty-seven-year-old Vincent Massey, an elegant Toronto aristocrat recently back from Balliol College at Oxford, putting in a pleasant couple of years before settling down to the serious business of running one of Canada's most impressive manufacturing concerns. Like other fashionable and elegant figures, Massey was spending the summer abroad, in the company of his younger brother Raymond, an aspiring actor. Having first sojourned in London, they set off in late July on a tour of the château country of the Loire, in a newly acquired Hupmobile, with, as Raymond later remembered, sadly defective tires. It is unlikely that they encountered Henri Bourassa, forty-six-year-old founder and editor of *Le Devoir*, and passionate Quebec nationalist, who was also in France that month on a pilgrimage to Lourdes. It's just possible, though, that when in England, the Masseys bumped into that controversial Canadian, Sir Max Aitken, who, having made his fortune before he was thirty, had moved to Britain in 1910. Aitken that summer was poring over the financial pages and sensing trouble ahead. "It was clear to anyone with a real knowledge of markets that some obscure and colossal movement was afoot," he wrote later. "There was no ordinary panic in the sense of a sudden and tremendous fall in prices; it simply became almost impossible to find buyers at all."

Few others shared Aitken's acumen or his curiosity. Then, as now, most Canadians were mainly preoccupied with domestic issues. They talked of Mackenzie and Mann, a pair of swashbuckling railway promoters who had recently pressured the Borden government into bailing their Canadian Northern line out of bankruptcy. They talked of the temperance movement, still gathering strength thanks to proselytizers like Nellie McClung, but dealt a sharp blow by the Ontario provincial election in June, when Premier Sir James Whitney's Tories defeated N. W. Rowell's Grits, who'd campaigned on the slogan, "Abolish the Bar!" They argued about women's suffrage, a movement much to the fore, again thanks largely to the irrepressible Mrs. McClung, who the previous winter had made headlines by writing, producing, and starring in a send-up of male politicians, notably Premier Sir Rodmond Roblin of Manitoba, that had played to packed houses in Winnipeg.

Subjects like these, though, divided social gatherings and even families. A more popular, and safer, topic of conversation was that of a marine disaster almost as epic as the *Titanic* and closer to home. On May 29, the Canadian Pacific liner, the *Empress of Ireland*, had gone to the bottom of the St. Lawrence with the loss of more than a thousand lives after a collision with a collier just east of Quebec City. As socially uncontroversial was the strange tale of another unhappy ship, this one a Japanese vessel named the *Komagata Maru*, which in early summer had arrived in Vancouver harbour bearing a cargo of 376 East Indian would-be immigrants. Not only were they refused permission to land, but the *Komagata Maru* – to general satisfaction – was chased into international waters by the single functioning warship in Canada's "tinpot navy," HMCS *Rainbow*. One reason Canadians were so unwelcoming was the presumption of racial superiority that then came as second nature to all English Canadians, Anglo-Saxons and Anglo-Celts alike. Another was that times were hard, and with industries working at less than two-thirds capacity, and less acreage under cultivation than in any year since 1910, immigrants were seen as a major cause of Canadian unemployment. A sign of the times was a poignant little poem given prominent space in the August issue of *The Canadian* magazine. It was titled "The Bread-line," and it spoke of "Thin, threadbare coats, buttoned across the breast . . . Pale faces stamped by hunger's seal and sign."

Most Canadians, though, were inclined to be optimistic. Silly, after all to be gloomy, when all the way from Cape Breton to Vancouver Island this was the loveliest summer anyone could remember. They flocked to band concerts, church picnics, lawn-bowling tournaments; rowed in regattas; hurled the caber at Highland Games. It was the kind of summer when, in the evocative description of one Ontario newspaper, "Many a young Leander spent the whole afternoon in the water or else lying on the sand, and basking in the sun."

The world that all of these people lived in was more like our own than we often suppose. During the opening years of the century, the framework of modern technology had been set in place. As early as 1900, electricity, indoor plumbing, and the telephone were all commonplace facts of urban life. By 1914, Canadians who lived in cities were also beginning to take for granted central heating, electric irons, and vacuum cleaners. Phones had become so commonplace that the Bell Telephone Company had started promoting the use of extension sets, not only in offices, but in households. True, there was no radio as yet, but Canadians went frequently to the moving pictures, which often starred Mary Pickford, formerly Gladys Smith of Toronto. Thanks to wireless telegraphy, an invention pioneered at Cape Breton by Guglielmo Marconi shortly after the turn of the century, newspapers reported the dreadful events at Sarajevo on June 29, only a day later. Cities were sprouting new suburbs – Westmount, Forest Hill Village, Shaughnessy Heights – and even in Ottawa, long a laggard when it came to municipal improvements, paved sidewalks were replacing the old wooden ones. The age of the horse and buggy was not quite over; in the capital, as everywhere else, there were still plenty of horse-drawn vehicles, but as early as 1912, as Ethel Chadwick noted in her diary, motorized taxis had already squeezed out most of the old hansom cabs.

The age of consumerism and mass marketing was well underway. Like baseball, most of the name brands that had already become household words – Shredded Wheat, Palmolive soap, Gillette safety razors, Heinz ketchup, and Coca Cola – were products of the more energetic style of enterprise that flourished south of the border. So also with popular culture: everyone laughed at Mutt and Jeff and the Katzenjammer Kids in the funny papers; everyone sang songs written in Tin Pan Alley. Still, when it came to the sentimental anthropomorphic animal tales that in those days dominated bestseller lists, Canadians could take pride in the fact that a novel titled *Beautiful Joe: A Dog's Own Story*, by a Halifax woman named Marshall Saunders, had sold more than a million copies in the decade and a half since it had been published. A source of even greater pride was that L. M. Montgomery's *Anne of Green Gables* was not only a huge international success, but had entranced the great Mark Twain. There were no antibiotics or sulpha drugs, and people still died in their thousands of pneumonia, tuberculosis, and even typhoid, one of whose victims a few years earlier had been Lady Victoria Grenfell, daughter of Connaught's immediate predecessor as Governor General. But thanks in great part to the efforts of Sir William Osler, whom many considered to be the greatest Canadian of his time, the practice and teaching of medicine had been revolutionized to the point that it had become almost fashionable to have one's appendix out.

But their world was also another world entirely. All these new developments were only a thin veneer of modernity on a structure that remained resolutely Victorian. Canadian society was still hierarchical and to a considerable degree, static. Religion and family were still the organizing principles of existence, and woe betide anyone who dared break the rules. In all the years since Confederation, less than a thousand divorces had been granted. Big families were the norm, but obviously pregnant women were rarely seen on the streets; so as not to give offence, they kept discreetly out of sight, venturing out only after dark for a stroll around the block on the arm of a husband. For single women, conventions were even more stifling. For all that Ethel Chadwick had become daring enough to smoke an after-dinner cigarette in the dining room at the Château Laurier, it would never have occurred to her, even at thirty-odd, to dine there alone with a man. Nor, as a devout Catholic, would she have dreamt of marrying a Protestant, let alone outside the church; indeed when a close friend who was also a Catholic married in a Presbyterian church, Ethel not only did not send a present but refused to have anything more to do with her.

Race and culture divided Canadians as deeply as religion, the two separating forces mutually reinforcing each other. Far from coming together as Macdonald and Laurier had hoped, French and English Canadians were drawing ever more apart. The wounds left by the long and bitter battle over bilingual education in Manitoba were still festering; for passionate Quebec nationalists like Henri Bourassa, the new decree from Queen's Park that outlawed French as a language of instruction in Ontario was one more sign that the only hope for his people was to withdraw from the mainstream of Canada into the fastness of Quebec. Others excluded from the mainstream included all Canadian native peoples (with the occasional romantic exception such as the poet E. Pauline Johnson); all Orientals, and, away off in their prairie sod huts, the "sturdy peasants in sheepskin coats." As for Jews, businessmen did admit that you had to hand it to them. But they handed out no invitations to join their clubs, much less house-party weekends at Blue Sea Lake.

As remote from our contemporary way of being was English Canada's attitude toward the Mother Country. The tie that bound was as simple as this: the British Empire, the greatest since the Roman, bestrode the world like a pink Colossus; Canada was a fiercely and unthinkingly proud part of that Empire, "daughter in her mother's house," as Kipling had put it, but "mistress in her own." The formula was sentimental, but it worked. Canadians accepted as a fact of life that Canadian treaties should be negotiated by British diplomats, and that the Governor General was not only the ceremonial link between Canada and Britain, but the major political link and channel of communication between Ottawa and Whitehall. (Not for more than another decade would the establishment of a British High Commission separate these functions, and while there was an embryonic Department of External Affairs and a handful of foreign representatives in Ottawa, they held only the rank of consul and were empowered to deal with only routine commercial business.) There was friction within the relationship. Individual Englishmen – no less, Englishwomen – were not especially popular, either because they were arrogant and patronizing or, in the instance of the remittance men who flocked to the Canadian West, because they were hopelessly incompetent. Indeed, when advertising for farmhands and chore boys, western farmers frequently inserted the warning, "No Englishmen need apply." As for the attitude of visiting Britishers to Canadians, these tended to be uncomplicated, as the example of Sir Arthur Conan Doyle demonstrates.

In the early summer of 1914, the creator of Sherlock Holmes had made a triumphal speaking tour of Canada that had included three nights in a teepee and an impromptu baseball game at Jasper, in the course of which he'd hit a homer. Soon after returning home, he gave an interview to a reporter from the London *Daily Chronicle* that was reprinted in a number of Canadian papers. According to the account relayed by the Ottawa *Citizen*,

Sir Arthur had discovered everywhere, "a very real and wide-spread element of loyalty and imperialism." As to the question of Canada becoming independent of Empire, "Perhaps by the end of the present century . . . this will come up in strong form . . . but in the meantime, Canada receives thirty-three percent of her invest-ment from Great Britain, as against fourteen percent from the United States and thirteen percent from within her own borders. Besides that, we give her free insurance in our navy, and the diplomatic service of the empire is at her disposal."

Then Conan Doyle added the kicker. "What Canada needs now are more women . . . she wants 100,000 women. . . . The popu-lation is not increasing because so many men in the west cannot get married . . . they toil on their farms alone and the moment things go wrong they get disheartened." As always, he had an ingenious solution. "We have a superfluity of women, and Canada is crying for them. An enormous matrimonial agency might be established, which would be of enormous benefit to us and to Canada. . . . If we send Canada our unwanted women, I think we might perhaps keep the farmhands for ourselves."

A more sensitive appraisal of Canada had been provided the year before by the poet Rupert Brooke. Before arriving by way of New York, Brooke had been warned by American friends that Canada was a dull, prosaic country "without a soul." After two months, travelling westward from Quebec to Victoria, he'd found something different, "an extremely individualistic national iden-tity." It wasn't that Brooke fell in love with Canada. It was, he con-sidered, "live, but not like the States, kicking." In Toronto, "wealthy, busy, commercial, Scotch, absorbent of whiskey," he was unable to resist sending up the members of the Arts and Let-ters Club who greeted him with awe. "One comes up and presses my hand, and says, 'Wal, sir you can not know what a memorable day in my life this is.' Then I do my boyish-modesty stunt and go pink all over; and everyone thinks it too delightful." In Alberta, he mocked the boosterism of westerners. "It is imperative to praise Edmonton in Edmonton. But it is sudden death to praise it in Cal-gary." Yet with his poet's eye, Brooke managed to see things that other outsiders did not. In Winnipeg, he remarked on how polite people were and was rather charmed by the "gauche pride" of its architecture, which while hideous was "cheerily and windily so."

In Ottawa, where he spent more than a week as a guest of the civil servant and poet Duncan Campbell Scott, he found "an atmosphere of safeness and honour and massive buildings and well-shaded walks. . . . What (it) leaves in the mind is a certain graciousness – dim, for it expresses a barely materialised national spirit – and the sight of kindly, English-looking faces and the rather lovely sound of the soft Canadian accent in the streets."

On a luminous afternoon in June, Scott and some friends took Brooke on a twenty-mile drive by motor-car into the Gatineau country so much beloved by Ethel Chadwick. They did not get as far as Blue Sea Lake; indeed, given the absence of roads that wasn't possible. But the trip inspired the most memorable passage in all of Brooke's writings on Canada. All of a sudden, the New Pagan from Cambridge got under the skin of this strange semi-wilderness.

"We went by little French villages and fields at first, and then through rocky, tangled woods of birch and poplar, rich with milkweed and blue cornflowers, and the aromatic thimbleberry blossom, and that romantic, light, purple-red flower which is called fireweed, because it is the first vegetation to spring up in the prairie after a fire has passed over, and so might be adopted as the emblematic flower of a sense of humour. They told me, casually, that there was nothing but a few villages between me and the North Pole. It is probably true of several commonly frequented places in this country. But it gives me a thrill to hear it."

Ethel's diary entry of July 27, 1914, "War is declared between Austria and Servia," marks the first intrusion upon her, and for all practical purposes upon all Canadians, of the gathering furies in Europe. Exactly how the news arrived is something that Ethel doesn't tell us. Perhaps, as an obliging houseguest, she'd rowed over to the public dock at the village to pick up the mail and found out from the postmistress, who had a telephone. Or perhaps some new member of the house party arrived off the evening train with an Ottawa newspaper. In any event, from that moment on, the tone of her entries changes abruptly. Swimming parties and picnics and bridge games went on as usual. But a far-off place in the Balkans that only a fortnight ago had seemed as remote as the *Prisoner of Zenda* had suddenly become immediate.

On July 30, as Russia moved to the aid of embattled Serbia, she wrote: "They say now that all the great powers may be involved in this war. It's awful. Great Britain, France, Servia, Russia, against Germany, Austria, Bavaria and Italy. I do hope not."

On July 31, as it began to dawn on Ethel that as Great Britain went, so also would Canada go, she wrote: "There seems now every prospect of an international war. Canada has offered a contingent at once. It's dreadful." As an afterthought, almost, Ethel added, "Read a lot of *Paradise Lost* this morning."

On August 1, word arrived of a drastic change in the Governor General's travel schedule, and Colonel Percy Sherwood's holiday was suddenly interrupted. "The Duke is returning from Banff by a special train. . . . Colonel Sherwood was sent for tonight to go down to Ottawa at once . . . within a week, the face of Europe has changed entirely."

On Sunday, August 2, the weather changed abruptly. The sun did not shine, it was humid and sultry with a grey pall of rain. By now, even at Blue Sea everyone realised that war was inevitable. "Germany has violated Belgian neutrality and marched in her troops. It's awful. What will a war of this kind and in this day mean?" Ethel wrote.

Late that evening, a violent thunderstorm broke and the temperature dropped sharply. Ethel added one line to her diary record of the day: "The north wind blew wildly all night. War was on it, blowing all over the world."

2

"An Irish Cinderella"

One can read a poem or a novel without coming to know its author, look at a painting and fail to get a sense of its painter; but one cannot read a diary and feel unacquainted with its writer. No form of expression more emphatically embodies the expresser: diaries are the flesh made word.

Thomas Mallon. *A Book of One's Own; People and Their Diaries*

Even this early on, Ethel Chadwick had sensed far more acutely than most people that the "war blowing all over the world" would not be a splendid little war that would be over by Christmas, would be instead a catastrophic event that would transform world history, and also the nature of Canada. Perhaps Ethel sensed also that the war would be the great divide in her own life, even though she would live through it safely in Ottawa. Thus far, she has revealed herself as a conventional belle of the period – frivolous, self-absorbed, and more than a little snobbish – and also as a highly intelligent young woman, far better read than most Canadians then and now. Since Ethel will be our principal guide to the home front for much of the war, it is time to reveal her more fully.

Like many good observers of society, Ethel was an insider-outsider, and not only because she lacked money. Although indisputably of the gentry, that she was Irish and Catholic meant that she was not quite of the same social order as members of those Old Ottawa families who took entrée to viceregal circles as a matter of right and not of privilege. In many respects, her background resembled that of another insider-outsider, the journalist Agnes Scott, who, at the turn of the century, had described capital society with wit and flair under the pseudonym Amaryllis. Though Agnes, now Mrs. W. P. Davis, was part of the older generation, the two were well acquainted.* Even more than Agnes, Ethel was a fervent admirer of all things British, for, unlike the Scotts, who retained a degree of native irreverence, the Chadwicks were best described as "Castle Catholics," a breed almost forgotten now, but of which in those days there were many examples, both in Ireland itself and scattered throughout the Empire. Like the seigneurs of Quebec, Castle Catholics saw devotion to the Crown as their best hedge against social disorder and atheistic republicanism. Being a Castle Catholic, as becomes evident time and again in Ethel's diaries, meant walking a perpetual tightrope between the dictates of one's religion and tribal instincts, and the social pressures of one's peers.

From both of her parents, Ethel had inherited her sparkling, Black Irish good looks and her passion for literature. Her father, Francis Chadwick, the son of a prosperous land-owning squire in County Meath, took great pride in having studied at the same Jesuit college as the poet Francis Thompson. Her mother Margaret Rose Sadlier, of Montreal, was the daughter of a family from County Cavan who had emigrated in the 1850s to found an Irish-Canadian publishing house and to become leading lights in the genial literary circle presided over by the great Thomas D'Arcy McGee. Indeed, not only in Montreal, but wherever there were Irish in North America, Ethel's grandmother, Mary Ann Sadlier, was one of the best-known women of her day, renowned for her uplifting tales of Irish emigrant life and for having edited the definitive posthumous edition of McGee's poetry. Her maiden aunt, Anna Theresa Sadlier, was equally well known for her inspirational religious romances and essays.

Francis and Margaret had met in 1880, when he crossed the

---

* The story of Agnes/Amaryllis is told in *The Private Capital: Ambition and Love in the Age of Macdonald and Laurier.*

Atlantic to investigate life in Montreal. Immediately after their marriage, they set out on a leisurely extended honeymoon which began on the continent and ended in Ireland. Ethel, the first of their six children, was born on March 25, 1882, in her paternal grandfather's big late-Georgian country house, surrounded by sweeping lawns and paddocks full of hunters. They named her after their favourite literary heroine, the delightful Ethel Newcome, in Thackeray's *The Newcomes*, although, as Ethel herself explains, a little adjustment was necessary. "Being Catholics, they needed to find a saint's name, and luckily, there turned out to be Saint Etheldreda."

The earliest years of Ethel's childhood were idyllic, and gave her a deep sense of entitlement that coloured the whole of her life. Having returned to Montreal shortly after her birth, the handsome and clever young Chadwicks established a lifestyle that while not ostentatious, was exceedingly pleasant. Thanks to a generous income from home, Francis had no need to work for a living, but could easily afford to house his growing family in a fine stone house on fashionable Sherbrooke Street and indulge a Victorian passion for scientific invention by spending most of his time pottering round the engineering department at McGill University. In a family memoir written when she was over eighty, Ethel remembered "trips by hansom cab to Scroggie's and Morgan's on St. Catherine Street where Mama did most of her shopping"; "a red haired Scotch nurse named Nana Ellen who took us to play in Dominion Square"; occasional trips to the theatre to see *Little Lord Fauntleroy,* and best of all, "a pink smocked cashmere party frock with hem touching the ground that I used to call my tip-toe dress."

Early in 1891, when Ethel was nine, this cosy and cossetted world vanished as abruptly as one in a Victorian melodrama. Save for a glancing reference – "Grandpa Chadwick's mills went badly" – she doesn't explain what happened. It has to be surmised that funds from Ireland dried up at the very moment that Canada plunged into a deep economic depression. Insofar as they could, the Irish of Montreal took care of their own. Thanks to Grandmother Sadlier's connection to D'Arcy McGee, Francis Chadwick was found a position, at $850 per annum, as Assistant Clerk of the Crown in Chancery. (A sleepy department within the House of

Commons, whose functions were later assumed by the Chief Electoral Officer, it was mostly responsible for the issuing of election writs and proclamations for the opening and closing of Parliament.) In June 1891, the Chadwicks moved to Ottawa and took up residence in a cramped little house on the shabbier fringe of Sandy Hill, in those days a bedroom suburb for civil servants. Save for occasional holidays that to her great regret never included a visit to her birthplace in Ireland, Ethel was destined to remain in Sandy Hill for the rest of her life.

Ethel began keeping her diary in 1895, when she was twelve, going on thirteen. "Papa gave me a little leather-covered book," she tells us that January. "He said to write down what I do every day and that I shall find it very interesting when I get old." So far as we can judge from these early, haphazard accounts written in a round, schoolgirlish hand, the first years in the new and impoverished environment slipped by contentedly enough. "Papa" and "Mama" were clearly tender and loving parents who put a brave face on misfortune. Since there was no money to spare for even the modest fees at Gloucester Street Convent, and since it would have been unthinkable to send their children to public schools, the Chadwicks provided them with a unique education at home, more dependent on after-supper readings from the classics than on formal lessons. By the age of fourteen, Ethel not only knew "dear books" like *Bleak House* and *Vanity Fair* almost by heart, but was conversant with Homer's *Iliad* and the essays of Macaulay. Ottawa itself, though in many respects a sub-arctic lumber village with muddy streets and wooden sidewalks, afforded excitements no other city could provide. In the capital, even a young girl couldn't avoid getting interested in the drama of politics. On June 23, 1896, when Laurier's Liberals swept to power "we stayed up til after midnight talking about the election," Ethel tells us, a discussion that was unlikely to have been marked by much enthusiasm because, as she tells us, "Papa voted for the Conservatives."

Most exciting of all was the proximity of Rideau Hall. As new additions to the local gentry, Francis and Margaret were quite often asked to balls and theatricals, and while most invitations had to be turned down for lack of appropriate clothes, once in a

Ethel Chadwick at eighteen in 1900. She made her bow to
society on the last night of the nineteenth century. This
is her formal debutante photograph. The slight cast in
her right eye, of which she was painfully conscious, can
be discerned.

while, as on February 23, 1897, they made a great effort. "Mama
got her hair dressed which cost 50 cents, and had her nails cut
and pointed," Ethel tells us. "She wore auntie's black satin and a
bunch of artificial violets." The following month, Ethel herself

attended her first viceregal function, a children's party hosted by Lady Marjorie Gordon, fifteen-year-old daughter of the Governor General, Lord Aberdeen. "I went down the big toboggan slide four times," she relates, "then we went in for refreshments. I took 3 glasses of lemonade and ice cream and 2 pieces of cake and I brought 2 cakes home in my pocket."

Ethel's formal debut to society coincided with that of the new century. On December 31, 1900, wearing "a white satin dress, and a green evening wrap with a big collar of rabbit fur," she was accompanied by her father to a debutante ball at Ottawa's Racquet Court, where "at the stroke of midnight everyone joined hands to sing Auld Lang Syne to the old century." Appropriately, her account of that epochal occasion, where Madame Emilie Lavergne, the great love of Wilfrid Laurier's life, was one of the chaperones, marks her true beginning as a diarist. From then on, she wrote daily and obsessively all the way up to 1971, when, in one of her last entries, written shortly before her eighty-ninth birthday, she remarked on another remarkable prime-ministerial romance: "Trudeau suddenly married a girl in Vancouver of 22, Margaret Sinclair." Throughout all of these years, Ethel's diaries would be her best friends. She read them over and over, frequently adding insertions and updates. Often, in the early years, she illustrated them with delicate watercolour sketches and decorative scrolls containing favourite quotations from Tennyson and Browning and Longfellow. She used them, not just to fix the experiences of her daily life but also as an emotional safety valve, to record an inner life that was frequently at variance with the carefully orchestrated persona she presented to the world.

Already by 1901, the discord between appearance and reality was becoming apparent. The full implications of the Chadwicks' financial situation were beginning to sink in. "There's no use being alive when one is so poor," she wrote despairingly, much in the manner of Amy March in *Little Women*. Indeed, it was only because of a providential cheque from her godmother in Ireland, that Ethel had been able to afford the white satin dress she'd worn to the ball. And while the parents of other eighteen-year-olds embellished their daughters' debuts with lavish theatre parties and private dances, the best the Chadwicks could afford was a humble tea party, to which, although two high-minded new arrivals in town named Mackenzie King and Bert Harper put in an appearance, "quite a few others," she noted sadly, "did not come."

Other girls in similar circumstances might have accepted reality, entered one of the socially acceptable female professions like teaching or genteel secretarial work, or, like Agnes Scott, gone in for journalism. But quite apart from the fact that Ethel's idiosyncratic education had provided her with none of the appropriate qualifications, she had no desire whatever to become a New Woman. She was ferociously ambitious, much more of a Sadlier than a Chadwick, yet a hard-working bluestocking career as a professional writer in the family tradition did not appeal to her at all. She was coming of age in an era when all the most glamorous role models were society figures: the exquisite Irene Langhorne of Virginia, who'd married Charles Dana Gibson and was the girl in his pictures; the swan-necked Consuelo Vanderbilt, who'd recently married the heir to the Duke of Marlborough. Mooning over rotogravure photographs of these heroines, Ethel yearned to be one of them. She was determined, at the very least, to make her mark within Ottawa society, to be part of the bright glittering world embodied by Rideau Hall. Here, the pattern set by another of Thackeray's heroines, less exemplary than Ethel Newcome, soon proved to be useful. Early in 1901, as a nineteenth-birthday treat, Ethel went to the Russell Theatre to see an actress named Gertrude Coffin play Becky Sharp in a dramatised version of *Vanity Fair.* "Oh my, it was lovely," she tells us. "It was wonderful to see characters whom I have known for so long." Like Becky, she began to hone all her talents carefully, and to use each and every one to her own best advantage.

The talent that Ethel could most easily exploit was her natural ability for skating. "The only thing that really matters in Ottawa is knowing how to skate," she confided to her diary. Far from being girlish prattle, this was an acute social insight.

Since the days of Lord Dufferin back in the 1870s, the ability to waltz on the ice and to execute elegant 3s and 8s had been a useful accomplishment for aspiring belles, much like being able to paint pretty watercolours, or tap out tunes on the piano. In 1898,

A skating party at Rideau Hall, *circa* 1911. "The only thing that matters in Ottawa is knowing how to skate," Ethel wrote in her diary. This snapshot from her own albums illustrates the point. In the years leading up to the Great War, viceregal skating parties were the organizing principle of Ottawa's social existence.

the advent of the Earl of Minto, whose countess was renowned as one of the best ice-waltzers in England had transformed skating into a social imperative. All the best parties at Rideau Hall took place on the rink; aides-de-camp were specially selected for their abilities on blades. On a more practical level, from October to March the new covered arena in Sandy Hill served as the fashionable meeting place for the younger unmarried set. Here, at the noon-hour, a period that in those leisurely days lasted two and a half hours, aspiring young lawyers and militia officers and civil servants – even, surprisingly often, the hard-working Mackenzie King – gathered to make eyes at the debutantes and to play Crack the Whip with them. In the season of her debut, having spent the last of her godmother's present on a new pair of fancy skates with serrated points and black leather boots that laced up to the knee,

Ethel set herself the task of becoming one of the best skaters in the capital, proficient enough to pass the rigid tests for entry into the inner sanctum, the Minto Skating Club, of which Lady Minto herself had been founder and patron. She also learned how to flirt, how to make small talk, how to amuse. For much of the next decade, her diaries reveal, skating was the organizing principle of Ethel's life. No matter that Minto's successor as Governor General, his brother-in-law, Earl Grey, was a terrible skater and a bit of a pincher, Ethel quickly became "the little Ottawa lovebird" he singled out to have pull him round the ice, and this led to a flood of invitations not only for skating parties but also for all the most exclusive Rideau Hall functions – dinner dances, supper parties, amateur theatricals – where she blossomed into "pretty, witty Miss Chadwick," the belle that the new crop of gold-braided aides – elegant Lord Bury, squeaky-voiced Lord Lascelles, gallant one-armed Captain Trotter – most liked to waltz and to chaff with.* It was also on the ice, in the winter of 1905, that Ethel commenced one of the most important relationships of her life: an exciting but troubling romantic friendship with the debonair Ottawa lawyer, D'Arcy Scott, whom we have already encountered in her company at Blue Sea Lake.

He was married, of course, and so it was a romance that could lead nowhere. Since they were both scrupulous Catholics, it was an affair that was entirely of the heart, not of the flesh: roses at Christmas, lilies of the valley on her birthday, a silly poem pressed into her hand at the end of a dreary Experimental Farm lecture on grain-growing, the swooning Indian love lyric, "Pale Hands I Loved, Beside the Shalimar," sung in a duet by moonlight in a canoe. In her diary, Ethel never discloses the truth of her feelings for D'Arcy, perhaps because she was afraid that her mother or one of her sisters might read it. But it's easy to guess that if circumstances had only been different she'd have married him in a

---

* Lascelles, heir to the Earl of Harewood, married Mary, the Princess Royal, daughter of George V, in 1922. At around the same time, Graham Trotter, nicknamed G, became a principal equerry to the Prince of Wales, later King Edward VIII, and still later the Duke of Windsor. "I learned from 'G' Trotter that life should be lived to the full," the duke remarked in his autobiography, *A King's Story*.

flash. Ten years older than Ethel, he was a man of commanding presence who had been elected Mayor of Ottawa by a landslide in 1906. D'Arcy, above all, possessed the background and breeding that mattered so greatly to Ethel. The Scotts were one of the most considerable political families in the Dominion, and in the early years of the century, D'Arcy's father, old Sir Richard Scott, continued to serve Laurier as a cabinet minister as vigorously as he had once served Alexander Mackenzie. But unlike dour old Sir Richard, D'Arcy was full of fun and and high spirits, a big powerful man brimming over with buoyant self-confidence, who was devilishly attractive to women, though bald as an egg. Like Ethel, D'Arcy was hugely ambitious, both politically and socially. Also like her – herein lay the rub – he lacked the resources to nourish his ambition, for the Scotts were not wealthy. Thus, in 1898, he had married "Queen" Davis, the well-dowried but otherwise unremarkable daughter of a local building contractor. Ostensibly, he had settled down to become the paterfamilias of a brood that by 1905 already numbered four and showed every promise of increasing exponentially.

"Mrs. D'Arcy does not skate," Ethel noted in her diary on March 11 of that year. Already by then, she and D'Arcy had been passing acquaintances for some time, since in the hugger-mugger style of Sandy Hill, old Sir Richard Scott's large red-brick establishment was right next door to the cramped duplex occupied by the Chadwicks. Up to this point, however, D'Arcy and "Mrs. D'Arcy" had seemed to belong to the world of the grown-ups, while she to him was no more than a pretty child. But the waltz at that Saturday-afternoon Rideau Hall skating party changed everything. Within days, they had another waltz together, this time at a ball at the Russell Hotel. On April 8, D'Arcy slipped into the pew behind Ethel at mass at St. Joseph's Church. "He whispered he was very glad to see me," she noted in her diary.

Accompanied by flowers and boxes of chocolates, slender volumes of poetry, and on one occasion, a trifle inappropriately, "a little devotional book about the importance of frequent communion," the flirtation soon gathered momentum. In the spring of 1906, casting aside all the accepted protocols with merry abandon, D'Arcy did the unthinkable. Unaccompanied by his wife, just

Another photograph from Ethel's albums, this one taken in February 1912, illustrates her prowess as a skater. Her partner on the Rideau Hall rink is the Ottawa lawyer D'Arcy Scott.

as if he were a single man, he paid a formal call on Ethel in the middle of the afternoon. "Mama of course said I was out," confides Ethel with shocked delight. "She said it was a dreadful thing for him to have done." Still, since Mrs. D'Arcy, *faute de mieux*, seems to have accepted the situation, there were few objections that Mrs. Chadwick could raise when an impeccably proper invitation arrived inviting Ethel to spend a weekend with the Scotts at their newly built summer house at Blue Sea Lake. Here, in the season when everyone was humming the waltz from *The Merry Widow*, Ethel and D'Arcy had a fine time. "The verandah is lovely," Ethel confides. "Everyone lay in hammocks and D'Arcy and I got into the same one."

By now, though, people were beginning to talk. They seem to have talked quite a lot; as late as the mid 1980s, members of the older generation could be found in the capital who, having eavesdropped as children on forbidden conversations, raised eyebrows and smiled at the mention of Ethel and D'Arcy. In 1908, when, having relinquished the mayorship, D'Arcy was appointed an assistant railway commissioner, a patronage plum that not only provided the princely sum of $9,000 annually, but also the use of a private railway car, Mrs. Chadwick put her foot down. "He wants to get up a party to go out to Winnipeg," Ethel lamented, "but Mama won't let me go." For a few years, meetings were less frequent, yet the friendship continued, and in any event, after Ethel turned thirty, she was much less prepared to accept parental dictums. Yet by 1914, when we meet them together at Blue Sea Lake, the relationship between Ethel and D'Arcy had mellowed from flirtation into friendship. Both in the interim had looked elsewhere, and Ethel, as we shall discover shortly, had fallen even more foolishly in love.

In the winter of 1911, shortly before Ethel's twenty-ninth birthday, her younger sister Rossie, who was neither as pretty nor as clever as she was, and who had never tried nearly as hard to be a social success, married in St. Joseph's Church. The groom, an Ottawa businessman named Joe McDougal, was not only good-looking but of impeccable character and all-around niceness. Moreoever, his financial position was such that his wedding present to his bride was a three-month honeymoon in Europe and a set of magnificent sable furs lined with ermine. Two months later, in a ceremony far more dazzling, Ethel's only real rival among Ottawa belles, the legendary Lola Powell, famous in viceregal circles for her lengthy flirtation with the Earl of Minto, married an officer in the British Regulars and sailed off to live in Dublin.

These twin events provided Ethel with an unwelcome opportunity for personal stock-taking. On the plus side, her attempt to conquer her personal *Vanity Fair* had succeeded far beyond all imaginings. The high point had come in June 1908, when Earl Grey had personally selected her to be one of the half-dozen local "love-birds" taking part in the event that was the high point of his own governor-generalcy: a magnificent week-long pageant on the Plains of Abraham marking the tercentenary of Champlain's arrival at Quebec. Cast as an aristocratic lady at the court of King Henry IV in a scene that depicted Champlain receiving his instructions, she'd worn a hooped gown of pink velvet and satin, with hand-painted roses on the skirt and a huge Medici collar, and had danced a stately pavanne on a carpet of royal blue covered with *fleurs-de-lys* spread down on the grass, to the music of hautboys and cymbals and lutes. "It was most impressive in every way," she remarked in her diary. "At the end of the pageant, the armies of Wolfe and Montcalm marched out on the plains together, but so as not to annoy the French people, there was no fight, only reconciliation." During this extraordinary week, an event that captured the imagination of Canadians in much the same way that Expo '67 would do six decades later, Ethel had truly arrived at the pinnacle. Thanks to the lumber king, Sir William Price, in whose lavish Grande Allée mansion she and Lola Powell were billeted, she'd had a Victoria and pair at her personal disposal. At the historical fancy-dress ball at the new Château Frontenac, Sir Montagu Allan, the Montreal king of shipping, had specially requested a waltz. For once, even being Catholic gave her a distinct social advantage, since the Duke of Norfolk, present at the festivities as first peer of the realm, was also one. After a special outdoor mass on the Plains of Abraham they had chatted easily, and, as she noted in her diary, Norfolk turned out "to know all about the English branch of the Chadwicks."

On the debit side, Ethel was no closer to her ultimate goal, which was to make a marriage that would both fulfil her romantic dreams and be financially advantageous. Indeed, she was considerably further away from it than she'd been a full decade earlier, and not entirely for lack of opportunity. As early as 1905, she'd turned down her first proposal, from Lieutenant Percy French, an officer of the Royal Engineers, whom she'd met on the Rideau Hall skating rink, and who had even agreed to turn Catholic for her sake. "He was very insistent, but I left him at the front door in the midst of all his questionings and arguments," she tells us with all the arrogance of being twenty-two and in the early power of her beauty. "It had started to snow and I didn't want to spoil my white wrap." A number of other suitors, including Mr. Clarence Pepler of the Dominion Bank and a "little Mr. Fitzsimmons" whose first name and occupation are not recorded, had been dismissed with even less ceremony, having neither the charm of D'Arcy Scott nor the glamour of Rideau Hall aides. But, by 1909, after a promising flirtation with the young newspaper publisher Harry Southam

("so nice and intelligent," she noted, "and a wonderful skater")
ended with the announcement of his engagement to the daughter
of Ottawa's King of Electricity, a note of realism had begun to
creep into her diaries. "Money marries money," she reflected. "A
poor girl has very little chance." For the first time, she began to
consider "that gloomy topic, the future," and to prepare for it.

At the top of the agenda was the unappetizing business of
earning a living. The nation was prospering, but the Chadwicks
were not, and no matter that Rossie and Joe were the souls of generosity, their goodwill and frequent lavish cheques could be
stretched only so far, especially now that Ethel's three younger
sisters, Beatrice, Helen, and Betty, had either made their debuts
to society or were on the brink of it, and Frankie, her only brother,
had to be seen through the Royal Military College at Kingston. No
more at twenty-nine than at nineteen would Ethel have considered taking a paying job, even less so, since within the viceregal
circle to which she'd grown accustomed, "going out to business"
was most decidedly not "the thing." But for the first time, she
began to think seriously of supporting herself by writing, and she
started churning out a stream of romantic poetry and short stories, even a 35,000-word novelette titled, revealingly, *An Irish Cinderella*. In return, she received a string of rejection slips, and
although none of her manuscripts survive, we can guess that
while Ethel was certainly not lacking in energy, she was gifted
with neither the family touch for religious romance, nor the ability to connect homespun reality with fantasy through vivid characters that was turning L. M. Montgomery into a celebrity. Still, by
dint of perseverance, she did begin to achieve a trickle of accep-
tances for articles on viceregal social life, mainly from British publications. "*Ladies Field* has sent me thirty-one shillings and
ninepence," she recorded with joy in 1911. "This is the first paper
to take anything of mine, and that's $7.75 in Canadian money." To
the end of Ethel's life, writing about Ottawa society would provide
her with a small income, and while she lacked the sense of irony
and daring to become a true successor to Amaryllis, she was
always a reliable reporter who, even in her late eighties, got all
the names right.

During these last years of her twenties, Ethel also began to broaden her horizons in other ways. Like all the other "autumn leaves," as aging post-debutantes were unkindly described, she did what was expected of her in the social round, paying innumerable calls, "assisting at the urns" at seemingly endless tea parties. She also began to cultivate an interest in public affairs and took part regularly in the Thursday morning debates held by the May Court Club, the service organization for well-bred young ladies founded by Lady Aberdeen. She struggled diligently on her own to learn Latin and French and, as always, found an escape from her constricted world through reading, now with a new sophistication. One find, raced through in a five-day marathon, was *War and Peace*, although it must be said that Ethel was neither the first nor the last to discover that "all those complicated Russian names rather slow one up," and to be a bit let down at the end to find "Natasha, humdrum and plump, married to that boring Pierre." More akin to her taste were the realistic and acerbic novels of New York society written by Edith Wharton. Ethel does not come right out and say so, but since we know that she gobbled up Wharton's masterpiece *The House of Mirth* in a single sitting, we can guess that she found in its tragic heroine Lily Bart, an ambitious girl of slender means who had developed a dangerous dependency on richer friends to accommodate her pleasures, an unsettling mirror image of herself. As for the compromising if entirely innocent visit to a bachelor's flat that triggered Lily's downfall, this was not all that far removed from some of Ethel's own indiscretions with D'Arcy Scott.

The great find was Henrik Ibsen. Unfulfilled heroines like Hedda Gabler and Nora in *The Doll's House* rang a bell inside Ethel. "There are so many things about them that are true to life," she remarked. Nora, in particular, was the clear inspiration for the first flickerings of a feminist consciousness. "I see that in Norway they are going to give votes to women," she noted with approval on May 31, 1910. "It seems strange that such a faraway place should be so go-ahead, but then again, this is Ibsen's country."

In other aspects of politics, Ethel maintained the family tradition of being staunchly Tory; indeed, but for certain reservations about John Diefenbaker, she remained a Conservative to the end of her life. As a passionate Imperialist, she was no great admirer of Laurier, who, in her opinion, "was always for Canada for herself and for letting the Empire's interest go to the wall." Thus on September 21, 1911, she was overjoyed when Sir Robert Borden defeated Laurier on the issue of reciprocity. A few days later, along with almost everyone else in town, she went down to Union Station to watch the triumphal entry of the new prime minister. "It was very exciting," she noted. "It looked as if the whole country were Conservative and Conservative only." Ethel being Ethel, she was far more excited by the prospect of another new arrival, the Duke of Connaught, who had recently been appointed to succeed Earl Grey as Governor General. "I wonder what they will be like, the Connaughts and their aides," she wrote. "Will I meet them? Will I know them?"

The advent of the Connaughts marked the apogee of the governor-generalcy. Never again would the viceregal court be as splendid. Not only was the new incumbent a prince of the blood – Queen Victoria's third son and favourite child, godson of the Iron Duke,

Princess Patricia. Younger daughter of the Duke and Duchess of Connaught, she accompanied her parents to Ottawa. A natural beauty, Patricia was also a painter of considerable talent. In the viceregal tradition, this photograph was sent to her acquaintances in Ottawa, including Ethel Chadwick, as a Christmas card in 1915.

(Opposite left)
Prince Arthur, Duke of Connaught. Youngest and favourite son of Queen Victoria and godson of the Duke of Wellington, he was appointed Governor General in 1911. An English diarist described Arthur as "the *only* gentleman royalty of manner and presence," but his elder brother, King Edward VII, was unimpressed by him.

(Opposite right)
Louise Margaret, Duchess of Connaught. A Prussian-born princess in her own right, she was autocratic and neurotic. Many Canadians, including the future prime minister, Mackenzie King, were amazed by her fondness for whiskey.

Wellington – he was far more regal and distinguished in his appearance than either his late elder brother, the paunchy and rheumy-eyed Edward VII, or his pedestrian nephew George V. Indeed, in the opinion of the English diarist Cynthia Asquith, Arthur of Connaught was "the *only* gentleman royalty with manner and presence." A youthful sixty-two, and a career army man, he was a tall, slender, and erect military figure with snowy-white hair and a wavy moustache. His duchess, Louise Margaret, was a princess in her own right, daughter of Prince Friedrich Karl of Prussia. The establishment that accompanied the Connaughts to Canada was far larger and more glittering than that of either the Mintos or the Greys, with its most glamorous member the twenty-five-year-old Princess Patricia, the duke's younger daughter, a natural beauty and a talented artist.

Or so it all seemed on the surface. In fact, as was well known in court circles in England, the Canadians were being fobbed off with a royal who had become something of an embarrassment. For Arthur himself, the appointment to Ottawa was the latest in a long string of personal disappointments. His military career had not gone nearly as well as he had hoped. Having commanded the Brigade of Guards at the battle of Tel-el-Kebir in 1882 and performed creditably, he'd expected to be named Commander-in-Chief of the British forces. Instead, he was passed over in favour of the Duke of Cambridge and shunted off to a succession of largely ceremonial posts in Ireland and Malta. Nor, on the available evidence, was his marriage a happy one, for Louise Margaret, having suffered a tormented childhood at the hands of a sadistic father, was frigid and neurotic and had a Prussian need to dominate. (Later, she would also startle Ottawans by her fondness for whiskey.) For many years, the only escape valve in Connaught's life had been provided by an extramarital relationship with the vivacious, dark-haired, American-born Leonie Leslie, wife of an Irish cavalry officer and youngest of the three beautiful Jerome sisters of Baltimore who had dazzled London society in the 1870s. (Jennie, the most beautiful of the sisters, had married Lord Randolph Churchill.) Their romance had begun in the mid-1890s when Leonie was in her middle thirties and he a decade older. From then on, he wrote to her every day for forty years, letters which all began "Beloved Leo," or "Dearest One," and were signed

either "Arthur," or by their private nickname "Pat." In these letters, "he expressed again and again his loneliness and his longing," according to Leonie's granddaughter, the Irish writer Anita
Leslie, who described the affair in her 1972 book, *Edwardians in
Love*. Whenever possible they were together, Anita Leslie continues, either in London or at Castle Leslie in Ireland. "The joy of his
life was gone when she was not there."

Thus for Connaught, Ottawa was tantamount to exile. Yet he
had no choice but to go. In 1909, he had infuriated King Edward
by abruptly resigning his position at Malta. It was all the fault of
the women, grumped His Majesty to a courtier: Arthur preferred
to idle around London boudoirs, and all he was good for was to be
the leader of cotillions. A few months later, he had blotted his
copybook yet more severely, aiming so low at a pheasant at a
Windsor Castle shooting party that in Anita Leslie's description,
"feathers waved on the Queen of Italy's hat." For the King, this
was the last straw. Intimates had rarely known him so angry. No
matter that by the time the Connaughts actually set sail across
the Atlantic, Edward had been dead for over a year, it had been
long since decided that Arthur was best enjoyed at a distance.

Needless to say, neither Ethel nor anyone else in Ottawa was
privy to this absorbing information. Much was made of the fact
that Arthur, as a young army officer back in the 1870s, had spent a
season in Montreal and had then expressed a desire to return
some day as Governor General. Like everyone else in town, she
reminded herself constantly that when addressing either the duke
or the duchess or the princess, it was necessary to say, "Your
Royal Highness," as opposed to "Your Excellency," as had sufficed
for the Aberdeens and the Mintos and the Greys. Her own first
encounter with the Connaughts – after some weeks of worry that
her name had been scratched off the invitation list – took place
on January 6, 1912, at the first Saturday-afternoon skating party of
their tenure. Thanks to her lengthy diary account, it is easy to picture the scene. "Terrible weather, 23 below zero all day," she tells
us. Instead of waltzing, most people played Crack the Whip and
Haulaway to keep warm. Mackenzie King was of the company and
as usual he buttered her up about her skating costume, which
was built around a paddy-green felt skirt and a purple sweater,
because the word was already out that the royals liked bright

Princess Patricia on the Rideau Hall skating rink in February 1914. Her partner in hi-jinks is Lieutenant-Colonel Worthington, the viceregal physician. Patricia was shy and aloof, but as this photograph is witness, she sparkled on the ice.

colours. She curtseyed to the duke, who was "nice looking with such white hair and very soldierly, with a deep strident voice," and to the duchess, who "isn't much to look at and speaks with a deep guttural German accent," as well as to Princess Patricia who turned out to be a bit less gorgeous than imagined. "Her face is a dream of beauty," Ethel reports, "but she is nearly six feet tall and her figure is big and lumbering."

Ethel turned her attention next to the members of the Royal Household. First, she was introduced to the naval aide, Lieutenant Ramsay, about whom and Princess Patricia romantic rumours were already flying, and "a nice little Captain Talbot who turned out to be a Catholic." She also met the duchess's lady-in-waiting, Miss Pelly, "said to be a power behind the throne, who rules the Duchess and runs the Duke." Then, midway through the party, warming her hands at the potbellied stove in the little hut by the rink, Ethel met Lord John Hamilton. It was a *coup de foudre*.

It took about three weeks for Ethel to stop referring reverentially in her diary to "Lord John," and to write of him simply as "John." In her most private references, she wrote of "Sweet Johnnie." Their romance lasted only a couple of months, yet there is no doubt she thought of him to the end as the great love of her life. He wasn't at all adept on the ice – indeed, as she writes of that first afternoon, "just as he was asking me to waltz, he fell down." Nor, as she discovered later, was he especially adept on the dance floor. He was, however, "very good-looking, tall and blond with blue eyes and a nice fresh open expression." By the time she went home, Ethel had further discovered that Hamilton was exactly the same age as she was, that he was a younger son of the Duke of Abercorn, and that his posting to Ottawa would, alas, be only a short one, to gain him experience for a much grander position as an equerry to King George v.

That winter season of 1912 continued to unfold like a fairy-tale come true. Recording it in her diary, Ethel sounds more like a starry-eyed colonial debutante than a sophisticated devotee of Ibsen. Hamilton continued to single her out from all of the other girls. "Lucy Kingsford says she thinks he loves me," she reports on January 11. Many of their meetings took place on the ski hills of Rockcliffe Park, where Ethel developed keen enthusiasm for a sport that up to now had never attracted her greatly. "All of the Royal party were out this afternoon," she tells us on January 16, "I wore a little red cap which I bought for the purpose of skiing. Lord John said he liked it. I stuck to a little hill, until Lord John asked me to try a hard one, so I did. Then he suggested we go down the long one, all the way down to the river, together. It was beautiful. A big red fat sun was just going down. He is so nice." Another afternoon was spent tumbling down the toboggan slide at Rideau Hall. Writing it up, she adapted the *Rubaiyat*: "Wilderness was Paradise indeed. It was lovely up at the top of the slide, the city clear and quiet below in the afternoon sunlight, and Lord John beside me."

Perhaps, in such isolated moments, he kissed her. Or then again, more likely not. As always, when dealing with matters of the heart, Ethel is better on the surrounding details than on the actual content. It is difficult even to know what they talked about, although it's unlikely that either Ibsen or women's suffrage were much in evidence, for Ethel hints early on that Hamilton was not much of an intellectual. Sometimes, they seem to have found common ground in the fact that they were both Irish and poor and "better at spending money than making it." Whether or not the burning issue of the day, home rule for Ireland, ever intruded, Ethel as a devout Castle Catholic would have had no difficulty coping with the fact that Hamilton's father, the Duke of Abercorn, was quasi-official spokesman for the Protestant landlord class. Much of the time, in any event, they seem to have engaged in "chaffing." "I was asking him about points of etiquette when speaking to the Princess," Ethel reports on one occasion, "and I said, 'What about you? Is it the thing to speak to you without your speaking first?' He chased me with a ski pole and pretended to be mad." One afternoon in February, around the time they began addressing each other by their first names, John amazed Ethel by calling in to see her in the middle of a bridge party at Rossie's flat in the Roxborough apartments. "He seemed to be quite embarrassed about interrupting, but Oh What Joy for me." On January 31, she took courage on the wing and invited him back to the Chadwicks' shabby establishment for a supper party, after a performance of that most romantic of operas, *La Bohème*, at the Russell Theatre. At first, she was horribly disappointed, "for it seems he has got to be on duty." Then, half an hour later, another aide was on the telephone. "He wanted to know if Lord John could come after all, as they had swapped places. He said John was too shy to ask himself. Then John came on the line and he didn't seem the least bit shy." The party, needless to say, was a huge success. "John is so sweet. When he was leaving, he paused in the hall as if he would like to stay longer."

By March 1, the weather was warmer and sunsets were later. A cliff in Rockcliffe Park overlooking the Ottawa River was *mis en scène* for one of the last viceregal skiing parties. "We boiled the kettle, gypsy-fashion, over a roaring bonfire and toasted crumpets on the end of ski-poles." By now, though, Hamilton's time in Canada was running out. "I was talking about his going and he said, 'Well, you needn't be so cheerful about it, you might at least pretend to be sorry.'" The agony was that Ethel, so gifted at small talk, couldn't find the right words to tell Hamilton what she really felt, which was simply, "I am heartbroken," as she wrote in her diary. On March 14, wearing her best blue satin with a bunch of real violets on her shoulder, she was one of sixty or so guests at a farewell dinner-dance at the new Country Club, hosted by his brother aides. "They were very sweet and put me next to John. He said he might come out to Canada again in the autumn. He asked me to be sure to wear a pretty hat for skating day after tomorrow, as he wants to take a photograph of me before he goes."

On Saturday, March 16, after a heavy snowfall, the Rideau Hall rink was fairyland. "The trees were almost all covered with white," Ethel tells us, "the sun shining through the white and green, and the sprays of feathery snow looked like diamonds falling when the branches moved." At this last meeting, Ethel asked Johnnie if he would try again to waltz with her. "He said, very sweetly, 'I'll do anything in the world you like, would you like me to jump off the roof, I'll do it.'" The music was the sweet, slow "Beautiful Lady" theme from the new Broadway hit, *The Pink Lady*, but even so it was a disaster. "We had a nasty fall, and I hurt myself quite badly," Ethel confides. "He said it was his fault, but I told him that it was mine, and that I'd tripped."

Later – Ethel was wearing her best winter hat, a confection made of "electric seal" that she'd fashioned out of a jacket that had been her godmother's 1905 Christmas present – Hamilton took some snaps with his Kodak. Afterwards, they sat down by the side of the rink, and talked until it got dark. This time, it is almost impossible to believe that they only shook hands. "I feel weary and blue," she wrote in her room that evening. "*Tout est fini*. If one could only say what one felt. I feel sure that I will never see him again."

Lord John Hamilton. A younger son of the Duke of Abercorn and an officer in the Irish Guards, he served briefly as an ADC at Rideau Hall in the winter of 1912, and later became an equerry to King George v. In the privacy of her diary, Ethel Chadwick described him as "Sweet Johnnie." This photograph, clipped from an English magazine, comes from her scrapbook.

John Hamilton did not return to Canada in the autumn. Nor did he send her the snaps – nor even a single postcard. For Ethel, continually on the lookout for the postman, this was not only an additional source of heartbreak but a continuing embarrassment, since, as she notes, "everybody keeps asking."

Whether Hamilton's behaviour was caddish, or whether, by his own lights, he had behaved as a gentleman by not misleading her, Ethel never held it against him. "During this year," she wrote on New Year's Eve, "I met and knew for a few brief weeks Sweet Lord Johnnie, and oh, that has been something to remember."

Ethel by now had learned nothing if not how to be resilient. Despite Hamilton's departure and the ever-increasing prospect of permanent spinsterhood, the years that immediately preceded the war continued to be the most pleasant of her life. The tiny income she had achieved through free-lance writing gave her a measure of independence, and a little more leeway at the dressmakers. She had never looked prettier, for the new style of simple high-waisted gowns and peacock colours made popular by Paul Poiret suited her figure and complexion, and so did the dramatic bird of paradise that quite often in the evenings she'd taken to wearing in her hair. What really made the difference was that never before had she been more assured of the entrée at Rideau Hall. The season of her romance with Hamilton had brought her to the attention of the duke. Before long, to her professed annoyance but great secret pleasure, she was dubbed "The Royal Favourite."

Perhaps something in Ethel's appearance and manner reminded Arthur of Leonie Leslie. Or perhaps he was simply glad to have someone to laugh at his jokes. Their special relationship began at a Rideau Hall tea party a few days after Hamilton had left Ottawa. Along with other members of the May Court Club, Ethel tells us, she'd gone down to Government House to enroll in a series of lectures on first aid organized by the viceregal physician. Later there was tea, and unexpectedly the duke came in. "He asked if I had had tea," Ethel continues. "I was just about to tell him yes, and then Captain Long, the chief aide, who was beside me, said in a loud whisper, '*Go With Him,*' so I did even though we were the only people in the room and even the servants had gone. He poured out the tea himself, and kept me talking. He said he supposed I would be coming down on Wednesday night, that they had decided to have a dance. I said I hadn't heard of it. He said, 'Oh, Miss Chadwick, you will certainly hear of it.'"

The Arthur–Ethel flirtation was entirely innocent and decorous. Unlike Earl Grey, Connaught did not go in for sudden squeezes in the viceregal conservatory. Ethel quickly discovered that what the duke enjoyed better than anything was a bit of chaff followed by some good-old-fashioned gossip. "He is not a bit careful of what he says, and very plainspoken," she reports on one occasion. "Today, he was laughing about a very ugly heiress who is staying with them. He said that any man who married her would have to swallow a gold coated pill." The duke was also amazingly thoughtful. When he discovered that she was particularly fond of the pink-and-white chequered Battenberg cake that was served regularly at post-skating tea parties, but that during Lent the strict rules of fasting forbade her to eat it, he arranged to have a whole cake sent round at Easter. "He is truly amazing," she preened another time. "I was the least important person in the room, not wealthy, not a cabinet minister's daughter or anything like that, and yet he spent the whole of the tea hour talking to me."

Everyone else at Rideau Hall took their cues from the duke. "Don't you notice how he always makes a beeline for you?" remarked Captain Long, with amused admiration at the first state ball of the Connaughts' tenure, when he came up to announce that the duke wished to partner her in the *galop*. Soon she became part of the high-spirited circle of courtiers presided over by "Toby" Long and his lively wife Sibyl, one of the handful of outsiders invited to the Long's flat in the Roxborough for a rare private supper party at which Princess Patricia put in an appearance. The high point, she reports "was a game called Musical Grab suggested by the Princess, where we all scribbled down the name of a song on a card and had to try to sing our partner's tune when the cards matched." And while Patricia herself was not greatly interested in making local friends and spent her happiest hours wearing a battered smock and painting still-lifes and landscapes, Ethel became a great chum of her lady-in-waiting, the Honourable Katharine Villiers. One afternoon in March 1914, she reports, their pleasant tête-à-tête over teacups was interrupted by mayhem committed by two of the most impudent of the younger aides, Lord Spencer Compton and Captain Boscawen. "They tied a thick cord from the handle of Miss Villiers' sitting-room door to the next door handle so that we couldn't get out. Finally, Miss V. had to ring for a footman to ask him to cut it, which he did, perfectly gravely."

In hindsight, Ethel's descriptions of the pre-war Connaught Court have a quality of bittersweet. The style was much like that of an Edwardian country-house party, at once enervating and ferociously energetic, and in some ways, surprisingly informal. In the description of Katharine Villiers, recalling it in a 1930s memoir, "Rideau Hall itself was rather like a cheery English country home, with its high white rooms, gay chintzes and great open fireplaces." The entrance, reconstructed in 1913 so as to provide an imposing façade, was pompously viceregal, but the rooms at

the back, overlooking the garden "opened onto a straggling verandah, where in the warm weather, the Staff was apt to idle in rows
in the sunshine, drinking coffee after lunch and watching the humming birds darting over the broad herbaceous borders." Except
for writing invitations, and donning gold braid on formal occasions, the young officers who served as aides had very little to do
and a great deal of time on their hands. These dashing young
bucks were aching for a splendid little war. "The uncivilized feroc-
ities of the future cast no shadow before," wrote Katharine Villiers. "Our ignorance raised so invulnerable a shield."

"Everything nice comes to an end," Ethel wrote in her diary on
May 7, 1914. That day the official announcement was in the
papers: the Connaughts were to leave at the end of the summer to
be replaced by the Duke of Teck, Queen Mary's younger brother,
and his duchess. "It is very sad," she continued. "They have been
very nice to me, the dear old Duke especially, and they had one
ADC whom I loved wildly." Thinking of the future was even more
depressing. "I dare say I won't be at all as much in with the Tecks,
for I am too old to make headway with new people now."

As it developed, this farewell to the viceregal court was premature. Immediately after war broke out, it was announced that
Connaught's term would be extended for at least another year.
Officially, the reason given was the importance in such perilous
times of continuity in viceregal tenure, along with the fact that the
Duke of Teck, who was only forty, wished to rejoin his regiment.
(Eventually, having renounced his German title and re-emerged as
the Earl of Athlone, he served as Governor General during
another war). The real reason was that the last thing that the War
Cabinet wished to have on its hands was a stubborn old soldier
whose ideas about warfare had been formed in the era of hollow
squares.

But the old order of hi-jinks and Battenberg cakes was gone
forever. No more would Lord Spencer Compton and Captain
Boscawen announce themselves over the phone as "Colonel Fog-
weather" and "Captain Slapcabbage" when inviting Ethel up for an
afternoon of skating, for they had already left for the Front by the
first boat available.

As for Lord John Hamilton, as Ethel discovered from the grapevine, he had resigned from his post at Buckingham Palace immediately after war was declared, and rejoined the Irish Guards. Along with the rest of the British Expeditionary Force, his regiment had crossed the Channel on August 10, and was moving towards the Belgian frontier to engage with the enemy.

3
Bugles in the Distance

*I hear a bugle in the distance. The soldiers have drill
and march out nearly every day now, in preparation for
going to the front.*

Ethel Chadwick. Diary entry; Monday, August 17, 1914

B y mid-August, when Ethel left Blue Sea Lake to return to the
capital, the war had begun in earnest. After a two-week
siege, during which the Belgian army under King Albert had
put up a much more spirited defence than anyone had expected,
the fortress city of Liège on Belgium's eastern frontier had fallen
to German artillery. Elsewhere, the French had made a disastrous
advance into Alsace. Everyone's eyes were on Belgium though:
the British Expeditionary Force, almost the whole of the standing
army, comprising 80,000 men, 30,000 horses, and 315 field guns
under the command of Field Marshal Sir John French, was moving
towards the Front, near the mining town of Mons, just north of the
Franco-Belgian frontier.

Ethel was no sooner back in town than she was engulfed by
the war. After the sparkle of Blue Sea, Ottawa itself seemed almost
under siege, stiflingly hot, and covered with a thick pall of smoke
from bush fires. The Chadwick household in Sandy Hill was in
uproar, for her only brother, much-cherished Frankie, aged
twenty-one, had rushed home from a summer job with an engineering survey party to announce that he'd volunteered and, as a
recent graduate of the Royal Military College, had been accepted
immediately. "Mama doesn't like it of course," wrote Ethel. "She

thinks that anyone going will never come back. But under the circumstances, it would have been rather peculiar not to have volunteered, for as he said, to be a soldier in peacetime and to back out
in war would be queer." The elder two of her three young unmarried sisters, Beatrice and Helen, were already enrolled in first-aid
courses, "hoping to get at least as far as Halifax as nursing assistants." Having already achieved a certificate from St. John Ambulance Association, thanks to the programme offered in 1912 at
Rideau Hall, Ethel had transitory dreams of something loftier. "I
would like to go as a nurse, but straight to the front."

Paradise Lost and the bored heroines of Ibsen were no longer
apropos. This was a season for learning how to knit Balaclava helmets and long winding belly bands called "cholera belts." A piece
of doggerel titled "Grey Knitting," by a woman named Katherine
Hale, that began with the lines, "All through the country, in the
autumn stillness,/ A web of grey spreads strangely, rim to rim,"
became hugely popular, and was printed in all the newspapers. It
was also a season of patriotic rallies. Perhaps by design, since
events that involved "a silver collection" were always a source of
embarrassment for Ethel, she'd managed to postpone her return
until after a huge gathering of local women held in the ballroom of
Government House under the auspices of the IODE to inaugurate
fund-raising for a Canadian hospital ship to be donated to the
Allies had taken place. But she was in plenty of time to go to a
packed meeting organized by the Canadian Club where the hero
of the hour was the Belgian Consul, Mr. Goor. "He was wildly
cheered, and no wonder . . . Belgium has made such a brave struggle, for such a little country." Mr Machado, the Japanese Consul,
the representative of another ally, if scarcely a front-line one, also
came in for applause; for musical accompaniment, the band of the
Governor General's Foot Guards played *Rule Britannia* and *The
British Grenadier*. This early on, it was too soon for *Tipperary*, the
music-hall ditty adopted by the British Expeditionary Force as its
marching song, to have taken hold, but by the end of September,
when Ethel attended a grand meeting to inaugurate the Canadian
Patriotic Fund, organized to provide financial aid to the wives and
children of servicemen, everyone knew not just the chorus, but
all the stanzas. "It was sung not just once, but many times," she
tells us. "Though the words and music are commonplace, it is, as

one speaker said, 'the slogan of the poor Tommies dying out in France.'"

So saucy and jaunty a song is *Tipperary* that it has created an indelible impression of a universally upbeat mood among Canadians, and among the peoples of all the combatant nations, as they marched off to a war that everyone knew would be over by Christmas. There was indeed a frantic eagerness to enlist, not only by single young men like Frankie Chadwick, but also by middle-aging family men like the Ottawa architect C. P. "Coly" Meredith, whose

"A great sea rolls between us and the battle," wrote one Canadian journalist in September 1914. "We cannot even hear the yelping dogs of war. [But] it is plain that the whole country is ready to make any sacrifice in maintaining the supremacy of Britain." This recruiting poster of 1914, by its emphasis on Canada's ties to the mother country, expresses the official Canadian attitude during the first months of the war.

wife Aldie was one of Ethel's closest friends. There was a wide-spread sense that war itself was a chivalrous enterprise. In *The Canadian* magazine, journalist Newton MacTavish echoed the sentiments of many. "A great sea rolls between us and the place of battle," he wrote. "We cannot even hear the yelping dogs of war . . . [but] it is plain that the whole country is ready to make any sacrifice in order to assist in maintaining the supremacy of Britain."

Yet there was also a more ambiguous response to the distant, but inexorably approaching bugles. Sir Wilfrid Laurier, the white-maned Leader of the Opposition was as close to being a pacifist as it was possible to be in those times, even though he dared not say so out loud. So also, and even more discreetly, was his trusted and thrusting adviser, the former Minister of Labour, Mackenzie King. So also, in her heart of hearts – witness her comment "It's awful. What will a war of this kind and in this day mean?" – was Ethel herself.

Other responses were less ambiguous. There was fear. There was opportunism. There was war profiteering, almost from the instant war was declared. Within Quebec, there was widespread opposition, if at this stage mostly silent, to a British war. (That it was also France's war made little difference, since that nation was secular, republican, and socialistic.)

The single most astonishing feature of the time was that the man primarily responsible for Canada's contribution to the war was all but certainly mad. In the opinion of the journalist Ralph Allen, Colonel Sam Hughes, Minister of Militia, "would have had the greatest difficulty passing a standard medical test for sanity." In their definitive study of the war, *Marching to Armageddon*, historians J. L. Granatstein and Desmond Morton describe him as "a mountebank."

Then sixty-one, the member for Lindsay, Ontario, and a stout Orangeman, Hughes had displayed a capacity for monomaniac paranoia early in his career. Having served efficiently, though without great distinction, during the South African war, he continued for years to insist that he had been promised the Victoria Cross, but had been denied it for nefarious reasons. He displayed his paranoia again, in public, just as the European conflict began. On August 3, 1914, the day before war was officially declared,

Colonel Sam Hughes, Minister of Militia. "There is only one feeling as to Sam, that he is mad," wrote one of Hughes's cabinet colleagues. Yet by his manic energies, Hughes got things done.

Hughes had been so infuriated with what he considered to be pussy-footing behaviour on the part of British politicians that he demanded that the Union Jack flying over militia headquarters be lowered to half-mast. "By God," the minister had roared to his military secretary. "England is going to skunk it. Oh, what a shameful state of things. I don't want to be a Britisher under such conditions." (Only after two hours' persuasion by the elderly quartermaster-general, was the flag restored to its position.)

But as is almost always the case with monomaniacs, Hughes possessed herculean energy and drive. The instant Canada was at war, he initiated a recruiting drive for a First Contingent of 20,000. "We are determined that the tyrant's heel shall never grind down upon the people of Canada," he proclaimed. The First Contingent, he made clear, would soon be followed by others. To accommodate all the recruits, he quickly turned the valley of the Jacques Cartier River near Quebec into a vast, tented training ground. And he began mobilizing supplies, equipment, rifles, guns, mortars, horses, and food and medical equipment.

Valcartier Camp, September 1914. One of Hughes's early achievements was to turn the valley of the Jacques Cartier River, near Quebec City, into a vast tented training ground. The telegraph poles seen in this photograph were clearly brand-new. The straggling figures in civilian clothes in the left foreground were probably new recruits, about to be taken in hand by the military men marching forward. It can also be noted that motorized transport was still virtually non-existent.

This imperious decisiveness got things done. More and more as the war progressed, it also undid them, and put paid, in short order, to other men's ambitions and *amour propre*. Coly Meredith, it developed, was to be one of Hughes' earliest victims. His tale of frustration, recorded years later in an unpublished memoir, reveals his own character as much as that of the Minister of Militia.

Meredith, who had just turned forty, was one of the most successful of the younger professional men in the capital. No matter
that his elders were still wont to measure his achievements
against those of his father – Edmund Allen Meredith had been
Sir John A. Macdonald's Deputy Minister of the Interior – Coly in
the eyes of his contemporaries had more than matched them.*
Just after the turn of the century, in his first big architectural
commission, he had skilfully updated Sir John's former residence,
Earnscliffe (nowadays the residence of British High Commissioners), to suit demanding new owners, without sacrificing its Gothic
Revival eccentricity. In 1909, he'd pioneered the technique of
poured-concrete construction for the new Murphy-Gamble department store on Sparks Street. The angular and yet cosy red brick
house on the edge of Sandy Hill that Coly had designed for himself
and Aldie suggests a certain kinship of spirit with the great Glasgow architect, Charles Rennie Mackintosh.

Like many young men of his generation, though, Coly's own
yardstick for achievement was his success in the militia. In 1914,
as a reserve lieutenant-colonel of engineers, he should have been
well placed. Yet the war for which he'd for so long been preparing
took him completely by surprise. In the latter part of July, while
Ethel was up at Blue Sea Lake, he and Aldie and their six-year-old
son Brian had embarked on a motor tour of New England in their
new Model T Ford. On the way back home, they'd stopped at
Brome Lake in Quebec's Eastern Townships to spend a few days
at the country estate of an Ottawa friend and neighbour, the
debonair bachelor, former Minister of Agriculture, Sydney Fisher.
"On Sunday August 2nd," Meredith tells us, "we were sitting
around the table having lunch when the phone rang. When Mr.
Fisher came back to the dining room, he said that it had been
Mackenzie King, to let him know that war was about to be
declared."

Straightaway, Meredith decided there was nothing for it but
to pack up and leave for home. The race to Montreal, fifty or so
miles away, was a bit like an episode in one of Charlie Chaplin's

---

* The story of Edmund Allen Meredith is told in *The Private Capital*.

films. "We got caught in thunderstorms, on clay roads, with no chains, but we finally caught the last ferry to Montreal Island and stopped at the Place Viger hotel. I was so busy thinking about the war that I didn't realize what a sight I looked walking into the lobby, all plastered over with mud." As soon as he'd registered, Meredith made a long-distance call to the Adjutant General, offering his services. He also fired off half a dozen telegrams to everyone he could think of with influence. Far from being a much-prized luxury, the Model T had become by now a terrible hindrance. "The roads being what they were in 1914, it would have taken two days to get to Ottawa, so next morning we left the car behind and took the train, so as to be on the spot to press for an appointment."

All this patriotic effort went for nothing. As Meredith quickly discovered, Hughes had already decided to dispense with the established militia structures. Instead he had invented one of his own in which most of the plummiest positions were reserved for either political cronies or members of his family. "I was told that the Honourable Sam Hughes intended that his son Garnet should have the appointment that I would have been in line for," Meredith reports mournfully. Nor did his offer to step down in rank get him anywhere. Instead of going overseas, he was destined to spend a dreary war in charge of engineering works at Camp Petawawa. Still, Meredith survived and lived on in Ottawa to the ripe age of ninety-three.

During these first weeks of the war, the air was thick with rumours. Many of these involved espionage and conspiracy, and a number got into the papers. On August 19 for instance, the *Citizen* reported a "mysterious aeroplane" that every night for a week had been flying up and down the Ottawa River. On August 21, "an unidentified body in officer's uniform" was found floating face down in the Rideau Canal. The most tantalizing mystery of all, and the one that sparked the wildest speculation, concerned the sudden disappearance of a young man-about-town named Joachim Ribbentrop. How had this elegant champagne salesman, much in favour at Rideau Hall, managed to avoid internment by slipping out of Ottawa and then across the border into the safety of the neutral United States? Eight decades later, this incident remains a curious footnote to history, since Ribbentrop later became Adolf Hitler's foreign minister and later still was hanged as a Nazi war criminal at Nuremberg.

Then in his early twenties, Ribbentrop had already been living in Canada for almost four years. Indeed, as he himself tells us in a lengthy memoir composed while awaiting execution in 1946, had the war not come along, he might have lived to a peaceful old age in the capital. "I had felt indescribably happy," he wrote. "I left behind business prospects, many friends, and a young girl whom I had wanted to marry." The son of a former Prussian staff officer, educated in France and in England, he had come out to Montreal in 1910, perhaps as a way of avoiding military service, and had found employment first as a bank clerk, later as a construction worker on the Quebec Bridge and on Mackenzie and Mann's new transcontinental railway. Far more impressive than Ribbentrop's career achievements, however, had been his swift rise in society. Gifted with elegant Teutonic good looks, a suave and impeccable manner, and considerable talent both for tennis and for playing the violin, he charmed the colonials in much the same way that a quarter-century later, as Ambassador to the Court of St. James, he would charm the far more worldly and knowledgeable Cliveden Set into the policy of appeasement. In the summer of 1913, his close friend, Arthur Fitzpatrick, son of the Chief Justice, encouraged him to move to Ottawa, where, having inherited a small legacy, he set up in business as a wine merchant. "I was introduced to Rideau Hall," he continues, "and spent many a pleasant hour in the company of the Duke of Connaught and his lady – who, as a German, was very kind to me."

Ethel herself had first met this new addition to Ottawa's slender corps of presentable bachelors on the Rideau Hall skating rink the previous February, and, as she later congratulated herself, she had not been greatly taken with him. "A little German who has come to live here called Riblondorf, or some such name," she'd recorded dismissively in her diary. Most others, though, responded to his charm and panache. Quickly, Ribbentrop became a fixture at all the best parties, and in December 1913 he helped Father Christmas hand out the presents at the May Court Club's annual party for needy children. On another occasion, in powdered wig and velvet breeches, he danced the minuet at a charity performance with Ethel's debutante sister, Betty. He was noted at all times for the elegance of his apparel, in particular for a white linen suit. Coly and Aldie Meredith greatly enjoyed his violin-playing and once, by Coly's account, took him for a picnic up the Gatineau in their Model T. Simultaneously, by his own account, Ribbentrop was absorbing information about *realpolitik* that would prove useful in the future. "Although I was only a young man, I appreciated the clever way in which England grants absolute independence to her Dominions but nevertheless – almost entirely through the person of the Governor General – preserves their close contact with the mother country." During the 1930s, he continues, he frequently cited the Canadian precedent when he and Hitler were discussing the framework of a new German empire. "Although business ties with the U.S.A. are strong, Canada remains loyal. . . . To maintain this cohesion is the great function of the English Royal House and one of the secrets of the British Empire – the product of evolution, built on the experience of many generations and a masterpiece of organization and the art of government."

Undoubtedly, it was Ribbentrop's friendship with the Connaughts, and particularly his cosy chats in German with the Prussian-born duchess, that prompted all the rumours that he must have been a spy. According to one widely held theory, to which Coly Meredith subscribed to the end of his life, shortly before war broke out, Princess Patricia, at the request of her mother, had arranged a meeting with Ribbentrop at a local tennis club, and forewarned him to get out of Canada as quickly as possible. The facts, unhappily, contradict this conspiratorial explanation, for the viceregal party had departed for Banff on July 23, well before war seemed a threat, and did not return to the capital until the very day war was declared, by which time Ribbentrop was already on the train for New York. In his memoir, he himself disposes of the spy theory with an unanswerable put-down. "An insane fairy-tale – what was there in those days for a German to spy on?"

The reason that Ribbentrop cites for his departure is probably the correct one. "I was a German through and through. . . . The homeland was magnetic. I was sure that every man would be needed in what promised to be a hard war." His departure, while speedy, was entirely legal; on August 4, like a number of other Canadian residents transformed overnight into enemy aliens, including the Austrian chef at the Château Laurier, he took the overnight train to New York. Indeed, being short of funds, he had even borrowed ten dollars from a friend named James Sherwood, son of Colonel Percy Sherwood of the Dominion Police. A few days later, he took ship to Rotterdam in neutral Holland and from there slipped into Germany. During the war, he served in the Blue Hussars and received the Iron Cross. In 1932, he joined the National Socialist Party and became a confidant of Hitler. To the end of his life, though, Ribbentrop retained a great affection for Canada, "a hospitable country so beautiful and rich in human relationships."

"What course would my life have taken had I stayed?" he asked rhetorically in his memoir. "Certainly I would not be in Nuremberg today."

On the afternoon of Tuesday, August 18, Ethel went up to the House of Commons to witness one of the most dramatic political events in the Dominion of Canada's forty-seven-year history: the opening of a special five-day War Parliament. This session had been summoned hastily to confer on the Dominion government extraordinary powers. Under the new Emergency War Measures Bill, announced in the Speech from the Throne by the Duke of Connaught, Ottawa would now have the right to dispense with habeas corpus if needed in order to suppress an "apprehended insurrection." Like most other people, Ethel paid considerably more attention to another provision: a new "war tax" was to be imposed immediately on coffee, sugar, spirits, and tobacco. It was also announced that Canada would send a million bags of flour to Britain.

It was a scorcher of a day, and standing in line for the public galleries Ethel had despaired of getting a seat. Luckily, she was accompanied by a friend who was the daughter of a former Liberal cabinet minister, and the two were spotted by Mademoiselle Yvonne Coutu, Lady Laurier's long-time companion, and beckoned into the section of seats reserved for the opposition leader. Here, Ethel found herself directly in front of Mackenzie King, then aged forty, who, despite his defeat in 1911, had continued to maintain a high profile in the capital as editor of the Liberal Party's official magazine and as a giver of dinner and tea parties in his comfortable suite at the Roxborough Apartments, with an excellent

Mackenzie King, June 1914. The former Minister of Labour and future prime minister had just turned forty. Despite having lost his parliamentary seat in 1911, he maintained a high profile in Ottawa.

view of Parliament Hill. Over the last fortnight, as he no doubt told Ethel, King had been working round the clock preparing an article on the war for *The Liberal Monthly*. In addition, as he would have been far too discreet to have said, though perhaps not to have hinted at, King had also appointed himself Laurier's principal strategist for coping with the rush of events. Indeed, as we know from King's own diary, it was due largely to his urging that Laurier had cut short his holiday at Arthabaska and returned to Ottawa late on the evening of August 3. Even then, by King's account, it was not until he'd patiently explained the full implications of Germany's violation of Belgian neutrality to his aging chief over sherry and biscuits in Laurier's dining room that Sir Wilfrid actually comprehended that war was inevitable. "Sir W. asked what was the need of summoning Parliament, that there would be no war, that Germany would not attack France by the North Sea coast."

Next morning, August 4, the day that war was declared, the two had met in Laurier's West Block office just after eleven o'clock. There, King waited impatiently while Sir Wilfrid went through a stack of letters. Holding one up, he said, "This has just come from France, no mention of war in it, it shows how suddenly everything has come." Then, in a lengthy discussion that was continued over lunch at the Rideau Club – "consommé and salad," King tells us, "at the furthest table in the corner of the dining room" – they discussed the Opposition's response to the war. While both were agreed that with war now a *fait accompli*, both parties must present a united stand, King noted that Laurier was apprehensive. "More and more as I talk with Sir W.," he wrote, "I find how much his thought is of Quebec, how hard he has tried to overcome its prejudices in the interests of British solidarity, and how painfully sensitive he is to the unjust treatment meted out from the French on the one side and the English on the other." Undoubtedly, as King was well aware, Laurier was thinking of the sad succession of events precipitated by his own reluctant decision to send troops to South Africa fifteen years earlier: the departure from Liberal ranks of his brilliant protégé Henri Bourassa, and his estrangement from Bourassa's fervent disciple, Armand Lavergne, who had been like a son to Sir Wilfrid, and who many believed truly was his son with his long-time close confidante Madame Emilie Lavergne. Yet, as King was also aware, there was rather more to it than that. Like everyone who was close to Laurier, King knew that in his heart of hearts his leader had the instincts of a pacifist. Well before the Boer War, when in Britain for Queen Victoria's Diamond Jubilee in 1897, Laurier had visited the Tower of London and had been revulsed by its bloodthirsty displays. "History has always made too much of kings and criminals," the prime minister had remarked to his startled guide.

In the course of lunch, King reports, Prime Minister Borden came over and shook hands with his predecessor. "He asked Sir W. if he was sorry not to be prime minister. Sir W. said, 'My lucky star has not deserted me; indeed, I am glad not to be in office.'"

Mackenzie King and Sir Wilfrid Laurier, *circa* 1914. While clumsily retouched, this photograph accurately describes King's relationship with Laurier on the eve of the war. As King makes clear in his diaries, he had appointed himself Sir Wilfrid's principal strategist. Later in 1914 he went to the United States to work as an adviser to the Rockefellers.

Another hail-fellow-well-met on the way out of the dining room, was Colonel Sam Hughes. Instead of returning immediately to the West Block, Laurier asked King to accompany him on a walk round Parliament Hill. For a time, they talked of conditions in Europe. Then – no doubt with the bellicose image of Hughes in mind – Laurier put the question to King: "Is it conceivable that men can want war? Is it conceivable that they can work for it, and against peace? Can you conceive how they can?"

King didn't record his answer. Probably it was equivocal, since the last thing he'd have wanted to do was to encourage Laurier not to support the government. Yet in his diaries, there is plenty of evidence to suggest that King himself shared Laurier's pacifism. On July 31, when he first read the war news while returning by train from a holiday in northern Ontario, he was incensed by "a diabolical article in the *Toronto News* suggesting England should throw down the gauntlet to Germany . . . the *Montreal Star* is as bad . . . I cannot believe knowing Asquith, Grey and Haldane to be the men they are, war will come with Germany. Winston Churchill is the one dangerous factor." On August 2, when it was clear that events were out of control: "The Tories at the Rideau Club . . . take the position that now is the time to destroy German power. It is devilish to my way of thinking, and madness having regard to the welfare of mankind. For the most highly civilized and cultured nations to destroy each other is scarcely believable, and yet at this moment, the danger . . . is so close as to make it appear to the mass of men that the step has already been taken." In a diary entry of August 3, in which he was deeply critical of an official telegram of support dispatched to the British government on behalf of the Dominion, King makes it clear that he was already questioning the need for Canada to say "Ready, aye ready." "It was right enough in tone and purpose," he wrote, "but vicious in one particular. It speaks of 'our' international relations and 'our' Empire, when there is no need for the first 'our' and 'the' would be a better word for the second. This is done to force Canada's hand in the matter of obligating her in advance to whatever England does."

Three weeks later, when the war was well underway, and the first companies were leaving Ottawa for Valcartier, King made his most telling entry. Standing on Wellington Street, next to the little statue of Sir Galahad that he'd had erected in memory of his close friend Bert Harper, drowned in the Ottawa River in 1901 in a futile attempt to save a young girl from drowning, he watched the troops parading to Union Station. "With the first sight of the regiment," he remarks, "I felt an emotion which made me desire to applaud the bravery of the men." Then he had taken a closer look. "Soon, I saw that the men going to the front were *not* those in the scarlet or in green, but with two or three exceptions only, a lot of men who looked as though they were unemployed and who had taken the work as an act of despair. They were poor in physique and badly drilled." Nor for that matter, were many of these volunteers native sons. "I should think 80% East Londoners or old country failures," King estimated. "It was a humiliating spectacle, nothing Canadian about them. What was most humiliating was not the sight of these poor fellows, they were brave enough, but the circumstances that the regular volunteers were the ones who stayed behind. They returned to the armouries, playing their bands and presenting a fine appearance, having left the others at the station to go to the front." It was, he concluded, "a commentary on soldiering in Canada . . . volunteering with no anticipation of the need for service is a farce. . . . I could not help thinking that the men who were not going might at least have given their uniforms to the men who were ready to give their lives."

King's observation was exceptionally astute. Despite all the flag-waving rhetoric, in Ottawa as everywhere else most of the volunteers for the First Contingent belonged to the ranks of the unemployed (of whom in the capital alone there were many thousands that summer), and, at a time when there was no welfare system, a private's pay of $1.10 a day would have seemed almost princely. As well, a good 65 per cent were recent immigrants of British origin, who had discovered that the streets of Canada were not paved with gold. As for the senior ranks, for every eager and idealistic Coly Meredith, there were perhaps half a dozen summer soldiers who'd joined for the fun and games of the mock battles, but not for the real ones. "They say it was very hard to get the officers," remarks Ethel, who had also witnessed the parade. A few weeks later, she was horrified to discover that one local man

Troop train leaving St. Thomas, Ontario. By September 1914, scenes like this were commonplace all over Canada. Most of the early recruits, though, were recent immigrants from the British Isles.

she knew well, who was a reserve officer in the Princess Louise Dragoon Guards, and who, indeed, had ridden with the regiment in London in the triumphal parade marking George V's coronation, had stayed home with the express purpose of making money out of the war. "He told me all about it," she informs, "his ways and means. He's rather a swine in some of the things he blurts out. He says he talks to me because I don't blab." And while Ethel leaves it at that, some indication of the profiteering potential presented by the war is contained in a letter to a Tory businessman, written on November 25, 1914, by John Bassett, a former newspaperman who had recently been appointed chief aide to Sam Hughes, at the Department of Militia and National Defence. "Contracts are sent to a great extent to those firms who have political pull," Bassett told his friend. "The only way to get anything is by coming to Ottawa, securing an interview with the minister, and if he thinks it worthwhile, keeping in touch with the contracts branch."

From Ethel's point of view, her chance encounter with Mackenzie King in the House of Commons gallery on August 18 wasn't a matter of great moment, since, as we know, they had been acquaintances for years and had frequently danced and skated together. Indeed, in 1906, when King had published *The Secret of Heroism*, the book he'd written to commemorate Bert Harper, he'd sent her an inscribed copy by special messenger. But like most of the capital's smart set, she considered him rather a bore, and worse, "a terrible butterer-up," forever paying florid compliments. "He said he liked my blue skating suit awfully, and then asked where the purple one had got to," she wrote in 1905. "Fool, if he would ask me to skate, instead of jawing." Still, on such an occasion it was nice to be in the company of someone who was in the political know. Together, they watched the proceedings, each making mental notes for the accounts they would later write.

Both were impressed by the solemn pageantry. Instead of his plumed hat, the Governor General was wearing his field marshal's uniform, and both Colonel Farquhar, Connaught's military secretary, and Captain Newton, the only viceregal aides left in the capital, were also in khaki. The ladies of the court were in sombre colours, and both Ethel and King took particular note of the Duchess of Connaught, who in Ethel's opinion lent a somewhat "ominous air" to the proceedings "since her country, Germany, has been the aggressor." King for his part, remarked on "the solemnity of the occasion, and the tragedy of the Duchess's position . . . she looked like a woman under great strain, who was nerving herself, and gaining power of self-command." Both admired the elegant Princess Patricia, and King, who was a little in love with her, not least because at a recent Rideau Hall dinner party they had engaged in a fascinating discussion about "psychic waves," took special note of her black dress. Both reserved their most fulsome comments for the duke's flawless delivery of the Throne Speech: "Earnest, manly, dignified, unassuming and gracious without being in any way condescending," was King's description, but Ethel was more artless. "The Duke looked so nice, as he always does." Later, Ethel tells us, the two compared notes. "Mackenzie King says the Duke was splendid and that his advice is really useful now, as from a soldier." King got the more important part of his message through, and would have been pleased to know that Ethel eschewed the possessive "our." "He said that for the first time Liberal ex-ministers attended a cabinet meeting this morning. All are united in the desire to uphold the great Empire."

Immediately after the ceremonies, King and Ethel bowed politely, and went their separate ways. He rushed off to rejoin Laurier; she went out to Parliament Hill to listen to the bands play. In fact, King's contribution to the war effort was already over. A few weeks later, he left Ottawa for the United States, where he spent much of the next four years working as an adviser to the Rockefellers on labour relations, and writing *Industry and Humanity*. While King also spent a good deal of time in Ottawa, he does not reappear in Ethel's diary until 1919, when he assumed the Liberal leadership.

For Ethel, as for most other capital residents, events on Parliament Hill were quite eclipsed during the first weeks of the war by events taking place at the agricultural exhibition grounds at Lansdowne Park. Here, under bell tents, were assembled the members of a glamorous new regiment, Princess Patricia's Canadian Light Infantry, named in honour of the princess, and of which she had agreed to be Colonel-in-Chief. Much in the manner of Lord Strathcona's Horse during the Boer War, this corps had sprung into being almost overnight. The "getter-up of the Regiment," in Ethel's inelegant phrase, was Hamilton Gault, a handsome and dashing thirty-three-year-old Montreal millionaire in dry goods, who had served in South Africa with the Canadian Mounted Rifles. On August 3, Gault had boarded the early-morning train to Ottawa with a proposal in his pocket and headed straight for Sam Hughes's office. If war broke out, he declared, he was ready to raise and equip a military unit at his own expense. It would be an elite group, composed of officers and men who, like him, had already seen active service. Hughes having tentatively approved the idea, Gault moved on to Rideau Hall. There he met with Lieutenant Colonel Francis Farquhar, Connaught's military secretary, a highly competent officer of the Coldstream Guards, who was also a man of imagination. Within days, Gault's scribbled notes

Hamilton Gault, founder of the Princess Patricia's Canadian Light Infantry. A Montreal millionaire who had served in South Africa, he took the morning train to Ottawa on August 3, 1914, determined to found a new regiment with an "irregular tang to it."

had been transformed into a detailed plan. Farquhar would command the new regiment and Gault would be senior major.

On Sunday, August 23, the regiment held its first church parade. Afterwards, in pouring rain, they marched to Parliament Hill to the tune of *All the Blue Bonnets Are Over the Border* to receive from the princess a banner to carry into battle that she herself had designed and embroidered. "I shall follow the fortunes of you all with the greatest interest," Patricia told her soldiers. "I wish every man good luck and a safe return."

Ethel, as it happened, had passed up this ceremony because of the weather. Thus, on the following Wednesday, she was quick to accept the suggestion of her next-door neighbour, Mary Scott, elder sister to D'Arcy, that they hike the mile or so out to Lansdowne Park to conduct their own private inspection. Save for occasional disagreements over politics, Mary, though a decade or so older than Ethel, was one of her closest friends. Like D'Arcy, she was gregarious and high-spirited, and had rather encouraged her brother's flirtation with Ethel. Mary, further, knew all about the pangs of unrequited love. It was common knowledge that for many years she had been carrying a torch for a man named Agar Adamson, who back in the 1890s had been the handsomest and most charming young buck in the capital, but who had married another and moved to Toronto.

Adamson and Mary had kept in touch though. Indeed, on this very afternoon, having secured a commission in Gault's regiment, he was waiting to meet her in Lansdowne Park. Whether or not Ethel felt slightly *de trop* on this occasion, cast against type in the role of a chaperone, she doesn't say. She tells us instead that Adamson very graciously showed them around and introduced them to Gault. Saying farewell in front of his tent, Adamson was his customary charming self. "He asked if there were any more at home like me."

On the way out of the encampment, Mary and Ethel bumped into Colonel Farquhar. Here, no introduction was necessary, since

Lieutenant-Colonel Francis Farquhar (*right*), first Commanding Officer of the PPCLI, with his adjutant, Captain E. S. Buller, who would succeed him as CO in 1915. This photograph was taken at Lansdowne Park in Ottawa on August 27, 1914, the day before the regiment left for the Front. The tent in the background was serving as battalion headquarters; to the far right is the celebrated "Ric-a-dam-doo," the regimental camp colour that Princess Patricia had designed and embroidered herself.

Ethel, as a viceregal regular, was already well used to chaffing with him. She had described him in her diary some months earlier, as "small, ugly, but delightfully easy to talk to." This time, however, Ethel did not engage in her usual social chit-chat, but was remarkably blunt. "I asked him if he were afraid, and he said, No, that he was such a little wisp he wouldn't be noticed."

Seven months later, on March 19, 1915, Farquhar was mortally wounded by a German sniper. Agar Adamson was destined to survive the war.

4

The Captain Returns

Now, God be thanked Who has matched us with His Hour

Rupert Brooke; 1914

A mong the 619,636 Canadians who served during the Great War, Agar Adamson was one of the most remarkable. He was forty-eight when he enlisted, one of the oldest to do so. He was one of the first to go overseas. He spent nearly three years in the trenches. He survived.

Within the context of our peaceable times, Adamson's reasons for volunteering make him appear at once vainglorious and a war-lover. "The little experience I had the good fortune to have as a Commander of a draft of Strathcona's Horse should count for something," he wrote in his application for a commission in the Princess Patricia's. "One might reasonably hope to see a little service under such glorious conditions as the European War."

The truth about Adamson is considerably more complex. Under the skin of this aging Edwardian buck dwelt a romantic who subscribed to the same code of chivalry that two years earlier had led Captain L. E. G. Oates, "a very gallant gentleman," in the description inscribed on his memorial, to limp to his death in an Antarctic blizzard so as not to be a burden to his comrades. This aspect of Adamson's character has been captured by his second son Anthony in a candid family memoir with the beguiling title, *Wasps in the Attic*, from which much of the information in this account is drawn. "He wore a uniform rather as a priest wears vestments. Duty was his ever-present thought. He could forgive his men for relaxing their sense of duty when not under fire –

drinking and a little quiet looting and attempted rape – but an officer and a gentleman in uniform was, in his opinion, never off duty."

What sets Adamson apart from the rest is the record he left of his war. From its start he kept a diary in the form of letters written daily to his wife Mabel. This was his way of exorcizing the horrors of the war: in his own words, "There seems to be something missing in my daily rounds if I have not included a line to you." Nearly eight decades later, the physical appearance of these letters – most were scribbled hastily in pencil, on any piece of paper that was available – convey instantly the chaotic conditions in which they were written. The fact that they exist at all conveys the theatre-of-the-absurd quality of the Great War: even in the thick of battle, the postal system functioned almost as efficiently as within central London. Every evening around six o'clock, letters were collected and delivered, even to the front line, along with *The Times* and the *Daily Mail*, usually a day late, but sometimes the same editions that Londoners had been reading that very morning. Adamson as a correspondent was not often literary, but he possessed a sharp eye for detail, a deep sense of irony, and was unfailingly honest and direct. His letters are one of the best Canadian accounts that exist of the Great War.

Circumstances had usually been kind to Agar Adamson. Born into the Canadian gentry and lucky enough to have married an heiress, he had had no need to scrabble for the comforts of life. Though not tall – he stood about five foot eight, with dark hair and moustache – he was undeniably handsome, his best features a fine Roman nose and extraordinarily bright blue eyes that gave no hint of his limited vision: he had no sight at all in one of them, thanks to a childhood encounter with a cinder, and was severely astigmatic in the other. By 1914 he was growing a bit tubby – a past master, according to one old friend, of ordering excellent dinners in fine restaurants, with a particular weakness for Pol Roger champagne – but he was nearly as fit as he had been in his twenties. A few weeks after joining the Patricias, he took part in a rugger game between officers and sergeants, and lasted the full hour and a half.

In 1914, the term *life-enhancer* had not yet been invented by the Bloomsbury circle, but Adamson assuredly fitted it. The most memorable of his attributes was his charm. This is always the most difficult of qualities to pin down – "if you have it," as J. M. Barrie wrote, "you don't need to have anything else; and if you don't have it, it doesn't much matter what else you have." Adamson's charm encompassed a sense of humour that was both prankish and ironic, a disarming candour, and, particularly appealing to men, an easy *bonhomie*. "In the mess, he was a most delightful dinner companion," a brother officer in the Princess Patricia's recalled after the war. "He had a resonant voice, a good accent, and an excellent vocabulary. His after-dinner speeches were not the less anticipated because he could indulge in pointed irony and was not particular whose toes he trod on . . . he refused to be bored." He was a man's man who got on famously with women; even now, more than sixty years after his death, Adamson refuses to be forgotten, even by those who encountered him only fleetingly. "I met him just once, in the late 1920s, in Ottawa, when I was a green young debutante, and yet I still think of him as one of the two or three most charming people I've ever encountered," recalls Eileen Scott Morley of London, England, now in her eighties and a niece of Adamson's old flame, Mary Scott. The setting for Eileen's encounter with Agar was a rather poky apartment in Ottawa's Sandy Hill, where Mary, as lively and witty as in her youth but grey-haired and crippled with arthritis, was entertaining her niece to tea and hearing all the news of the jazz-age social whirl. Colonel Adamson turned up unexpectedly. "He was still very good-looking, but that wasn't really the point," Eileen Morley recalls. "It was a quality of sheer personal magnetism, of allure if you like. I wanted to stay, but much to my amazement – to my eighteen-year-old mind these were really *old* people – I picked up clear signals from Aunt Mary that they wanted to be alone, and that I was *de trop*."

For much of his personal style, Adamson was indebted to his grandfathers, both of whom had arrived in British North America three-quarters of a century earlier, in the turbulent era that followed the rebellions of 1837. Both had made small but distinctive marks on Canadian history. On the paternal side, William Agar

Adamson, a sporting parson educated at Trinity College, Dublin, had come out in 1840 as chaplain to the Governor General, Lord Sydenham. He later became librarian and chaplain to the Senate but is best remembered for his 1860 treatise, *Salmon Fishing in Canada*, which contained not only sage advice for anglers – "servants you must have who deal with fires, cooking, wet clothes and pickling or smoking the fish caught" – but also the complete words and music to "*Ma Boule Roulant,*" one of the favourite songs of his voyageur guides. "[William] was one of the best type of Irish gentlemen, one who if he had $5,000 a year would spend $5,500," one of his legions of female admirers remembered after his death. Adamson's maternal grandfather, Stewart Derbishire, was equally a bon vivant, and, more intriguingly, a figure surrounded by controversy. The son of a Northamptonshire doctor and a Scottish mother who, in her girlhood, had been celebrated in a poem by Robbie Burns called "Bonny Ann," he became a lawyer, and a keen observer of revolutions, sometimes an actual partaker. In 1832, he defended without fee the group of Dorset farm labourers who had dared to form a primitive union and had become known as the Tolpuddle Martyrs. Later, he became a war correspondent and covered the Carlist war in Spain for the *Morning Chronicle*. In 1838, Derbishire arrived in Canada as a confidential agent in the service of Lord Durham: he prepared a long investigative memo on the sources of the recent rebellions in Upper and Lower Canada that provided much of the underpinning for Durham's own famous conclusion about "two nations warring within the bosom of a single state." He stayed on to become simultaneously Queen's Printer and member for Bytown (soon to be renamed Ottawa) in the first legislature of the united Canadas.

As civil service contemporaries, and also as fellow Epicureans in the wilderness, Stewart Derbishire and William Agar Adamson cultivated a pleasant friendship; probably it was on one of the many occasions when these two wined and dined each other that William Agar's son James met Derbishire's second daughter, Mary Julia. As is so often the case with offspring of flamboyant parents, this pair seem to have been rather a colourless couple who left little mark even upon family history. James, an unambitious civil servant, moved his family to Ottawa when it became the capital in 1865, and died there in 1891 at the age of sixty-four, having risen only to the position of clerk assistant to the Senate. Still, thanks to Mary Julia's private means – Stewart Derbishire's wife, who chose not to join him in Canada, had been a considerable heiress – they were able to live in somewhat grander style than James's salary would have allowed. They built a fine two-and-a-half-storey brick mansion on Metcalfe Street that later became the home of Prime Minister Sir John Thompson and, later still, of Laurier's Minister of the Interior, Clifford Sifton. Three sons were born of the marriage, of whom the eldest and youngest vanished early from Canadian history by emigrating south of the border. The middle son became the real heir of his grandfathers. He was named for them both and also for his maternal great-grandfather, Allan Masterton, "Bonny Ann's" father and a close friend of Robbie Burns: Agar Stewart Allan Masterton Adamson, born in Ottawa on Christmas Day 1865.

Little survives in family records to tell us much about Adamson's childhood, but thanks to accounts kept by others, we have a fair idea of how it was to grow up in the immediate-post-Confederation capital. Like all the other civil service families so rudely removed from the civilities of Quebec City, Agar's parents and grandparents grumbled incessantly about the mud in the streets and the bad smells from drains, the yammering of the mills at the Chaudière, the stacks of newly sawn lumber at virtually every street corner. For their children, however, the ugly little lumber-town was a vast adventure playground. Two rivers, the majestic, fast-flowing Ottawa and the gentle meandering Rideau, flowed right through the heart of the town, not to mention the Rideau Canal. There were boundless opportunities for skating and snow-shoeing and rowing and swimming or simply tumbling around in the vast piles of sawdust. Parliament Hill offered an ever-changing array of attractions: the fireworks and military reviews that marked the Queen's Birthday on May 24, the ascensions by balloon on Dominion Day, the stately viceregal processions that signalled the opening of Parliament. Along with all the other nicely brought-up children of government officials, Agar would have been invited to children's parties at Sir John A. Macdonald's big, gabled, grey stone house, Earnscliffe, and carefully instructed not to gawp at Mary Macdonald, the prime minister's retarded and painfully deformed daughter, but always to include her in their games. Much more fun were the many viceregal children's parties held at Government House. Here, during the 1870s, Agar made a lasting chum of Governor General Lord Dufferin's quicksilver son and heir, the Honourable Archie Blackwood, later to become Lord Ava. In 1900, when Archie Ava died at Ladysmith, in the early months of the war in South Africa, Adamson, by now thirty-four and hearing the news in the midst of his honeymoon in Mexico, mourned him like a brother. "So few really good genuine men in this world," he wrote in his diary. "It seems hard that a Boer bullet should find its way to him."

Like many other sons of the Canadian gentry in Victorian times, Agar grew up thinking of himself not as a Canadian, nor even as a Colonial, but as an Overseas Englishman. This attitude was underscored by his numerous doting – and best of all, wealthy – relations in England. His mother's three unmarried Derbishire sisters kept luxurious spinsters' hall in a vast corner house on the fashionable side of Hyde Park in London. Her brother, John Montagu, who, in the best Victorian tradition, had reverted to his mother's maiden name in order to inherit the bulk of the family fortune, had a splendid country seat called Downe Hall in Dorset. By the time Agar reached his teens he had already crossed the Atlantic half a dozen times, and in the early 1880s Uncle John staked him to several delightful and uproarious years at Cambridge. Though he did not shine academically and left without a degree, he was a great success as an athlete, particularly in sports involving horses. Among many equestrian accomplishments, he won the prestigious Newmarket stakes, and a delightful period photograph shows him at the reins of a coach and four, about to embark from Cambridge to London, presumably at the start of a carriage race. He had a wonderful time and got into a good many scrapes. Once, he was fined the considerable sum of £10 for "driving furiously." Another time, after a riotous evening with too much champagne, he fell down a flight of stairs at his college and suffered a severe concussion. Soon afterwards – a curious choice for one of his temperament, but Adamson was not always as he appeared on the surface – he embarked on a career in the ministry. This avenue closed suddenly, however, when, supposedly taking a final retreat before ordination in order to meditate on matters spiritual, he slipped off to a race meeting where he had the bad luck to encounter his bishop. So Agar returned to Ottawa in 1890 and joined his father in the Senate as a junior clerk, at a salary of $650 per annum. There were, in fact, few other options. Not only was Uncle John Montagu now in declining health, the many drains upon his fortune had diminished it severely. Even for a favourite nephew, the reading of the avuncular will was unlikely to prove a rewarding experience.

The prospect of a life of genteel poverty appealed to Adamson no more than it would to Ethel Chadwick. Still, better to be poor as a buck than as a belle – unlike ball-gowns, one reasonably well-tailored set of evening clothes could survive many seasons, provided one's linen was fresh. Thanks to his natural ebullience, so different from Ethel's tendency to melancholy, Agar accepted his altered fortunes with good grace and, during the 1890s, surmounted them by becoming one of the most popular and sought-after young men in the capital. In 1892, following the death of both his parents within a few months of each other, his mother's sister, "Auntie Bob" Derbishire, came out from England to keep house for him. They sold the fine mansion on Metcalfe Street and moved round the corner to a modest brick house on Nepean Street. Like all the other young bloods, Agar joined the militia, and in 1893 he was commissioned a lieutenant in the Governor General's Foot Guards. While no great shakes at passing exams at the annual summer staff courses – an 1895 Certificate of Military Instruction accords him a "Gentleman's C" of 55 per cent – he shone as a horseman even though he could not afford a mount of his own. In 1899, aboard a charger borrowed from Ottawa's Chief of Police, he beat out seventeen other candidates for top marks in army equitation trials. Thanks to this achievement he was given the plum post of "galloper" to General Edward Hutton, the British officer commanding the Canadian militia at that year's military manoeuvres.

Along with riding, Adamson enjoyed skating, canoeing, sailing, shooting birds and moose, going to parties, and gambling for

higher stakes than he could afford. Unlike his grandfather Derbishire, he had slight interest in politics and no ambition whatever to wield power behind the scenes as a bureaucrat. During his
late twenties and early thirties, his main goal seems to have been
to lead a gregarious, happy-go-lucky life. Time and again he turns
up as a star in the society columns, most notably those written by
Mary Scott's cousin, Agnes, the renowned "Amaryllis." On one
memorable occasion, he won top prize in a charity bazaar competition where gents trimmed ladies' hats. "Mr. Adamson has various talents but one never fancied a talent for millinery among
them," Amaryllis noted indulgently. Towards the end of the
decade, when the Earl and Countess of Minto arrived to reinvent
Rideau Hall in their own stylish and slightly *louche* image, he
became a particular favourite at the viceregal court. Amaryllis
informs us that once, at a skating carnival, he jumped through a
paper hoop and waltzed away with the Countess. He enjoyed
many flirtations; Mary Scott – "Minnie," he always called her –
was certainly only one of legions of belles who found his charm
irresistable. Theirs, though, was a serious romance and not just a
flirtation, for she never married and, as Eileen Scott Morley is witness, a current of electricity remained between them all their
days. But the fact that she was a Catholic and he was a Protestant
constituted an almost immovable impediment to marriage. As
grave an impediment was that even though Minnie occupied an
influential social position as the daughter of a senior cabinet minister and as his stylish and effervescent political hostess, she, like
Adamson, was poor as a churchmouse.

Eventually, Agar Adamson, being the charmer he was, managed to
marry for money as well as love. In 1895, en route home from militia exercises at Niagara, he went to a dinner party in Toronto and
met Mabel Cawthra, a member of one of that city's richest and
most powerful families; before long, they were being seen often in
each other's company, most notably at a magnificent costume ball
marking Queen Victoria's Diamond Jubilee, to which they part-
nered each other as Napoleon and Madame Récamier. Mabel was
not a conventional beauty – her features were too firm and her
jaw too pronounced – but she was striking and full of vitality, with

fine eyes, an elegant figure, and glorious auburn hair. Talented, self-possessed, and a world traveller, she had studied painting and sculpture in Paris, sailed up the Nile in a felucca, dined with the Viceroy in Calcutta, taken part in a tea ceremony at Kyoto. In her mid-twenties, Mabel was the kind of financially secure, independent-minded young woman who might have interested Henry James. Like Isabel Archer in *The Portrait of a Lady*, "she did not look to a man to furnish her with her destiny . . . but had a system and orbit of her own." Mabel's outlook on life was that of a turn-of-the-century New Woman: her unconventional attitudes about religion and marriage challenged Adamson and put him on his mettle. "Can't one have honour and truth and love without a God to regulate them?" she wrote him on one occasion; on another, "You know that I am no believer in marriage ceremonies, and think divorce ought to be encouraged, and marriage made a yearly contract." Unlike Agar – uneasy portent for the future – Mabel had little taste for what she described as "the game of society." But they shared a passion for horses; indeed, if anything, she was a more daredevil rider even than he.

The courtship was stormy. Mabel's widowed mother, the formidable Mrs. John Cawthra, convinced that Adamson was a fortune-hunter, was dead-set against the match. Mabel herself, as a free spirit, took a long time to overcome her skepticism about matrimony. "I do not know what I want," she wrote him. "I feel as if I were a combination of dozens of people all demanding different things." But she was head-over-heels in love and at last, in the late summer of 1899, she accepted him, exorcising all of her own last doubts in an extraordinarily brave letter. "I want you to feel that marriage is not the hard and fast hopelessly binding thing most people think it is. . . . I am simply going to live with you because I want to, and if I cease to want to I shall leave and hope that you will do the same." The wedding, a lavish white and silver affair, took place on November 15, at St. George's Church in Toronto. "I married the dearest woman in the world who alone approved of the match," Adamson noted in his diary. Immediately afterwards, they set off to Mexico for a honeymoon on horseback.

Their life together commenced in the context of war. Five weeks earlier, on October 11, 1899, a ragged army of Boer irregulars

Agar Adamson and Mabel Cawthra Adamson, January 1900. This photograph was taken in New York, en route home from their honeymoon in Mexico. They had just consulted a clairvoyant, who promised them happiness.

had invaded the British colonies of Natal and Cape Province in South Africa. Wedding or no, Agar and Mabel were quickly swept up by the patriotic fever that gripped all of English Canada. She, as on the hunting field, was even more of a hothead than he. "Why was I not born a man?" she lamented to him in a letter. With her eager approval, he volunteered for the First Canadian Contingent, and both were deeply disappointed that he missed being selected. "Should we go anyway, on spec?" she wrote impulsively. "We could say we had changed our minds [about Mexico], go to England instead and then sneak off by the first boat to the Cape." Common sense prevailed, but as soon as they returned to Ottawa at the end of January 1900, they developed a more orderly strategy. In March, as a first step, Agar took leave from his job in the Senate, and took a commission in a special service regiment raised from the militia to man the Imperial Garrison at Halifax, thereby relieving the British regulars for duty at the Front. Mabel – already it was clear that this was a partnership of equals – stayed in Ottawa to lobby members of cabinet, most notably Postmaster General William Mulock, who was her first cousin, and the Minister of Militia, Frederick Borden, well known to have a weakness for good-looking women. The golden opportunity presented itself in mid-April: Agar was offered a commission as a lieutenant in Strathcona's Horse, the glamorous new regiment of mounted rifles chiefly recruited from the ranks of the North-West Mounted Police, and financed by Lord Strathcona, then Canada's High Commissioner in London. The main body of the regiment having left for the Cape six weeks earlier, he was put in charge of a fifty-man draft of reinforcements. Accompanied by Mabel, and also by his mother-in-law Mrs. Cawthra, who, despite her grave and ongoing reservations about Agar was never one to miss out on the excitement, he and his men sailed for Liverpool early in May. Immediately on arrival, they travelled by special train to the London docks and boarded the South Africa-bound troopship, HMS *Assaye*. The following afternoon, they sailed for the Cape, with Mabel, Mrs. Cawthra, and Lord Strathcona waving from the jetty.

Out on the veldt, Agar served with gallantry and distinction. During his first engagement under fire, a skirmish near Standerton in the southern Transvaal between his small group of troopers and a much larger contingent of Boers, he won a mention in dispatches for not losing a single man and for bringing back all his wounded. To his great pride, he successfully recommended one of his sergeants, Arthur Richardson, for Canada's first Victoria Cross of the war. "The enemy did their best to make you, my sweetheart, a widow, but only succeeded in wounding my horse," he wrote to Mabel. "A bullet makes a most curious sound as it passes you, very much like an Elephantine humming bee. I do not think I was afraid."*

By now, much to Adamson's regret, all the big setpiece battles were over, but the extraordinary Boer generals, Smuts, Botha, and De Wet, had developed an entirely new form of war – guerrilla war: small groups of men riding hard, shooting fast, and then vanishing to live by their wits and off the land. Throughout the long cold South African winter of 1900 – Mabel, back in England, had passed up the fripperies of the London season to enrol in a nursing course in a bleak hospital at Kidderminster in the Midlands – Adamson

---

* A more detailed account of Adamson's time in South Africa is contained in *The Private Capital*.

and the Strathconas pursued the Boers into the northern Transvaal wilderness. "We are on short rations, three dog biscuits a day
and a little bully beef," he wrote her. "Washing impossible, one
night in bed out of every three, with the marrow of one's bones
almost frozen." In August, as the chase gained momentum, the regiment galloped through towns along the railway line, endeavouring
to cut the Boers' last link with the sea. At Amersfoort, he wrote
Mabel, "I had the advance guard, and two small galloping guns . . .
we rode very hard, the bullets simply rained in upon us." At
Ermelo, "we rushed to the Town Hall, pulled down the Transvaal
flag." The chill and the dust and the wind were all relentless. "I
hope this will reach you," he wrote from a camp by the Komatic

Agar Adamson in 1900, shortly before going out to South
Africa as a lieutenant in Strathcona's Horse. Out on the
veldt, he discovered that soldiering was his true calling.

River. "It is being written under difficulties, with a sputtering candle. . . . It is too cold to write more and alas, your sleeping cap was stolen from my haversack."

Adamson, as these letters bear witness, was beginning to discover that soldiering was his true calling. He had a natural gift for command. What mattered out on the veldt was not bravura displays of horsemanship, but being cool and resourceful under fire. What mattered as much was to be respected by one's men and to hold them in respect. At first, Agar admired the Commanding Officer of the Strathconas, the legendary Colonel Sam Steele, as a bold and innovative leader in the field. Before long, though, he came to despise Steele as a coarse bully who treated the troops like animals. "Men suffering dreadfully from bad boots," he noted in his diary on October 7, 1900. "The OC will not allow a single man to ride on wagons. Most unjust." On October 18, as the regiment moved into rest camp at Pretoria, Adamson noted, "CO and most of the officers disgracefully drunk, making idiots of themselves at the club. The men left absolutely alone."

To his immense chagrin, Adamson's war ended abruptly in November 1900, when he contracted typhoid fever. Invalided back to Britain, he enjoyed a rapturous reunion with Mabel and a long, recuperative holiday in the south of France, during which they conceived their first child, a son whom they named Rodney. Back in Ottawa, he found it difficult to readjust to his sinecure in the Senate, all the more because, despite his war record and despite the assiduous lobbying of both Mabel and of Minnie Scott (an unlikely and no doubt uneasy alliance), he was passed over for promotion to the prestigious position of Gentleman Usher of the Black Rod. Thus, early in 1902, shortly before the peace treaty was signed, he made a second sortie to South Africa, with Mabel's approval, this time as a captain in the 6th Canadian Mounted Rifles, hoping to transfer to a permanent commission in a British regiment. "If I depend on you or anyone else for income I lose my self respect," he wrote her. "I'm sure if we could once get into an Imperial Regiment, it would suit us both down to the ground." She closed up the house in Ottawa and embarked with the baby for England, intending to sail shortly from there to South Africa herself, "to start life afresh under the Southern Cross." Alas, none of these plans came to anything. Within the British Regulars, there was no room for Overseas Englishmen, no matter how keen and courageous. "I have tried in vain, but they are firm," he wrote Mabel. "They will not employ Colonials."

The next dozen years were the most frustrating of Adamson's life. For a time, he and Mabel thought of settling in England; while he took an unsuccessful stab at learning gentleman-farming near Bath, she enrolled in a course in the applied arts at the noted Arts and Crafts Guild workshop at Chipping Camden in the Cotswolds. In 1903, they dragged back to Ottawa, but within a couple of years Agar and the Senate decided by mutual agreement to sever a relationship that was growing less and less productive. The family moved to Toronto, where Mabel had always wanted to be. In October 1906 their second son Anthony was born. Shortly thereafter, Mabel used a chunk of her capital to establish the Canadian franchise of an English antiques and decorating business, the Thornton-Smith Company, with the intention that it would absorb both their energies. The venture flourished, winning contracts to refurbish the Senate Chamber and to decorate the interior of the new Royal Alexandra Theatre, but Adamson did not. His fabled charm did not extend to chatting up clients; indeed, thanks to his candour and pointed irony, he quite often drove them away. He was now well into his forties and in his own eyes and in those of his in-laws, he was a failure, a man content not only to live off his wife's income, but also to live in his in-law's houses: during the winter months, he and Mabel and the children shared a large mansion on Beverley Street with her mother; in the summer, they lived at the farm property near Port Credit, thirteen miles west of Toronto on the Lakeshore Road, that had been deeded to Mabel's great-grandfather eight decades earlier. Agar and Mabel had not fallen out of love with each other, but with each passing year it became more evident how little they had in common. While she attended to the business and in her spare time founded the Society for Applied Art and the Heliconian Club for like-minded women interested in culture, he whiled away the time drinking too much champagne in gentlemen's clubs with companions of whom she nearly always disapproved. Quite often, he slipped up to Ottawa under the pretext of taking in the races or the annual horse show, but most likely also to see Minnie Scott, who did not make judgements.

By the summer of 1914, the gulf between Agar and Mabel had never been wider. In a profile in a Toronto paper, she was celebrated as "a Canadian woman of genius, who makes homes and buildings beautiful." He, meanwhile, was pottering around aimlessly at Port Credit, supervising the construction of an ornamental rustic bridge of small tree trunks arching over the driveway. The German invasion of Belgium provided him not only with a desperately needed challenge – the last chance to make something of himself – but also with an escape route from a life that was increasingly pointless. As a member of the Arts and Letters Club, Adamson may have been one of the Torontonians who had met Rupert Brooke when he was entertained there during the previous summer. Certainly, in 1914, the first line of Brooke's famous war sonnet would have struck a chord. "Now, God be thanked who has matched us with His Hour."

The day after war was declared, Adamson set out post-haste for Ottawa. There – quite possibly from Minnie Scott – he learned of Gault's plan to found a new regiment. Since the two were not yet acquainted, he sent his letter of application to a chum of his youth: Arthur Sladen, known informally as "Slads," private secretary to the Governor General. At once candid and jocular, the style was Agar himself.

> Being in the neighbourhood of forty-nine, though neither looking or feeling it and being totally blind of one eye and being a bit dotty in the other, and weighing in the neighbourhood of one hundred and eighty-five pounds in the lightest possible pyjamas, it often appears to me that I might be considered rather a waiste [sic], than an advantage to any expeditionary force, but I do think that the little experience I had the good fortune to have as a Commander of a draft of Strathcona's Horse, and the experience of seeing troops in the field, should count for something, and one might reasonably hope to see a little service under such glorious conditions as the European War.

Presumably, Sladen passed this communication, together with a personal recommendation, along to Colonel Farquhar, who in turn had a word with Gault. Whatever happened, the magic worked: Adamson was offered a captaincy in the Princess Patricia's. Within a day or so, he returned to Port Credit to pack up his kit. On Monday, August 10, he left home, not to return for nearly five years.

On that day, as it happened, Mabel was entertaining the local chapter of the Women's Institute at an outdoor tea party by the lake. Adamson was waved off to war in the manner of a patriotic tableau: twenty-five Ontario ladies in summery shirtwaists and wide-brimmed straw hats, all fluttering handkerchiefs.

5

The Unlikely Lieutenant

My profession is speeching, not fighting.
Talbot Papineau. A letter to a friend; 1915

The Princess Patricia's Canadian Light Infantry left Ottawa on the morning of Friday, August 28, 1914. Thousands of citizens waved and cheered as the regiment marched briskly to the skirl of the pipes from Lansdowne Park to Union Station. Yet the mood was sombre, for the grim news of the British retreat from Mons was just beginning to sink in: there was no formal send-off on Parliament Hill and no dallying on the platform. "They were embarked in a very few minutes," reported Ethel Chadwick, who had managed to secure an excellent vantage point not far from the viceregal party. "I didn't see anyone I knew to say goodbye."

Though less than a month old, the regiment had begun to develop a mystique. Its designation *Light* Infantry had been chosen by Hamilton Gault because, in his words, it had an "irregular tang" to it. The regimental colour, soon to be nicknamed the "Ric-a-dam-doo," was not an official colour, approved by the College of Heralds, but the simple red, blue, and gold "Camp Colour" that Princess Patricia had designed and embroidered herself. Before long, it would take on almost mystical significance as the only regimental colour actually carried into battle by any British or Colonial unit, even if inadvertently. The crest on the cap and collar badges, also designed by the princess, harked back to the age of chivalry: a single daisy, in honour of Gault's elegant wife, whose name was Marguerite.

Princess Patricia's design for her regiment's cap and collar badges. The single daisy was in honour of Hamilton Gault's wife, Marguerite. Later, the design was to cause problems and would be changed.

This initial complement, soon to be known as "The Originals," comprised thirty-one officers and about eleven hundred other ranks. Already, they referred to themselves as "the Patricias," or "the PPCLI," or simply as "The Regiment," the term Adamson most often used in his letters, rather than by the popular abbreviation, "Princess Pat's," for this was considered *lèse-majesté*. By any standards, they were an unusual body of men: a mixed bag of prospectors, trappers, guides, cow-punchers, prize-fighters, farmers, adventurers, and remittance men, assembled in less than a fortnight and already bonding into a self-defined elite brotherhood. Three times as many had volunteered as had been chosen. Nearly all had put in some time with the British regulars; about half had seen service in the field, either in South Africa or on the Northwest Frontier of India. This latter experience derived from the fact that almost all were relatively recent immigrants from the British Isles; only about a hundred were Canadian-born. According to a rumour well on the way to being transformed into a legend, one group of old sweats anxious to get back in action had hijacked a train and forced it to go to Ottawa at the point of a gun; another party, who described themselves as the "Legion of Frontiersmen," banded together in the west even before the recruiting posters were up, and enlisted in a body, already wearing a makeshift uniform of cowboy hats, khaki shirts, and neckerchiefs. The pipe band, led by a gallant old Highlander named

Jock Colville, had arrived unsolicited from Edmonton, in full Highland kit and the Hunting Stewart tartan, donated by the local St. Andrew's Society.

Among the officers, the proportion of Canadians was much higher: almost a third. Of the Britishers, a handful, including Farquhar himself and Captains Buller and Newton, who had also been seconded from the Duke of Connaught's staff of aides, were upper-class, spit-and-polish former members of the Brigade of Guards. A more typical member was Captain J. S. Ward, formerly of the British Army in India, more recently a fruit farmer in the Okanagan Valley.

Of the Canadian-born officers, a number were problematic choices, the reason being that Farquhar and Gault had been prohibited from recruiting active members of the militia, who were all

The PPCLI leaving Lansdowne Park en route to the troop train on Friday, August 28, 1914. The pipe band had arrived unsolicited from Edmonton. The small boy just in front of the band seems almost a symbol of innocence soon to be lost.

to be commandeered for the First Canadian Contingent, and so had had to accommodate certain handicaps. Adamson himself, nearly a decade over-age, was one example. Captain George Bennett, a former Regina bank clerk who had been gazetted paymaster was another: as the brother of the Conservative Member of Parliament, R. B. Bennett, he'd got in through political pull. There was also Captain Charlie Stewart, a tall, rakish Nova Scotia bachelor, whose chequered career, as described by his nephew, the diplomat and diarist Charles Ritchie, included expulsion from the Royal Military College for gambling, dismissal from the mounted police for striking a corporal, a spell in the Yukon during which he had not struck it rich, and numerous affairs with women, married and otherwise. Already, to his six-year-old namesake, Uncle Charlie was a legend. "He had been bold and adventurous; feats of

Officers of the Princess Patricia's Canadian Light Infantry assembled at Lansdowne Park in Ottawa on August 27, 1914. Within months, those who had survived would become known as the "Originals." Approximately a third were Canadian-born. Farquhar is tenth from the right in the second row with Buller to his immediate left. Hamilton Gault is on Farquhar's immediate right. Agar Adamson, wearing his service ribbons from South Africa, is fourth from the right. Talbot Papineau, yet to start growing a moustache, is fifth from the right in the row of junior offices seated on the ground. Charlie Stewart is fourth from the right, next to Papineau. Papineau and Stewart and numerous other officers are wearing brand-new wristwatches, still at that date an innovation, probably given to them as parting gifts.

nerve and truant defiance were his," Ritchie wrote many years later.

The most unlikely Patricia of all was Talbot Papineau. He had no military experience whatever, in fact was known to have expressed disapproval of the Boy Scouts because of that organization's militaristic overtones. As might have been a more considerable disqualification for a regiment whose tone was so thoroughly British, he was a French Canadian, indeed was the great-grandson of Louis-Joseph Papineau, leader of the *patriote* rebels of 1837. Yet, the same day that Adamson sent in his letter of application, Papineau applied to Hamilton Gault to be allowed to join by way of a telegram sent all the way from Vancouver where he was speaking at a Canadian Club convention; he was immediately accepted, and gazetted as a lieutenant. It is time to introduce Papineau properly, for he is the tragic hero of this book.

Then thirty-one, Papineau was a clever, self-assured Montreal lawyer, brimming over with *joie de vivre* and clearly cut out for stardom. His full name was Talbot Mercer Papineau; as it suggests, he was the product of two cultures, in some ways prefiguring Pierre Elliott Trudeau. From his father's people – rooted in Quebec for more than two centuries – he had inherited much of his intellect, his profound sense of place, his passion for politics, his not inconsiderable vanity and, perhaps, his sense of irony. From his mother, the former Caroline Rogers of Philadelphia, a strong-willed member of the Yankee aristocracy, and a descendant of a signer of the Declaration of Independence, he had inherited additional intelligence, along with his vaulting ambition and so far as we can judge, much of his physical appearance. "I fear my mould is not heroic," he once mocked himself. "I am neither an Apollo, nor a Penseur nor a David . . . I am neither tall nor short, sadly I am four inches lower than my six-foot ideal." This however, was a bit disingenuous for he was extremely good-looking, with crisp wavy hair brushed back from a widow's peak that would have done credit to a matinée idol, with a full sensual mouth and intense brown eyes. No less charming than Agar Adamson, and equally well aware of it, Papineau possessed all the appropriate athletic and social graces: a fine horseman, a champion canoeist, an excellent dancer. He fascinated women, but those who fell in love with him did so to their cost, for he was restless and elusive.

He was born on March 25, 1883, in the idyllic surroundings of Montebello, the ancestral Papineau seigneurie, originally known as Petit Nation, on the north shore of the Ottawa River about halfway between Montreal and Ottawa. An informal family snapshot taken a couple of years later, in which Talbot appears as a toddler, sitting on a wooden sled and wearing a blanket coat and sash, suggests not so much late-nineteenth-century Canada, as the Russia of Turgenev and Chekhov. In the background, set on a sweeping, snow-covered lawn, is the graceful, turretted manor house built in 1850 by Louis-Joseph Papineau after his return from exile in the United States. Talbot's father, also called Louis-Joseph, stands nearest the house, a tall, elegant, bearded man in a voluminous fur coat and broad-brimmed hat. Caroline Papineau, a small, slim woman with exquisite carriage, fashionably dressed in a long, close-fitting jacket and flared, three-tiered sporting skirt, looks straight at the camera. Two other children appear in the picture: Talbot's elder brother, once again Louis-Joseph in the family tradition, and his younger brother Westcott. A fourth son, Philip, would be born a few years later.

As in *The Cherry Orchard*, however, the impression of serenity and contentment provided in this opening setpiece was an illusion. Before Talbot entered his teens, his parents had become estranged. Louis-Joseph appears to have been both alcoholic and spendthrift. Parcel after parcel of the original 250,000 acres had to be sold off to pay the bills, until only about 800 acres of woodland remained. Nevertheless, Talbot's childhood was a happy one, and it was to Montebello that he returned time and again in his thoughts during the worst tours of duty in the trenches. "There I was born and there my heart is," he wrote to an American girl with whom he had fallen a little in love. "What games we used to play, how often as Indians we crept through the underbrush to attack the settlement, or paddled in tense silence through the shadows to pass the waiting foe."

He grew up completely at home in either culture, playing
Hereward the Wake in the reeds on the riverbank, as often as Dollard at the Long Sault. The Papineaus had long been free-thinkers,
so he was not brought up Catholic, and, thanks to Caroline's influence (cleverest and handsomest of her sons, Talbot was the apple
of her eye, and she to him was "rather a deity"), he was educated
almost exclusively in English alongside the sons of the Montreal
Anglo-Scottish ascendancy at Montreal High School, McGill University, and subsequently, Oxford. In the opinion of his doting
grandfather in Philadelphia, Talbot Mercer Rogers, he was
"sprightly, keen, quick to see, quick to reply in well-chosen language . . . he has naturally many popular elements and would
make a first-class jury lawyer." Classmates remembered him as
gregarious, competitive, cocky, and handy, when need be, with his
fists. As editor of the McGill student newspaper, he deliberately
stirred up a row by writing an article arguing that the students

Talbot Papineau as an infant. Even this early on, he seemed destined for stardom.

Three generations of Papineaus gathered at Montebello, *circa* 1885. Louis-Joseph Papineau (1786–1871), leader of the *patriote* rebels in 1837, had built the manor house in 1850, after returning from exile in the United States. The family had many American connections: the *grand patriote*'s son, also named Louis-Joseph (on the left wearing a fur hat), had married Mary Eleanor Westcott of Saratoga Springs, New York. Their son, again Louis-Joseph (closest to the house in a fur coat), married Caroline Rogers of Philadelphia, whose mother had been Mary Eleanor's closest friend. Caroline, still remembered by her granddaughters as a "tiny but indomitable presence," is shown pushing a sleigh containing her third son Westcott. Her eldest son Louis-Joseph wears a tuque with a pom-pom. Her second son Talbot Mercer Papineau, named for his Philadelphia grandfather, is in the foreground, wearing a blanket coat and sash. (A fourth son, Philip, would be born a few years later.)

Montebello is on the north shore of the Ottawa River, about halfway between Montreal and Ottawa. The estate is now a hotel complex, the Château Montebello, but the manor house has been preserved largely unchanged.

themselves were the best judges of their professors, and then answering himself in an angry reply signed with a pseudonym. He studied political economy under Stephen Leacock – "his description of how some heads winked as they fell in the basket from the guillotine was extremely amusing," Papineau recalled – and the two became good friends. But he was not overawed by Leacock's fame – indeed, much in the manner of Pierre Trudeau, there was little that overawed Papineau – and his character assessment of Leacock is revealing not only of the professor but also of the student. "I do not call him a success," he continued. "I sometimes think he simply wants to be merry and entertaining without serious intentions of getting anywhere."

By the time he left McGill in 1905, covered with glory as one of the first Canadian Rhodes Scholars, Talbot's fame was beginning to spread. "Young Papineau . . . is able, with English ideals and a French temperament and wit. If he has ambition, he may go far," the Governor General, Earl Grey, wrote to a friend in England. He had expanded his knowledge and sense of Canada by spending one summer on a geographical survey party around James Bay; another laying track for the CPR west of Moose Jaw. Already, he and Caroline were planning his career in public life. Beyond being an ardent Liberal – a Papineau could scarcely be otherwise – his political ideas were vague, although, thanks to Leacock's influence and perhaps also Caroline's, he was a committed free-trader. "The U.S. has only survived its choking tariffs because it happens to be within itself the biggest free-trade area in the world," he wrote later to a friend.

At Oxford, where he read international law at Brasenose College, Papineau encountered a diametrically opposed set of ideas. This was the heyday of the Imperial Federalists, those who believed in the Kiplingesque ideal of a Parliament at Westminster expanded to include representatives from all the Old Colonies (i.e., white ones). He got to know the most messianic Imperialist of them all, Lionel Curtis, professor of colonial history at New College, who, in the words of another undergraduate of the era, the aspiring historian, Arnold Toynbee, "had an unerring eye for potential converts whose conversion might turn the tide of public opinion." Little remembered now, Curtis's singular achievement was to resurrect the seventeenth-century word, *Commonwealth*, coined by Oliver Cromwell, and to pioneer its usage as a circumspect substitute for *Empire*. Curtis never made a true disciple out of Papineau, but they became lasting friends, and a few years later, when Curtis hit on the idea of founding "The Round Table," a discussion forum composed of groups of influential young men in cities all over the Empire, Talbot introduced him around Montreal, and, while declining the local chairmanship, agreed to become a member.

On the whole, though, the creamy English charm of Edwardian Oxford, reflected in novels like Max Beerbohm's *Zuleika Dobson*, left Papineau unenchanted. One reason, no doubt, was that as a Colonial, he found himself a very small fish in a very large pond. The other was that he was homesick for Montebello. "How I longed to be going back with Westcott," he wrote Caroline in 1906, after a visit from his younger brother. "But I am more than ever determined to see this thing through with the best grace possible and the greatest benefit." To the detriment of scholarship – much to his chagrin, he emerged with a Second instead of the First that he and Caroline had banked on – his happiest hours were spent on the river, where he rowed stroke for the College Eight and became secretary of the Boating Club. On the last day of his Finals in June 1908 – "all is over now, and I am delightfully and happily free" – he celebrated by hiring a canoe and paddling all the way down to Richmond in the company of a newly acquired puppy. "I am tremendously pleased to leave Oxford and delighted beyond expression to be returning home," he told Caroline. "I am so anxious to see the stables and the horses and all the improvements, and to be there generally with you again."

Back in Montreal, Talbot began his political apprenticeship in earnest. He set up a law practice in partnership with his close friend and fellow Liberal, Andrew McMaster, in the Canada Life Building on St. James Street and though at twenty-eight was considered a little too young (and perhaps, in Laurier's view, a little too cocky) to contest a seat in the election of 1911, he campaigned actively for the party's policy of reciprocity with the United States. He read voraciously, particularly enjoying the works of H. G. Wells and Anatole France whom he described as "investigators of the future." He sometimes engaged in long discussions about the future of Canada with his first cousin once removed, Henri Bourassa,* the passionate Quebec nationalist who had recently founded *Le Devoir*, and it may have been through Bourassa's influence that he began to cultivate an interest in Quebec folksongs and culture. Simultaneously, Papineau's own view of Canada began to take shape. While he remained a free-trader – he took Leacock to task for abandoning ship in 1911 and was gratified to wring an admission out of his former mentor that this had been a mistake – his experiences at Oxford had also had an effect, if not quite the one that Lionel Curtis had hoped. "I am before all Canadian," he wrote later. "Especially, I want to see Canadian pride based on substantial achievements, and not on the supercilious and fallacious sense of self-satisfaction we have borrowed from England." He became president of the Montreal branch of the Canadian Club, an organization founded in 1904 to promote a cautious version of nationalism, and was soon one of its most popular speakers, specializing in explaining Quebec to the rest of the country.

He played as hard as he worked. No Montreal bachelor was more sought after, the ornament of many ballrooms and tennis parties and weekends in the Laurentians. His own house parties at Montebello were legendary, as photographs and guestbook reveal. Once, Laurier himself dropped by for the day, and wrote, "Trop court sejour!" Yet there is reason to suspect that during the years leading up to the war, Papineau was beginning to feel nearly as frustrated as Agar Adamson, if for quite different reasons. The crushing Liberal defeat of 1911 had put a spoke in his wheel. In 1913, he turned thirty – and still seemed to be marking time. Increasingly, he became a compulsive traveller, testing his mettle climbing mountains in Switzerland and driving the terrifying corniche road along the Amalfi coast of Italy at breakneck speed, "shouting for the sheer joy of it," as he wrote to a friend.

Papineau spent the first part of his 1914 summer holiday

---

* Bourassa was the maternal grandson of *le grande patriote*, Louis-Joseph Papineau. His mother Azèlie, had married Napoleon Bourassa, a well-known Quebec artist.

The style is the man himself. These photographs from a Papineau family album were taken at one of Talbot's legendary house parties. Among the figures dancing with the flag, he is third from the left; his younger brother Westcott is second from the right.

south of the border, in the Hamptons of Long Island, but the outbreak of war found him, as we know, in Vancouver. His behaviour
that weekend baffled the Canadian Club organizers. In the midst
of his address to the annual meeting – the subject was *The Nationalist Idea in Quebec* – he departed from his text to make a sharp
comment about current events, "Canada did not have one word to
say in the diplomatic negotiations leading up to the war, nor in
the declaration of war." Yet he cancelled an additional speaking
engagement in Victoria and rushed straight back to Ottawa to
enlist, after having telegraphed his close friend "Hammie" Gault,
and having had a favourable reply.

In fact, Papineau's reasons for volunteering were straightfor-
ward. The war was an adventure and a calculated risk. Unlike so
many young British aristocrats, he was not half in love with the
idea of dying a hero. Instead, he wanted to have a brilliant career.
A "good war," as the saying went, would enable him to leap up the
ladder, bearing battle-honours. Even Laurier seemed to agree, or
so Talbot hinted in a letter to his mother, who naturally, was horrified by his decision. "I had luncheon yesterday in private with
Sir Wilfrid – very interesting," he wrote from Lansdowne Park on
August 27. Further to cheer Caroline, he also described a farewell
dinner for the regiment tendered by the members of the Rideau
Club. "I made a long speech and was much congratulated. Some
men said I should be Premier one day."

Papineau proved to be almost as copious a war-correspondent
as Agar Adamson. He dispatched great convoys of letters – to his
mother nearly every day and, from mid-1915 onwards, to a particular woman friend. Nearly all of these letters survive. Papineau's
style is alive and assured, his observation acute. "Writing near
midnight by light of a candle," begins one letter of 1915. "Outside it
is inky black. I have to feel ahead with my cane as I walk along the
trenches. At each bay stands a silent black sentinel who chal-
lenges me as I pass. Occasionally we send up a flare and then peer
anxiously behind our wire entanglements for signs of the foe . . .
for two days and nights there has been a thunderous cannonade to
the north of us, but we have no news."

Reading Papineau's accounts in tandem with Adamson's, we
have an uncanny sense of moving along through the war in their

presence. Yet these two brother officers scarcely ever turn up in each other's letters. The gap between them was both generational and cultural. Like many military men, Adamson was suspicious of intellectuals and politicians; like most English Canadians of the time, he was even more suspicious of French Canadians. Papineau was not only all of these things, he was also in Adamson's opinion, an apple-polisher and a glory-hunter, even a "self-seeking bounder," as he put it in a 1917 letter to Mabel. Yet Adamson, even at his most Waspish, was too much a good soldier not to give credit where it was due. "Papineau is really very good," he admitted a few weeks later, praising his steadiness under fire.

In the last week of August, when the train carrying the Patricias pulled out of Ottawa, Adamson and Papineau and everyone in the regiment expected to be at the Front in a matter of weeks. At Montreal, after a brisk and wildly cheered march along Sherbrooke Street, they boarded the Canadian Pacific liner *Megantic*. They sailed the next morning, to the toots and whistles of every ship in the St. Lawrence. At Quebec, though, they were intercepted by a telegram from the Admiralty. Because of the new submarine warfare, no troops were to cross the Atlantic except in a convoy. This meant that the Patricias, ready and eager for action, would have to cool their heels until the raw recruits of the First Canadian Contingent were ready. Colonel Farquhar – "Fanny" Farquhar, as he was already affectionately dubbed by both officers and men – brought the news to the messrooms. "This is our first knock," he told his men. "Take it like soldiers." By means of some deft string-pulling, he managed to save them from the indignity of having to bivouac with *hoi-polloi* at Valcartier, that instant city of 6,000 bell tents and 32,000 men over which Sam Hughes ruled like a despot. Instead, they remained on the south shore of the St. Lawrence at Lévis, where an old militia camp was put at their disposal.

They waited there nearly a month. In Europe, Paris was saved at the Battle of the Marne, and the Russian army suffered a terrible defeat at Tannenberg. For Papineau, the additional training at Lévis was an opportunity to discover how little he knew. "I spend as much time as possible reading my manuals," he wrote to his mother. "The other day I tied my platoon all up and had an awful time getting it straightened out. I seem to get along well with the men but I make a good many mistakes in drill, which is most annoying." He was growing a moustache, he added. "I do not think it is very becoming, however it is the Colonel's wish that we should all have them." Presciently, much effort was devoted to surveying and digging practise trenches. Even more time was spent on the rifle range, testing the Ross Rifle, the Quebec-manu-factured sporting rifle that Hughes was demanding be used at the Front. Much to the minister's fury, the Patricias rejected it, choos-ing instead the standard British Lee Enfield. "The experience which we have had with the Ross," wrote Farquhar in an official memo, "can hardly fail to have shaken the confidence of the men in that rifle." (Though an excellent target weapon, the Ross jammed repeatedly under rugged conditions, or when fired rapidly).

For Agar Adamson, the month at Lévis was a bit like being a "summer soldier" back in the 1890s. There was even plenty of riding, for, while the Patricias were an infantry regiment, wealthy admirers had provided the officers with excellent mounts. The first of his wartime letters were directed, not to Mabel, but to his sons. In hindsight, these read like cheery, *Boys' Own* chronicles, but they were the log of a middle-aged man's joyful recapturing of youth.

"We had a great night march a few nights ago," he told thir-teen-year-old Rodney, going on to describe, *con brio*, how he had led his company through three miles of thick woods and under-brush, with only a tiny, radium-illuminated compass as guide, and emerged triumphantly at dawn precisely at the point where the white flag was posted. "I was quite pleased with the result," he continued, "because you know that, as your mother says, I can lose my way in the daytime anywhere in Toronto, but it is a differ-ent game we are playing just now." There was also the challenge of mastering semaphore – "you can send long messages by moving your arms in certain directions" – a forced march during which he carried "a sword, a greatcoat, a pistol and fifty rounds of ammunition, a blanket, a waterproof sheet, a water bottle, a haversack and a pair of field-glasses" for twenty-seven miles, the last five miles non-stop, and of the rugger game with the sergeants, an extraordinary performance for a man of nearly fifty. "The next morning I felt as if every bone in my body had been broken," he wrote, "but we won by one goal to a try."

Adamson took the training in earnest. As in South Africa, what mattered most to him, as second-in-command of Company C, was to gain the respect of his men. He in turn gave them his deep respect. "They are a fine lot," he told Rodney. "They never complain no matter how wet or tired or cold they are, and very often, they are all three."

On September 28, 1914, a rainy Wednesday, embarkation orders were posted at last. The Patricias marched aboard the liner *Royal George*, hastily painted battleship grey, and set sail on September 30. The first stop was the Gaspé Basin, where they anchored for two days, while the full convoy assembled. In all there were 36 transports carrying 32,000 men, 105 nursing sisters, and 34 chaplains, Adamson reported to Rodney in a letter accompanied by a neat diagram. "We will all start off at once, four abreast, with four men-of-war conveying us, one in front, one behind, and one on each side." Everyone was gripped by a sense of awe and of occasion. Each ship that arrived was greeted by a great roar of cheers from the men aboard the others. Sam Hughes buzzed around in a tugboat, distributing pamphlets and offering good wishes. When, on his orders, the revenue cutter *Canada* moved through the fleet, offering to take the last mail and post it in Halifax, hundreds of men rushed to the rails and sent down great blizzards of letters. But since it was windy, many were left floating on the water. Papineau made several pencil sketches of the ships and the river, and these survive among his papers.

The voyage to England took over a fortnight. "Owing to some ships being slow, we have not been able to make more than nine knots an hour," Adamson explained in a letter to Mabel. There was a curious feeling of being isolated in a crowd, for while nearly all the other ships could be seen nearly all the time, and indeed, collisions were sometimes perilously close, no communication between them was allowed, except for orders from the flagship. On October 5, they were joined off Cape Race by ss *Florizel*, a small passenger steamer carrying a contingent of troops raised

Talbot Papineau titled this pencil sketch "A part of the fleet in Gaspé Basin." He drew it from the deck of the *Royal George* as the convoy carrying the Canadian Expeditionary Force was assembling. In the absence of a sketching pad, he used a sheet of official regimental stationery, as the crest at the left indicates.

An artist's view of the Canadian armada. This painting, by F. S. Challenor, is more professional than Papineau's work, but since it was done later from photographs, lacks the quality of immediacy.

The ss *Florizel* leaving St. John's with the Newfoundland Regiment aboard. Its members, nicknamed "The Blue Puttees," would become as legendary as the Patricias. Three years later, the *Florizel* struck a reef and went down with great loss of life during a peaceful civilian passage between St. John's and New York.

by the independent colony of Newfoundland, oldest member of the British Empire. The Newfoundland Regiment would soon become as legendary as the Patricias; further along, we shall encounter two of its members. Much to the relief of Adamson, who had never been a good sailor, and who had equipped himself with a good supply of Mothersill's tablets, the seas were calm all the way, and the weather was sunny. Much less to his pleasure, he was required to enrol in a course of French lessons under Papineau's instruction. "I am in the Booby class, and it is an awful grind," he complained in a letter to six-year-old Anthony. "But Colonel Farquhar refuses to take any officer to France who can't speak enough to be understood, and send an ordinary written message." This sense of being at a disadvantage with a much younger man wounded Adamson's *amour propre* and was undoubtedly one of the reasons why the relationship between the two got off to a bad start.

In most other respects, the trip was almost a luxury cruise. Only the occasional sight of a dead horse jettisoned from one of the crowded animal transports served as *memento mori*. Adamson had a cabin all to himself, complete with "a brass bed, all sorts of electric lights, a writing table, in fact everything but a piano and a clock." Every evening, the officers were piped into dinner in the glittering dining salon. Rather to his disapproval – "there is no doubt women are a mistake aboard a troopship" – a number of officers were accompanied by their wives. Nevertheless he enjoyed chatting them up. One Mrs. McKinery, married to the major in command of Company C, was a De Wet, he told Mabel, "full of South African money obtained from mines and feathers, but with a very limited range of conversation." The elegant Marguerite Gault "is very nice generally, sings a bit, is very much in love with her husband, wears a new dress every night for dinner." As for Lady Evelyn Farquhar, Adamson was one of the few not to be intimidated by her, for like many brave but unassuming soldiers, the CO had chosen to marry a bit of a dragon. "She is full of ability, upper gum and seasickness," he reported. "She is reported to be very mean, this I know nothing of, and so far have found her most interesting. She is writing a letter to each man's wife or mother, and trying to make them all different." After dinner, there was usually a concert – Adamson remarked in particular on an excellent rendition of "The Preacher and the Bear" – and a splendid trivial pursuit called "The War Game" played on a board six feet by twelve, that he described as "very much like toy soldiering."

On Wednesday, October 14, the convoy passed the Scilly Isles and began steaming up Plymouth Sound. Their port of entry had been kept secret, but as *The Times* reported, "the news spread like wildfire and no ship was allowed to pass by the Hoe without a popular demonstration." The cadets aboard the old, full-rigged training ship HMS *Impregnable* mustered on the rigging to shout "Hip-Hip-Hurrah." As the fleet anchored in the Hamoaze, off Plymouth Dockyard, bands played and the crowds on shore sang "Tipperary." (The Canadians didn't respond by singing it back, since this was the first time they'd heard it.) "Nothing like the Canadian contingent has been landed in this country since the time of William the Conqueror," noted the gentleman from *The Times*, getting a bit carried away. The arrival was none too soon, noted Adamson, since tobacco and whiskey had run out three days earlier aboard the *Royal George*.

At noon on Friday, October 16, he disembarked with letters to post. "I will put this in a pillar box, and also one to Anthony," he signed off to Mabel. "I hope you miss me as much as I miss you at all times."

The Canadian armada standing off Plymouth on October 14, 1914. "Nothing like the Canadian con- tingent has been landed in this country since the time of William the Conqueror," noted *The Times*.

The letter, in fact, took months to reach her. Instead, to Adamson's astonishment, they were reunited in person in less than a fortnight. A cable, rather than the letter he had been expecting, awaited him at Plymouth. Rodney was in boarding school at Ridley College in St. Catharine's, Ontario. Mabel and Anthony were in New York, about to cross the Atlantic aboard the *Mauretania*. "Why was I not born a man!" she had lamented at the time of the Boer War, resentful about missing all the action. This time, Mabel Cawthra Adamson had every intention of having a war of her own.

6

The View From Basil Mansions

This is a time of war, and rumours of war – especially rumours. No one knows what is going on. You just get ready and wait.

Mabel Adamson. A letter to her mother, Mrs. Cawthra; November 23, 1914

Wars disrupt and devastate societies, turn upside down and sometimes destroy the lives of individuals. But wars also shake up and energize societies, and open up opportunities that would never otherwise exist for some individuals. Mabel Adamson was quick to recognize this. Her decision to follow Agar to England wasn't unusual in itself. Every army wife who could afford it was doing the same, with Lady Evelyn Farquhar and Marguerite Gault at the head of the list: when visiting Agar at Salisbury Plain a few weeks later, Mabel had difficulty booking a room, since all the nearby hotels were filled with acquaintances from Toronto. Indeed, by 1917, according to one estimate, about thirty thousand Canadian wives and sweethearts, accompanied by a good many others whose standing was more questionable, had "drifted to England mainly for social reasons," as the *Canadian Annual Review* for 1917 noted with acerbity.

Mabel's intentions were entirely different. The feverish, almost macabre gaiety that soon became one of the characteristics of wartime London held no attraction for her. ("We danced every night," one belle of the era recalled many years later. "It was only when someone you knew well or with whom you were in love was killed, that you minded really dreadfully.") Nor, unlike many of her own contemporaries, had Mabel any intention of whiling away the war in a furnished flat, ticking off the days between Agar's leaves, justifying long afternoons of bridge and rumour exchange and too much sherry with a little desultory bandage-rolling. From the day she booked passage for seven-year-old Anthony and herself aboard the *Mauretania*, Mabel was determined to do something of significance for the war effort. She began as she meant to go on. Accompanying her aboard ship, labelled "Not Wanted on Voyage," were half a dozen steamer trunks filled with clothes, hastily collected on a whip-round of fashionable houses in Toronto, and intended to be distributed to the thousands of Belgian refugees now pouring into Britain.

Mabel was now forty-five. The Jamesian heroine of the 1890s had matured into a self-assured matron and businesswoman. If her marriage had worked out less well than she'd hoped, this was a sadness she kept to herself. Never, even in the heat of their worst arguments, had she told Agar how close she had come not to marrying him at all; how, on the night before their wedding, she had tried desperately but unsuccessfully to reach him by telephone to suggest that neither of them turn up at the church. Yet Mabel, under the skin, was in some respects the same coltish girl who had confessed to being "a combination of dozens of people, all demanding different things." These contradictions in her character had their roots in Mabel's background. On the one hand, she was irrevocably a Cawthra, a bred-in-the-bone member of a clan of stolid, utterly conventional Canadian Forsytes who were good at making money, and – herein lay the real point of friction between herself and Agar – were passionate only in their adherence to the work ethic. But on her mother's side – John Cawthra having been uncharacteristically venturesome in his choice of bride – Mabel was an Elwell of Bristol. They were a quite different breed: an intellectual and creative family of civil engineers imbued with the spirit of adventure and a flair for the arts. From this side of the family, Mabel had inherited her own artistic talent, her zest for travel, and her disregard, when need be, for convention. The genes inherited from the Elwells must also have been the reason that Mabel had fallen in love with Agar, because a true Cawthra would have been far too sensible.

Mabel's impulsive decision to follow Agar to England was also her Elwell side speaking. She had no clear idea of what she would do when she arrived. In the event, the doing of it would put both her health and her marriage at risk. Yet it is impossible not to conclude that Mabel never felt more alive or more fulfilled than during the war. "I was really too young to understand what was going on," her son Anthony Adamson recalls. "But I do know that she was totally consumed with what she always described as 'her work,' and that it seemed to matter to her much more than art, or horses, or even the Thornton-Smith Company had ever done."

Mabel was not much given to introspection, and kept no diaries. And while an excellent correspondent, none of the letters she wrote almost daily to Agar survive, since army regulations demanded that all personal correspondence be destroyed immediately after being read. Her fullest accounts date from the first months of the war and are contained in long newsy letters she wrote home to Mrs. Cawthra, before that redoubtable woman herself decided to move to London.

The first thing Mabel remarked on, when the *Mauretania* docked at Liverpool on October 27, were the new immigration restrictions. "It is very difficult getting into England now," she reported to Mrs. Cawthra. "All the passengers were assembled in the saloon and no one is allowed off until they are cross-questioned as to their nationality, business, etc, and all foreigners have to have passports." As Canadians, and thereby British subjects, she and Anthony whisked through without difficulty, but the era of free and easy travel was irrevocably over. Within a year, passports would be demanded even of native Britons, and this emergency regulation was never rescinded.* There was also the flimsy new paper money to get used to, replacing Britain's gold coinage, the weighty, reassuring sovereigns and half-sovereigns, that as much as "Rule Britannia" had been a hallmark of Empire.

---

* Prior to the war, the only European countries that required passports for entry were Turkey and tsarist Russia.

In August, during the brief financial panic that accompanied the declaration of war, virtually everyone with money in the bank had withdrawn it in gold, and when by government fiat this was returned to the banks, the first pound and ten-shilling notes were issued in exchange.

London itself, that first wartime autumn, was decked out as gaudily as for a coronation. The flags of the Allies – the Union Jack, the tricolour, the Golden Eagles of tsarist Russia, the red-and-black-and-yellow of Belgium – festooned almost every lamp-post and omnibus, and were massed in the windows of Selfridge's and all the other big shops. Red Cross collection boxes were everywhere; recruiting posters showing War Minister Lord Kitchener pointing his finger were pasted to every hoarding; newsagents offered French papers. In *The Times*, Harrod's suggested silver cigarette cases and efficient "tinder lighters" as suitable presents for departing officers, while "to help Tommy Atkins," a flask of Horlick's Malted Milk Tablets was recommended. Yet despite all the patriotic folderol, Mabel found herself less than impressed: most Londoners she encountered seemed curiously disengaged from events, much less involved than Torontonians. "You really have to read the papers to know there is a war on," she told her mother. "The city seems perfectly normal, except at night when it is very dark. There are no large street lamps, and the [traffic] islands have red lanterns hanging on them, and the big shop window lights are covered with either red or blue papers. There is a big search light on the entrance to Hyde Park. I presume it is useful, but to the ordinary observer it only seems to illuminate the fog for a very short time."

Mabel was by no means alone in deploring the air of normality. "It requires some effort to realize that London is almost within hearing distance of the great battle of the Aisne," wrote an unnamed columnist in, of all places, the October 15 issue of the society journal, *The Lady*. "Business proceeds very much as usual . . . the shops are crowded with busy, animated but very matter-of-fact shoppers . . . one has to wait for a table in a popular cafe . . . the only real reminder is the sign 'Quiet for the Wounded' that swings outside Charing Cross Hospital." Before long, the sight of walking wounded in bright blue convalescent uniforms, and of women wearing black, would be as much a part of the London scene as pigeons in Trafalgar Square, but this early on, apart from men in khaki, the only people whose lives seemed really touched by the war were the dejected clusters of Belgian refugees wandering aimlessly round the West End and queuing up at the museums of South Kensington. By mid-October, more than a hundred thousand had flooded across the channel in dredgers, yachts, fishing smacks, and even rowboats. Most wound up in London, where they were sometimes paraded through the streets in shooting brakes en route to temporary shelters at Alexandra Palace and Earl's Court. Later, a large colony of Belgians settled in Soho and opened shops, introducing Londoners to the pleasures of fine *pâtisserie* and, less successfully, of horsemeat.

Unlike the Belgians, Mabel had no worries about accommodation. The peripatetic Mrs. Cawthra had always maintained a *pied-à-terre* in London, and a couple of years earlier, she had taken a long lease on a first-floor flat, Number 16 Basil Mansions, in a new red-brick mansion block on Basil Street in Knightsbridge, close to Harrod's. Except for the now-horrendous traffic, this fashionable Edwardian *quartier* has changed little down the years: it is easy to stand on the doorstep of Basil Mansions and imagine Mabel bustling in briskly. Thanks to Anthony Adamson, then barely eight but possessed of an exceptional memory, we can follow her inside, and picture the flat in detail, from the mahogany barometer that hung just inside the door, to the Delft plaques that decorated the front hall. "The drawing room was pink and full of spindly furniture and floral chintz," he recalls, "and since that wasn't my mother's style at all, she hardly ever used it." Mabel much preferred the dining room, which was blue with art nouveau touches and had a cosy fireplace and a long window overlooking the street, with a writing table in front of it. "This became my mother's command post," Anthony Adamson continues. "Here, every morning, she would read my father's letters, and write him in return, using a Swan fountain pen, and deal with other correspondence. There was always a lot of paper in the dining room – files and bulging manila envelopes."

Despite Mabel's attempts to liven it up, Number 16 left much to be desired as a permanent residence. Even the front rooms got little sun, since they faced north, and the bedrooms, opening off a long dark corridor, looked out on a gloomy light well. But it was spacious, handy to the Underground, and, most unusually, was equipped with central heating. "This is the warmest place I have ever been in, in England," Mabel noted to her mother. "There are days when I don't even light the dining room fire." To add to the convenience, Number 16 also came equipped with an efficient pair of household retainers, Mr. and Mrs. Fletcher, who kept a parrot in the kitchen, Anthony recalls, and also a shiny black automobile complete with speaking tube and vase for flowers and a chauffeur called Porter.

The day after moving into Basil Mansions, Mabel spent the morning sorting and labelling the clothes she had amassed for the Belgian refugees. In the afternoon, Porter brought the car round, and having already ascertained by telephone that the Catholic Women's League on Victoria Street was the agency best organized to identify the neediest, Mabel delivered the parcels there. She then went on to Westminster Hospital, where large numbers of wounded Belgian soldiers were being cared for, and took two with broken legs on a sightseeing tour of London. "I put them in the back with their legs up on the little seats, and I told them what all the places were," she reported. "They were most cheerful and awfully pleased to be taken out."

Her next and pressing duty was to get Anthony settled. Though her relationship with her younger son had always been particularly affectionate, it would never have occurred to Mabel to depart from the customs of her class and do other than pack him off to boarding school. "I couldn't possibly keep him in London," she told her mother. "He is not a town child, and can't stand stuffy places. The tube upset him. A moving picture theatre near Marble Arch, quite a large airy place, I thought, made him feel so sick that I had to take him home in a taxi." Within ten days, after a trip to an outfitter on Bond Street during which, in Mabel's account, "Anthony was immensely pleased with himself in an Eton suit and a top hat," he was deposited at a prep school near Sevenoaks in Kent. He himself recalls: "I was a very foreign body. I talked through my nose like a Canadian, so an English boy was told off to 'teach me English.'" Eventually he adapted, being by nature cheerful and, as mattered most, a promising rugger player.

Thus far – well into November 1914 – Agar and Mabel had been reunited only briefly. The Patricias were under canvas at Camp Bustard, a few miles from Stonehenge, on the southwest reach of Salisbury Plain, a two-hundred-square-mile stretch of gently rolling downland in Wiltshire, long used as a training ground. The best Agar had been able to manage was a three-day leave, much of which they'd spent in Harrod's and the Army and Navy stores, replenishing his kit. Already, she confided to her

Going to the wars, 1915. Agar Adamson, never shy of having his picture taken, posed for this photograph shortly before leaving for the Front. His equipment weighed sixty-six pounds and included an expensive compass, an electric torch, and – as can be seen – an elaborate periscope. He lost most of this kit during his first tour of duty in the trenches.

mother, the deficiencies of Sam Hughes's hastily assembled war machinery were manifest. "Agar does not want to be quoted as saying things are no good . . . but their boots have worn out already and their uniforms are not much better." Nor, in her description, "does he give a very attractive account of conditions at camp." For the Canadians, Salisbury Plain had become a horror story. While perfectly adequate for splendid little wars, it was quite unequipped for a total war bringing with it a mass invasion by thirty-two thousand Canadians. Shooting ranges, transportation, and mess facilities were all at a premium. So, most pressingly, were qualified instructors. "Agar said he met a company the other day forming a hollow square and preparing to receive cavalry," she reported, "a thing which has not been done since the Crimean war." As well, the Canadian regiments were scattered in camps separated by vast distances so that communication was difficult: a taxi into the cathedral town of Salisbury itself, fifteen miles away, cost an appalling twenty-five shillings.

The worst problem was the weather. The Canadians had arrived in salubrious autumn sunshine. Within a week, a relentless, driving rain that presaged the worst winter in living memory had set in, accompanied by persistent high winds. "The men never have dry clothes, day or night," continues Mabel's report to Mrs. Cawthra. "According to Agar, the only way to dry your clothes including your boots is to sleep in them, well covered up with blankets. There are no lights but candles, and everybody goes to bed at eight o'clock."

On Saturday, November 8, well before it was light, Mabel set out by car, driven by Porter, to see Salisbury Plain for herself. Agar's instructions promised an adventurous journey. "On reaching Bustard Village," he'd wired, "ask for Princess Patricia's Regiment, 1 mile over the down, the going is a bit poached. Bring chains for the hind wheels. Don't get out until you reach my tent, or you will get lost." Despite the driving rain, the forty or so miles between London and Stonehenge were easy to negotiate; in Mabel's opinion the English roads, while not in that era paved, were "beautiful, compared to any Canadian road, though cut up at the side by all the military traffic." But once they were out on "the vast wet windy plain," the road narrowed to a single-lane muddy track, and Porter, in Mabel's description, "turned white and shook like a leaf." Time and again, they met head-on with military convoys, "immense troop transports, gun carriers etc., ten to thirty of these vehicles all at once," that forced them off the road into axle-deep mud that Mabel, with the journey from Toronto to Port Credit in mind, described as equalling "the Lakeshore road at its worst." Past Bustard Village, then as now a handful of houses and a pub, the road disappeared entirely; after stopping to put on the chains they slithered the rest of the way over slippery wet grass. When not engaged in cheering up the by now thoroughly demoralized Porter ("He says that by the time I am finished with him, he will either be a real man or a nervous wreck") Mabel peered out the window and discovered that Agar's descriptions had not been exaggerated. "There is simply no place for the men to get dry," she noted. "They route-march through the pouring rain, and come back to leaky tents, twelve to fifteen men in each." She was equally appalled by the messing arrangements. "The cooking is done out in the open, with a blanket hung up on the windward side of the stove. The men have no mess tents, a big black pot of food is deposited in front of each tent, out of which they dig their respective portions." Most distressing of all, she reported, was the condition of the horses. "They are most miserable, tethered in the awful wind and rain with no protection whatsoever. They are said to be dying at the rate of thirty a day."

When at last they reached Agar's tent, he was nowhere in sight. Instead, a subaltern rushed up with a message: Captain Adamson was detained on the shooting range, and would join her later at the Old George Hotel in Salisbury. It was nearly 11:00 PM before he turned up, and by then Mabel had made a number of other alarming discoveries. "Salisbury looks as if it were in the hands of the Germans," she relates. "A picket goes around every night dragging drunken Canadians out of pubs. The night I was there, there were 100 arrests, including 22 officers. The fault is with the officers. They have no control over the men, in fact are just as bad. Managers of London theatres have written to the authorities, demanding to know what they are to do with drunken officers, civilians they know what to do with, and also the Tommies, but drunken officers, they have no precedent for." Although never mentioned in the newspapers, this problem of the drunken-ness – equally the ineptitude – of many of the original Canadian officers was quite widely known back home because of all the let-ters like Mabel's that were crossing the Atlantic. Britishers also knew of the problem. In *Marching to Armageddon* Desmond Morton and J. L. Granatstein quote a British officer who, having been assigned to help the CEF disembark at Plymouth, and having been told that Canadians were not "coolies" and would not unload their own ships, remarked that "the Canadians would make fine soldiers if all their officers were shot."

Much of the blame rested with Sam Hughes. He'd appointed political cronies to key posts; as a passionate teetotaller he'd banned "wet canteens" from the training grounds. The underlying problem was that the Canadians were far from home, suffering "culture shock" – magnified by the patronizing attitudes of the British – and they were caught in that most difficult of all military situations – due to be sent into action and so anticipating all its horrors, but not yet in action, when the heat of battle itself can cool fear. A scrap of doggerel written about Salisbury Plain by one Captain Ambrose of the Canadian Expeditionary Force was designed as a chin-lifter, but it reveals more about the mood of that autumn than the author intended.

> . . . *In the morn when we arise*
> *There are but the rainy skies –*
> *And the mud*
> *Nine inches deep it lies,*
> *We are mud up to our eyes,*
> *In our cakes and in our pies*
> *There is mud.*

"This is a time of war and rumours of war – especially rumours," wrote Mabel to Mrs. Cawthra on November 23. "No one knows what is being done or what is going to be done. You just get ready and wait." After parting with Agar at Salisbury, she'd fully expected not to see him again before the regiment left for the trenches. Instead, on November 16, the Patricias were detached from the Canadians and posted to a camp just outside Winches-ter, where, along with four battalions of British regulars just back from India, they formed a brigade of the 27th Division. Conditions here were more congenial – "Agar is very pleased at being brigaded with such a lot of good troops," Mabel reported – but the weather, if anything, was worse. Agar's tent had no floor, and breaking ice in a canvas bucket every morning in order to shave reminded him of conditions on the veldt in South Africa. Mabel noted "the sorrowful sight of troops from the Indian Army in pith helmets and shorts standing around in the rain." As the weeks dragged by without embarkation orders, the waiting game rubbed nerves and tempers raw.

On the night of December 3, a freak accident resulted in Charlie Stewart's and Talbot Papineau's tent going up in flames, with both of them lucky to escape with only severe burns. In the gentlemanly manner of the day, no inquiry was held. Papineau's explanation to his mother was, "I was sound asleep. Charlie came in about eleven o'clock. He smoked a cigarette and went to sleep. Since he and his side of the tent were more severely burned, it is probable his cigarette or a candle started it." In the event, while the burns to Papineau's face and right hand were extremely painful, and for a few days Stewart's life was actually feared for, both officers recovered quickly.

At last, in mid-December, the orders arrived. On December 21, the Patricias crossed the English Channel to Le Havre in an open cattleboat. From there, they travelled in boxcars to the railhead at St. Omer, a pleasant town in northern France that served as British General Headquarters. Christmas Day found them dining on bully beef in the village of Blaringhem, in the area where the Hazebrouck defensive line was being constructed; the regiment spent the last week of the year digging trenches in the water-logged soil of Flanders. But Agar Adamson, to his great desolation and fury, was not with the regiment. (Neither for that matter, were Talbot Papineau and Charlie Stewart, who were still recovering from their burns.) Instead, Agar ate goose and plum pudding with Elwell relations at Bristol. Two days prior to embarkation, Colonel Farquhar had called him aside and delivered the blow: as senior captain, staff-wallahs had decreed, Adamson was to stay in England and supervise the training of a draft of 500 men expected shortly from Canada. "The CO was very nice, and said he regretted it very much," wrote Agar to Mabel. "But you have only a small idea of what this means to me and I am wretched. I offered to drop my rank and go as a subaltern or do anything rather than remain behind." He also sent a wire begging Mabel not to come down and visit. "I should be too unhappy." She went anyway, accompanied by Anthony who was by now on his Christmas vacation, and found Agar almost frantic with rage and frustration. The journey from Winchester to Bristol did not contribute to Yuletide merriment. "It took 6 1/2 hours to do a 3 hour trip," wrote Mabel to her mother. "There were floods all along the line; at Bath, the only evidence of the road was a lighted street lamp sticking up in the midst of a roaring torrent." Anthony cried because there were no Christmas stockings. "My mother explained about Sam Hughes and the Kaiser and the general busy-ness," he recalls, "but I was inconsolate." Eventually, it was the equally inconsolate Agar who pulled himself together to rescue the situation with a bravura display of charm. "He came up to my room all happiness and said he was so proud because at last I was recognized as being an Adamson, and Irish. In Ireland, Santa Claus came on St. Patrick's Day instead. I went to sleep all proud, and when March 17, 1915, came, I never noticed it."

The New Year brought fresh disasters. From Flanders, where the Patricias had entered the front line for the first time on January 7, Colonel Farquhar wrote encouragingly, "Let me know as soon as you consider things are on a workable basis. I will then get you a successor and will ask for a draft from 200 to 300 men under yourself." But back on Salisbury Plain at the reinforcement depot at Tidworth, Agar by now was embroiled in a ferocious battle with his new commanding officer, an elderly martinet named Colonel James, recently "dug-out" from St. Helena where he had been military governor. No sooner had the new draft arrived on the Plain than James, with imperial high-handedness (but probably also acting in collusion with General Alderson, commander-in-chief of the Canadian Division who, as we know from a comment of Mabel's, was "very bitter" about the glamour and mystique attached to the PPCLI), transferred it to a general pool of Canadian reinforcements. To add insult to injury, Agar himself was detached from the regiment and put into a pool of surplus Canadian officers. "This is the last straw," he wrote Mabel early in February. "I have written and protested, but James wrote back that any suggestion from me is out of order."

Nothing in Adamson's experience had prepared him for political warfare. Somehow, though, he managed to get an SOS to Farquhar, who replied that he would return post-haste from the front line and sort matters out with the higher-ups at the War Office: could Adamson meet him in London and brief him? James, aware that something was up, rejected Agar's request for leave. With daring born of desperation, and also the cool resourcefulness of a natural warrior, Agar did the next best thing. Under cover of night on February 4, he disguised his most trusted NCO, a former steward at the Toronto Club named Sergeant A. B. Cork, in a suit of his own mufti and smuggled him out of camp with a long memo addressed to Farquhar in care of Mabel. "Sending man up to meet Fanny," he wired Mabel, using the colonel's nickname as code. "Expect tonight after ten and put him up." For the next forty-eight hours, Cork waited for the Colonel in the unaccustomed splendour of the spare room at Basil Mansions. "He is afraid to go out for fear of the Colonel turning up and telephoning," wrote Mabel to her mother, "and I think also because he looks so funny in Agar's clothes. Mrs. Fletcher and I had a great laugh when he first turned up . . . I had expected a man in uniform and when this apparition turned up I did not at first feel like letting him in. We feel as if we are co-conspirators."

Thanks to Farquhar's adroitness, the episode ended happily for all but Colonel James. On February 9, instead of facing a court-martial as he'd half expected, Agar found himself whizzing down to Salisbury in a staff car in "Fanny's" reassuring presence, to meet the General of Southern Command. "All my actions were upheld and approved of," he wrote Mabel. "We are, as of today, a separate self-contained unit." Less than a week later, as was even better, he and a draft of 200 men – "a heterogenous lot to have come from Canada including two Servians, a Roumanian who was an interpreter in the Balkan wars, and two sailors who were recently in the U.S. Navy" – embarked for France aboard a battered tramp steamer called the *Manchester Engineer*. Mabel, in a flamboyant gesture that few other wives would have dared, met him at Salisbury and travelled down to the Southampton docks aboard the troop-train. "The embarkation officer and the guard of the train were very much upset when they found me and I was hustled off at once," she reported to her mother. Prevented from bidding her a proper farewell, Agar wrote one from France, en route to rejoin the regiment. "Goodbye old girl," he told her. "Don't worry about me. Lots of hardships are due after so many years of undeserved comforts, and there are a great many men and officers here who must find it harder to stand than I will." He signed off with the gallant, old-fashioned endearment that he had once used in South Africa and that he would continue to use throughout the war: "Ever thine."

7

The Belgian Canal
Boat Fund

For Relief of Civil Population Behind Firing Lines
Send Them Something
Text on a poster commissioned by Mabel Adamson. Spring 1915

T he point at which Agar's and Mabel's characters intersected
was their unswerving commitment to the British Empire and
to the advancement of its interests. His departure for the
Front was her cue to proceed with her own war. Since early
November, she had been laying the groundwork: updating the
nursing skills learned in 1900 at Kidderminster Infirmary with a
crash course of Red Cross lectures; brushing up the knowledge of
French acquired even longer ago as an art student in Paris by daily
lessons with a congenial tutor, Madame Pesci, a recent evacuee
from Paris and the wife of a sculptor. "They were living on the outskirts of the city," Mabel reported to Mrs. Cawthra. "In September,
at the time of the Battle of the Marne, their house and his studio
were blown up by the French to clear the way for fortifications.
They were given two days to get out, and lost nearly everything.
Now he has gone to the U.S. to look for work and she, poor
woman, not speaking a word of English is marooned here with a
six-year-old daughter." With her customary blend of generosity
and efficiency, Mabel took the Pescis under her wing. Helping
settle the little girl at a convent in Hampstead, she was reminded,
perhaps uncomfortably, of her own experience with Anthony. "I

felt awfully sorry for the child," she reported, "she had a cold and an earache and her mother left her in an immense, bare chilly convent. We went through a dormitory, which I am sure had sixty beds in it, in rows touching each other end to end. The only comfortable looking thing about the place was an old nun, a Belgian, who took us in charge. Earlier, Madame Pesci had put the child in a convent kept by nuns at Earl's Court, and one day she went there and found the nuns all dressed up in ordinary clothes with hats on, and much made up. It gave her such a shock, she took the child away. This time, she has got the real thing in convents."

Most afternoons, Mabel practised her French by escorting wounded Belgians on automobile outings around London. "On the whole, I find it easier to understand the Belgians speaking French than the British Tommies speaking English," she noted, for at this time the regional dialects of the British Isles, still decades away from being homogenized by radio and television, were almost different languages. "I have heard some wonderful tales of the War," she went on. "One man told me he had been 23 days in a trench, in water up to his knees. He had nothing hot to eat for a month, not even a cup of tea." Other days, she helped civilian refugees find their feet in a foreign country. "Today I took two Belgian women out to the hostel at Alexandra Palace to look for relatives," she wrote on December 2. "Poor things, they had had an awful time and none of them knew where their husbands were." In between times, she continued to process the shipments of clothing continually arriving from Toronto, not all of which were well selected. "Some people send such useless stuff," she remarked. "I have a large case packed with men's bowler hats, also a lot of women's hats, all of which are quite useless to Belgians of the peasant class who don't wear hats even in London." Every fortnight or so she joined other expatriate regimental wives at the Farquhars' townhouse in Mayfair to help Lady Evelyn – "thoroughly sloppy and untidy but extremely amusing" – pack parcels of comforts for the Patricias. Socks and shirts and cigarettes were the items that were really useful, she noted, as opposed to the tidal wave of cholera belts and Balaclavas with which they were inundated. "I should think *one* muffler, *one* belt, *one* Balaclava helmet, would see most men through the war." A few months

later, when the true nature of trench warfare had become apparent, she realized otherwise. "The waste in war is simply
appalling," runs a letter of mid-March 1915. "All the officers who
went to the front with their most expensive kit – the best com-
passes, periscopes, electric lights, etc., having lost everything
they are now wanting the cheapest things possible. They have
discovered how impossible it is to save anything in a trench, you
are lucky if you save your life."

On such occasions, and also at the many concerts and musi-
cales held to raise funds for the war effort, much information was
traded, most of it wildly inaccurate, for London far outdistanced
Ottawa as a capital of rumour. In early November, it was said that a
whole army of Russians had landed in Scotland and passed
through England en route to the Front, stamping the snow off their
boots at Berwick-on-Tweed and jamming the penny-in-a-slot cigarette machines with roubles. In mid-December Mabel reported
ironically, "it is known for a fact that Prince Louis of Battenberg,
former First Sea Lord, is shut up in the Tower and due to be shot at
any moment."* Then there was a story emanating out of the military camp at Winchester that Mabel picked up on November 20.
"Eight regiments were hustled off last week to Scotland, as there
was a scare that the Germans were landing there. It proved a false
alarm and they came back, but it goes to show that the War Office
looks on it as a possibility."

None of these activities came anywhere close to absorbing
Mabel's energies, still less to accomplishing her purpose, but finding the right outlet proved more difficult than she had expected.
London was swarming with organizations in support of the war
effort – most of which had also declared war upon each other. "It is
awful the way the Army Medical, and the Red Cross, and St. John's
Ambulance fight," she wrote Mrs. Cawthra. "Each one thinks that
any new effort is a reflection on their capability." Being a Colonial,

---

* Prince Louis of Battenberg soon changed his family name to Mountbatten and
became the Marquis of Milford Haven. He was the father of Lord Louis Mountbatten and the great-uncle of the Duke of Edinburgh. Needless to say, he was not
locked up in the Tower but *was* forced to resign his position because of his
German background.

albeit a wealthy one, was a disadvantage. "They are both supercilious and indifferent towards offers to help – in any form except money," she continued, describing a rebuff in mid-November when, as the casualties from the first battle of Ypres came flooding in, she volunteered both her car and herself for ambulance duty. "They wanted the car all right – but not me, at any price. . . . There are so many people offering their services that it seems impossible to get anything to do. Yet it is very curious, with all these thousands of people willing to work, that one still reads in the papers of wounded men lying for two or three days without attention."

Being a woman was an additional disadvantage, as Mabel was quick to discover. "The English government is hipped on the subject of women," she reports early in 1915. "They seem to try and purposely squash every individual effort." Ironically enough, the tactics of militant suffragettes in the years leading up to the war had probably compounded the prejudice: having been beleaguered and embarrassed, masculine officialdom was determined to get its own back, no matter that even firebrands like Emmeline and Christabel Pankhurst had buried the hatchet for the duration. Later, as more and more men were conscripted and labour shortages began to bite, things would change dramatically: women would become farm-labourers, munitions workers, even drivers of double-decker buses, and after the war they would be rewarded with the vote. But this early on, save for qualified nurses who wore the halo of Florence Nightingale and in any case were indispensable, the contribution of women was not taken seriously. The first real shift in official attitudes didn't come until July 1915, when the suffrage societies organized a massive procession of thirty thousand women through London demanding their right to be employed in the war effort. "Their spirit is splendid," said the press, which was not what it had said about earlier demonstrations by suffragettes. "This procession will educate public opinion," declared Lloyd George, then Chancellor of the Exchequer and soon to become prime minister.

Mabel's easiest option would have been to do as many of her contemporaries did, and spend her war working in the familiar, female surroundings of the Canadian Red Cross Society. Already its offices had been opened in Cockspur Street, just off Trafalgar Square, and while the commissioner, Colonel Hodgetts, was a man, everyone knew that the real power was in the hands of the assistant commissioner, the formidable Lady Drummond of Montreal, whose handsome twenty-six-year-old son Guy, a good friend of Talbot Papineau's serving in the Royal Highlanders, was being groomed for great things in Tory politics. A strikingly tall woman

Grace, Lady Drummond, Assistant Commissioner of the Canadian Red Cross Society in London, takes Sir Robert Borden on a tour of Maple Leaf canteens in 1915. A tall and commanding presence, she was one of the best-known Canadian women of her day. The woman in the background wearing a Red Cross uniform is Lady Perley, wife of the Canadian High Commissioner to Britain.

in her mid-fifties, the widow of Sir George Drummond, former president of the Bank of Montreal, Grace Julia Drummond was one of the best-known Canadian women of the day. Instrumental in helping Lady Aberdeen found the National Council of Women back in the 1890s, she had been praised by that indomitable activist for "her distinguished presence, great personal charm, gifts of rare eloquence and the power of clothing her thoughts in the most expressive language." Lady Drummond was clearly a consummate and tough-minded bureaucrat: thanks to her skills, the Red Cross Society, though staffed entirely by volunteers, soon became an organization immensely more efficient and responsive than the notoriously muddled Canadian military bureaucracy at Argyll House near Oxford Circus. By the middle of the war, it encompassed a dozen separate departments, administering everything from Maple Leaf canteens and hostels for soldiers on leave, to writing letters for wounded soldiers in hospital, to supplying troops in the trenches with hometown newspapers. But Mabel had not the least interest in becoming one of Grace Drummond's lieutenants. Indeed, the absence of even a passing reference to the Canadian Red Cross suggests that the possibility never even occurred to her – most likely because she knew she would have little scope for her own initiative.

The more Mabel pondered her war effort, the more its nature became obvious. Her own inclination and flair for the unorthodox, plus the considerable expertise she'd already acquired, plus her increasing command of French, all best fitted her to keep on helping the Belgian refugees. Now that the basic needs of those who had crossed the channel were in hand, her attention began to turn to those who had stayed behind: the civilian population in the small fraction of Belgium still in the hands of the Allies, a narrow strip about thirty miles long and ten miles wide, running inwards from the coast to the beleaguered city of Ypres, centred round the medieval market town of Furnes (nowadays known by its Flemish name, Veurne). Here, just behind the firing lines, tens of thousands of families lived daily within range of the guns. Many were homeless; all were constantly in danger of being shelled; food, clothing, and medical attention were all in desperately short supply. But even as Mabel's heart went out to these unfortunates, in particular the women and children, it took her a while to figure out how best to help them.

Sometime in late February 1915, a fortuitous encounter with a passing acquaintance from Toronto, a Mrs. Innes-Taylor, pointed the way to a solution. Beyond the fact that she too was the wife of a Canadian officer, that she spoke French like a native, and was in Mabel's description "a most enthusiastic person," we know very little about her; even Anthony Adamson's exceptional memory cannot summon up her first name. What *is* clear from Mabel's letters is that like had met like: the two were kindred spirits and would continue to be so all through the war. So far as we can piece things together, it seems to have been Mrs. Innes-Taylor who first came up with the idea – why not equip a canal barge as a relief ship, distributing food and comfort along the network of waterways traversing the war-torn area of Belgium? Mabel, for her part, provided the organizational skills and undoubtedly the first act of faith in the form of a sizeable donation. She was also equipped with the right connections and a knowledge of how best to use them.

Within a fortnight, the Belgian Canal Boat Fund had been born and christened, and a prospectus drawn up. Mabel would serve as London-based president and treasurer, Mrs. Innes-Taylor as hands-on organizer in Belgium, later they would rotate. An impressive honorary committee was mustered, Mabel having roped in Lady Perley, wife of the Canadian High Commissioner, who in turn had roped in the Dowager Marchioness of Londonderry, one of London's most powerful hostesses. To underline the professional nature of the venture, an office was rented at 71 Duke Street, between Oxford Street and Grosvenor Square. When going to "her work" on Duke Street, Anthony Adamson recalls, his mother eschewed her usual stylish clothes, wearing instead a no-nonsense blue broadcloth smock.

The next hurdle was to convince the Belgian authorities that the scheme was both serious and feasible. Having enlisted one M. Raemakers of the Belgian Embassy as an ally, Mabel and Mrs. Innes-Taylor set about the difficult business of securing visas to cross the channel. After a number of false starts, they embarked on March 30 for De Panne, the small seaport just north of the French border that, with Brussels in the hands of the enemy, was temporarily serving as the portable capital of Belgium. "We are going to interview the Belgian government," she reported to her mother. "They evidently think we have the whole of Canada behind us, which is a little disconcerting, but I have hope that Canada will back me up." On April 5 she reported on the trip. "I don't think I have ever put in such a day in my life. To meet five ministers consecutively, and have pretty speeches on tap about the *Entente Cordiale* etc., and to do it a little differently each time is really an awful strain. . . . We talked French all the time, another

Sir George and Lady Perley visit an IODE hospital. The leading members of Canada's overseas community during the war, they entertained lavishly and were criticized for being preoccupied with the social aspects of their position.

hour would have given me paralysis." But the mission had been a triumph. "The tangible result is a letter from Monsieur Berryer, the Minister of the Interior, praying the English and French authorities to give us every facility."

All was not yet smooth sailing – in fact, it was not to be sailing at all. British military authorities refused to authorize a relief ship to operate in the War Zone, despite a personal intervention by Sir George Perley engineered by Mabel over dinner at the Carlton Hotel. "I thought the backing of the entire Belgian government would have been quite sufficient," she remarked crossly, "but it seems the Great Powers consider Belgium a negligible quantity." There is also reason to suspect that Perley may have been less than effective. Able enough, he was still new in the job, having been appointed only six months earlier to replace Lord Strathcona, and he was painfully deferential to imperial authority. "The High Commissioner's success is largely due to his gift of silence," wrote the acerbic Canadian journalist H. F. Gadsby in a profile for the March 1915 issue of *Maclean's*. "Outside of one or two undertakers, I know of no man in Canada who combines chronic reserve and abiding gloom in such just proportions . . . so far he has done nothing out of the routine, except to move the High Commissioner's office from the middle of the block to the corner of Victoria Street."*

By now, though, there was no going back. Mabel and Mrs.

---

* The leading member of Canada's overseas community during the war, Perley (b. 1857) was the Harvard-educated son of an Ottawa Valley lumbering dynasty. As High Commissioner, he continued to serve as a Conservative Member of Parliament and as a cabinet minister without portfolio. His second wife, the former Millie White, was the daughter of Borden's finance minister, Sir Thomas White, and a former president of Ottawa's May Court Club. The Perleys, who had a fine house in Park Lane and entertained lavishly, were widely criticized for being preoccupied with the social aspects of their position. "Social graces counted for a great deal more than the welfare of the common soldier," editorialized *Saturday Night*, in 1919. After 1917, and the appointment of Sir Edward Kemp as Overseas Minister, Perley lost much of his influence. He left London in 1922, and continued to serve as MP for Argenteuil until his death in 1938. The house known as Stornoway in Ottawa's Rockcliffe Park that he built for his daughter Ethel Perley-Robertson is now the official residence of the Leader of the Opposition.

Innes-Taylor quickly regrouped and decided to establish their headquarters on the outskirts of Furnes, in a hut close to a temporary school, out of the range of the artillery. Here, for the next four years, the Belgian Canal Boat Fund – while not strictly accurate, it was decided to keep the original name – would not only undertake to feed and clothe all 370 pupils of the school on a continuing basis, it would also distribute food and clothing to hundreds of refugees in the vicinity and establish a medical clinic. Far more helpful than Perley in getting things going was the American businessman Herbert Hoover, later to become president and at that time London-based chairman of the American Committee for Belgian relief. Skilled in personal diplomacy, he negotiated a number of agreements which permitted the passage of food, clothing, and medical supplies through both the allied naval blockade and the German front line. "Mr. Hoover handles all the U.S. supplies and agrees that our Canadian supplies can go through him too," Mabel reported. "But what will the Belgians do if Germany and the States go to war?"

By late April 1915, Mabel was confident enough of the scheme to commission a fund-raising poster. Given the intense competition among war charities, she knew that in order to command attention, this must be both dramatic and unique. Thus she went to considerable pains to seek out John Hassall, one of the leading commercial artists of the day, best known for his eye-catching advertisements for Colman's Mustard. The image that Hassall came up with did not disappoint. Even today, his chiaroscuro portrayal of an anguished Belgian mother and her children against the background of a canal and a windmill stands out as a superb example of propaganda art.

The appearance of Mabel's poster on hoardings and in tube stations all over London coincided with the sudden reappearance of Agar. The official notice from the War Office, dated May 14, 1915 – "Dear Madam, I regret to inform you," and going on to report that he had been wounded – turned up at Basil Mansions three days later than a message from Agar himself, pushed through the letter slot just as Mabel had settled down with a cup of coffee and the *Daily Mail*. "I arrived last night and am in Lady Ridley's hospital at 10 Carlton Terrace," this hastily scrawled letter read. "I am

By the spring of 1915, so many war charities were competing for attention that it was important to stand out from the crowd. Even today, the poster that Mabel Adamson commissioned from John Hassall, the commercial artist who made Colman's Mustard famous, would command attention in London's tube stations.

only slightly wounded, in the shoulder. Please bring a toothbrush
and tooth powder and a package of Auto Strop razor blades."

The jaunty, unconcerned tone of the note did not fool Mabel.
She set off straight away for the hospital, knowing she would find
there a man who would be radically different from the one she
had seen off at Southampton three months earlier. Thanks to
Agar's almost daily letters from the Front, she already knew far
more than most civilians about the obscenities of trench warfare.

8

Fortunes of War

*Canada will begin now I think to recognize her
sacrifice. Her casualties have begun.*

Talbot Papineau. A letter to his mother; January 1915

I nstead of ending by Christmas, the war had ended in a "race to
the sea" that itself had ended in a draw. The famed Schlieffen
Plan, a strategy derived from Hannibal's victory at the Battle of
Cannae, by which the Germans planned to crush the allied armies
by a pincer-like assault, had failed – just – because there weren't
quite enough Germans to bring it off and because the French had
rushed reinforcements out of Paris in taxi-cabs. Barbed wire and
the machine gun now ruled the battlefield. Nothing could get
through them, nor, later, at Gallipoli, around them. Both sides,
their generals weaned on Alexander, Caesar, Marlborough, Frederick the Great, Napoleon, still believed in "the breakthrough." Both
maintained their regiments of cavalry, ready to be unleashed in
one glorious charge across open fields. To prepare for that day,
both dug protectively into the earth, unfurled strands of barbed
wire, and set up strongpoints for their machine guns. These were
merely temporary bastions from which the breakthrough would
be launched.

Trapped in a technological timewarp, the two armies settled
into a war like none before or since. From just south of the mouth
of the Yser, on the coast of Belgium, down to Beurnevisin on the
Swiss frontier, stretched four hundred miles of twisting, looping,
but roughly parallel lines of trenches. Into this immensely long

but narrow space were compressed more men and more armaments than had ever been assembled before in even the widest of spaces. Three and a half years, and millions of dead young men, later, the lines followed almost exactly the same looping course between the mouth of the Yser and the hamlet of Beurnevisin. At times, as at Verdun or at Passchendaele, the line did shift a few miles eastwards or westwards. Later, it shifted back the same number of miles. "This isn't war," said Lord Kitchener early in 1915. He was right. It was mutual suicide.

"The *idea* of the trenches," writes Paul Fussell in his 1975 masterpiece, *The Great War and Modern Memory*, "has been assimilated so successfully in metaphor and myth that it is not easy now to recover a feeling for the actualities." A front-line trench could be as close as a few dozen yards from its enemy counterpart, although, quite randomly, the gap between them was sometimes as wide as a mile. In theory (as we shall discover shortly, practice was often quite different) a trench was about eight feet deep and four or five feet wide, thickly surrounded by barbed-wire entanglements, and the floors covered with wooden duckboards (in the damp soil of Flanders, these were often covered with a foot or more of sludgy water). To the front and rear were parapets of sandbags. Along the top of the parapet there were snipers' plates made of thick steel, with holes just large enough to accomodate a rifle barrel and the human eye. At the back of the trenches there was usually a row of dugouts, reached by dirt stairs and used for officers' quarters. (Officers' meals were usually provided by a cook; other ranks did their own cooking, such as it was, sometimes using coal braziers and towards the end of the war, Primus stoves. Mostly, they simply opened tins of bully beef or the infamous meat-and-vegetable Maconochie stew.) A well-built trench did not run straight but zigzagged every few yards so that a shell or bomb that landed in it could kill only those in each "zig." With all these zigs, the allied front alone encompassed some twelve thousand miles of trenches. Communication trenches, running roughly at right angles to the front line, served to bring up supplies such as food and ammunition, and to bring back the dead and wounded. Behind these were more trenches parallel with the front line, to serve as a defence in depth for up to half a mile to the rear. Forward of the front line,

THE WESTERN FRONT, 1914-1918
CANADIAN OPERATIONS

ENGLISH CHANNEL

• Ostend   • Bruges

BELGIUM   • Ghent   Scheldt

Furnes

Dunkirk
(FLANDERS)   Lys

• Calais   F
                      Passchendaele
Voormezele →   A   Hooge
Ypres   • Mt Sorrel   BRUSSELS ●
St Eloi   B C
St Omer •   Escaut

Hazebrouck • Armentières   ARMISTICE LINE,
                                11 NOV. 1918
Festubert →   LILLE
• Etaples   Givenchy   • Tournai

          Béthune   • Lens   Mons •
                    • Vimy   Scarpe
FRANCE   E
                    • Douai   Valenciennes
Arras   H   Sensée
        I   ← Canal du Nord   N
        Beaumont-   • Cambrai
        Hamel
Thiepval •   Bapaume
Somme   D
          • Courcelette
Ancre / • Albert
Amiens •   G
        / Luce

10   0   10   20   30
|—|—|—|—|—|
        Miles

Oise

——— ALLIED FRONT, 15 DEC. 1914

•••••••• ALLIED FRONT, 20 MAR. 1918   Compiègne •   Soissons   Vesle

– – – ALLIED FRONT, AFTER
THE GERMAN OFFENSIVES OF
MARCH-JULY 1918   Reims

PARIS   Marne   Epernay
●
                Château Thierry

A The Battles of Ypres. April-May 1915   E Vimy Ridge. 9-12 April 1917
B St Eloi. February-March 1915; March-April 1916   F Passchendaele. 26 October-10 November 1917
C Mount Sorrel. 2-13 June 1916   G Amiens. 8-11 August 1918
D The Battles of the Somme. July-November 1916;   H Arras. 26 August-3 September 1918
  Beaumont-Hamel, July 1, 1916   I Canal du Nord. 27 September-11 October 1918

shallow ditches known as "saps" thrust out into no man's land and served as posts for observation and grenade-throwing. In some instances, as at Vimy, as visitors can still see today, opposed "saps" might be less than twenty yards apart. A standard tour of duty in the front line was about four days. It was spent entirely head-down. To look up and out, other than through a periscope, was to die to a sniper or to a burst of machine-gun fire.

Within this "Troglodyte World," in Fussell's phrase, normal biorhythms were turned upside-down. His description of trench routine speaks for the Canadians as well as for the British. "During the day, men cleaned weapons and repaired those parts of the trench damaged during the night. Or they wrote letters, deloused themselves, or slept. The officers inspected, encouraged, and strolled around looking nonchalant to inspire the men. They censored the men's letters and dealt with the quantities of official inquiries brought to them by runner. . . . Daily 'returns' of the amount of ammunition and the quantities of trench stores had to be made. Reports of the nightly casualties had to be sent back. And letters of condolence, which as the war went on became form-letters of condolence, had to be written to the relatives of the killed and wounded." After evening stand-to, the real work began. No man's land came alive as small parties of men inched through the wire, scurrying from shell-hole to shell-hole, hugging the ground when a flare arched up, trying to pick up intelligence by listening to the enemy's whispered conversations, trying to snatch a prisoner, trying to demoralize the enemy with a sudden storm of hand grenades upon his trenches, or, as the textbooks demanded, just trying to keep up their own aggressive spirits. To relieve the tension and the monotony, almost everyone became a chain-smoker. Cigarettes were smoked behind cupped hands; no one, except newcomers, lit more than one from a single match. Only with the dawn could everyone begin to relax: its coming meant there would be no attack – except when it did come.

The first forty miles of the allied line of trenches, a mainly quiescent sector north of Ypres, was held by the Belgians. The next ninety miles, down to the river Ancre in northwest France, was held by the British and Colonial forces. The French manned the rest, to the south, their stronghold the fortress of Verdun on

the River Meuse. The British and Colonial part of the line nor-
mally comprised some eight hundred battalions of about a thousand men each. They were concentrated in two main sectors: the
Somme area in Picardy, which would take centre stage in 1916,
and the Ypres Salient in Flanders. This latter was an untidy bulge,
about nine miles long at its widest point and protruding about
four miles eastward into the German lines. Vulnerable to attack on
three sides, and under constant artillery fire on its exposed
flanks, the Salient was a military insanity but a political necessity:
it encompassed almost all of the little bit of Belgium that had
been held onto at such an appalling cost, and therefore had to go
on being held no matter how appalling the future cost. It was here
that the Patricias first entered the line, on January 7, 1915, as part
of the British 27th Division.

One of the best ways to recapture the *idea* of the trenches is
to make a pilgrimage through the Ypres Salient. At first, the placid
and prosperous Flemish farm country evokes little that's resonant. Only the occasional shell craters, now serving as water-
holes for cattle and geese, or an unnatural wave in a field of
cabbage or corn, serve as reminders of battles long ago. Even the
daily sunset ceremony at the Menin Gate in Ypres, although
moving, lacks a quality of immediacy. Then, when the suburbs of
Ypres are still in the rear-view mirror, the road-signs marked
"Passchendaele" flash into view. Suddenly, the tragic dimension of
the war becomes recognizable as the pilgrim realizes how small
was the battlefield over which so much blood was spilled. The
description that best sets it in context for Canadians is that of
Ralph Allen in *Ordeal By Fire*:

> During the three years between early 1915 and early 1918, the
> whole of the Canadian ground forces fought and died, and if
> fortunate, lived, in an area hardly bigger than three or four
> Saskatchewan townships. Their every value and perspective
> had to be adjusted accordingly. From one small piece of quag-
> mire, another piece of quagmire fifty yards away could look as
> enticing as the towers of Cathay. The slightest bulge on the
> flat, sodden, dangerous plains became a hill or a mountain.
> On a reverse slope, a company or a battalion could buy

respite from the incessant artillery barrages. On a forward slope, it could be wiped out. In the desperate lore of the front, hummocks not large enough to make a toboggan slide became as high and as famous as Everest or the Matterhorn.

The other quality of the Ypres Salient that soon intrudes upon a visitor is the ambience. Brooding and melancholy, it is that of a vast graveyard. Meticulously maintained cemeteries and memorials encroach everywhere upon the farmland: the huge British cemetery at Tyne Cot, close to Passchendaele; the giant statue of the "Brooding Soldier" at Vancouver Corner commemorating the 18,000 Canadians who faced the enemy nearby after the first German gas attacks in April 1915. As memorials go, the regimental cemetery of the Princess Patricia's at Voormezele, a village about four miles south of Ypres, is one of the smaller, mentioned in few of the official guidebooks. For us, though, because a number of our characters are now at rest there, it is a place filled with resonance.

Talbot Papineau and Charlie Stewart, recovered from the burns and accompanied by a detachment of forty men, caught up with the Patricias on Febuary 1; Agar Adamson and his draft of two hundred arrived by way of Rouen three weeks later. They found the regiment near the village of St. Eloi, at the extreme southeast elbow of the Salient, engaged in a stubborn defence of a strongpoint that had been christened "The Mound" and that was just that, a hump of brickmakers' clay some twenty feet high and seventy feet long, standing beside the road at the southern approach to Ypres. Elsewhere in the area, the Germans held the high ground. "You never saw such a scene of utter desolation and destruction," was Papineau's first impression on arriving at regimental headquarters in the cellar of a ruined farmhouse that Colonel Farquhar had christened Shelley Farm, not in honour of the poet. "Every barn and house has been smashed to pieces. We passed a whole village smashed to ruins, church and all, not a stray dog or cat living. The Germans would throw up their famous lightning rockets and our whole party would throw themselves down flat in the mud til the darkness came again." Yet his first tour of front-line duty was an easy one, without casualties, and being young and full of mettle, he found it exhilarating. "It's like a game," he wrote his mother on Febuary 5, "dodging and running and creeping and lying down. As it grows dusk we meet our guides and in the dark, in a single file, we are led silently across the fields. All about is the sharp crack of rifle fire. We follow hedgerows and avoid the open. Then we creep up to the opening of the trench, and one by one jump in. I wait until my men are all in and jump after. I have not been badly frightened yet. That will come, I suppose. This is so much like a *fête-de-nuit*, a thunderstorm and duck shooting, that I positively like it."

We can suspect that Papineau was being economical with the truth to spare Caroline's feelings. Soon – "I have faith in your courage" – he began telling her more. Yet he did not describe in detail the horrors that soon became routine, still less the black mood of hopelessness that after six weeks of fruitless fighting was starting to creep up on the regiment.

Adamson spared Mabel nothing. "At the present moment, the Germans have the best of it," he wrote within days of arriving. "Their bomb and mortar throwing is perfect, also their flares, and we are infants at it. Their trenches are beautifully made, they have their men do nothing else, and they are drained and all communicate with each other. Their sniping is organized, the snipers having fixed rifles with telescopic sights firing from about 300 yards Their particular game is to enfilade the trenches. They fire all day, picking certain points where they know the men will be working, and at night keep up a steady fire about every 30 seconds, generally from both sides of the advance trenches."

The trenches inherited by the Patricias beggared description. Recently taken over from French troops, who had relied much more heavily upon their artillery than their infantry, they weren't trenches at all, only shallow ditches knee-deep in water, protected by a few sandbags and isolated from one another. Number 21, the most notorious death-trap of all, in which Adamson found himself in his first day in the line, "consisted of sandbags about 5 feet high and no trench whatever." Getting in and out involved crawling zigzag through half a mile or more of the mud, and was the most dangerous part. "We lose a lot of men in this way," he continued. "The routes have to be changed constantly as the Germans always find out, and the only way of knowing is by our number of casualties."

We can imagine Mabel shuddering as she read such reports by the dining room fire at Basil Street. Each letter she opened was grimmer. The putrefying stench of wet and decaying human and animal flesh, Agar told her, was incomparably worse than he'd anticipated, and far beyond the power of the smelling salts she'd sent him. "I counted seven dead horses just outside my trench yesterday," he wrote on March 3. "There is also a dead Frenchman there and has been for a long time. We got orders reading, 'Keep the Shelley Farm on your right, and pass between the broken tree and the dead Frenchman on your right,' so the poor fellow was being of some use in death. . . . One of the most disgusting sights was a couple of pigs deliberately feeding on the decomposed body of a soldier. You will be glad to hear it was their last meal, and they remain to add to the stench." A few days later, making improvements to a trench, his men dug into a mass grave. "We had to get the correct depth to give the living men shelter. The only thing to be done was to dig right on regardless of what we went through. The grave was some months old and it was a most horrible operation, especially when the flares were turned on and you saw the awful sights you were digging and picking to pieces. It was too much for some men who had to be relieved."

Almost as bad as the stench and the sights was the continual pounding of the artillery. "It affects the strongest of us," Agar went on. "The noise and the shaking of the earth gives us the most dreadful headaches and turns us deaf." Even on an uneventful day, the tension of being in the front lines was ever-present. "It gets on one's nerves, always having to be on the alert, as one never knows where or what they will do, and I think when you find they have not done anything, and you have really got out with the whole company safe, the relief is almost as bad as the strain."

Thus far, physical casualties to the Patricias had been relatively slight: seventy killed and wounded since early January. But the dreadful conditions produced much sickness – pneumonia,

Canadian soldiers examining a skull. This photograph was taken later in the war, on Vimy Ridge, but as early as 1915 such discoveries were routine. Far more disturbing, but far beyond the ability of the camera to convey, was the putrefying stench of wet and decaying human and animal flesh and the constant pounding of the artillery. In his letters to his wife, Agar Adamson provided some of the most graphic descriptions ever written of the ambience of the Front.

typhoid, rheumatism, a condition called "trench foot," a low-grade form of frostbite produced by standing for hours in cold water – so that by the time Adamson arrived, the regiment was nearly four hundred men under strength. "The suffering of the men is very great after they come out of the trenches," he reported. "Their hands and feet are all swelled up and a stiffening of the joints sets in." As damaging to morale in these early days was the large number of deaths that were caused by carelessness and inexperience. The first officer to be killed, Captain D. O. C. Newton, a former aide to the Governor General and a great beau around Ottawa, lost his way at night in no man's land and was shot by one of his own sentries. A fortnight later, a Captain Fitzgerald jumped out of his trench in broad daylight to inspect a dead body and was instantly shot dead by a sniper. "He practically committed suicide, so foolish was he," Papineau wrote home. On the same day, he continued, "Lieutenant Price was killed. His guide led him incorrectly into the trenches, and he was shot in the chest." The moment when Talbot himself stopped thinking of the war as a *fête-de-nuit* came shortly before noon on March 3, when Captain J. S. Ward, the Okanagan fruit farmer who had become his close friend, jumped up too hastily to inspect the neighbouring trench. "He sank back in my arms," wrote Talbot. "He had been shot in the back of the head. He bled frightfully. The brain matter was easing out. I loved old Ward. He was one of the best fellows I know. It was terrible for me to see him like that so suddenly. He was conscious and could recognize me, although his mind wandered. He was in great pain, and I gave him a good deal of morphine. He would hold my hand sometimes. He said, 'Talbot, you're an angel.' He called for 'Alice, where's Alice?' A terrific snowstorm blew up. I never saw such darkness and such wind. Flocks of birds flew before it. Later there was thunder and lightning. How long those hours were. It was not until 8:30 PM that the stretcher party came." Ward died a few days later.

Two other casualties not recorded in official regimental records dealt the Patricias another blow. On January 7, the first day the regiment was in the front line, two officers had broken under the strain. One was a Captain Smith, "accused of lying and cold feet," as Papineau reported. The other was Major J. W. H. McKinery, a big blustery man, Adamson's former company commander. "It appears that he 'blew up,'" Agar wrote Mabel. "He hid himself in the only safe place in the trench for 48 hours, cursing and swearing at his subalterns and NCOs all the time, and as soon as he got out bolted for the dressing station to have imaginary wounds attended to. The NCOs told the CO that if they were ordered to go into the trenches with him again, they would refuse and stand a courtmartial." As a cover story, it was put out that both men had been sent back to England on sick leave. Few people believed this – "It is surprising how men come back from the front just ill or tired out," Mabel noted skeptically in a letter to her mother – and the resulting gossip damaged the regiment's reputation. (Both men subsequently were struck "off strength" and reassigned to low-echelon staff duties.)

There were additional pressures upon Farquhar. The future of the regiment itself was now at risk. Six months earlier, when the Patricias had marched out from Ottawa, neither he nor Hamilton Gault nor anyone else had given much thought to reinforcements, but the matter now was becoming critical. Adamson's draft of two hundred had exhausted all the reserves in sight. Neither Sam Hughes nor General Alderson, commander of the Canadian forces, had any great love for the Patricias, a wild card among regiments over which they had no control. Henceforth, they decreed, all Canadian troops arriving in England would go to reinforce Alderson's Canadian Division. New recruits back home would be reserved for an additional Canadian Division. In order to establish itself as indispensable, as well as to erase the blot on its honour left by McKinery and Smith, the regiment needed urgently to distinguish itself.

Farquhar's response, on Febuary 27, was to conceive of a way to hit at the enemy before being hit by him. He requested permission to make a sudden local attack on a new trench that the Germans were sapping directly in front of The Mound, and so less than twenty yards away from the Patricias' line. Described as a "reconnaissance in force," this was the first engagement fought by a Canadian regiment in Europe. It was also the first of the "trench raids" for which the Canadians were to become famous. Talbot Papineau was one of the ninety or so men chosen to take part.

Nearly eight decades later, his private account, a sixteen-page letter to his mother scribbled hastily in pencil, remains the most riveting account of this singular Canadian military initiative.

"We have made an attack at last and I have led it," begins Papineau's letter. At midnight, he and the other raiders had assembled at Shelley Farm. Already, Hamilton Gault and another officer, Lieutenant Colquhoun, who unfortunately had been spotted by the enemy and taken prisoner, had reconnoitred the territory. They were divided into three groups. The first, led by Lieutenant C. E. Crabbe, consisted of about thirty snipers and riflemen, plus three grenade-throwers headed by Papineau. Their objective was to rush the German sap and clear it. The other two parties were to act as cover, and to break down the enemy parapet. "The moon was well down and dawn was coming," continued Papineau. "The colonel said, 'There are six snipers that will go ahead of you then you will go with your bomber-throwers. Crabbe will be behind you with his men. All right! Lead on!'"

> I was pretty scared! My stomach seemed hollow. I called my men and we fell into line and began creeping forward flat on our bellies. I had a bomb ready in my hand. We lay for a moment exposed and then suddenly we were all up and rushing forward. My legs caught in barbed wire, but I stumbled through somehow. I set my fuse and hurled my bomb ahead of me. From that moment, all hell broke loose. I never thought there could be such noise. I had my revolver out. A German was silhouetted and I saw the flash of his rifle. I dropped on my knees and fired point blank. He disappeared. I said to myself, "I have shot him." I fired into the trench at whatever I thought was there. Then my revolver stopped. I lay flat and began to reload. I was against the German parapet. I looked behind me and could see only one man apparently wounded or dead near me. I thought, "The attack has failed. I am alone. I will never get out." A machine gun was going and the noise was awful.
>
> Then I saw Crabbe coming. He knelt near me and fired over me with a rifle. I had got a cartridge home by this time and Crabbe and I went over the edge into the trench. It was deep and narrow, beautifully built, dried by a big pump, sides

supported by planks, looked like a mine shaft. A German was lying in front of me. I pushed his head down to see if he was dead. He wasn't. I told a man to watch him. Then I began to pull down some of the parapet and sandbags. Three or four men were there too with shovels. The German machine guns were going like mad. It was beginning to grow light.

Presently we were told to evacuate the trench. I passed the order, then climbed out and made a run for our own line. Another man and I went over head first. The man that came after me was shot through the lungs. The next man got it in the stomach. They fell on me in the mud. I could not budge. Then over on top of us all came a German! He held up his hands and a couple of our men took him away. Gault was there and he worked pulling the wounded men off each other. One or two men came piling over with fixed bayonets and almost put our eyes out. I was finally pulled out of the mud. It was not quite light. I had to get back to my own trench. I beat it across the open expecting to get it any minute. I was so exhausted I wobbled from side to side in the mud. However, I reached home and dived for cover. I was tired but mostly glad to be back.

The stretcher bearers were carrying the wounded out past the back of my trench. The last party got halfway, then dropped their stretcher and ran. Gault crawled out to the man with a couple of volunteers and they dragged the stretcher into a ditch and then to a hedge. Gault was shot through the wrist. He will probably get the VC.

In practical terms, the raid achieved little, at a cost of twenty casualties. No ground was gained; the damage inflicted upon the German trench was slight; indeed, within minutes, as Papineau noted, the enemy was back in it throwing bombs. For the next three days, infuriated at having been outwitted even briefly, the Germans battered the regiment with mortar, rifle fire, and grenades and gave Adamson, now McKinery's replacement as commander of No. 2 Company, what he described as "the most awful day I ever put in."

"I could do nothing," he told Mabel. "There was only one rifle working owing to the mud and the debris knocked up by the bombs. We just lay there all day huddled together with constant fire pulling our breastwork down inch by inch. I lost 6 killed and 21 wounded." Nor was there any long-term gain; a fortnight later, after more severe fighting and many more casualties – including Charlie Stewart, badly hit in the stomach – the Germans captured The Mound and the first battle of St. Eloi was lost.

Yet within the context of early 1915, the raid was an important achievement. It demonstrated enterprise and daring. The Divisional Commander telegraphed "Well done PPCLI." Field Marshal Sir John French himself telegraphed "his great appreciation." Within the regiment itself, morale had been recouped and honour restored. Papineau and Crabbe both received the new decoration for junior officers, the Military Cross, and were the first Canadians to do so. Hamilton Gault won the first Canadian DSO for his gallant rescue of the wounded soldier. As mattered most of all, the newspapers having reported the affair, the future of the Patricias was secure at least for the time being.

This was to be "Fanny" Farquhar's last legacy to the Patricias. On March 19, shortly after receiving instructions to leave St. Eloi for the centre of the Salient, Farquhar was hit by a chance bullet while showing the commanding officer of the relieving battalion around. Adamson, leading his own company back to billets after a hard forty-eight hours in the trenches, learned what had happened when he stopped briefly at the dressing station. "I found the Colonel on the floor," he wrote Mabel. "The surgeon was dressing his wound. He was groaning and suffering a great deal. From the very first there was no hope." That same day, Adamson was also mourning the death of Sergeant Cork, his trusted emissary during the battle with Colonel James. "I had just spoken to him," he told Mabel. "He said he had received your remedy for chilblains and was going to write to thank you for it. He was shot through the spine a few minutes afterwards."

Two nights later the Patricias buried their colonel in the new regimental cemetery at Voormezele, a few yards away from Sergeant Cork's grave. "We all seem to think he would like to be with his men," Adamson wrote. "It was his own idea to rope off a separate piece of ground for them." Only forty officers and men were allowed to attend since the ground was continually raked by enemy fire. Nowadays, for the contemporary visitor, thanks to an eloquent letter that Papineau wrote Lady Evelyn, it requires no stretch of the imagination for the tidy rows of poplars around the cemetery and the well-tended rosebushes surrounding the graves, to dissolve into that long-ago muddy field just back of the front lines. "We paid our last respects to the Colonel. It was the first beautiful evening we have had. The lovely sunset still tinged the sky, a new moon and little stars were quiet and clear overhead. A warm stillness and peacefulness seemed with us as we stood by the grave, but just beyond there was the constant crackle of rifles, now and then the whine of a bullet or the loud explosion of a bomb. Peace upon one side, war upon the other . . ."

Papineau's letter went on to say all the right things. "As a Canadian, I feel a national debt of gratitude to him. An Imperial officer, who could have commanded the highest position in the British army, he accepted the task of creating as well as commanding a new and untried Canadian regiment. He knew how to combine the discipline and dignity of the regular British army with the easy independence and democracy of a volunteer Canadian regiment. . . . He himself is with us no longer but his influence and his memory will endure."

Yet, nearly eighty years on, Agar's stumbling description of his own feeling is the more telling. "We are all very much depressed but have to keep up an appearance of cheerfulness, and speak of it as if it were only the fortunes of war. . . . What really makes a real man is something very hard to fathom. I suppose it is a case of training, but I really think it is more than that. It must be a matter as difficult as the definition and reason for the production of a real genius."

On March 25, the Patricias marched to Poperinghe, a peaceful market town turned into a bustling transport centre and forward base. There they spent the next week luxuriating in hot baths and the first change of clothes in a month. (Adamson and the other officers had their baths in a hotel: the men splashed around in huge converted beer vats in the main square.) There was even a divisional race meeting with a steeplechase in which both Adamson and Papineau took part. Everyone roared with laughter at the regimental four-in-hand, a carriage painted yellow and black, with two men inside dressed up as a bride and bridegroom. A few moments later, recounted Adamson, "a very fat French nurse and a fatter priest turned up. General Plumer said it was the most perfect makeup job he had ever seen. He was quite upset when he found out it was a real woman and priest and that she was the matron of the hospital at Poperinghe."

Soon the Second Battle of Ypres would begin. Compared to it, the desperate weeks at St. Eloi would seem like a militia manoeuvre.

9

Pluck Against Science

*We trust to pluck and luck, while the Germans trust to
science and munitions with able leadership.*
Mabel Adamson. A letter to her mother; May 1915

In most Canadian accounts of the Great War, the story begins
with the Second Battle of Ypres, the six terrible days in late
April 1915, when the First Canadian Division, with an open
flank, choked by gas, and badly outnumbered, fought a desperate
and ultimately successful defensive battle against superior forces
at St. Julien, Langemarck, and Gravenstafel Ridge. "I understand
that the Canadians were used in some heavy fighting last night
and there will be many sad hearts," Talbot Papineau wrote on
April 23. Three days later, he continued, "Some reports are
appalling. I should feel dreadfully if they are true, yet what a glorious history they will have made for Canada. These may be the
birth pangs of our nationality." They had indeed been savage
pangs. Casualties exceeded six thousand; among them was Papineau's friend, Guy Drummond, son of Lady Drummond, who died
of a bullet wound in the neck on the first day of the battle.

The role soon to be played by the Patricias within Second
Ypres would be of a quite different nature, although equally devastating. Instead of poison gas, they would encounter "the most
overwhelming superiority of artillery fire ever concentrated upon
British trenches," in the words of the official regimental history.
At Bellewaerde Ridge on May 8, the British 27th Division, of which
the Patricias were a unit, had its left flank laid bare, as had happened to the Canadians at St. Julien. It too suffered a terrible bat-
tering, but stood its ground.

For the Patricias, the prelude to battle was uneventful, indeed, almost a holiday. On April 5, now under the command of Lieutenant-Colonel E. S. Buller, "Teta" to his friends and yet another member of the viceregal contingent from Ottawa, the regiment marched out of Poperinghe and into billets in Ypres itself. Although by now the railway station, the cathedral, and the four-teenth-century Cloth Hall – that had served as inspiration for the original Centre Block on Parliament Hill – had suffered heavy pounding, the city was still functional. "There are still some beautiful churches standing here and the carving is very fine," Adamson reported to Mabel. For a few days, he and other officers were billeted in a women's polytechnique. Agar's detailed descriptions suggest that more about the decorating business had sunk in than she had given him credit for. "The lady principals must have done themselves very well, as there are several very large and beautifully furnished bedrooms which must have been vacated in a very big hurry. I have one with every possible comfort, including sheets and a beautiful Circassian walnut bedroom set, a fireplace, 4 cupboards full of women's dresses, a great quantity of hats, some very smart underclothes and the most delightful smelling facepowder." Later, they moved to the town house of a merchant. "He was a church candle maker and a bleacher of linen. The woman was a bride of only a few months. They have a beautiful formal garden and glass houses, nine bedrooms intact, electric bells and telephones in the rooms." Yet more splendid were Colonel Buller's accommodations. "He is in a house decorated by a swagger Austrian firm of decorators. It looks very much like the rooms you see in *The Studio*, even the glasses are long, thin creatures, the leather-embossed wallpaper looks as if it came from Germany."

Even the new trenches in Polygon Wood, about four miles east of Ypres, were a tremendous improvement on those at St. Eloi, well sandbagged and passably dry. Best of all, reported Adamson, "there is a wonderful communication trench that can be used quite safely even in daylight. It is a great boon to be able to get in without being fired at." Spring was beginning and leaves were coming out on the trees; Adamson dispatched the smelly, mud-encrusted fur linings of his mackintosh and battle vest back to

London. Along the quiet line, the only real excitement was a Zeppelin raid behind the lines on April 12 that inflicted no damage. "She was a wonderful looking thing on a starlit night," Adamson wrote. He used the peaceful interlude to bombard Mabel with requests for replenishments to the kit either lost or destroyed in the mud at St. Eloi. He needed socks, cigarettes, a new leather holster for his revolver, field-glasses ("like the ones left in No. 21"), and an additional supply of periscopes. "If they are very cheap, about £1/6, please send me two dozen. They are most useful and keep the men interested and me informed of wherever the fire is coming from." He also thought a portable typewriter might come in handy. "They are of the greatest use and cost, I think, £7 and go into a case about the size of a small dispatch box. I wonder if you would make me a present of one, including paper and carbon paper." On Easter Sunday, April 18, Agar hugely enjoyed raspberry jam, a tub of Devonshire cream, a tinned ham, and a traditional chocolate fish with Easter eggs inside, all sent by Mabel, and in return he sent Anthony a bird-feeder. "All the little boys and girls here are very fond of birds and tame the wild ones, they all use these little hoppers." Despite his forty-nine years, he was feeling as fit as a fiddle. "Even after three nights without a real doze I am not half as tired as I have been after a late night at the club. I suppose it is the fresh air and no whiskey. I have not drunk a tumblerful since being out here." He was also pleased as punch about a description of himself that he'd come across while censoring his men's letters. "Our captain whose name is Adamson is a dear good fat old man who crawls about in the trenches like a porpus and speaks to us like men."

The battle began two days later. Around mid-morning on April 20, German shells began falling on Ypres, catching the Patricias in their billets. "A very heavy bombardment of the town," wrote Adamson. "A shell fell in the backyard killing two horses. About one o'clock, they commenced firing 15-inch shells knocking down a large part of the town. The large square was littered with debris and wounded civilians. A great many women and children were killed and wounded. The whole town was a continuous stream of stretcher bearers."

At 4:00 PM orders came to evacuate the infantry barracks.

"We took the men to a vacant field outside the town and scattered them and watched the shelling. Had it not meant death to so many people it would have been a magnificent sight. The 15-inch shells weigh 1,400 pounds; on exploding, large pieces will land 200 yards away from where the shell landed. The pieces are red hot. The effect of these shells is amazing. The walls of the houses are generally four bricks thick, very well mortared together and pieces the size of a horse are hurled in all directions. . . . Our men did very good work in getting people out of the ruins. One family of nine was killed in one house. A little boy we all knew who used to sell picture postcards and who had lost his entire family in November was killed. An officer in the next billet to me had both his legs blown off above the knees. The poor unfortunate Leicesters had 56 men knocked out by one shell and many others buried. These are only a few instances that came under my eye."

Later that day, the regiment marched to the advance trenches for a three-day tour. During it, they received muddled and garbled but not inaccurate word of the great German attack to the northwest. First, a gas attack. "The Germans broke through the lines held by the French North African troops, who bolted all the way to Ypres in great disorder, bleeding from the noses, from the fumes from the German shells," wrote Adamson. "The Canadian Division, although out of their own line, counter-attacked and held them from advancing further."

By April 27, thanks mainly to the Canadians, the German attempt to capture Ypres from the north had failed. By now though, the ferocious attacks had played such havoc with the allied line that on Monday, May 3, orders were issued to the 27th Division to retreat a mile or more to new, hastily prepared positions at Bellewaerde Ridge, the last high ground outside Ypres to the east. Agar and his company moved back accordingly. But for the first time he was beginning to have serious doubts about the generalship of those who were giving the orders. "For the last three months," he told Mabel, "the regiments at rest have been building a magnificent back line of trenches, with drains, cement, bomb-proof dugouts and everything that could be devised, including wonderful wire entanglements. . . . They now find that it is not facing the right way, instead of facing the enemy is almost at the right angle to it. It is things like this that make one very angry and wonder how we are ever going to win the war against so skilled and alert an enemy who leaves nothing to chance, while we muddle ahead in the same old British way, losing the magnificent men for the want of a little commonsense or at least judgement."

Another shock, closer to home, happened on May 6, the eve of the attack on the new position. Colonel Buller was shot in the right eye by a sniper and put out of commission. Hamilton Gault, just back on the active list after his wound at St. Eloi, took over command of the Patricias. As senior captain, Adamson suddenly found himself second-in-command.

"We moved last night from our support dugouts," wrote Adamson to Mabel on May 7, from Bellewaerde Ridge. Here, there were two lines of trenches, about fifty yards apart, the second line a shallow ditch following a hedgerow, in which there had been a field battery. Through some incredible blunder, the battery had been removed and sent further south. One of the dugouts originally constructed for the gunners was designated battalion headquarters, and here the precious regimental colour made by Princess Patricia was placed. Already, Adamson reported "heavy artillery fire . . . 5 killed, 11 wounded, 2 machine guns smashed to pieces and crews buried and wounded. . . . Enemy in front of us advancing their line of trenches and sniping force in every direction, fire from Maxims and artillery come from 3 different directions. . . . Two men have gone mad and have had to be disarmed. . . . It seems certain that this line cannot be held, and that we are only making a bluff at it . . . I think a trapped rat would be a more accurate simile than the Knight in *Alice in Wonderland*."

This hasty disjointed letter was the last Adamson had time to scribble. To find out what happened the next day, we have to turn to the official regimental history.

The battle began about 7:00 AM. Shrapnel and enfiladed machine gun fire were devastating to the garrisons of the inadequate trenches. Shells blew in whole bays at a time. The main assault was launched at 9:00 AM and was beaten back mainly by rifle fire. All day the Germans kept up the pressure, mounting attack after attack, each preceded by accurate concentrations

of artillery fire. Casualties were appalling. By noon, ammunition
was running short and a gallant company of the Rifle Brigade
came forward, through the artillery fire with boxes of ammunition and two machine guns. At about 3:00 PM, when a platoon of
the Shropshires brought forward more ammunition, 80% of the
Patricias were casualties. There was a great gap on the left flank
and the holes and ditches which the remnants of the battalion
occupied were under fire from three sides. Shortly afterwards,
a final German assault was beaten back and about 5:00 PM the
artillery fire ceased. The Kings Royal Rifle Corps relieved what
was left of the Regiment, 4 officers and 150 men.

The discreet official references to the Patricias trying to
match concentrated artillery fire with their rifles indicates how
poor the generalship was on that day. Our own sources suggest
that the real story was even worse.

"What they went through in that bombardment is almost
incredible," Mabel wrote later to her mother, reporting what Agar
had told her. "The Germans brought a battery right out in the
open without any attempt to hide it and fired all the guns at once
and as hard as they could fire. They got the range from aeroplanes who flew over our trenches quite unmolested. The con-
necting trenches were heaped with wounded and dead. Eleven
wounded men were put in a dugout for safety. A shell struck it and
all were killed. They got orders to hold the trench at all cost and
they did. But the cost was appalling."

Through much of the day, Adamson was in command of the
Patricias, Gault having been wounded in thigh and right arm
around 9:00 AM. "He lay all day at the bottom of a trench with his
feet on a dead man, constantly buried in mud and dirt by shells,"
Mabel recounted. About 10:00 AM, Agar himself received a bad
shrapnel wound in the shoulder. But it was not until nightfall that
he went to a dressing station to have it bound up. Here, the seri-
ousness of the wound was recognized and he was put on a
stretcher and sent on his way back to England. Papineau, for his
part, survived the day unscathed, although at one point the men
to his immediate left and right were killed. "Sergeant-Major Fraser
was hit while I was talking to him," Papineau wrote later. "I wore

his cap with a hole through it afterwards for three weeks." His singular achievement was to rescue the regimental colours, after the dugout serving as headquarters had been destroyed. "Our second line had become our front line," he went on. "I found the colours lying on the parados. I wrote a note to Hugh Niven, then the senior officer remaining, asking him what I should do with them. The note was handed down the trench hand to hand and in a few moments I had his reply telling me to take charge of them. Shortly after this the colours were hit by shrapnel and a hole about 2" square made in them."

Back in London, heaved off a hospital train at Charing Cross Station, lying on a stretcher on the platform, Adamson found himself the victim of yet more official confusion. As Anthony Adamson reports in his family memoir, "Orderlies went to each stretcher and asked name, rank, unit and denomination. My father answered the question as to his denomination with 'Church of Ireland.' As this church had been disestablished for fifty years, his form could not be completed. He therefore remained on the platform. At last he was picked up and taken to the private house of Lady Ridley in Carlton House Terrace, who had graciously offered it for the care of officers, preferably titled officers. . . . He got a bed in the dining room with eight or ten others."

Here, a few days later, Agar was informed that he had been awarded the DSO for conspicuous bravery. A letter that pleased him much was addressed to Mabel and written by the regimental surgeon, C. B. Keenan. "I am glad to hear Agar is comfy. He deserves everything good in this world. He is an honour to the Regiment." Then Keenan added a postscript. "There is no Regiment left, only a few rifles. I do not know what the future holds for us."

Agar's wound turned out to be really two wounds: a gaping four-inch hole in the left shoulder where the shrapnel had entered and a smaller hole under the armpit where it had come out. While not really serious, it took much longer to heal than he had expected, and for more than a fortnight had to be dressed every three hours. "It is not a clean wound," Mabel reported to her mother, "and in fact very few are, since they are so long unattended and get so full of dirt. Agar says the soil of Belgium is so rich that if you get any in you, you promptly grow wild oats." Still, the surroundings for his convalescence could scarcely have been improved on: the walls of Lady Ridley's dining room were covered with green silk brocade and a number of Old Master paintings and he and the other officers retained the services of her chef and servants. He was able to be up and about, indeed on the first day after he arrived, Mabel and Porter brought the car round and whisked him off to the oculist to replace the two pairs of spectacles lost in the debacle at Bellewaerde Ridge. "His costume consisted of a mackintosh ending in a fringe around his knees and a pair of rubber boots with the top cut off, a pale blue cotton sling for his arm," recounted Mabel, "but one gets accustomed in London to sights like Agar. It is quite usual to see the soldiers out in dressing gowns and bedroom slippers."

Less easily consoled were Agar's spirits. He spent much of the next few weeks writing letters to relatives of the members of his company who had perished. As painful as writing such letters was receiving the replies. "The loss of my only son is hard for me to bear, as he was always a good son, but I am proud to know that he did his duty and carried out the work he had set himself to do," wrote Mrs. Grace Lognon of Montreal. Agar also wrote to all of his men who like him were in hospital. "It was a very pleasant surprise for me to receive such a kind letter from you, also the cigarettes for which I thank you very much," responded one of his sergeants.

Now that the Second Battle of Ypres had ended in the same bloody stalemate as the first, the anger that Adamson had begun to feel on Bellewaerde Ridge intensified. "Ypres was held purely for sentimental reasons," he wrote to a friend in Toronto. "General Smith-Dorrien wanted to fall back on the canal and even if necessary not to hold the town. French insisted upon our remaining in the exposed position, and Smith-Dorrien is in England having been relieved of his command. It is and always will be a question if we did not pay too big a price." Mabel's letters home also reflect the mood of that gloomy summer, when the first Zeppelin raids were killing civilians in London and even the jingoistic *Daily Mail* was beginning to make sharp criticisms of the conduct of the war. "Agar takes a very pessimistic view," she wrote in early June. "The

Government and the 'High Commands' are muddling things so dreadfully. The waste of life and material is awful and most soldiers think they are losing four men to the Germans' one. It is simply a question of time until you get hit. We trust to pluck and luck, while the Germans trust to science and munitions with able leadership."

Above all, Agar worried about the future of his beloved regiment. "It may be that I am growing old," he wrote in a long reflective letter to another Toronto friend, "but though I have always thought the finest thing in the world had to wear a petticoat, I have yet to see a more magnificent sight than the remnant of a regiment, dirty, tired and silently marching back after an attack, the set stare in each man's eyes, the knowledge of his reduced ranks, the determination to stick it, which is apparent in his every movement, the absolute silence and fatigue makes one realize that there are still real men in the world, and the finest specimen is the underpaid, much abused and often drunken Tommy Atkins." The one bright spot was the news that the Patricias would, after all, survive. Friends in Canada solved the problem of reinforcements by recruiting through the universities, with the Students' Union at McGill the main mobilization centre. The first new companies arrived in late summer to join the remnants of the battalion, resting in a quiet sector of the line near Armentières.

In mid-July 1915, Mabel decided it was best for them both to get out of London for a while. They found a delightful furnished flat overlooking the sea at Folkestone, the south-coast resort close by the huge new Canadian base at Shorncliffe. By now, she herself was feeling ground down, not only because of Agar and the Zeppelins but also because of the many disasters that had befallen the growing Canadian community in London. On May 7, the day before the battle of Bellewaerde Ridge, the *Lusitania* had been torpedoed off Ireland. Numerous Canadians were among the two thousand casualties, including some acquaintances, most prominently the two younger daughters of Sir Montagu Allan, the Montreal shipping magnate. "The calamities have brought us all very much together," Mabel wrote to her mother. "Lady Allan herself is seriously injured. Poor Mrs. Hay has gone to Queenstown to search for the body of the Braithwaite girl who was lost." Overarching everything were the dreadful losses suffered by the Canadian Division. On May 10, Mabel went to St. Paul's Cathedral for a massive memorial service for the Canadians and found herself sitting right behind Winston Churchill. "The church was jammed," she reported, "the music was magnificent. I have never heard anything more impressive than the Guards' Band rendering of the *'Dead March from Saul'* and *'The Last Post.'*"

As soon as school was out, Anthony joined his parents at Folkestone. For him, the six weeks spent there were blissfully happy. "There were thousands of Canadians and lots of warships and even airships and I was beginning to be mesmerized by the beauty of the English countryside and its history. There was also an amusement pier, which we did not have at Port Credit." In August, Agar was gazetted a major; in September he went back to France. By then, thanks to sea air and native resilience, he was almost back to being his usual ebullient self, sufficiently restored to dash off a letter to his sister-in-law, Maud Cawthra, in which he described wartime fashions. "Now that the women are wearing short skirts and in effect, flat feet, they take such tremendous strides that even you would have difficulty keeping pace . . . I cannot tell you about their clothes from the waist up as there are not any . . . they are called X-Ray blouses." As for the effects of the war upon Mabel, "a busy day in Toronto, between the Exhibition, Thornton-Smith, Heliconian Club and weeding garden, is as child's play to one of her days now keeping barges afloat."

In that same letter, Agar also included a biting but no doubt perfectly accurate assessment of the Canadian military establishment at leisure. "My enforced respite gave me many opportunities for the study of human nature. Everybody hates everybody else like the very devil, all the good wives think their husbands ought to be Brigadier Generals and give you their reasons why. The question of the order of precedence at Buckingham Palace is nothing to that of the seniority of the officer's lady in the Canadian colony. Even Sam Hughes is afraid to tackle it. A woman with a husband in France does not approve of one who has a husband nursing a staff job in Shorncliffe while *she* knows, because she has been told, that

Agar Adamson and his son Anthony at Folkestone in the
summer of 1915. Adamson had been awarded the DSO
for bravery at Bellewaerde Ridge and was convalescing
from his wound. Despite his jaunty appearance, he was
becoming increasingly pessimistic about the war. Eight-
year-old Anthony, however, hugely enjoyed the summer.

her husband's ability would be thrown away merely commanding an infantry regiment – and she may be quite right."

Had Adamson known about the manifestations of human nature now making their appearance at home, he would have been even more acerbic. To investigate that scene, we must return to Ethel Chadwick as she observes the goings-on in Ottawa as a member of the viceregal court's inner circle.

10

Home Fires Burning

In those days I knew, of course, nothing of psychology ...
I was still too young to realize how much vicarious
excitement the war provided for frustrated women cut
off from vision and opportunity in small provincial
towns, or to understand that the deliberate contempla-
tion of horror and agony might strangely compensate a
thwarted nature for the very real grief of having no one
at the front for whom to grieve.

Vera Brittain. *Testament of Youth*; 1931

In Canada, the aftermath of Ypres was disbelief, followed by grief and then anger. More than six thousand Canadians were casualties, about 60 per cent of those who had taken part in the battle; 66 officers and 1,784 other ranks had been killed. And while the cities were most deeply affected (the Montreal and Toronto Highland battalions and the "Little Black Devils" of Winnipeg had all suffered almost as badly as the Patricias), no part of the Dominion was left untouched. In most places, spring had come unusually early that year – "the heat has already forced out the buds on the trees," Ethel Chadwick wrote on April 27. Years later, the contrast between green leaves unfurling and black-bordered casualty lists was the thing she remembered most.

The immediate response to Ypres was a fresh surge of patriotism. No longer an adventure, the war had become a crusade. "This baptism of blood will arouse amongst us a deeper consciousness of national duty," said the Reverend W. D. Herridge of Ottawa, in a widely reprinted sermon that was the centrepiece of a massive

memorial service held on Parliament Hill on April 29, attended by
the Duke of Connaught and Prime Minister Borden. Enlistment figures, which had been sluggish all winter, soared. One new recruit
was Westcott Papineau, Talbot's younger brother, who gave up his
job at the Ogilvy Flour Mills in Montreal to join the artillery as a
private. Another was John Thompson, son of a late prime minister
and an occasional beau of Ethel's, an intellectual and somewhat
iconoclastic lawyer in his mid-thirties, who in the past had frequently ruffled her feathers by mocking her slavish devotion to
Empire. "He is certainly determined about going to France," she
noted in her diary, "and since he never thought much of soldiering
before, it is remarkable." One Toronto regiment hired a streetcar to
tour the city carrying recruiting officers and bearing placards:
"Your King Calls You, How Will You Answer Him?" and "If You Want
to Enlist, Jump on This Car." At the end of the summer, the Canadian National Exhibition featured model trenches and a display of
"Blood-stained and torn clothing worn by soldiers who have given
their lives in the service of their country."

By now, many Canadian women were wearing mourning, or
at least, eschewing bright colours. ("It is entirely a matter of personal preference," the Ottawa department store, Murphy-Gamble,
counselled in large newspaper advertisements. "Those in authority in England are said to have pronounced against full trappings
of grief because of its depressing effect. But Black and White is
fashionable, and many will wear it out of courtesy to a friend's
sorrow.") Yet it was frowned on to show pain in public: the example to be followed was that of Lady Drummond, who had
appeared for duty as usual at the Canadian Red Cross offices in
London the very day after her son had been killed at St. Julien. In
mid-1915, to the general satisfaction, the 1914 regulation that married men and those under twenty-one needed their wives' or parents' approval to enlist was rescinded. "If we hold back our men
we are courting defeat," ran an open letter on the subject, issued
by the National Committee of Women for Patriotic Service. "The
most compelling call for sacrifice rings out from the graves of
those who on the fields of Flanders have blazed the trail to glory
with their lifeblood. Can we make their self-surrender of no avail
by holding back the men who would take up and complete their
splendid task?" Some women became as bellicose as Sam Hughes:

Recruiting Poster, 1915. Less than a year separates this poster from the imperial lion of 1914, but the style has changed markedly. After Second Ypres, when the raw and untried Canadian Division held the line against gas attack, the appeal was to *Canadian* pride.

Muriel K. Bruce of Toronto composed a song entitled "Why Aren't You in Khaki?" that became the official anthem of the Recruiting League; another Toronto woman, Jessie McNab, established a Women's Home Guard attired in khaki-coloured short skirts and Norfolk jackets; others began handing out white feathers, implying cowardice, to able-bodied men not in uniform. South of the border, in the neutral United States, women were singing a plaintive new song, "I Didn't Raise My Boy to Be a Soldier," and in the spring of 1915, many of them travelled to The Hague to attend an international women's congress for peace chaired by Jane Addams of Hull House in Chicago, the pioneer social reformer who had greatly impressed Mackenzie King during his student days. But the single Canadian woman who attended – Laura Hughes of Toronto; Sam Hughes was her uncle – found herself ostracized at home, as did Alice Chown, a pacifist and feminist who had written articles praising the conference. Indeed, even Nellie McClung had suspended her pacifism, although not her feminism, for the duration. As McClung saw it, bloodshed might even be God's way of saving humankind. "By the time we have emerged from the furnace of war," she wrote, "the clear, sacrificial fire may have purified us, burned away the dross, and prepared us for simpler living and simpler pleasures."*

Such were the public attitudes, conditioned by social pressures, by propaganda, by the examples set by role models such as Lady Drummond. Less easy to describe is the private mood: what people on the home front were actually thinking and feeling. Living memory has almost died out. Canada, sad to say, did not produce a wartime diarist with the intensity and perception of Vera Brittain; one ransacks the archives in vain to find a 1914-18 equivalent to Edmund Allen Meredith, in whose journals the early

---

* Although Laura Hughes was not an official delegate to the Women's Peace Conference, she was granted time to deliver an address that undoubtedly horrified her Uncle Sam. According to the account that appeared in the Canadian papers on May 1, 1915, Laura Hughes argued that cabinets should include a Minister for Peace, and also that "the time had come when women should re-occupy the position of peacemakers they held in prehistoric ages. Then, when women thought men had fought enough, they went out and stopped the strife."

post-Confederation years come alive. Apart from Ethel Chad-wick's, one of the most revealing journals to survive is that of the novelist Lucy Maud Montgomery. Recently turned forty and in mid-career, the busy wife of a Presbyterian minister in Leaskdale, Ontario, a hamlet in the hilly countryside about sixty miles north-east of Toronto, she was as dedicated an Imperialist as anyone else. Yet her private diary – her "life document" as she described it – reveals Montgomery's inner anguish. "I said I dreaded the spring for what the war news might be," she wrote on April 26, as the first news of the gas attack at Ypres came in. "My dread has been justified." Ten days later, chancing to visit Toronto the day after the *Lusitania* was sunk, she wrote, "I shall never forget the scene as I walked up Yonge Street. . . . As usual it was crowded, and every man and woman on it held a morning paper and blun-dered along reading it, indifferent to everything but the news it contained. For myself, when I read of those scores of murdered babies and pictured their dear little dead bodies floating about in that pitiless ice-cold water, I felt a hideous nausea of life. I wanted to get out of a world where such a thing could happen and shake its accursed dust from my soul." The following year, visiting family connections in Indiana, Montgomery reflected how, for Canadians, the war by now had become almost *ordinary*. "It seems so strange to be in a country that is not at war! I did not realize until I came here how deeply Canada *is* at war, how normal a condition war has to come to be with us. It seems strange to go out – on the street or to some public place – and see no Khaki uni-forms, no posters of appeal for recruits, no bulletin boards or war dispatches."

Soon after the end of the war, in 1920, Montgomery produced a novel, *Rilla of Ingleside*, based on her wartime diaries. Though sentimental and jingoistic, it is in some ways her most interesting book, virtually the only Canadian work of fiction to describe everyday life on the home front from direct personal experience. Rilla herself, a frivolous, self-absorbed teenager transformed by the war into a sacrificial model of womanhood, is one of Mont-gomery's less successful heroines: the author, one senses, was straining too hard to make her into a metaphor for Canada's own coming of age. But through its well-observed detail, the novel takes us under the skin of smalltown wartime life: anguished farewells on railway platforms; the complicated politics of Red Cross meetings (whether or not it was patriotic to serve "eats" was of considerable importance); the assiduous struggle to master the map of Europe and get one's tongue around foreign place-names like Przemysl, and Ypres and Brest-Litovsk. "Three months ago I didn't know there was such a place in the world as Lodz," Rilla tells us. "Now I know its size, its standing, its military significance." In an era without mass communications, the arrival of the postman was the central event of the day. "Father just snatches the paper – I never saw Father snatch before – and the rest of us crowd around and look at the headlines over his shoulder." Answering the telephone was a matter of trepidation. "The moment between saying 'Hello' and hearing the response seems a hundred years long, for I am always dreading to hear, *There is a telegram.*"*

Ethel Chadwick's wartime diaries lead us into much the same kind of territory, but also into a set of circumstances considerably more sophisticated and complex – all the more complex because all the social givens Ethel had spent her youth mastering were soon to be stood on their heads. No matter that Ottawa was still a dowdy colonial capital, it was undergoing a transformational change in mores and manners. Better than she herself ever realized, Ethel's diaries of 1915 and early 1916 chronicle this social change from the point of view of one who was totally unfitted, by background and inclination, to adapt to it. Thus, while Ethel, as we know, started the war immersed in Milton and the Greek classics, by mid-1915 she had fallen in love with the Russians. Dostoevsky was the one who impressed her most. But it was Chekhov,

---

* That *Rilla of Ingleside* is in fact "the only contemporary fictionalized women's account of the First World War," is confirmed by a new scholarly study, *The Fragrance of Sweet Grass; L. M. Montgomery's Heroines and the Pursuit of Romance* by Elizabeth Rollins Epperly (University of Toronto Press, 1992) published just as this book was being completed. Epperly devotes a full chapter, *Womanhood and War* to *Rilla of Ingleside*. She also points out that Montgomery's 1919 novel, *Rainbow Valley* "was another response to the war . . . this is a novel about the children who were to mature into the soldiers and the workers of the war."

past master of tragicomedy who could truly have written her story.

Every now and then, as on April 29, 1915, when she arrived at Parliament Hill too late to hear Herridge's sermon, but in time to spot a friend of her youth marching past the reviewing stand wearing the smart kit of an army nurse about to go overseas, Ethel wished she had followed her earlier patriotic instincts and taken courage on the wing. "I wish I could have been a nurse or somehow gotten out to the front," she wrote in her diary. But Ethel, who possessed no qualification beyond a St. John's Ambulance Certificate, had long since settled into the conventional war work favoured by most of her smart-set contemporaries. By the end of 1914, the routine had become second nature: Tuesday and Wednesday mornings at the May Court clubrooms overlooking Sparks Street, cutting out and basting pyjama bottoms and dressing-gowns for the Red Cross, or else rolling bandages, a couple of afternoons at the new "Women's Exchange" established by the May Court Club to raise money for soldiers' comforts by the sale of home baking and handicrafts ("The Princess herself contributed several framed pictures," Ethel tells us, "and the Duchess a number of knitted silk scarves which very fortunately are nearly all sold"); a couple of days a month venturing into the shabby, working-class houses of Ottawa under the auspices of the National Committee of Women for Patriotic Service, visiting soldiers' families. "The family on Wilbrod Street badly needed some wood and coal so I got them sent some from the Relief Committee, also a turkey and a lot of groceries," she noted with satisfaction on Christmas Eve. There was also the disagreeable but necessary chore of putting in duty on tagdays. "I collected at the door of the Château Laurier for two hours for the Red Cross," she reports in late October, "but didn't get much." Later, reinforced by two friends, she moved on to the dark, cavernous basement bar, heavy with cigar-smoke. "Here, everyone gave something, but they looked sheepish. I think they hated our going in." Like all self-respecting females, Ethel went nowhere unaccompanied by her wooden-handled knitting bag. Though unhandy with her needles, she could cope well

enough with Balaclava helmets, and by early October, had completed her fifth. But it was another six months before she produced a pair of socks good enough to satisfy the eagle-eyed Red
Cross examiner. "Mrs. Rivers praised them immensely, said the
heels are beautifully turned," she reported in April.

During these early months, Ethel slogged through her tasks
with a heavy heart. Once, when serving refreshments at a social
club for new recruits, she almost broke down and cried. "Some of
them are so young, just golden-haired boys and they are on their
way to be killed." Even books were no longer an escape. "I was
reading part of the *Agamemnon*, *the Seven Against Thebes*, but in
the middle I began to think of our own war and its horrors," she
wrote early in December. "Somehow everything comes back to
that."

For her, as for all members of the viceregal inner circle, the
real meaning of trench warfare had sunk in early. Almost all of the
former Connaught aides, save for those fighting with the Patricias,
were members of the original British Expeditionary Force, the
"Old Contemptibles." Many former skating partners were dead
before Christmas: Captain Tommy Rivers-Bulkeley in October;
Colonel George Paley in November; Commander Ling of the Royal
Navy down with HMS *Formidable* in the same month. When Captain
Newton of the Patricias was killed in January – naturally, it was
not revealed that he had been shot by his own sentry – she wrote
sombrely. "He is the 5th man I know killed in this dreadful war.
Apparently he had told a friend that he wasn't awfully keen to go
as he had never cared for the soldier's life, but felt it his duty."

For Ethel herself, by far the worst blow had fallen already. On
December 9, 1914, a day when, in the way of such things, she'd
been feeling more upbeat than usual, news had come of the death
of "sweet Johnnie Hamilton." The previous night, there'd been a
gala concert and charity auction in aid of Belgian Relief at the
Château: the high point was provided by the witty lawyer Dick
Ritchie who acted as auctioneer and extracted the considerable
sum of $175 for a landscape painted and donated by Princess
Patricia. In the morning, Ethel had walked into town, and lucked
into several yards of "tomato-coloured crêpe de Chine" at a bargain price. In mid-afternoon, just as she was pinning out a pattern

for a blouse on the dining-room table, the telephone rang. At the other end of the line was one of the best-informed of her friends, Maud Francis, sister-in-law to the Governor General's secretary, Arthur Sladen. She informed Ethel that Hamilton had been killed fighting with the Irish Guards at a place called Zwartelen. The Duke had been told the previous evening, but had ordered that the ladies of the court not be told, so as not to spoil the concert.

Whether or not Ethel managed to finish her cutting out, she doesn't tell us. Most likely she did, since the last thing she'd have wanted to deal with was her mother and sisters coming in from their own war work and fussing about the mess. We do know that she put the last touches on "an appreciation of the Greek poet Sappho" due to be delivered at the May Court's literary meeting the following morning, and "typewrote it out." Later that evening, she retreated to her room and poured out her heart to her diary:

> He was such a darling . . . the nicest man I ever knew. I never knew anyone take chaff so well, I remember he said that never had anyone been chaffed by anyone as he had by me. I loved him. I can't get him out of my mind. I remember the day he asked me to put on a pretty hat as he wanted to take a picture of me and when he took it, he said it was typical of me that in it I looked as if I were saying something nasty to him. All the time I loved him so; it will be 3 years in January since I met him. I said when he left, "*Tout est fini*," and indeed it was. I loved him. I can't get him out of my mind. Never more on earth.

For the next several weeks, Ethel's diaries reflect her emotional desolation. Her pain was all the more difficult to bear because she was in the thankless position of being a mourner without official status. Everyone in the viceregal circle, including the duke, the duchess, and the princess, knew that she'd been hopelessly in love with Hamilton, knew also that he, in some unresolved way, had cared for her and yet, since his departure from Ottawa in March 1912, had never sent her so much as a single postcard. Thus most of her friends were too embarrassed to say anything. Since the worst way of handling grief is not to talk about it, Ethel was grateful when, at a mid-December dinner party, a bluff old British adviser to the Canadian militia, Colonel "Four-eyes" Macdonald, "who loved John as much as I did," plunged right into the subject and even suggested that the "missing believed killed" listing might have been a mistake. Indeed, for a time – Hamilton's body was one of the many that were never found – there was reason to hope that he might have been wounded and then taken prisoner. But by New Year's Eve, as the duke himself gently told her at the first skating party of the season, there could no longer be any doubt. "He gave me such a nice greeting, and said it was so long since he had seen me. He stood talking, but made me sit down and then sat down beside me all during tea. He told me about Lord John being killed, and I remembered the first Connaught skating party three years ago, the day I met John, him getting me tea in that very same drawing room." *Faute de mieux*, she later attended a Country Club dinner-dance organized by her old friend, D'Arcy Scott. Then in the small hours she came home and wept. "I just sobbed and sobbed, thinking of the men I knew, especially sweet JH. Nothing is known of him; his skeleton is probably lying on some battlefield. If he had even been killed in some glorious moment. However, he was just as brave, but hadn't luck."

"Last of January, rather a pleasant month," noted Ethel just over four weeks later. Probably she was just as surprised to find herself writing this entry as we are to read it. Yet, much as she mourned Johnnie Hamilton, for her, he had already died three years earlier. Meantime, in Ottawa as in London, the febrile gaiety of wartime was catching, and with the viceregal court giving the lead, who could resist? "I'm rather amazed that they are having skating parties as usual," remarked Ethel on January 16, "but I suppose it's allright."* Almost in spite of herself, she started to get back her sparkle. "Met the two new aides at the skating

---

* Ethel wasn't the only one amazed. During his sojourns in Ottawa, Mackenzie King similarly wrestled with his conscience: "I am sensitive to comment, not caring to be seen skating at a social function when others are away fighting," he tells us on one occasion. Still, King usually accepted.

Ethel Chadwick and Dorothy Yorke, lady-in-waiting to
the Duchess of Connaught, on the rink at Rideau Hall,
winter 1915. By then, half a dozen former viceregal
aides, including Lord John Hamilton, had died in the
war, but skating parties continued as usual.

today," she tells us that same day, "Major Arthur Duff and Colonel
Stanton. They haven't much looks between them, but may turn
out to be nice."

This new pair of courtiers, as Ethel would discover to her
cost, were of a quite different order than the puppyish aristocrats
who'd peopled the Connaught Court in the years before the war.
They were older and more worldly, and, it would develop, they
were looking for something rather more substantial by way of
female companionship than instruction in skating and a bit of

chaff. Duff, who took an immediate shine to Ethel's beautiful married sister, Rossie McDougal, was in his late thirties, and bore a livid zigzag scar on his forehead. Having been wounded and taken prisoner at Cambrai in late August, he'd made a daring escape from hospital and stumbled his way across France and Belgium to the safety of the allied lines. "He told Rossie he will probably go back when his sick leave is over. He can't want to, but knows it is his duty to do so," Ethel recorded. Stanton, who from the start fancied Ethel, was Farquhar's replacement in the senior position of Military Secretary, "a short fat, red-haired man about forty-five," she relates. "He served with Kitchener at Omdurman and has been on the reserve list of officers. He volunteered for the front but was not accepted due to some friction at the War Office and so got this job." Almost as an afterthought she added, "Colonel S. is married but his wife has not come out."

No previous admirer, viceregal or otherwise, had ever invited Ethel out to tea on such short acquaintance. Yet the following week – "it seems funny when we know them so slightly, but as they say, it is wartime" – we find her and Rossie joining Stanton and Duff at the Château Laurier, with the sporty, jolly-hockey-sticks lady-in-waiting, Dorothy Yorke, another new arrival, along to play gooseberry. "It was delightful. Colonel S. ordered everything he could think of, later we smoked." As delightful, for Ethel and Rossie, were the envious glances cast their way across the tearoom. While the quintet attracted attention, it did not, at that stage, raise eyebrows. Even in pre-war Ottawa, it had long been permissible for attractive young matrons like Rossie to compete with each other to acquire a viceregal courtier as an admirer, rather in the manner of a *cavaliere servente*. Provided things didn't get out of hand, it was even acceptable to display a large signed photograph of one's cavalier, replete with medals, upon one's piano. As for Ethel, while the rules for single women were stricter, her long flirtation with D'Arcy Scott had given her at least some experience in the tricky business of conducting a decorous relationship with a married man. Thus, a few days later, we find Rossie giving a large dinner party to introduce the major and the colonel to local society. "I wore a new dress I manufactured

myself," Ethel tells us, "a tight black satin skirt and a new fashioned black velvet waist. It was a very pleasant party, although
Stanton and Duff appeared before Rossie was quite ready."

From then on, Stanton-and-Duff became the stars of her
diary for the best part of a year, featured nearly every day against
backdrops that range from lunch parties at the Country Club
("Colonel S. had the most delightful place cards, paper swans in a
little lake") to theatre parties to see the notorious Mrs. Patrick
Campbell play Eliza Doolittle in Shaw's *Pygmalion* ("After all I had
heard about her, I was rather disappointed. She is probably better
in more emotional parts as a woman with a past than as a guttersnipe") to a visit to a maple-sugar bush in a hired omnibus that
Ethel went to great pains to organize herself. "The afternoon was
exquisite," she relates. "Some leaves of last year hanging like pale
skeletons in the trees, and the cans catching the sap shining out
like copper in the sunlight. We watched the sugar being made in
the hut, and the men, especially Duff, played with the sticky taffy
just like children." Her most evocative wartime setpieces take
place in a log tea-house recently opened amid the ski-hills of
Rockcliffe Park to raise funds for the Red Cross, where she and
Rossie volunteered as waitresses a couple of afternoons a week.
Thanks to a detailed description Ethel wrote for the English
Ladies' Pictorial, we can picture it perfectly.

> There is always a cheerful log fire blazing hospitably, and a
> large inglenook with cushioned seats on either side. The walls
> have been artistically finished with brown beaverboard. Large
> flags of the Allies, resting against the rustic pillars supporting
> the roof add a bright touch of colour, and lights shaded alter
> nately with white and red cast a softened glow upon the numer
> ous tea tables with their tempting dishes and dainty services of
> china. A rustic winding staircase occupies the centre of the
> room leading to a cosy upper room where patrons can have
> their tea served if they wish for a trifling extra charge. The win
> dows here give a magnificent view of the surrounding country.

On the days when she and Rossie donned frilly aprons, Duff

and Stanton would almost always ski over from Rideau Hall for tea, usually accompanied by Dorothy Yorke and occasionally by Princess Patricia. "As always, there was a good deal of badinage," she reports after a typical mid-February tea-party. "They were talking about 'muffins,' as the English officers used to call their best girls out in Canada in the old days. Colonel Stanton was asking if I had been anybody's muffin. He said he thought I only pretended to be prim, but really wasn't."

Reading between the lines, one senses that Ethel, for the first time, felt vaguely uneasy about where things were heading. In any event, Stanton was grievously mistaken: despite her veneer of sophistication, Ethel was still as innocent and prudish at thirty-three as she had been as a debutante. Sexually, she was entirely inexperienced; indeed, we can suspect that like many spinsters of her era she had only a very shadowy notion of what the facts of life were. If, thanks to Rossie's whispered confidences, she did know, she was probably repelled. And yet – here no doubt lay the source of Stanton's confusion – Ethel was never more alive than when in the company of men, flirting and being flirted with, being paid compliments. Nor, judging by the evidence of photographs taken in 1915, had she ever looked lovelier. The winds of war had liberated fashion; on the skating rink in winter, on the golf links in spring, her skirts now edged up to mid-calf, exposing her elegant ankles. The most intriguing series of snapshots from that period date from the middle of July, and were taken by Stanton himself. This time the backdrop is Camp Petawawa, the artillery training camp on the shores of the Ottawa River, about 150 miles to the northwest of the capital. The occasion was a fishing trip organized by Coly Meredith, who, frustrated in his attempts to get overseas, had been posted there as commandant.

That Ethel, on the afternoon of Friday, July 9, 1915, found herself boarding the westbound CPR train with Colonel Stanton, whom she now addressed by his nickname, Carl, is a measure of how much, even for her, standards of behaviour had loosened. They were not, of course, travelling à deux; with them in the private compartment – Rossie was out of town and Duff otherwise occupied – was a married friend of Ethel's, Maud Macoun, daughter of a former minister of militia, Sir Frederick Borden. Upon arrival, they would acquire an additional chaperone, Meredith's wife Aldie, who was spending the summer with her husband. All the same, even a year earlier, Ethel would never have dreamt of setting out on such a lark, all the more since Maud had a slightly fast reputation, indeed, Ethel tells us, "was rather going in for Stanton" herself. Yet the hint of indiscretion added to the excitement of the journey. "I think the conductor thought that the Colonel was the Duke himself since all his luggage had Government House labels," she relates. Over tea and ices in the refreshment car, he became "very confidential and told me how he and his wife had grown apart."

Equally dashing was being met at the station by Meredith's official car, a splendid McLaughlin-Buick of the same kind used by staff officers in France. Ethel, Maud, and Aldie piled into the back seat, and, "smoked glasses," as they were called, not yet being in common use, squinted smiling into the sunlight while Stanton

Ethel Chadwick (*centre*) and Maud Macoun (*right*) arriving at Petawawa station on July 9, 1915. On the left is Aldie Meredith, whose husband Lieutenant-Colonel "Coly" Meredith was in charge of the artillery training camp. This snapshot was taken by Ethel's beau Colonel Edward Stanton, Military Secretary to the Duke of Connaught.

snapped their picture. Sweeping into the camp was a bit like sweeping into a foreign country as royalty. "The guard saluted us at the entrance," Ethel tells us, "and we drove through a large motley crowd of Austrians and Hungarians." (From Meredith's own memoir of his time at Petawawa, we know that these were aliens from enemy countries rounded up from all over Canada, and interned at the camp to build roads and bridges and ranges for artillery practice. "One could write a long and interesting story about these people," he noted, "for while most were labourers, there were engineers and bankers and musicians among them.") More delightful still was the discovery that the staff-house in which the ladies would be quartered, a simple wooden building designed four years earlier by Meredith himself in the days when Petawawa was no more than a militia training camp, had the romantic name, Cupid's Nest. "Many people who are now

Camp Petawawa, 1915. Interned aliens, most of whom were Austrians and Hungarians, were rounded up all over Canada and sent to Petawawa to build roads and bridges and ranges for artillery practice. "One could write a long and interesting story about these people," Coly Meredith noted in his memoir, "for while most were labourers, there were bankers and musicians among them."

Siberian Battery Exercising at Petawawa. Other wartime visitors to Petawawa included a group of Russian "ballistic experts" dispatched to oversee the testing of shells being manufactured for the Tsar's army by Canadian munitions plants. This romanticized depiction is one of a series executed by the noted Canadian illustrator, C. W. Jefferys. Interpreter for the Russians was a dashing Baron von Rumel whom Ethel Chadwick found fascinating.

celebrities have stayed there," Ethel recorded, "including Sir John French and Sir Ian Hamilton. The view is very pretty, overlooking the river, which at this point is very wide." After dinner on the verandah, they took a spin up the river in Meredith's official launch. No one, so it would appear, got much sleep. "Maud and I were in the sitting room on camp cots. We talked and giggled greatly. The men slept outside in huts. We heard the *Last Post*, and the guard calling out 'All's Well' at half-hour intervals all through the night."

The sun rose on a typical Ottawa Valley scorcher. After queuing up for "shower baths" – for Ethel this was a great novelty that involved much splashing and more giggles – the party set out to travel twenty-eight miles into the wilderness to fish on Lake Cartier. They motored the first part of the way over rough logging roads; at the point where the going began to be impassible for automobiles, they were met by great buckboards drawn by horses commandeered from the artillery. "It was only a trail really," Ethel tells us, "high rocks and awful mud, the wheels up on one side and down on the other. One had to hold on for dear life but it was rather exciting." Matched against this great wilderness, Blue Sea Lake seemed almost suburban. "One of the guides we had with us, a man named Paquette, a perfect wonder they say, in his knowledge of the woods, came and whispered and asked if we would like to see a moose. So we went silently on foot to a little lake, called Long Lake, and there in the water just opposite us was a bull moose with huge antlers; he looked at us for a bit, then swam away to the opposite shore." Here it was decided to have lunch – Aldie had brought along her cook, "a Spaniard called, oddly, Angus Gordon." By now, though, the expedition was beginning to turn into a disaster. "I started suffering terribly from hay fever, but Colonel Meredith was even worse." It was decided not to proceed any further, but to return to Petawawa. "I didn't much care, but Carl Stanton, I think, was terribly disappointed." Much more than with Ethel, we sympathize with the maladroit Coly Meredith, for whom nothing ever seems to have turned out as he had envisaged, and for whom the meticulous staffwork involved in organizing a perfect Canadian weekend for the Governor General's Military Secretary – down to the buckboards meeting the motor without a moment of overlap – was evaporating as the result of his own wheezing and sneezing. Still, Stanton was easy going, "very good on an expedition of this sort," Ethel relates, "very tactful and diplomatic." In any event, excellent fishing was provided next day on a mostly pollen-free lake accessible by launch. "I caught two fish," Ethel reports, "Carl got a large four- or five-pound pike. Then back to 8:00 dinner on the verandah. The sunset was a most glorious one. Fuchsia clouds of glowing red and purple wonderfully reflected in the water."

On the third day of the long weekend, everyone lolled around. "After breakfast, we sat out in camp chairs," Ethel tells us. "Carl Stanton did some sketching. Around 11:30, we went in for a swim, and then Coly Meredith motored us down in the launch to a faraway beach for a picnic lunch. My wet hair was flying wildly in the wind. Carl said I should always wear it down as it is becoming. He is always praising one's looks and clothes and so on." Then, in the lazy interlude after lunch, Stanton said something in a low voice that was distinctly disquieting. "We were speaking about Duff. Carl says that Rossie is very fond of him, and that Joe is jealous." In the immediate – " 'Absurd,' I told him" – Ethel pretended to pay no heed and turned her mind to the pleasures ahead, a tea party with exotic visitors that the Merediths had arranged as highlight of the holiday. "I decided to wear a white skirt and a simple blue middy-blouse from two years ago. Carl said I looked very smart and that no doubt I wore it for someone else's benefit and not his." Yet again everyone piled into the launch, setting out this time for the opposite shore of the river, a spot called Burnt Bridge. "There was another wooden building, like Cupid's Nest," Ethel tells us. "Out on the verandah, three Imperial Officers of the Tsar's army were waiting to meet us."

So bouleversée was Ethel by the prospect before her, that for the moment all of her talent for description deserted her. Still, it's a reasonable guess that these figures, who seemed to have stepped directly out of Tolstoy, were wearing high-collared white cotton shirts buttoned on one side in the manner of the Imperial Court relaxing at Tsarskoe Selo. From Coly Meredith's memoir, we learn that these Russian officers constitute a brief, quirky footnote to Canadian history. They were "ballistic experts," dispatched to the Canadian wilderness to oversee the testing of shells being manufactured for the Imperial Army by the Canadian Car and Foundry Company of Toronto. In Meredith's view, they were mostly a pain in the neck. "From the start, they made one understand that they were 'Imperial Russian Officers.' When they first arrived, in the early summer of 1915, having been instructed to do everything I could for them, I had tents put up on a knoll in a beautiful spot overlooking the river. They at once informed me, however, that as 'Imperial Russian Officers' they could not be put into tents, so I put them into the mess building. The Russians were always having trouble with Colonel Mackie, who represented the Canadian Car Company, and as Mackie was very friendly with Colonel Sam Hughes, the Minister of Militia, it led to great complications. One morning the phone in headquarters rang, it was the Russians wishing to see me. In a few moments, they arrived, and after much clicking of heels, standing with stiff backs, and refusing to sit down, one of them said, 'Sir, it has been reported to us that the Minister of Militia, the Honourable Sam Hughes, has said that we, the Imperial Russian Army, can "go to hell."' I knew this to have been said, but it was necessary for me to deny it, and I said it was quite untrue."

Thus, for Meredith, engineering an opportunity to introduce the querulous Russians to the Governor General's Military Secretary represented a considerable exercise in diplomacy. Yet, once again, nothing went entirely to plan. Only one of the officers – a Captain von Rumel – spoke any English. And instead of acting as interpreter he appears to have spent the entire evening chatting up Ethel. "He is actually a Baron," begins her account, "very tall, with brown, tanned skin and lovely blue eyes, though a cast in one of them. Of German ancestry, he enlisted with the Russian army as a private and as he was a motor expert, he went as a driver. He distinguished himself greatly at Tannenberg by blowing up the motor-cars under heavy fire, when otherwise the Germans would have captured them, and received the Cross of St. Michael for this. Unfortunately, he hit a superior officer in the face in an argument which in wartime meant death, but on account of his family, or perhaps his prestige, he was smuggled out here to be an interpreter."

Skipped over lightly in Ethel's six-page account of their encounter, is the fact that von Rumel, at twenty-three, was a full decade younger than she. Also briefly dispensed with are descriptions of his two brother officers. "Captain Chkowviski [*sic*] is a tall blond with a heavy face and lumpy mouth. Captain Godima, the engineering expert is fat and uninteresting." Recounted in detail however, is the ride back to Cupid's Nest just after sunset. "Aldie and Maud and Col. Stanton and I were in the prow. Then we asked the other two Russians to come up and sing. The Colonel went back to sit with Colonel Meredith and the orderlies. I think he was not charmed at the Russians coming on the scene as he had been the only pebble. The Russians sang some of their folksongs. Queer, mournful things, like the sadness of Russia, I was thinking, and strange to hear out here on a Canadian river."

Over a late supper at Cupid's Nest, von Rumel continued to monopolize her. "He is from Petrograd, but was educated in Brussels. He was deploring the illiteracy of the lower class in Russia, but said there is to be compulsory education there after the war. We talked about Tolstoy. He told me how to pronounce Turgenev, whom he loves even better. When I said we were leaving in the morning, he seemed surprised and sorry and said in his fascinating voice, which has a sort of singing, or purring sound, 'Ah no, you mustn't go,' with great regret. Later, he sat beside me on the verandah. Before they left, he and the two others sang another of their songs, very simply and without self-consciousness. Colonel Stanton remarked that he could never have done such a thing. Then they clicked their heels together, and bowed in unison, very politely."

There remained one more scene to be played out the next morning. "I had said that I had never seen a samovar, so just after nine o'clock, von Rumel sent a message asking us to motor over to the Russian officers' quarters. He showed me the samovar, a big copper urn, with biscuits and fruit on one table. He was terribly sweet and glided about everywhere. He gave us all cigarettes to smoke and then they played for us, he on the piano, the other two on the guitar and the balalaika. They played the '*Barcarolle*,' very beautifully, and then something from the Russian composer Tchaikovsky. Then we all went for a last swim. The Baron held a pole while I sat on it, and rolled off into the water. Colonel S. took a lot of photographs. I had my hair down my back, looking awful probably, but Colonel S. said I reminded him of Ondine. Then we bade sad goodbye."

From Coly Meredith's point of view, the weekend had perhaps been a success after all. "The Russians appeared to have appreciated all that I had tried to do for them," he wrote many years later, "and recommended me to their Government for the Order of St. Stanislaus (second class)." But unfortunately, he adds, "the Revolution came before it went through."

As to the fate of von Rumel and the others, we can only

Swimming party at Petawawa, July 1915. Baron von
Rumel, on the far left holds Ethel's hand. Colonel Stanton took the snapshot but was not best pleased to be
upstaged.

wonder. Perhaps they perished fighting with the White Russian
Army, or re-emerged in the 1920s as waiters in Shanghai, restaura-
teurs in Hollywood, or taxi-drivers in Paris. About Ethel, we do
know for certain. Her own days as a belle were dwindling to a precious few. Soon, events would turn away from her, leaving her an
exile from everything she cared about. So let us linger, and look
one last time at Etheldreda Mary Chadwick in her prime. Catching
the train back to Ottawa, she was wearing her white linen skirt
and middy-blouse. Her waist-length hair, still too damp to be

Another of Stanton's Petawawa snapshots. "Colonel S. took a lot," Ethel tells us. Faded though they are, these entries in Ethel's album capture something of the style of that languorous, long-ago weekend. Baron von Rumel is looking towards Ethel, but Maud Macoun is clearly trying to get a "look-in." "I had my hair down my back, looking awful probably, but Colonel S. said I reminded him of Ondine."

pinned up properly, was tied back with a ribbon. She was still pink and glowing from her great success with the Baron. "Maud was insinuating that he was rather taken with her, as she always does about men, but in fact, she didn't get a look-in," Ethel writes. Nor,

to her equal satisfaction, had the predatory Maud got a look-in
with Stanton, who, from start to finish, save for that odd, insinuating remark about Rossie, had never been nicer or more attentive.
"When I got out my knitting," Ethel tells us, "he offered to hold out
his thumbs so I could wind the wool."

11

The Naughty Nine

*How swiftly in our own land came the changes wrought
by war! One grew inured to bobbed hair, knee-length
skirts, universal smoking, Einstein, trousered women,
camouflage, expensive economy and economical
extravagance, unashamed macquillage, weddings* à la
volée, *War Babies, and appetency for divorce.*

Madge Macbeth (under the pseudonym Gilbert Knox).
The Land of Afternoon; 1924

When Macbeth's *roman à clef* about Ottawa during the
Borden era was published in 1924, it electrified the capital. Quite apart from the fact that the golden-tongued,
ferociously ambitious Raymond Dilling and his well-meaning but
maladroit wife Marjorie, could easily be identified as the then
Conservative leader Arthur Meighen and his wife Isabel, everyone
knew that Sir Eric Denby, "who affirmed his stand on the Temperance question with the zeal of a Hebrew prophet," was Borden's
venerable finance minister, Sir George Foster, and that Honourable Godfrey Gough, "who sought to mould a policy for his
Party that would have made Machiavelli blush," was the Honourable Robert Rogers, the notoriously corrupt Minister of the
Interior, later of Public Works. As for the Angus-McCallums, "two
sisters with generous, florid faces who seemed to lie fatly on the
surface of every function, rather like cream on a pan of milk," they
were Ethel's great friends of the Rideau Hall skating rink, Annie
and Jessie McLeod-Clarke; while the much-feared Mrs. Long, "who
found the columns of her husband's paper a convenient medium

for the maintaining of discipline and the administration of justice,"
was Mrs. P. D. Ross, wife of the editor of the Ottawa *Journal*.

The Land of Afternoon deals with the war itself only tangen-
tially. It is apropos instead in two other ways. Such a novel, unin-
hibitedly lampooning some of the most esteemed public figures of
the day, could never have been written, and most assuredly
would never have been published, pre-war. Macbeth herself exemplified the new kind of person who could do these new kinds of
things. A spirited Philadelphia-born widow, who supported her
young family by free-lance journalism, she elevated herself during
the war into the category of a celebrity. In 1916, along with the
poet Duncan Campbell Scott, she founded the Ottawa Drama
League. Later, she became a key figure in the Canadian Women's
Press Club and the Canadian Authors Association. By the mid-
1920s – a slight aura of notoriety helped rather than hindered –
she'd become a regular within the viceregal circle. Indeed, by the
time of her death in 1965, Macbeth had long been a folkloric figure
in the capital, described by B. K. Sandwell in *Saturday Night* as "a
professional diner-out who knows everybody and has always
known everybody."

Ethel, when *The Land of Afternoon* came out, made no reference to it in her diary. We can surmise that one reason was that
while she herself was not caricatured openly, she could find
unsettling traces of herself in the impecunious Azalea Deane ("a
much be-familied young woman who was leaving 'mile 30' behind
so rapidly that it was already quite blurred in the distance") and
also in the brittle and snobbish Pamela de Latour. The deeper
reason, it's easy to guess, is that Ethel had come to see in Macbeth's uninterrupted social success, the achievement she had
reached for, had grasped, but by then had lost. When the back-
eddies of the tide of war brought to Ottawa the new mores of
"bobbed hair," "unashamed maquillage," and "knee-length skirts,"
Ethel Chadwick was too stiff, too old in her spirit, to bend to
them, let alone to embrace them. By her own hand, she made herself into a casualty of war.

She could have had no inkling of this when she returned from
Petawawa full of high spirits and energy. In that autumn of 1915,

she agreed, almost to her own surprise, to become one of the principal convenors of a three-day "Patriotic Entertainment" at the Russell Theatre in aid of the Red Cross, described in the Ottawa papers as "the most wonderful volunteer effort so far produced." Demonstrating an unsuspected talent for organization, Ethel not only planned, directed, and appeared in a series of elaborate *tableaux vivants* based on scenes from *The Rubaiyat* – ("I wore bare feet, an ankle bracelet, and a spangled veil and while holding a jug on my shoulder kept a tragic expression") she also compiled and designed the programmes and played the part of Australia in the grand finale, a spectacular setpiece titled, *At Your Service, Britannia*. "I wore a gold dress, and gold nuggets in my hair to represent the gold mines. Rossie, wearing a head-dress shaped as a pyramid, was Egypt." Later in the season, this time for the benefit of the Duchess of Connaught's Fund for Prisoners of War, she dressed up in gypsy costume and read palms at a May Court fête. "I had a mask and a veil over my face, and talked in a slow foreign voice, rather imitating Baron von Rumel, and made $13.40." One appreciative customer was her Petawawa partner Colonel Stanton. "He called me Cassandra, after the Greek lady who prophesied truly but was never believed."

During these "busy, busy days," as Ethel describes them, the pace of the social round remained frantic. Duff-and-Stanton kept up their attentions to her and to Rossie; the highlights of the fall season, and the source of much merriment, were visits to a local dance studio to learn the one-step and the foxtrot. "Carl says I dance like a dream, and if only the Russian baron could see me." In mid-October, Rideau Hall itself was enlivened by the arrival of yet another wounded hero as aide: one Captain Angus Mackintosh, heir to the Scottish title, The Mackintosh. "He is rather good-looking," she tells us, "about 32, good complexion, light brown hair, very gay and bright and full of fun. He was wounded in the lung and the bullet just missed his heart."

On Christmas Eve, Ethel was one of the privileged few invited to a private viceregal tea party to meet Dame Nellie Melba, the great Australian singer, who, at Their Royal Highnesses special request, had given a gala war-charity concert at the Russell the previous evening. She describes the event in a diary entry. "The

Major Arthur Duff (*left*), Rossie McDougal (*centre*), and Ethel Chadwick at the Royal Ottawa Golf Club, 1915. Ethel worried about Rossie's flirtation with Duff.

scene inside the theatre was brilliant. Every seat was taken, and large numbers of people had to be accommodated at the back of the stage. Behind them hung a huge red cross on a white field. Every member of the audience carried a small Union Jack, which was given out with the programme. As the Royal party stepped into their box, Melba came to the front of the stage and sang 'God Save the King,' asking us all to join in." Next day, in the blue drawing room at Government House, the duchess herself introduced Ethel to the diva. "She is fat, and rather wrinkled, not good-looking any more, but easy to talk to. I remarked that I had specially loved her 'Adio,' from *La Bohème*, which she had sung with great expression. She told me that they had asked her to sing her famous 'Home, Sweet Home' as an encore, but that at this time, after all the terrible happenings of the war, she dared not do it, for fear of breaking down. She also said that the hitherto meaningless words of 'God Save the King' now mean so much to her. Then Colonel Stanton, who was standing nearby, asked her to sign an autograph for me. She borrowed his fountain pen and wrote, '*L'art est un ami qui ne trompe jamais.*'"

Never again, for Ethel, glad confident morning. A few weeks later, on Wednesday, January 26, 1916, yet another wartime fundraiser, billed as a "Cabaret de Vogue," was held in the ballroom of the Château Laurier. By the time it was over, Ethel was a social has-been. She herself is a poor guide to what happened. Years later, she excised from her diary the pages that described the event, leaving behind only a much bowdlerized version that appeared in the Ottawa *Journal* in 1963, when, in her eighties, Ethel was eking out her old-age pension with discreetly edited excerpts. But by reading between the lines of this account, supplemented by contemporary newspaper stories, we can assemble enough pieces to restructure the evening that was perhaps the most fateful of her life.

It all began so comfortably and so familiarly. The usual primping at the mirror; the usual dither about what to wear. Ethel settled on "a furbished-up blue brocade evening dress, very short, with bead trimming, blue shoes." The finishing touches were a billowing scarf of blue tulle – "swathing oneself in tulle is very fashionable at the moment" – purchased at Murphy-Gamble that very morning, and shimmery blue silk stockings, bought at the rival department store, A. J. Freiman. Shortly after nine on this subzero evening, Rossie and Joe McDougal called for her in a taxi. They joined the long queue of hooting motor-cars, interspersed with the occasional sleigh lined with buffalo robes, converging on the entrance to the Château Laurier. Observing the scene – huge snowbanks flanking the porte-cochère, silk top hats gleaming over raccoon coats, ladies clutching their fur wraps around their bare shoulders, officers in long swooping greatcoats – Ethel must have been reminded of glittering nights in St. Petersburg, for, thanks to the Baron's influence, she was currently deep in the Russian novelists.

Among the five hundred guests was everyone who mattered. Most of them were well known to Ethel: all of her friends in the smart set; many "politicals," as she still described them, including Mackenzie King, up from the States for a spell, the consuls of Belgium and Japan representing the Allies. The military contingent was led by the short, bespectacled but impressive figure of the Chief of Staff, Major General Sir Willoughby Gwatkin, a particular favourite of Ethel's, a British officer who apart from being a delightful dinner companion, also enjoyed birdwatching and writing light verse. Conspicuous by their absence, as she was quick to notice, were the duke, duchess, and princess, even though the affair was in aid of the duchess's Prisoner of War Fund. "Perhaps they won't come to any dance in wartime," she wrote in her diary, adding with relish, "but they all came to *my* entertainment at the Russell." The rest of the viceregal contingent, though, was out in force, Dorothy Yorke, Stanton, and Duff and the new aide Mackintosh, both of whom, Ethel noted, "looked particularly resplendent in their full-dress kilts."

Yet as soon as she entered the ballroom, Ethel would have sensed the first warning signal. Clearly, this "Cabaret de Vogue" was going to be of entirely different order from her own lovingly prepared programme of "living pictures" two months earlier. The room had been got up in a way that prefigured nightclubs of the 1920s: instead of perching in rows on little gilt chairs, the audience was dispersed among separate tables in parties of a dozen or so. Moreover, the organizers of the show, who had commandeered the best tables, and were bustling around greeting everyone, were *not* people Ethel either knew or cared to know. They were newcomers, a pair of cabinet wives with slightly *louche* reputations, Mrs. Bob Rogers and Madame T. Chase Casgrain, recently acquired second wife of the Postmaster General. (Mrs. Bob, it was rumoured, had employed a tutor in etiquette to prepare her for Ottawa; as for Mme Casgrain, she later manifested in *The Land of Afternoon* as the culture-crazed, whisky-drinking temptress, Hebe Barrington.) The programme contained additional unwelcome information. When choosing the cast for their cabaret, Mesdames Rogers and Casgrain had skipped more than half a generation. The performers belonged to the youngest of the younger set, nine girls still in their teens, barely old enough to put up their hair, if indeed, they hadn't already bobbed it. Even their names – Jean, Sheila, Evy, Bee, Clare – had a chic, futuristic ring: not a Maud nor a Muriel nor an Ethel among them.

There were other portents. "Oddly enough, both Rossie and I were wearing blue, and so were all the women at our table," Ethel writes, adding, "When Major Duff and Colonel Stanton came over to talk, they called us 'Bluebirds.'" What she is conveying obliquely is that, for the first time in over a year, a major social event was taking place without Duff-and-Stanton sitting next to her and Rossie. Instead, along with Mackintosh, they were seated a couple of tables away, "hosting a party for a number of the young girls taking part in the entertainment."

The programme included the one-step, the two-step, the sinuous tango. Each time the young dancers appeared, their costumes were more outrageous. For a "fishing dance," they disguised themselves as boys "in blue-jean overalls, and rough straw hats, with bamboo rods with little frogs attached," as the reporter for the *Citizen* described. In her "chic little dance and song" titled "I'm Just Crazy Over You," Miss Clare Walters wore "a ballet costume of yellow gauze, with a bodice of black velvet and large butterfly bow of tulle at the back, and introduced several odd but attractive steps." The only number that Ethel seems actually to have enjoyed was an old-fashioned waltz, with "the noted soprano, Mrs. George Patterson Murphy singing, 'I'm Forever Blowing Bubbles,' and the girls softly swaying, each with a dozen balloons attached to the hem of her skirt, each holding in her hand a wand to which more balloons were attached." In between the sets, the audience took to the floor. "We bumped along as well as we could between all the tables," she records. "My partners got enveloped in my tulle scarf. They were laughing about it. I trying, unsuccessfully, alas, to entrap them like a spider in her web." These partners, so far as we can tell, included neither Stanton nor Duff; instead, several social notches down, they were mostly Joe McDougal and her old friend from the Lord John Hamilton era, the elderly British officer, Colonel "Four-eyes" MacDonald. It's painful to imagine Ethel, smile growing ever tighter as she pretended not to notice the whoops of hilarity issuing from the viceregal table as champagne overflowed into Clare's or Evy's, or was that Sheila's glass?

The show-stopper came near to midnight. Titled *Surprise Flirtation,* the production values of this boffo finale suggest that it was adapted from *Ziegfield Follies* watered down to suit a provincial audience. To the beat of a saucy foxtrot, three huge bandboxes, painted shiny black and festooned with cerise ribbons, glided into the ballroom, "bumping into chairs and tables en route," as the *Citizen* reported. "Then entered three charming young ladies in pages' costume, dressed in black satin knickerbockers, short black velvet capes and black velvet toques. They untied the ribbons, opened the boxes, and drew forth three pretty young girls, also attired in black satin, with whom they danced." In Ethel's terse description, "The costumes of the girls were *very* abbreviated. They pranced around the room."

Cabaret de Vogue concluded, naturally, with "God Save the King." Ethel and the McDougals left soon afterwards. It's unlikely, though, that they retreated quickly enough to avoid seeing the young ladies of the cast, flushed with their triumph, rushing across the room, in a great whirl of giggles, and flinging their arms around the seated officers, tugging them off to the dance floor. "The orchestra continued to play til the small hours," the *Journal* reported the next day. "All the young people danced on and on."

It was General Gwatkin who gave the evening its signature. Over at Mrs. Bob Rogers' table, the company was roaring with laughter. The General had just christened the dancers, "The Naughty Nine."

They were the first of the flappers in Ottawa, harbingers of the Jazz Age, forerunners of all the "Bright Young Things" with rouged knees and rolled stockings. In hindsight, what's really remarkable about the Naughty Nine is that they should have turned up so early in this most conventional of capitals. Within days of the cabaret, the social ecology of Ottawa had been transformed: "That rowdy little bunch," in Ethel's description, were not only the talk of the town, but the toast of it; the *sine qua non* of ADC skating parties and Country Club dances. Their particular style, as Macbeth satirizes in *The Land of Afternoon*, was "getting up stunts": doing cartwheels in the middle of sedate tea parties, or seeing how many olives they could stuff into their mouths at one go. When troop trains left town, they would rush down to Union Station in a body and hug the officers goodbye. When the Governor General reviewed regiments, they would position themselves opposite the reviewing stand and make funny faces at Duff, Stanton, and Mackintosh. According to Macbeth, they also invented a private slang. "Dee-Dee," for instance, was short for "damn dull." No doubt they applied it to Ethel.

All this was silly stuff. Yet it was also real. The Naughty Nine and those who copied them understood that when the smell of death was in the air, chaffing, the occasional peck on the cheek, and allowing oneself to be addressed by one's first name were no longer enough. Men familiar with the horrors of war, as Duff, Stanton, and Mackintosh all were, and men just about to depart to encounter them, could no longer be expected to behave as John Hamilton had behaved in 1912. This said, it was still only 1916. The Naughty Nine were all girls from good families: several were the younger sisters of friends of Ethel. It's most unlikely that any of them was naughty enough to "go all the way." Yet, by their hugs and kisses, they dared to cross a long insuperable barrier, making physical contact in public respectable. As remarkable, in the heightened atmosphere of wartime, they beguiled most of society into accepting the new standard.

Ethel remained unbeguiled. As a single woman approaching her mid-thirties and without means, her social position was bound to become vulnerable. Her response to the Naughty Nine was tantamount to suicide. She – and Rossie, most probably at Ethel's urging – decided to boycott all future social gatherings to which any or all of the "objectionable girls" had been invited. A fortnight later, having remarked the sisters' absence at, among other things, two skiing parties and a dinner-dance at the Country Club, Stanton approached Ethel on the Rideau Hall skating rink. "He said, 'Rossie and I were too good to live.' I said, 'How would you and Duff like it if *we* started throwing our arms around your necks?' He said, 'We should like it.'"

The last thing Stanton wanted was for Ethel to disappear from his life. Fun as the Naughty Nine may have been to romp

with, they could neither play decent bridge nor discuss Dostoevsky. A week later he tried again and this time he was more tactful. "He said, 'Now, be sensible, and come along on Sunday to
another little skiing party.' When I refused, he said we were silly,
silly, that we wanted to be the only ones to have fun. I said not at
all, it was all for the sake of propriety." Then like a wounded
animal, she lashed out blindly. "I asked him please not to call me
Ethel any more. From now on, I said, it's Miss Chadwick."

By now, the behaviour of Ethel and Rossie was producing
nearly as much gossip as that of the Naughty Nine. The young girls
christened the sisters "The Prudish Pickles," and when this got
back to Ethel she responded with an affected shrug. "I don't at all
mind 'Prudish,'" she wrote in her diary. "But 'Pickle' sounds too
frivolous for us." Old friends tried to intervene. "Can't you compro-
mise?" implored Maud Macoun, her companion on the trip to
Petawawa. "You, above all, who have practically lived at Government House?" On Ethel's thirty-fourth birthday, the old friend who
mattered the most, D'Arcy Scott, made a bit of headway. Calling
round with a bunch of sweet peas, always her favourite flower, he
persuaded her to go to a dinner-dance at the Country Club. But
when Ethel walked into the room and discovered that "two of the
objectionables" were also there, she took it as a personal insult
and refused to dance, even with D'Arcy. "He was furious and got
quite rude," she informs. "He as much as called me an old frump.
He said did I think I was Royalty to have a guest list submitted in
advance?" That night's quarrel, it's sad to have to report, marked
the start of a breach between Ethel and D'Arcy that lasted until his
death in 1924. Meantime, for much of the next two years, she continued to record each encounter with one or other of the Naughty
Nine as if they were sightings of the Hun.

Hurt pride, miscalculation, and a fair bit of frumpishness
aside, there may have been one justifying motive in Ethel's self-
destructive behaviour. While her own relationship with Stanton
was entirely above suspicion, that between Rossie and Duff had
raised quite a few eyebrows: witness Stanton's comment up at
Petawawa, about Joe McDougal being jealous. Rossie, moreover,
was sexually experienced. Less knowing than her sister, Ethel was
in some ways more worldly. Thanks to her omnivorous reading,

she knew what had happened to Anna Karenina and to Emma Bovary. Perhaps, in part, by boycotting all gatherings involving the Naughty Nine, Ethel was trying to prise Rossie away from Duff and thereby prevent scandal. The phrase she uses time and again when defending her actions – "above all, propriety" – lends some credence to this theory. So does the tone of satisfaction with which she reports, in mid-March, "Rossie has given Duff the throw-down."

Whatever her motive, Ethel paid for her actions with the ultimate price – her position as a viceregal courtier. "Everything now is either BC (Before Cabaret) or AC," she wrote in her diary. She didn't tumble right out of the social hierarchy. In the spring of 1916, she organized a flower market in aid of the Red Cross, and in the fall, a harvest market. In November, she got up another Patriotic Entertainment, and even wrote the script for one of the skits, a playlet called *The Shirker*, in which, in her description, "a society girl jeers at a young man not in uniform only to discover that he is really a wounded VC." Inevitably though, her position dwindled to that of her station, a spinster in her advancing thirties without means. Her last farewell to her youth and to the golden years of her belledom can be found between the lines of her last conversation with Stanton. It took place at a viceregal tea party, held on October 9, 1916, just before the Connaughts departed from Ottawa, he and Duff along with them. "I said goodbye and told him I was sorry he was going. He said, 'You know perfectly well that you are glad.' I told him I bore him no evil, although I had heard nasty things he had said about my being prim. He said, 'that was all I ever said against you, and you *are* confoundedly prim.' I wished him a happy life, as I would never see him again."

In fact, as we discover with a little more digging, Stanton deserves a bit more space in Canadian history than Ethel allots him. On duty as well as off, Connaught's Military Secretary had attracted controversy; indeed, Prime Minister Borden was just as happy to see the back of him as Ethel was. Throughout 1916, Stanton had played a key part in a Britain–Canada confrontation over the running of the war that led to the premature retirement of the Governor General and to the sacking of the Minister of Militia, Sam

Hughes. "I was perfectly convinced that the Duke had been led into his actions through the influence of Colonel Stanton," Borden wrote in his 1938 autobiography. "That gentleman had been Governor of some small Crown Colony or dependency and seemed to be under the impression that Canada occupied the same status as the territory he had governed."

Borden's case against Stanton was not without substance. An archetypal Imperial officer, ambitious and able, but also arrogant and high-handed, he must have been appalled by the muddle and confusion of Canada's war effort. He had, in fact, been military governor of Khartoum, in the Sudan, and no doubt saw in Sam Hughes a combination of the worst features of both the Mahdi and General Gordon: he would have been contemptuous of Borden for putting up with him. Stanton drafted most of the critical memos with which Connaught bombarded Borden; stretching his authority to the limit, he sometimes signed them himself. He also encouraged General Gwatkin and other British staff officers to leak confidential information to Rideau Hall, much of which was then leaked to friends in high places in England.

In truth, the aging Connaught needed little urging to step beyond the bounds of constitutional propriety. From the moment of his arrival in Canada in 1911, he and Hughes had been daggers drawn. In the duke's opinion, the minister was "an impossible fellow . . . eaten up with conceits and . . . very ignorant in military matters." On one memorable full-dress occasion in 1912, the minister barged into the Royal Box at the Russell Theatre, wearing a bright blue suit, shouting imprecations at the duke at the top of his voice. The irony was, no two men loved the army more. But they loved it as polar opposites. Connaught, the godson of Wellington, dandled on the Iron Duke's knee as an infant, was a stickler for tradition, so much of an authority on the details of regimental uniforms that he could tell at a glance if the spurs a man wore or the colour of his sword slings were incorrect. Hughes, no matter that both his own grandfathers were veterans of Waterloo, was a populist Orangeman, a self-styled Agricola, whose hatred of "Sandhurst-trained regulars" dated all the way back to the Northwest Rebellion of 1885, when his application to lead a company to Batoche had been turned down in Ottawa.

The Duke of Connaught in full viceregal regalia. He cut a splendid figure, but in the opinion of Sir Robert Borden was "by no means a brilliant intellect." By late 1916, Borden had succeeded in having him replaced as Governor General, although not with the man of his choice.

Prior to 1914, the Hughes–Connaught imbroglio could be enjoyed as comic opera, perhaps even by Borden, who did not lack for a dry sense of humour despite his gruff mien. The guns of August changed everything: the prime minister not only had to cope with a war but with a pair of choleric warriors each convinced that he alone knew how to wage it. In the first week of hostilities Borden invited Connaught to sit in on cabinet meetings – a gesture he quickly regretted and put a stop to after a fortnight. Hughes was the more wearisome problem, insisting on running the war as a one-man band, creating Valcartier as a personal fiefdom, establishing the notorious "Shell Committee" to oversee munitions production, and staffing it with dubious political cronies dubbed "Honorary Colonels."

By early 1915, Government House and Hughes's Militia

Department resembled two rival armed camps. Discretion was
not a feature of either side's conduct. Connaught, as Ethel is witness, bad-mouthed Hughes to everyone within earshot. "He com-
plains how the Minister makes things so hard and unpleasant as
he is utterly incompetent." Hughes was one of the chief promulga-
tors of the rumour that the Prussian-born Duchess of Connaught
was a spy, even suggesting to reporters that she was using her
Prisoners of War fund as a cover for transmitting messages to the
enemy, by means of notes rolled up in handknitted socks.

Stanton's arrival escalated hostilities. He attempted neither
to quiet down Connaught, nor to find ways to short-circuit
Hughes. To make matters worse, he got off on the wrong foot with
Borden by making a hash of the introductions at the annual
viceregal levée on New Year's Day 1915. "He had great difficulty
deciphering the cards," Sir Robert wrote in his diary. "He angli-
cized *Gagnon* and gallicized *Anglin.*"

The crisis broke early in the spring of 1916. The details are
convoluted, but the gist of what happened is that Hughes, at a
meeting of staff officers, made remarks about the Governor General that far exceeded the usual limit even of his invective. When
these got back to Connaught, the duke, no doubt egged on by Stanton, threatened to resign unless Hughes apologized publicly.
Borden's reaction, so far as we can tell from the cautious entries in
his diary, was to call Connaught's bluff, thereby sending a discreet
signal to Whitehall that the Duke should be recalled. "I suggested
that he himself had spoken disparagingly of Hughes," the prime
minister wrote of an audience with Connaught on March 18. "Told
him that Stanton has a disposition to be meddlesome and offi-
cious." On March 24 "HRH still insists on apology or resignation but
is really guilty himself as he admits that he discussed Hughes' conduct with other persons. He is by no means a brilliant intellect."
Late in May, Whitehall responded to Borden's signal. "HRH . . . told
me in confidence that he is taking his leave early in October." In
fact, Borden had already been informed of Connaught's impending
departure six weeks earlier through unofficial channels, by means
of a message passed from the Colonial Secretary, Bonar Law, to
their mutual friend Sir Max Aitken, then the most influential Canadian in London, who sent the word on by coded telegram. By now,
Borden himself had moved so far forward in his constitutional

thinking that he confided to the High Commissioner in London, Sir George Perley, that the next Governor General should be a Canadian: the ideal candidate, he suggested, would be Sir Wilfrid Laurier. Instead, at the end of June, word was transmitted across the Atlantic that the ninth Duke of Devonshire would be Connaught's successor. "Choice seems very good, but they have not asked our approval," wrote Borden in some irritation.

Connaught himself left Ottawa on October 12, angry and embittered. "I am chased out of the country," he reportedly remarked to Sir Wilfrid Laurier. "Your Minister of Militia is the embodiment of impertinence and your Premier is the personification of weakness." On his return to England, he sent the Lauriers a loving-cup of remembrance, but pointedly sent no mementos to the Bordens. He was given no further official positions, but lived on cheerily to the ripe age of ninety-two, ever a great hand with the ladies and remembering Ethel Chadwick with annual Christmas cards.

Having extracted one thorn from his flesh, Borden was now emboldened to get rid of the other. In late October 1916, shortly after the Connaughts departed, he created a new Overseas Ministry, based in London, to be responsible both for the troops in the trenches and reinforcements in Britain. This seemingly mundane bureaucratic shuffle had the effect of stripping Hughes of much of his effective power. Hughes's response was so intemperate that Borden was able to seize upon it as an excuse to demand his resignation. "The mad mullah of Canada has been deposed," wrote a Canadian officer at the Front. "We walk with sprightlier step."

Despite Stanton's role in this sorry affair, on balance he did Canada a service by speeding events to a head. Nor did his own career suffer. In 1918, he was appointed to the important post of Military Governor of Palestine. "The new appointment comes as welcome news to Colonel Stanton's many friends in the capital. His admirable qualifications are well known," reported the Ottawa *Journal* in a story that Ethel pasted into her scrapbook. He died in 1947, the epochal year of the granting of independence to India and of the end of the British Empire.

The close of the Connaught era is also our cue to leave Ethel. From then on, she ceased being a good observer. Indeed, within days of the fateful cabaret, the sparkle had gone from her diary. On February 3, 1916, she has little to say about the event that for everyone else was a great home-front catastrophe of the war years: the huge fire on Parliament Hill that in the space of a few hours destroyed the half-century-old Centre Block. Nor does she comment at all on an issue that throughout 1916 had the whole city up in arms, and that would have affected her directly as an Irish Catholic: a row over bilingualism in Ottawa separate schools that produced bitter enmity between French and Irish and fed directly into the even more divisive battle over conscription the following year. Ethel's journals for 1917 are sketchy and attenuated: those for 1918 have disappeared entirely. The entries that do exist are mainly a record of tea and self-pity; "I think a blight has descended on me," she wrote at one point, "I may just as well stay in the mud where I am." The Devonshires, no surprise, did not take her up; instead they took up the Naughty Nine, who were just the right age to be chums with their debutante daughter, Lady Maud Cavendish. Indeed, much to Ethel's horror, before the year was out, Lady Maud married Angus Mackintosh, the one holdover aide from the Connaught era and, in Ethel's opinion, the most disreputable of the lot.*

And yet. Even if, like Stanton and D'Arcy Scott, we've lost patience with Ethel for being silly, we can't help feeling guilty about abandoning her. Every now and then, moreover, she gives us a glimpse of her old self. In April 1917 she tells us how, having been inspired by the Ottawa screening of D. W Griffith's masterpiece, *Intolerance*, she sat up three nights running and wrote a "photoplay scenario" to enter in a contest sponsored by the Ottawa *Journal*, with a munificent prize of $50. Over the next fortnight, her entry, titled *A Day Among the Spuds*, a comedy about a

---

* The marriage lasted barely a year. Mackintosh, by then an attaché at the British Embassy in Washington, died in the great flu epidemic of 1918. Of longer duration, but equally star-crossed, was the marriage of Maud's younger sister, Lady Dorothy Cavendish, to Captain Harold Macmillan, the future British prime minister, whom she met at Rideau Hall when he was posted there as an aide shortly after the war. In the 1930s, Lady Dorothy began a lifelong affair with another Conservative politician, Robert Boothby.

society girl's patriotic attempt to become a wartime "land girl," first makes the short list – "it's down to eight out of forty, and the paper says all of them are excellent" – and then – "wonder of wonders" – is selected as one of the two finalists. When Ethel loses to a more sensational entry titled *The Spy* – "Of course, it's my usual damned luck" – it's impossible not to speculate that success might have given her the confidence to launch herself into a career.

Six months later, in mid-November, shortly before the Khaki Election, Ethel again touches a chord in us. As the sister of a serviceman – her brother Frankie served throughout the war in the motorcycle corps – she actually has a vote. Naturally, she intends to cast it for Borden and conscription, and she has thrown herself heart and soul into the campaign. "I've been asked to help with the programme for a mass meeting of women voters," she tells us. "They're going to have 'In Flanders Fields' recited to a tableau. This will surely appeal to any woman to vote for conscription." Just as we're about to close the volume – this is almost the last entry in Ethel's account of her war – we notice that there's an addition. In much more careful script than usual, she has written down from memory the last verse of the poem by the Canadian army doctor, John McCrae, composed in the aftermath of Ypres, that had become the anthem of the Allies. It's hard to doubt, all these years later, that there were tears in Ethel's eyes, as she set down the lines, now in the aftermath of Passchendaele.

> *Take up our quarrel with the foe*
> *To you, from falling hands we throw*
> *The torch, be yours to hold it high*
> *If ye break faith with us who die*
> *We shall not sleep though poppies grow*
> *In Flanders Fields.*

After the war, Ethel picked up the pieces of her life as best she could. Now that she was coming up to forty, marriage, children, a real home of her own were no longer in prospect. There were, of course, countless other women like her: so many potential husbands had died in the trenches that middle-aging spinsters of

slender means constituted a distinct post-war social phenomenon. Some, like Ethel's and Agar Adamson's friend Minnie Scott,
profited from the example of Madge Macbeth and turned themselves into "characters": jolly, voluble, wisecracking forerunners
of Auntie Mame who were invaluable at dinner parties, even when
they made the numbers uneven. Others swallowed their pride
and went out to work as late-blooming secretaries, book-keepers,
and clerical assistants. Some even launched businesses of their
own, surprising bank managers and relatives by demonstrating
that excellent dress sense or a knowledge of fine furniture could
be turned into a "little shop around the corner" that could at least
break even.

Ethel was too much a prisoner of the past to reinvent herself.
Until her parents died in the mid-1930s, she lived with them, after
that in a succession of cramped bed-sitting rooms and later,
studio apartments. Except for Rossie and Joe, who remained
steadfast, her immediate family was of little comfort. She was not
close either to Frankie or to her three youngest sisters; since
none of them married, and Rossie herself remained childless,
there were no nieces and nephews to watch growing up. Even
Ethel's celebrated looks faded early: the elegant slenderness
turned to scrawniness, henna rinses unable to conceal the grey in
her hair. Her small pleasures, as we know from her carefully kept
account books, included a packet of Craven A cigarettes every
couple of days and a bottle of cheap Australian sherry scrimped
out to last a week.

Her later diaries, chronicling an ever-narrowing life, convey
nonetheless some of the spunkiness of those magic years when
by her skill at chaff and on skates, she could keep up with the
stiffest competition. She plugged away at writing social notes for
British periodicals, became a frequent contributor to the Canadian society magazine, *Mayfair* (a 1935 story about Blue Sea Lake
has particular poignancy), and as late as the 1960s religiously
chronicled the doings of Ottawa's "Rockcliffe Set" for the *Montreal
Gazette*. (Ever a staunch Imperialist, Ethel diminished her useful-
ness as a society reporter by refusing to attend functions at
Rideau Hall after 1952, when Vincent Massey was appointed the

first Canadian-born Governor General.) During the years between the wars, she resurrected the talent for illustration that had enlivened her earliest diaries, and decorated lamp shades and tea trays in floral motifs to sell on consignment at local gift shops. The Second World War gave Ethel a brief reprise: once again she organized annual flower markets in aid of the Red Cross and, while the era of patriotic tableaux was long gone, wrote a couple of patriotic sketches that were broadcast on local radio. Reading, as always, was her great bulwark against loneliness. In these years, Virginia Woolf was the great revelation. "To think, she and I were born within two months of each other," she wrote after reading *A Room of One's Own*.

Close to the end of her life, Ethel's luck changed for the better. In 1962, a chance conversation with an Ottawa *Journal* editor led to the publication of a few excerpts from her earliest diaries. The feature was an instant hit – with Centennial Year in the offing, nostalgia was suddenly the fashion – and ran for the next several years, enlivened by photos supplied by Ethel from her albums. Old friends got a kick out of seeing their younger selves in print (naturally Ethel carefully excised all unflattering references), young people were charmed by the quaintness of it all. In a modest way, she became a celebrity. In 1966, a reporter from Canadian Press called to do an interview that appeared in newspapers across the nation: "A diary begun by a little girl in 1895 has become one of the few records of a golden period in Ottawa's social history," ran the lead of the story, accompanied by a photograph (carefully retouched at Ethel's insistence) that showed her dressed to the nines, proudly holding open a volume of her journals. Even in the flat, news-agency style of the story, her sense of might-have-been came through. "It was all changed after the Great War," the reporter quoted her as saying. "It never came back the same way."

Ethel's diaries end in mid-1971, when she was eighty-nine. She lived for another four years, so either the last volumes have gone missing or she no longer had the energy to write. In those last years, she was living in a small apartment in Sandy Hill, just down the street from the house she'd grown up in. Soon after her death – whether fulfilling her last instructions, or acting on his own initiative is uncertain – the caretaker of her building parcelled up the cargo of journals and scrapbooks and photo albums and deposited them at the National Archives. There she survives for posterity in a long row of brown cardboard boxes.

A last gracenote is in order. Unlike her heroine, Virginia Woolf, Etheldreda Mary Chadwick wasn't a diarist of brilliance or wit. The world she knew was provincial and circumscribed, and Ethel herself was too much the architect of her own misfortunes to be able to transcend it. Yet simply by being her own artless and often silly self, she carved out her own niche in history: there seems to be no other record of Canada during the Great War and the years leading up to it that takes us under our old colonial skin with so much immediacy, no one else, that's to say, who was *there*, and who would write: "Read *Paradise Lost*; the north wind blew all day. . . . War is declared between Austria and Servia."

If Ethel is a symbol of our colonial past, Talbot Papineau embodies the new kind of Canada that was being forged by the war. We left him early in May 1915, in the midst of the dreadful battle of Bellewaerde Ridge. We find him again six weeks later, on June 24, in the relatively quiet sector of the British line around Armentières, sitting in a dugout writing a letter. We know that it was a fine day, and that when Papineau looked up, he saw "the fringe of a wheatfield filled with blood red poppies, below the earth is brown and muddy." We know further that Papineau, always a gifted correspondent, is having a lot more trouble than usual getting going. He is in fact, introducing himself to a woman he has never met. "My Dear Miss Fox," reads the salutation. "You will be surprised to receive this letter."

12

Letters to an Unknown Woman

*The fresh adventure of writing to an unknown rather
appealed to me. Would you forbid me the appeal and
deny a poor soldier?*

Talbot Papineau to Beatrice Fox. June 24, 1915

Despite his carapace of cool confidence – the governing style of the trenches was " 'British Phlegm' . . . the trick was to be entirely unflappable," as Fussell has observed – the battle of Bellewaerde Ridge had left Talbot Papineau shattered. In the immediate aftermath, still wearing the bullet-holed cap of Sergeant-Major Fraser, he'd written no letters at all. In mid-May, he dispatched to his mother only a couple of the pre-printed Field Service Postcards that were standard issue, and upon which it was necessary only to put a tick beside whichever lines were appropriate: "I am quite well"; "I have been wounded"; "letter follows at first opportunity." An unexpected six-day leave scarcely helped; he spent much of it plodding around London, calling upon the wounded and the bereaved.

In some ways, the springtime city must have seemed a continuation of the nightmare he'd just left, for the furies of war had descended upon the expatriate community of "Square Mile" Montrealers with particular destructiveness. At Lady Drummond's flat in Mayfair, Talbot encountered a veritable roundelay of death; not only had Grace Drummond lost her son Guy at Ypres, Guy had also left behind his young bride of less than a year, the former

Mary Braithwaite. Mary, in turn, was mourning the loss of her sister Dorothy who, having booked passage to Britain immediately upon hearing of Guy's death, had perished aboard the *Lusitania*. Lady Allan, wife of the shipping magnate, Sir Montagu Allan, was equally in shock: she herself had survived the *Lusitania* with severe exposure and a broken leg, but her two younger daughters, Anna and Gwen, had drowned. The only part of Talbot's leave that he seems actually to have enjoyed were a couple of days up at Oxford, when he browsed around Brasenose and rowed a scull on the Isis.

In late May, promoted to captain and having rejoined the remnants of the Patricias near Armentières, Talbot resumed writing to his mother almost daily. The feverish quality of these letters suggests a man living on his nerve ends. As recently as April, still on a high from the trench raid at St. Eloi, he'd written Caroline jauntily, even a little calculatingly – about his Military Cross. "It is very pleasant to have such a fuss made, and when I come home it will be a help, I am sure, 'in my business.'" Now, he was sombre. "It is a good thing to have this ribbon on my chest. I cannot show fear, can I, when I am labelled brave?" In a long letter on May 26, Talbot made an attempt to tell her what had really happened at Bellewaerde Ridge but abandoned it halfway through. "Even now, I cannot hope to go over those awful days, the memory is confused and imperfect . . . the worst day was May 8, when we had about 450 casualties . . . I had the man on each side of me killed. . . ." At the end of the letter, he reached deep into himself. "Any courage I have comes from you and not the Papineaus. I am tired of this grandfather business. . . . On that awful 8th of May, it was your confidence that again and again gave me the courage to go on."

Reading such passages, hastily scribbled in pencil, we can't help but feel like voyeurs upon another's pain. Yet, by their very intimacy, these letters give us a much better appreciation of the bond between Talbot and his mother and a better appreciation of Caroline herself. "Dear, dear little mother," he wrote. "So wonderfully unselfish and loving, with every thought for us and none for herself, bearing a crushing burden of sadness and shame and yet so bravely protecting us and assuring us a childhood of comfort and joy." However much the intensity of their relationship jars our post-Freudian sensibility, we begin to perceive Caroline as Talbot perceived her, a hard-pressed single mother, undignified by widowhood, bringing up a quartet of young sons after being abandoned by a profligate husband, dependent upon a monthly allowance from her father-in-law. In Caroline's day, there were no court-ordered maintenance payments; no mutually supportive Al-Anon groups; indeed, since Quebec had no divorce law, the process of getting one would have involved a special Act of Parliament and a humiliating public hearing by a Senate committee. A less determined woman would have gone home to Philadelphia, where Caroline's family, though not particularly wealthy, had plenty of social position. Instead, she stayed on at Montebello even in the face of such embarrassments as the failure of her errant husband to show up for his own father's funeral in 1903 because, as the newspapers snidely reported, "he was unavoidably detained by illness." Above all, Caroline clung onto Montebello for the sake of her beloved Talbot who loved the woods and the hills and the river as much as life itself.

To the end of her own life, in 1951, Caroline Papineau could console herself with the knowledge that by preserving Montebello as long as she did, she'd preserved the thing that Talbot most wanted to live for. All through that summer of 1915, his letters brim over with references to home. "How I long to hear about the place," he wrote her in June. "I look forward to seeing all sorts of improvements, a tennis court, a boathouse, new gates at the Lodge. . . . I think continually how I shall sink into the old landau when it meets me at the station." A bunch of pressed pansies that she'd picked from the garden arrived in perfect condition and were pinned to the wall of his dug-out. The news that his younger brother Westcott had enlisted in the artillery, and that his youngest brother Philip was also thinking of doing so, made him fearful about the survival of all that Montebello stood for. "Don't let them come," he wrote Caroline. "Their duty is there. Canada must not be too seriously hurt. I am afraid and depressed today – not for myself, but for our civilization, our people, our world."

Even for Talbot, there was a limit to how often he could write to his mother – or for that matter, to his law partner, Andrew

McMaster, or Lionel Curtis, or the numerous old friends from McGill and Oxford with whom he also corresponded. In the trenches, particularly in quiet sectors of the line, time yawned out interminably. Days and days could slide by with little more excitement than was generated by someone shooting at a rat. To stretch out the time still further, the atmosphere was never free from tension, all the more because ever since Ypres there was the continual threat of a sudden gas attack. "It's like a bad boy walking behind you with a hard snowball, always ready to throw, but not throwing," was Talbot's description to Caroline.

Along with being bored, Talbot was also "wild for want of exercise"; more directly, he was sexually frustrated. Like most officers, he worked off some of his surplus energy through endless intense games of bridge, occasionally poker. (Other ranks played Crown and Anchor, a kind of floating crap game that was officially outlawed but that many officers pretended not to notice.) Like many officers and men, he lavished affection on a pet, in his case a black-and-white mongrel puppy christened 'Bobs' whom he'd bought from a little girl by the roadside for five francs. Yet for Talbot, as for Agar Adamson, writing letters, and just as much, receiving letters, was the most effective therapy. The difficulty was, to whom could Talbot write other than Caroline, who could understand him so well? Montreal and London were filled with girls with whom he'd flirted and danced, and who would have been delighted to become his romantic confidante, yet to correspond with any of them could create complications, assumptions, even commitments. Instead, he was in search of a relationship that, as he later put it, "could be free from the artificialities which surround so generally the intercourse between men and women." So on June 24, 1915, he sent his first letter to "My dear Miss Fox," and embarked upon one of the most extraordinary of all the correspondences engendered by the war.

Her full name was Cecelia Beatrice Fox, but she was always known as Beatrice. She was seven years younger than Talbot, just coming up to twenty-five. By coincidence, she lived in Philadelphia. By greater coincidence, as Talbot later discovered, he'd just missed meeting her a year or so earlier when, on one of his frequent visits

"My Dear Miss Fox, You will be surprised to receive this letter." Give or take a few days, this snapshot, probably taken by a brother officer, shows Talbot Papineau precisely as he looked when he began his correspondence with the Philadelphia sculptress and society belle, Beatrice Fox. The puppy's name was "Bobs"; Talbot had bought him for five francs. Both men and officers lavished attention on pets and often carried them into the front line. After four months in the trenches, Talbot's experiences are written on his face and in his mien. By now, he was the only officer of the PPCLI Originals not to have been killed or wounded or sent off sick.

to that city, his uncle, Jay Rogers, had invited her to dinner only to learn that she was out of town. But it wasn't the Philadelphia connection that connected Beatrice to Talbot. Rather, it was the Dowager Countess of Donoughmore, an eccentric Anglo-Irish grande dame, the mother-in-law of his former commanding officer, Francis Farquhar. The previous winter, when Talbot was recuperating from the burns suffered in the tent fire at Winchester, Lady Donoughmore had taken him up. "She is very original and to me the most amusing and delightful character," he reported to his mother. "She has made sort of protegés of Charlie Stewart and myself. She is knitting us socks and will send us a package to the front from time to time." The countess also had the instincts of a matchmaker. Over tea at her house in South Audley Street, she spoke rhapsodically of Beatrice. "Lady D's son married an American, a Miss Grace who is now the Countess of Donoughmore," Talbot explained to Caroline.* "The old lady hates Americans. She seems fond, though, of a Philadelphia girl, a Miss Fox. Perhaps May [Jay Rogers's wife] may know her. If so, she can tell her I have heard her praises sung for an hour."

For the next several months, Talbot was too busy fighting battles to think of Miss Fox. But during his post-Bellewaerde Ridge leave in London, another *tête-à-tête* with Lady Donoughmore renewed his interest. Beatrice, he was reminded, was slender and willowy, with coppery hair, a society girl who was also a talented sculptress. "I was told you were many things I find it difficult to believe a woman can be, all at the same time," he wrote to her in that first letter. "Intelligent, lovely and amiable, talented without freakishness." It must be said, though, that Talbot was not one to fling his cap heedlessly over the windmill: by then, a letter to his Philadelphia relatives had produced similar rave reviews, the information that Beatrice was the daughter of a noted ophthalmologist and two photographs clipped from the society pages of

---

* Elena Grace was a shipping heiress, one of many wealthy American girls who married impoverished aristocrats in the early years of the century. On her marriage to Richard Hely-Hutchison, 6th Earl of Donoughmore, she enriched the family treasury by £100,000 – about £2 million in today's money.

the Philadelphia *Inquirer*. "The one in which you fondle a bust and wear a big apron I did not care for," he continued. "The other, a full face in evening dress with a glint of sunlight in your hair I liked and have kept." Whether or not Talbot had worked through several drafts of this letter, his final version managed the difficult feat of being both spontaneous and eloquent; half a dozen pages of pale blue quarto notepaper, written in pencil in his orderly, easily decipherable handwriting without a single crossing out. "If I am a little obscure or erratic you must forgive me as I am in a dugout within a hundred yards of the Boche and they send an occasional rifle grenade or whizz-bang in my direction. . . . Since August I have been a licensed killer, since January I have tried to kill – I have succeeded in not being killed at any rate. Out of forty officers I am the only one neither killed nor wounded nor sick, rather a record of good fortune but a record which may be broken this evening or in ten minutes for all I know. Living on such volcanoes destroys my sense of decorum." He closed with an entreaty that was irresistable. "I should sleep, but the fresh adventure of writing to an unknown rather appealed to me. Would you forbid me the appeal, and deny a poor soldier?"

Beatrice's answer arrived on July 29 with the 6:00 PM rations party. (Usually, provided no torpedoes intervened, trans-Atlantic communication was swifter: about a fortnight for a letter to arrive at an eastern seaboard destination; another two weeks for the response. Most correspondents numbered their letters, so that gaps and non-sequiturs could be accounted for. But Talbot had sent his first letter in care of Lady Donoughmore for her to forward.) In the meantime, on July 8, back of the line in billets, he'd dashed off another, and this one was more impetuous. "I am in a bad temper this evening, and have tried in vain every other sort of amusement so I shall write to you. You are the victim of my mood. You may well ask why I do not inflict myself on some seasoned friend instead of your unoffending self. I suppose because the others can hold no surprises for me. They are dear creatures but labelled and pigeonholed, just as I am for them, I daresay. . . . They would not be shocked to get an erratic letter from me. While you, having been swept by curious chance across my orbit, present possibilities." Then he spoke freely about his raw nerves.

"We have ridden all afternoon. I am a little tired. We get so little exercise sitting in the trenches that an afternoon's ride is actually fatiguing. A few moments ago, several shells whistled overhead and exploded down the street. A good bag, I understand, an old woman and a baby killed and a little girl of seven has lost the fingers of her right hand. . . . However, we give more than we take and the only way to finally stop these Germans is to keep killing them. But how I hate it!! . . . This time last year I was at East Hampton, Long Island, and I had a splendid time. I long for a holiday now. You are probably modelling clay, playing golf, and learning some new dances."

Beatrice's first letter seems to have struck just the right note. "I feel quite triumphant," Talbot responded *con brio*. "I have succeeded in my venture to draw you into the vortex of my correspondence." Sadly, we have no way of knowing exactly what she wrote: like Mabel Adamson's letters to Agar, and Caroline's to Talbot, Beatrice's letters did not survive the war, but were destroyed in compliance with army regulations. But from Talbot's reply it is evident that in a manner that was both charming and disarming, she had told him a good deal about herself. "When you accuse your hair of being red, and your eyes a nondescript grey and your complexion freckled, I can accuse you of false modesty. . . . "I understand you to possess chameleon hair and eyes . . . my artistic sense is not outraged by freckles. . . . You confess to a fondness for ice-cream sodas. Hail fellow mortal. Well met kindred spirit. May we some day cluster around a fountain – my tongue is flannel at the thought. Here I enliven water with lime juice – from Lady D – but usually slacken thirst with enormous quantities of indifferent tea, in brimful canteens like tannery vats." If there was a section of Beatrice's letter that bored him a trifle – Talbot was a man of his own time – it was the one in which she expressed her wish to be perceived as a serious artist. Still, at this early stage of their relationship, this could be skipped over lightly. "I quite like what you said about yourself and your 'art,'" ran his reply. "I thought you might be wedded to it, or else be the 'trailing green gown' variety as you so well express it. I entirely approve of girls having some more knowledge than Mrs. Malaprop considered necessary, and where they can control talent without losing balance, I favour its development and exercise."

In this first letter, Beatrice had tucked in a pair of four-leaf clovers. "Despite these, I shall probably be hit one of these days," continued Talbot's reply. All the rest of that long hot summer, with the war in a curious lull, he wrote to her nearly every day, about anything that popped into his head. Knowing that they had in common a strong visual sense, he often sketched vivid word-pictures of trench life. "Breakfast has just been eaten; our oil-clothed table looks like a cheap boarding-house board," he wrote from his dugout early in August. "I have had porridge and real milk and sugar, then a boiled egg and another green one I didn't have . . . topped off with a cigarette, what more could a man desire? Even the morning paper will soon be here, only a day old – much younger than the egg." Then, perhaps testing Beatrice for shockability, he added a couple of racier details. "We have some daring ladies from *The Sketch* and illustrated weeklies pinned to the walls – one balanced on a diving board in a diminutive bathing suit of flaming red with black borders . . . another with piled-up yellow hair plucking feathers from Cupid for her hat. These ladies are often the subject of comment. We discuss their characters. They are attractive but disturbing and create restless wishes for home or Piccadilly."

As racy – perhaps even a bit unnerving to a Philadelphia belle – were Talbot's descriptions of the rough male camaraderie that characterized the trenches and sometimes erupted into wild horseplay as a way of letting off steam when the regiment was out of the line. "We live now in a sort of a hut," he explained in mid-August. "It is built of coloured canvas to deceive aviators. Eight of us live in each hut in two rows with a lane down the middle. Our sleeping bags are spread upon the uneven earth and we each have a soapbox to support a candle in a bottle and small articles. The 'Baron,' i.e., Captain Van Den Berg, lives opposite to me. Last night I was rolling off my puttees when the Baron, who is a pugnacious devil, suddenly swung round and batted me on the foot with his cane. I naturally went for his throat. We each secured a stranglehold and for several moments dust and clothes and legs and arms rose and fell in confusion. Eventually we arranged terms of peace. Later, for some reason which I cannot recall I fired five rounds of ammunition with accuracy against Barclay's candle, which was extinguished; Barclay then retaliated on my bottle with equal success. . . . We behaved disgracefully, I admit."*

Often, he regaled her with tales of the exploits of his closest friend among the officers, the devil-may-care Charlie Stewart. "He is the most pronounced character I have ever met. . . . He has the vitality and appearance of Hercules but remains normal by constant undermining operations – such as fifty cigarettes a day and the output of a whiskey factory. He plays a perfect game of bridge, and recently took £90 from Bonar Law and Sir Edward Grey. On the 14th of March, he was shot through the chest while we were withdrawing across the open. The Colonel told me to get him in. He was very heavy, I and 3 other men nearly failed. . . . He protested violently and made an awful noise about the pain. I promised to write to his various sweethearts and finally left him to die in the dressing station – a cellar of a ruined house – with the tears rolling down my face. The 'padre' asked him if he wished him to pray. 'Yes,' he said, 'Pray like hell.' But he didn't die. He was taken to the Duchess of Westminster's hospital and raved so against what he called her 'beauty chorus' and their open-worked stockings and patent leather shoes that she had him transferred. . . . He came back a few days ago, much to my delight."

Other letters were sombre, and spoke of the horrors of war. To the unseen Beatrice, far away in the city of brotherly love, Talbot found himself writing more openly than even to Caroline. "I hate this murderous business," he told her. "My profession is 'speeching' not fighting. I have seen so much death – and brains and blood – and marvellous human machines suddenly smashed like Humpty Dumpty. I have had a man in agony bite my finger while I tried to give him morphine. I have bound up a man without

<hr>

* Captain J. W. H. Van Den Berg was a soldier of fortune of Dutch origins who joined the PPCLI in March 1915, and for a brief time was suspected of being a spy. He was awarded the Military Cross and served with the regiment until June 1917.

Captain Gregor Barclay, of Montreal, joined the regiment through the McGill recruitment scheme. He served with the PPCLI until February 1916.

a face. I have tied a man's foot to his knee while he told me to save his leg and knew nothing of the few helpless shreds that remained . . . I have had a man apparently uninjured die from the shock of the explosion as his elbow touched mine. . . . Never shall I shoot duck again, or draw a speckled trout to gasp in my basket – I would not wish to see the death of a spider."

A few days later, he wrote yet more mordantly. "It is over a year now since I volunteered and since then life has seemed like a ball in a game of roulette, trembling uncertain on the edge of either Beginning or End. For in effect Life will again be at the Beginning if I survive. All opinions, ambitions, decisions hang suspended awaiting the verdict of chance. In the meantime, I have moments of gaiety with companions, moments of sadness when I think of home, moments of terrific anxiety and black, black moments when I question myself, my courage, and even the final success of our cause. Recently, I have been tired but more confident and ready to face the issues. For a while I thought too vividly. I pictured the homecoming, the glad celebrations which you too promise, the widened fields of action, the possible realization of some ambition, then the wish to live became maddenly dear. The wider my horizon, the keener my perception of self and the possibilities of life, the more horrible appeared death, the less I wished to put my head above the parapet and the more acute the inner throb when a machine gun barked and I thought of the time to come when I should have to charge into that rain of bullets and then suddenly cease to be, or slowly in pain realize the coming end of all things."

Almost as if he were unburdening himself to a psychiatrist, Talbot then went off on a journey into himself: "It is a great mistake for a soldier to have too keen an imagination or to allow his thoughts to dwell morbidly on his dangers. I now cultivate a sort of daredevil carelessness. I am not by nature intrepid, nor even quarrelsome enough to make fighting enjoyable. On the contrary, I shrink from the naked disclosure of human passions – I dislike intensely loss of control, drunkenness, insanity, hatred, anger, they fill me with a cold horror and dread. But to see a man afraid would be worse than all. To have to kill a man in whose eyes I saw the wild fear of death would be awful. I almost think I should stop and let the fellow kill me instead. There should be no heroism in war. No glorification – no reward. For us, it should be the simple execution of an abhorrent duty, a thing almost to be ashamed of since by reason of our human imperfection . . . we would rather kill and torture than accept conditions of life that we have not been taught to regard as good. Had I been born under Prussian influence I should have believed their cause and fought for it, but I have been differently trained and so I fight against it."

These remarkable letters, prefiguring Hemingway's famous description of courage as "grace under pressure," suggest that in years to come, Talbot might have written an account of the war to rank with Robert Graves' *Goodbye to All That*, or Edmund Blunden's *Undertones of War*. Indeed, when writing to Beatrice he often revealed a touch of the poet. A letter of August 26, 1915, is really a pastoral ode in which, like many wartime poets, he evoked the obscenity and the absurdity of the war, by describing its antithesis: the timeless, Breughel-like world that still existed, scarcely changed, on either side of the lines.

The day has been gloriously warm and flooded with sunshine. The observation balloons have hung motionless in the hazy unclouded blue. I fretted and fussed all morning. We are confined to billets to be ready in case of attacks so I cannot roam. After luncheon the restraint became unbearable. I was wild for want of exercise. All about us there are these marvellously cultivated fields bearing crops utterly unknown to us in Canada. Some are green where potatoes have been grown, otherwise they are peroxide blondes. The grain is being cut by hand and piled in small stacks of smaller bundles. In one field I saw an old man with two enormous loads of sheaves building a wheat stack. It was irresistable. I tramped over, took off my cap and belt and coat, rolled up my sleeves and told the old chap that I would take his place. He capitulated at once. I climbed on the load and seized his long-handled pitchfork. The heads of grain were so full and ripe I hardly dared move and felt clumsy and brutal to stand upon them. My task was to spear a sheaf and toss it to a boy who stood near the top of the stack. In turn he tossed the sheaves to a couple of ancient farmers who shaped them and placed them, building the stack in a solid sturdy mass that would resist storms and wind and rain and protect the grain until threshing time. I began very merrily chatting with the men. I learned how to move my feet so I should not stand on the end of the sheaf I was trying to toss. I learned to shorten or lengthen the handle to reduce the effort. I learned to give a little shove at the end of the stroke to disengage the fork, just as we used to hoist the pole at Oxford when punting . . .

We finished the first load very pleasantly. The farmer's wife came out with a jug of cool beer and a china bowl. I hate beer. I've never taken more than a mouthful in all my life but I felt too much a part of the picture not to join in the drinking. So we all sat wiping our brows and passing the china bowl. Then the horses drew the huge lumbering wagon away. Close by another fully loaded waited its turn. Once more I climbed up and we commenced with a swing. I wondered if they would notice I was tossing more slowly. To my shame, blisters came on what I thought were my calloused hands. The perspiration soaked and dripped about me and the sheaves grew heavier and heavier. But it was magnificent. It was an adventure in contentment.

This marvellous description brought to a close the first phase of Talbot's relationship with Beatrice. Clearly they were destined to be soulmates. "You are the best correspondent I have ever had," he told her. "You are almost a dream come true." Her fresh and spontaneous letters, arriving most often in batches, connected him with the land of lost content, a world of stability and charm that he had always taken for granted and now might never know again. "You have the artist's faculty of seizing upon the salients," he told her. "Your pen pictures and your little hap-hazard illustrations are like a moving picture machine. And you speak and describe feelingly. Like you, I have received a number of letters at the same time, and I too have read too quickly, but certain things made an immediate impression. Do you remember writing outside at breakfast – fearing smudges from the buttered toast – and feeding the squirrels and blue jays? The essential thing is that my silly eyes grew warm and moist when I read your description of the woods and of the wild things. I wonder if you love them as I do?"

The next set of letters from Talbot would demand more of Beatrice. Written from London, where he spent much of September on leave, they reveal a side of his nature that was more unsettling. They also take us under the skin of the capital in wartime.

13

The City of Earthly Delights

How I have come to hate London! Not so much London's fault, I suppose, as my own, but for me it has come to mean – long walking in an alien crowd, the ceaseless flow of money, innumerable dashes in taxi-cabs, feverish excitements of nightclubs and music halls, health-destroying restaurants and lounges, and the ceaseless passing of painted faces, the hideous pageantry of commercial affection. If I have been drawn into this side of life I blame myself a great deal, but I also blame disturbing influences of the war, and generally, the extraordinary moral laxity of the people.

Talbot Papineau. A letter to Beatrice Fox; October 3, 1915

War is always an aphrodisiac. Even in dowdy Ottawa, the thrill of danger, the sense of impermanence, the glamour of men in uniform produced the Naughty Nine. By late 1915, London was in the full flush of hedonism. Memoirs of the period are notable for their accounts of reckless behaviour: dancing 'til dawn, excessive drinking and gambling, eager experimentation with morphine and chloroform, both easily available. "Looking back on these nightmare years of tragic hysteria, it is frightening to live them again in memory," Lady Diana Cooper, the reigning belle of the era, wrote nearly half a century later. "The young were dancing a tarantella frenziedly to combat any pause that would let death conquer their morale." A more matter-of-fact observer, Mrs. C. S. Peel, biographer and social historian, tells us in her 1929 book, *How We Lived Then*, that "as the casualty lists lengthened, 'Life is Short; Let us enjoy it while we may' became the motto of the young. The mental strain, the desire to forget horror led to an increase of drinking, drugging, smoking, gambling and dancing. . . . A young man dined with a gay party, danced, drank, got through the early morning hours as best he might, and then the leave train took him and maybe the girl who loved him never saw him again."

A particular wartime phenomenon was the proliferation of nightclubs, a species almost unknown before 1914. "By the winter of 1915, there were 150 in Soho alone," writes Mrs. Peel. "Drink was sold after hours for preposterous prices. The style of dancing altered during these years and jazz bands multiplied and flourished. Girls who had never before earned money or been free of chaperonage found themselves independent, and their elders were sometimes horrified."

Nor was the frenetic new lifestyle confined to the upper and middle classes. In mid-1915, a serious shortage of shells, coupled with rumours that too many munitions workers flush with new money were spending their afternoons carousing in pubs, led to the introduction of early closing hours – a measure that, since the British always revere the established, remained in force until 1989. King George V did give up alcohol for the duration, switching to barley water, but as the Bishop of Durham soon observed of a social occasion, "We drank champagne in spite of the King's example."

Some Londoners' lives went on almost as usual. The diaries of Virginia Woolf, then living in the suburb of Richmond, are remarkable for the rarity of references to the war. It was possible also for new arrivals from Canada and the other dominions to arrive in the great capital of the Empire, race round the tourist sights, marvel at the tube trains, and even more at the moving staircases that led to them, and be almost oblivious to the highly charged atmosphere. "The way the taxi drivers tear around on the wet pavement and on crowded streets in the dark is a revelation," wrote Don Brophy of Ottawa, a young pilot attached to the Royal Flying Corps. "There are dozens of hotels, better than any Canadian hotels I have seen, with the possible exception of the Château Laurier." The more usual reaction was shock. "I've just about come to the conclusion that there are a few people in this town trying to lead a decent life," wrote another Canadian pilot, Harold Price, of Toronto, after his first leave in London. "It shakes a fellow's faith in humanity." Price's stout Methodist faith had been shaken in particular by a musical revue titled *Vanity Fair*. "Parts are good but parts are as sensual as ever. I like pretty flowers. I like pretty girls, but I hate legs above the knee."

More than any other factor, it was the sheer nearness of the trenches – their "ridiculous proximity" – in Fussell's phrase, that accounted for London's behaviour. Previously, "going off to war" had meant departing for far-flung battlelines in South Africa or on the Northwest Frontier. Later, during the Second World War, the battlefronts would be as distant as North Africa or Burma; at the same time, the experience of being under fire during the Blitz would fuse civilians and soldiers together. In the Great War, though, it was as if a pair of vast cities were each other's mad twin: one a City of Destruction, constructed out of mud, peopled by rats, lice, corpses, and frightened men in filthy uniforms; the other, a City of Earthly Delights, awash in music and champagne and pretty women. The source of the tension was that these two "cities" were less than a day's journey apart, and that those who lived in the City of Destruction came on leave to the City of Earthly Delights. For Talbot Papineau, as for many other soldiers, the juxtaposition was often unbearable. "I disliked everyone and everybody," he wrote Beatrice at the end of his leave, after gorging himself with a last slap-up tea at the fashionable Piccadilly Hotel. "I hated the contrast between the soft lights and comfort at the tea room and the trenches. I grew especially angry with the women – some very pretty ones too – who seemed so pleased and placid with themselves while I knew of the carnage at that moment going on." His lonely departure from Charing Cross station aboard the leave train intensified these feelings. "There were crowds of soldiers returning by the same train, and many officers. A larger crowd still of weeping women. I was so bitter I laughed at them all and their silly tears. What difference does it make if a few more of us are killed?"

There was an additional reason for Talbot's bitterness. He

was equally angry at himself. His long-awaited leave had been largely a disaster because there had been no one with whom he wanted to share it. The weather had been gorgeous – after a long chilly summer, London was steeped in golden sunshine, the parks full of roses in bounteous second bloom. "If You Were the Only Girl in the World," Jerome Kern's sweet lilting waltz from *The Bing Boys* was the song everyone was humming. But Beatrice was on the other side of the Atlantic and even Lady Donoughmore was out of town. Thus Talbot too had abandoned himself to hedonism, and in a great rush of remorse, he told Beatrice all about it.

He'd left Armentières in the highest of spirits. "I plan a rather strenuous round of baths, lunches, and dining at night clubs," he wrote Beatrice, "I principally look forward to getting my soiled old uniform off and into white collars and a pretty blue suit." The first social engagement of his leave – a weekend houseparty on the Isle of Wight, given by an old Montreal girlfriend who'd married a British businessman – promised an excursion into pre-war sybaritism. There would be tennis and croquet and sailing, baccarat and bridge after dinner. Whether or not the highlight of the weekend – a "costume party, everyone dressed under 8 years of age and acting accordingly," as Talbot informed Beatrice – struck him as a trifle grotesque, cast against the scene he'd just left, he flung himself into it with gusto. "I bought a little sailor suit with white shoes and socks and a big straw hat, and little short white trousers." As a single, healthy male, and a hero to boot, he was the lion of the evening. "There were seven women whose husbands were at the war, only four real men, one with arm in a sling and another with crutches. However, a number of girls were dressed as boys and one mother wore her own thirteen-year-old son's Boy Scout uniform."

Predictably, the party got out of hand. "We were given cocktails in feeding bottles," Talbot continued. "I was the bad boy . . . I pulled the girls' hair and slipped under the table and pinched their legs, so that everyone jumped screaming onto their chairs. One sober mother pursued me beneath and took my shoe. I captured hers and filled it with champagne, and she filled mine with jelly." Later, the hi-jinks overflowed into the garden, leaving Talbot not only with a gigantic hangover but with a badly sprained ankle.

As a result, he spent four more days on the Isle of Wight, being ministered to by his hostess, who "bathed and bandaged my foot" and who also, in keeping with the reckless new *zeitgeist*, seems to have signalled her willingness to do more besides. "She . . . has a baby face and a little cupid's bow but her heart is cold and calculating," he wrote Beatrice. "Her husband is very wealthy but fat and fifty. I felt sorry for him. He does not look at home in his own home. She will be faithful by expediency, not principle."

Because of the accident to his ankle, Talbot's leave was extended for another fortnight. But the recollection of his giddy behaviour on the Isle of Wight, coupled with bleak news from the Front, where the disastrous battle of Loos was now engaged, cancelled his enjoyment. Back in London, sharing digs with an old friend from McGill and Oxford, John Archibald, he was restive and bored. "I hobbled along Brompton Road wondering what to do next. Then I took a taxi to Piccadilly. There are a great many men still in the streets, and a great many soldiers, but the general impression is women, women, women. They swarm everywhere, breezing about the shop windows, standing at bus stops, dashing across the road and flashing by in cars. I must say that the majority are pretty and attractive but what are their purposes? They still seem curiously ineffective and inane and luxuries rather than necessaries, despite nursing and munitions and a rare post-woman or ticket-collectoress. Yet I should have liked to have had a pretty companion – to admire her smartness and see the flash of her smile and be stimulated by her possible appreciation."

To this comment, there was probably also a subtext. By the standards of the day, Talbot wasn't a prude – witness his information to Beatrice about the pin-ups on his dugout wall. But like most young men of his generation and class, he drew a distinct line between Good Girls and Bad Girls – all the more because the example provided by Caroline had instilled such an exalted ideal of womanhood. Before the war, the notion of nicely brought up young girls venturing into London's West End unaccompanied by a chaperone was unthinkable. The fact that so many now were on the loose, exalting in their new freedom without having taken on the responsibility of war work, angered him, even more, it exacerbated his sexual frustration.

The following day, a long afternoon on the river – "lonely but agreeable" – partially restored Talbot's spirits. At Richmond, on the south bank of the Thames, he rented "a fairly respectable canoe" and set out upstream towards Hampton Court. For the next several hours, he was almost his old self again, and painted a dreamy word picture for Beatrice. "The river was crowded with craft, principally punts and clinker-built skiffs. Occasionally a canoe with its occupant sitting on the bottom at the stern, the bow high in the air. They do not know how to paddle over here. They will never learn. And yet the paddling is wonderful. There are not our tiresome distances and turbulent waters but smooth going, and every foot has beauty and interest. Along both banks picnickers were moored peeling hard-boiled eggs, feeding the swans and the ducks . . . fawns came to the water's edge and there were flowers and drooping trees. Many men rowed uncomfortably in khaki, and many self-conscious wounded Tommies in their brilliant blue suits were escorted by nurses and patronesses. Everything was in movement, and yet everything seemed stationary and localized."

By evening, though, Talbot was restive again. "I dined at the Carlton and then sauntered in silk topper along the blackened streets, the usual crowd, innumerable young officers and young women, taxi-cabs flying through the darkness. I went on to the 400 Club, of which I am a member. I sat alone, and watched the dancing and ordered peach melba and cider cup."

Inevitably – he was young, good-looking, an officer – Talbot ceased being alone. "I have recently done much that I would not care to write you about," he told Beatrice in an emotional, twelve-page letter written on October 3, 1915, the next-to-last day of his leave. "Because with war I had ceased to dream, I have sought the hollow shams of easy and immediate gratifications. Because life might suddenly end, I have not waited for the slow and doubtful realizations. I wanted affection – beauty – laughter – companionship – I wanted them immediately and so I bought them – the cheap, ready-made articles, and so I have cheapened myself until I was sick with disappointment and glad that tomorrow I go back to the front and so perhaps end it all."

In truth, Talbot was flagellating himself unnecessarily. So far as we can fill in the dots, all he seems to have done was to have slept with a couple of ladies of easy virtue – given his fastidious nature, pretty showgirls or actresses are more likely than Piccadilly tarts. Or like many other officers, he may have adjourned to the Cavendish Hotel, where the proprietress, the famous Rosa Lewis (later to be celebrated as "The Duchess of Duke Street"), was renowned for her patriotic ability to provide handsome heroes with all they wanted, including a "a nice clean tart." On one disastrous evening, we do know, he shocked some Canadian friends by making a bit of a spectacle of himself at the Savoy. "I will tell you why the Siftons have refused to dine with me again," he continued to Beatrice. "It cannot be a greater shock to you than it was to me. I dropped in to see them at the Carlton to arrange details. Wyn only came to see me. He said Mrs. Sifton would not dine with me because of what happened at the Savoy last Friday. I said, 'What did happen?' I was utterly dumbfounded. So I learned that after supper I had danced with Mrs. Sifton and we were walking to her table when the girl I had brought with me suddenly grasped my arm and I left Mrs. Sifton alone without a word and went off dancing with the girl. Upon my soul, I can remember no such occurrence, though Wyn says he saw the whole thing himself. Of course, I had had champagne but I pride myself upon my manners under all circumstances, and I cannot conceive of such an action. I do know the girl was furious because I danced with anybody else and it is possible she came up and interfered – but I must have believed Mrs. Sifton was at her table before turning away. However, there you are . . . I solemnly authorize you, if you ever learn of my touching any form of wine again, to abandon me utterly and immediately."

This long *mea culpa*, as we discover, had been prompted by the arrival of a packet of letters from Beatrice, unexpectedly forwarded from the Front. "I have been almost ashamed to open them," Talbot told her. "I have to the present been ashamed to answer them." Above all, he was upset by a line in which she remarked that she demanded of her friends "clean bodies and clean minds." "I could not write you," he went on, "until I had bathed in cold clean water and shaved and brushed myself and dressed as particularly as if you were here, for these things seemed necessary. . . . My resolutions have already taken place. I shall be different whether you write to me again or not . . . but you have crystallized some of my uncertainties, you have cleared the clouded atmosphere which obscured my star. Now if I must die I shall die as I would have liked to live, and if I live I shall not have destroyed utterly my ability to live cleanly."

Then, in an exquisite passage that suggests metaphysical poetry, Talbot told Beatrice what she had come to mean to him. "I was first interested in the texture of your hair, the colour of your eyes, the expression of your face – and even as to how you dressed. And now I do not care, that part of you has ceased to exist, you have become only a mind, a mind answering to mine . . . I want to know what you think, not what you wear. . . . If I were actually with you my senses are much too acute not to be attracted by your outer charms, but away from you I can only think of your inner nature, some of which you have shown to me, much of which still remains to be known. . . . Very timidly I have written, fearful that I should not have discovered you and yet so far I have known only a joyful and exultant satisfaction with everything you have replied. These are things I can say without sentiment because between us there can have been no interfering sex-attraction. It is not love – it is understanding."

Shortly after midnight, Talbot added a long postscript to his letter. It was concerned with the most practical of matters – his own career, which on the last evening of his leave, he had managed to advance quite spectacularly. The refusal of the Siftons to dine with him had turned out to be a blessing in disguise: on the spur of the moment, after dining alone at Simpsons in the Strand, Talbot had telephoned Sir Max Aitken at the Hyde Park Hotel, and was immediately invited round.

In fact, it was a bit more than impulse that had spurred him to make the call. Aitken, better known to us as Lord Beaverbrook, was the most powerful Canadian in London. An influential Conservative Member of Parliament at Westminster, he was also Sam Hughes's personal representative at the centre of the Empire, and the official Canadian "Eyewitness," or war correspondent, accredited to the Front. The next chapter will chart Aitken's course at this make-or-break stage in his turbulent career. Here, it's enough to note that while he and Talbot were not friends – for one thing, they were on opposite sides of the political fence – they were cordial acquaintances. The previous winter, while recuperating from their burns, he and Charlie Stewart had spent a pleasant couple of days at Aitken's country estate, Cherkley Court, just outside Leatherhead in Surrey. Several months later, in the aftermath of Bellewaerde Ridge, as we discover from a letter written to Caroline, he'd written to Aitken suggesting that his talent for "speeching," in both French and English, could be usefully employed in making a recruiting tour of Canada. While Aitken's reply had been noncommittal, it had at least been encouraging.

More to the point of their present encounter, Talbot Papineau and Max Aitken were both ambitious young men of affairs. Aitken was several laps in the lead, but he would have recognized that Talbot was similarly determined to make his name (as a Papineau, he already had a name) and, like all who are ambitious, would have responded to someone possessed of the same drive and energy, but who was not likely to provide direct competition, since Talbot's horizons were limited to Canada.

Arriving at the opulent fifth-floor suite at the Hyde Park Hotel, overlooking Knightsbridge and Hyde Park, that served as Aitken's London headquarters, Talbot had found himself in exalted company. Bonar Law, Conservative opposition leader at Westminster was there. So was Lord Rothermere, then proprietor of the *Sunday Pictorial* and various other newspapers, younger brother of Lord Northcliffe, owner of *The Times* and the *Daily Mail*. "I gathered a good deal of exclusive news which the papers would be glad to have," Talbot reported to Beatrice. "On the whole, the atmosphere was gloomy. Sir Max is just back from the Front. As usual, there has been much staff bungling. [During the offensive at Loos] the First and Twenty-Fourth Divisions took up advanced positions but were left without food and drink for 48 hours and eventually had to retire with heavy losses. Our casualties have been between fifty and sixty thousand." Equally distressing was the news from the Eastern Front, at Gallipoli. "The situation in the Dardanelles is desperate. The Australians feel bitterly the manner in which they have been misused and Bonar Law seriously suggested they would be driven from the Empire. Sir Max said it was most depressing to belong to a decaying Empire."

As always in that era, much of the evening was devoted to bridge. As partners, he and Bonar Law were not a success, Talbot reported. "I went down £1/10 to Lady Aitken." From his point of view, the most profitable part of the conversation was introduced by a comment from Rothermere. "He said the young men should be promoted, and generals should be 30 and 35 years of age, as in all great wars." Perhaps it was at this point that Talbot's glance coincided with Aitken's and the same thought occurred to both of them. Certainly, it was a measure of Aitken's power that he was able to operate so swiftly and confidently. "I have been offered a staff appointment with promotion," Talbot signed off to Beatrice. "However, in the meantime, I rejoin the regiment tomorrow."

While Talbot was on leave, the Patricias had shifted south into France, to a sector of the Somme Front about ten miles from the cathedral city of Amiens. He arrived there by way of Boulogne – "the quays are lined with thousands of Red Cross ambulances," he wrote Beatrice, "the streets are in almost total darkness" – thence by train to Amiens; from there by a combination of lifts on army vehicles and shank's mare to the regiment. All the way along he mulled over Aitken's offer, but arrived still in a ferment of indecision. Accepting a staff job would mean further promotion, and a far better use of his talents. As important, it would mean safety: Caroline's mind set at rest; the probability of meeting Beatrice, and perhaps – who knew? – even sweeping her off to Montebello as his bride; the certainty of returning to Canada and going into politics. The brief meeting with Bonar Law had sent Talbot's imagination racing into the future. "He is an intelligent man, but weak in force – no vitality," he told Beatrice. "In a few years I shall love to measure with him – Tariff Reform and Imperial Federation indeed!"

Going to a staff job would create difficulties, though. It would mean abandoning the regiment; the embarrassment of having to explain to Charlie Stewart and Agar Adamson and Hamilton Gault why he was going, all the while knowing that none of them would for an instant have considered such an offer. In 1915, the hostility

felt towards staff officers by those doing the actual fighting was
not yet as visceral as it would become after the Somme and Passchendaele; even so, as Talbot was undoubtedly aware, Shakespeare's famous lines from *Henry IV* expressed the general
attitude:

> *But I remember when the fight was done*
> *When I was dry with rage and extreme toil*
> *Breathless and faint, leaning upon my sword*
> *Came there a certain lord, neat and trimly dressed*
> *Fresh as a bridegroom and his chin new reap'd . . . He made*
>   *me mad to see him shine so brisk and smell so sweet*
> *And talk so like a waiting gentlewoman*
> *Of guns and drums, and wounds – God save the mark!*

In the event, the decision was easier to make than Talbot had
anticipated. The ambience of the regiment was different now.
Adamson and Gault were back, well of their wounds, and Charlie
Stewart, as always, was in ebullient spirits. "Whiskey has always
been short, and Charlie has been distressed," Talbot reported.
"Yesterday a bottle came by mail and Charlie, leaping and danc-
ing, unpacked it, and put it upon the mantelpiece and then bowed
and salaams made. 'How d'do Mr. Bottle. Glad to see you, Mr.
Bottle. Welcome O Bottle, O Great and Glorious Bottle.'" Most
other officers, however, were newcomers, recent recruits from
McGill and other universities, who were not part of the quasi-mystical band of brothers who had fought at St. Eloi and Bellewaerde
Ridge. "I feel like a senior among a lot of freshmen," Talbot wrote
Beatrice. Simultaneously, the aura of chivalry had been tarnished.
The beauteous Marguerite Gault, in honour of whom the regimental crest was a single white daisy, had betrayed both the Patricias
and her husband by having an affair with one of his brother officers, a certain Captain Bainsmith. "Hamilton has instituted
divorce proceedings," Talbot wrote Beatrice. "But he won't let me
speak to him about it. Marguerite wrote me a long letter telling me
quite frankly her position. I think she was inconsiderate in continuing a friendship with this man when gossip was injuring both her
and her husband. But I know them all so well that I refuse to

believe that there was anything but a thoughtless wartime flirtation." Whatever the rights and wrongs of the situation, it cast a
deep pall of gloom over the regiment. "Gault tries to be cheery
and hard-working," wrote Adamson to Mabel, "but he has always
been very self-contained. I always felt confident that something
was up, but thought she would cover up her tricks."* To add to
the disquietude, the future of the Patricias was once again up in
the air. As a Canadian regiment attached to a British division, it
had always been something of an anomaly; now that it had covered itself with glory, Sam Hughes and Aitken were determined
that it should be transferred to the Canadian division. As a Canadian nationalist, and perhaps also with an ambitious eye to the
biases of his new patron, Talbot was all in favour. Gault, as the
regiment's founder, disagreed strongly and was backed up by a
number of other officers, making the atmosphere in the mess
uncomfortable. "We will all be better soldiers by sticking where
we are," wrote Adamson to Mabel. (Politics prevailed: early in
1916, the Patricias became part of the 3rd Canadian Division.)

---

* Since the Gaults had been married in Quebec, their divorce could be granted
only by an Act of Parliament after hearings by a Senate Committee. The case was
heard on March 10, 1916, in the privacy of the office of the Minister of Finance Sir
Thomas White. It was a measure of the notoriety attached to it that Borden himself made a rare private comment in his diary. "Very unwholesome. . . . Great
interest by members of Parliament. Saw Mrs. G. after she had given evidence. She
looked pale but brave. Think she was very indiscreet but not guilty." In the event,
adultery was not proven and the divorce was not granted. After the war, the
Gaults obtained an amicable, uncontested divorce in France. Shortly thereafter,
Gault married an Englishwoman, Dorothy Shuckburgh, settled in a splendid
country house, Hatch Court, near Taunton in Somerset, and became a Conservative MP at Westminster. He died in 1958.

   The end of the marriage presented the Patricias with a delicate problem. The
regimental cap and collar badges bearing the insignia of a single white daisy had
been designed by Princess Patricia in honour of Marguerite, and Gault was
determined that these should be changed. But the princess, as Colonel-in-Chief,
proved obstinate. "Is this not a difficult job to tackle?" Adamson wrote Mabel.
"The Princess refused and Gault wants me to write asking her to change her
mind. . . . The men love the badge and I don't think after so many good fellows
have died with it, if not for it, it should be changed because one lady has lost
her bed and board." In the end, though, Patricia was persuaded to replace the
marguerite with a more impersonal design.

Nor was Talbot himself in good shape, either physically or mentally. The new tour of duty had begun well enough; the change of venue from Flanders to another relatively quiet sector of the line in Picardy seemed at first glance a change for the better. "Our present line runs through the heart of a pretty little village on the border of a canal and we simply occupy the houses," he wrote Beatrice. "You would never believe I was in the trenches to see me . . . I am seated at a nice mahogany round table before a crackling wood fire." His little dog Bobs, having been entrusted to the care of his batman, had jumped all over him in welcome. Better still, a packet of letters from Beatrice was awaiting him, which also contained a number of photographs and a lock of her auburn hair. "You have reawakened my interest in your hair and eyes and I shall not be content 'til I have seen the mass as well as the uptorn individuals," he told her. "Equally I am pinned to realities, very pleasant ones, by your photographs . . . I like the firm mouth and the honest intelligent eyes." Talbot, indeed, was in such an expansive frame of mind that he decided to respond to Beatrice's remarks about her work. "You seem to know what you are talking about. I confess that I was skeptical at first. I have known so many girls uplifted to a plane they were not really entitled to by an expensive education and the assiduous assistance of a good master. With an artist always at their shoulders they would seem to produce a picture, by themselves they could do very little. But I am inclined to give you the benefit of my doubt . . . I like your fun and I like your serious criticism and I like your opinions so far as I know them." A few days later, he made a few pencil sketches of his own of brother officers, and sent them along to her. "They are the first I have attempted since the war. I thought you might be interested."

But as the autumn rains set in, and the regiment shifted constantly and seemingly aimlessly from one set of rat-infested trenches to another, Talbot slumped into despondency. "Confound this war. It's horrible. I hate it," he told Beatrice, after getting soaked to the bone on yet another route march. "I am going steadily to believe that it will be over by Christmas and when that hope proves vain I shall believe something else." As depressing as slogging through mud was the necessity of having to destroy all her letters. "My baggage is limited to 35 lbs; what I have I have to

Captain R. A. S. "Beau" Nash of the Princess Patricia's Canadian Light Infantry. Talbot Papineau made this sketch on October 19, 1915, and sent it to Beatrice Fox, adding the information that the book Nash is reading is Stephen Leacock's *Nonsense Novels*.

carry on my back, so there is little room for accumulation. I try to memorize your letters but I am sure I must forget a lot." Like most soldiers, albeit in a way that would have horrified his pre-war agnostic intellectual self, he'd begun making fetishes of such small objects as he could carry with him: her "copper silk" lock of hair; a photograph of Caroline in the garden at Montebello; in particular a pearl-handled pen-knife given to him by his elder brother Louis just before the Patricias left Canada. "This is the only thing I still retain except life and health," he told Beatrice. "I have grown so superstitious that I am inclined to connect the two, just as a poor savage would." The most important talisman was Bobs: in mid-October, when the dog went missing one night in no man's land, Talbot risked life and limb to crawl over the parapet and retrieve him. Ten days afterwards, when Bobs went missing for good, he was greatly distressed. "He has in all likelihood been carried away by some of the troops that are constantly passing through this village," he wrote Beatrice from the hamlet of Morcourt. "It's all in the game, all a part of this horrible procession of events to which our hearts must be hardened and our mind deadened." The disappearance of Bobs seems to have been the last straw: the following week, Talbot himself was packed off to hospital in Le Havre, officially the victim of acute bronchitis, but by his own account, "more hurt in mind than in body." It was as if all the dread and horror of the past nine months had suddenly caught up with him and overwhelmed him.

In hospital, where he remained for nearly two months, until mid-January 1916, Talbot occupied himself by writing a "treatise on trench warfare" and letters to Beatrice. On November 23, marking yet another development in their relationship, he addressed her for the first time as "My Dear Beatrice" instead of "My Dear Miss Fox." "What has our correspondence meant to me?" he wrote, echoing a question she seems to have posed. "It has meant receiving frequent letters and so being kept cheered and interested in trying times. It has meant the charm of a possible romance, it has stimulated my imagination and has given me letters to write, which as they seemed to touch an answering chord, added fresh fuel to my enthusiasm. . . . Love and war, are they not inseparable? And here I was at war and not in love. Why should I not grasp at the form even if I were denied the substance? . . . Please keep on amusing a soldier no matter what he says or does."

By early February, when the staff appointment eventually came through – even for Aitken, it took a while to work through the official channels – Talbot had long since made up his mind to accept. As it developed, Sir Max had pulled out all the stops. Talbot's appointment was a glittering one: ADC to the Commander of the Canadian Corps, Major-General Sir Edwin Alderson, a British officer who had commanded Canadian troops in South Africa. "So far as I can make out, I am a combination between a

fashion plate and an orderly," he wrote Beatrice, in a rather trans-
parent attempt at modesty. "We are in an enormous house and the
translation from the trenches is stunning! We have napkins at all
meals and I am so unaccustomed that mine slips continually to
the floor." At the last moment, though, a brief farewell tour with
the regiment had been almost enough to make him wish the temptation had never come his way. "Yesterday I cried like a baby
when it came time to say goodbye. . . . All the NCOs in my company paraded to say goodbye and I couldn't say a word. I felt like
the devil! Now I would return if I could, but I cannot give this position up until I have made good at it."

Talbot's letter to Caroline about leaving the Patricias was
much more hard-headed. "I have had a long talk with the Corps
Commander . . . I gather from him he will use me effectively. . . . It
is no doubt a great compliment to me to have been selected, but
the water is deep and there may be rocks. I have to steer a difficult course."

As always, it was Caroline who understood Talbot better
than anyone else. What they both knew, as Beatrice could not
have, was that the price of escaping from the fog and thunder of
war into safety would be Talbot's own self-respect. As long as he
stayed on the staff, he would no longer be his own man. Instead,
he would be hostaging his fortunes to those of Max Aitken, a man
whom everyone agreed would go far, and whom some wished
would go all the way to hell.

14

"An Odour of Genius"

I did not make situations. I turned them to account.

Lord Beaverbrook. Quoted by his biographer
A. J. P. Taylor in *Beaverbrook*, 1972

Nearly three decades after his death, the name *Beaverbrook* still conjures up sharply defined images: brilliant but ruthless publisher with frustrated political ambitions, much in the manner of Citizen Kane; tycoon with some of his gains achieved by dubious means; wild colonial boy turned imperialist crusader; compulsive womanizer; a force of nature, often coarse and bullying, who demanded deference from others, yet, in contradiction, at times sweet-natured and generous, quite often vulnerable.

As we meet him in 1915, Beaverbrook was still Sir Max Aitken. He was already wealthy, and as a a *wunderkind* financier from the Colonies, he'd made some important contacts, including Bonar Law, a future British prime minister, and Rudyard Kipling, relationships nurtured with excellent tips about investments. But he was still only in his mid-thirties, still in the process of inventing himself. Despite his knighthood, purchased, in his own blunt description, for "services to come" to the British Conservative Party, he had ascended only to the lowest rung of British politics, as a backbench MP best known for seldom attending the Commons and for speaking there scarcely at all. As yet, he owned no newspapers and so could command no sycophancy. Much of the British establishment shrugged him off as just another colonial upstart on the make, one best to be kept at a distance since at any moment some financial upset or scandal might unmake him.

Yet Aitken was already a force of nature, "a strange attractive gnome with an odour of genius about him," in the description given by Lady Diana Cooper, who first met him during the war. A trio of informal photographs taken around this time captures the

Sir Max Aitken, later Lord Beaverbrook, with an unidentified group of Canadian officers and their wives, *circa* 1916. The gathering may have been a garden party at Aitken's country house, Cherkley Court. He was still in the process of inventing himself. In the description of one admirer, he was "a strange attractive gnome with an odour of genius about him."

quality. Amid a company of jocund, short-back-and-sides staff officers and pretty women in straw hats and flowing chiffon, Aitken is the centrifugal figure, crackling with energy and vitality. Then and later, he provoked extraordinarily strong reactions among all who encountered him, frequently coming from opposite directions. To his official biographer, A. J. P. Taylor, usually the most skeptical of historians, Aitken was, "the human being I had most loved," the result being that this 1972 biography is virtually a hagiography. To Malcolm Muggeridge, he was "a bad man . . . someone who'd sold his soul to the devil . . . a man who enjoyed stimulating in people what was basest in them." Most revealing, perhaps, is that Beaverbrook evoked extreme reactions among people who viewed him from the same perspective. Clement Attlee, Britain's post-war Labour prime minister, called him "the man in public life most distrusted by men of all parties." Michael Foot, Labour leader in the early 1980s, described him as "a second father . . . a figure of bewitching interest . . . [who] has not received his due honour."

Not in dispute is that no other Canadian carved his name so large upon his times. Even Muggeridge conceded, "Nobody would be able to write the story of the first half of the twentieth century, and leave him out." The full dimension of Beaverbrook lies far beyond the scope of this book. Instead, we set out to snapshot the young Max Aitken on the wing, at a transformational moment in his career. As master propagandist and backroom kingmaker, his actions during the war would cut the pattern for the whole of his future life.

As soon as the war broke out, Aitken had seized it as an opportunity for personal advancement. By the end of 1916, he'd succeeded brilliantly, having catapulted himself into the inner sanctum of power by playing a key role in the coup that forced Prime Minister H. H. Asquith to resign in favour of Lloyd George. Along the way to that dénouement, and perhaps as a half-intended dress rehearsal for it, he executed a similar kind of coup at the top of the Canadian military establishment. The sheer bald-faced gall and adroit ruthlessness by which he did this, a thirty-five-year-old with some money but with many suspicions attached to its source and fully as many doubts about his character and intentions, provides a case illustration of Aitken's own summary valediction of his career, "I did not make situations. I turned them to account."

Max Aitken was ever an original, a "one-off," as the British say, his character too complex and contradictory to be fully explained by background and heredity. Yet New Brunswick was forever his Rosebud – as no one in that province was ever allowed to forget. During his lifetime, he showered it with benefits that were also monuments to his own greatness – the Beaverbrook Library, the Beaverbrook Art Gallery, Beaverbrook scholarships. After his death, on his instructions, his ashes were placed in the bust of himself by Oscar Nemon that stands in the town square at Newcastle, the north-shore lumbering town at the mouth of the Miramichi where he grew up. It was as if the whole of his life had been a long series of efforts to "show them"; an endless quest for approval.

In fact, Aitken was born not in New Brunswick, but in Ontario, in the small community of Maple, long since swallowed up by suburban Toronto. The date was May 25, 1879, a day after the holiday that all over the Empire marked Queen Victoria's sixty-first birthday. His father, William Aitken, a tall and impressive figure with a long beard, was a Church of Scotland minister who had emigrated from Torphichen in the Lowlands in the 1860s; his mother, the former Jane Noble, was the daughter of a prosperous local merchant. William Maxwell Aitken, Max, as he was known from the beginning, was the fifth of their ten children, nine of whom lived to grow up. Shortly before Max's first birthday, William answered a call to the parish of Newcastle. There, the family moved into a handsome, newly completed clapboard manse with a mansard roof that nowadays is the civic library, needless to say, thanks to Beaverbrook.

In Canada, in those days, such a background was nearer to rule than exception for upwardly mobile young men. From similar manses all over the Dominion, in the decades that bracketed the last of the old century and the beginning of the new one, they marched out in their hundreds – Lester Bowles Pearson, Beaverbrook's only real Canadian rival on the world stage as

the apotheosis – to people the professions and to form the man-
darin class of the embryonic civil service. But in London, as
Aitken was quick to grasp, all the more since it never occurred
to him to be the least bit apologetic about them, his origins
made him intriguing. "He was always ready to talk of his early
youth, and of his Calvinist upbringing," wrote Lady Diana
Cooper. She recalled how he loved to recite from memory that
gloomiest of all Presbyterian hymns, "I know that God is wrath
in me/For I was born in sin," a performance invariably followed
by the comment, "Beautiful, isn't it?" Like his contemporaries
all over the Empire, he grew up on the tales of G. A. Henty and
Sir Walter Scott; though William Aitken was a Clear Grit in the
tradition of George Brown and Alexander Mackenzie, Max himself always claimed to have been converted by the rhetoric of
the epochal 1891 election over free trade – "The Old Man; the
Old Flag; The Old Policy" – to Sir John A. Macdonald's brand of
romantic conservatism, and also to the doctrine of imperial
protectionism. But it was from William Aitken, possessed of
considerable erudition though little ambition, that Max inherited his high intelligence and probably also the courtly, ornate
style of expression – never "Hello, how are you," always "Good-
day to you" – that Lady Diana and others found so beguiling,
especially when uttered in the rough New Brunswick accent –
closer to "G'day t' ya" – that he resisted all suggestions to
soften. From Jane Noble Aitken, who was by far the dominant
parent, Max inherited, as he recalled, "energy and drive,
courage, determination and high spirits," and less happily the
curse of asthma. As important to his development was the
primeval landscape of New Brunswick itself, "a country of
rolling forests, with distant glimpses of hills and valleys and of
broad rivers, full of big salmon running down over rapids past
tree-clad islands to meet the great tides sweeping up from the
Miramichi bay," as he described in old age the sense of place he
never lost.

There were fishing expeditions; log-rolling competitions; a
pet spaniel named Tasso. Early on, demonstrating a talent for
deal-making, Max cornered the schoolyard market in marbles;
much in the manner of Tom Sawyer, he conned others into

making the deliveries on his paper route, while reaping the lion's share of the profits. Yet it was also a boyhood full of discord. In later years, Aitken himself blamed this on too many people jammed into too small a space. "Try to accommodate eleven members of one family in a house of six bedrooms," he wrote in his memoir, *My Early Life*. "It does not make for harmony." The deeper problem was that tenderness and affection do not seem to have been prominent features of life in the manse. William was austere and reclusive, much given to burying himself in his study; Jane was domineering and a strict disciplinarian."It is diffi-cult to recollect any evidence of warmth in the relations of my parents," he tells us. "My mother invariably spoke of her hus-band and to him as Mr. Aitken, and I cannot recall any time when my mother was called Jane." As the middle child in a huge family, he was inevitably the odd one out, all the more because he was undersized, funny-looking – "God couldn't make your mouth any bigger without removing your ears," one schoolmate taunted – and asthmatic. Early on, he began to exhibit most of the classic symptoms of emotional deprivation: a mischief-maker, a bit of a bully, "the devil to live with," in the description of one of his brothers. One of his sisters once flung him downstairs in a rage. In school, he was incurably idle – when he bothered to turn up at all. "There was never any doubt about his ability," one teacher commented later. "But I never believed that he would be in any way successful."

The opening stages of his career bore out this assessment. Having failed the entrance exam for Dalhousie University – an event that engendered a lifelong hatred for that institution – he worked for a while in a Newcastle drugstore for all of $1 a week, then apprenticed unsuccessfully in a law firm, next turned to sell-ing insurance. His energy and zest were infectious, however unco-ordinated, and he did better for a while, attaching himself to a rising young local lawyer, R. B. Bennett, a future prime minister. When Bennett went to Calgary to start his political career, Aitken went along as a kind of executive assistant. But his penchant for getting into trouble – too much poker, too much whiskey, a couple of disastrous business ventures – embarrassed the straight-laced Bennett ("If only your character equalled your ability.") and soon he was given his congé.* Back in New Brunswick he did little, at one point getting so seriously in debt that a warrant was issued for his arrest.

By Aitken's own account, the turning point was his twenty-first birthday, May 25, 1900. While sitting around the campfire on a fishing party, with a bottle of whiskey on the go, he listened to the tales of a young Canadian who'd gone to the States and made good. "His delineation of new ideas of effort and achievement set the match to the tow of latent and fiery ambition." He made the instant decision. "I'm going to make some money quickly. I am going to sell what makes money."

Less than a decade later, he was a millionaire several times over.

The details of how Aitken made his fortune have been recounted by Taylor and others, including William Kilbourn in his study of the Steel Company of Canada, *The Elements Combined*, and more recently, by Christopher Armstrong and H. V. Nelles in *Southern Exposure: Canadian Promoters in Latin America and the Caribbean, 1896–1930*. Relevant here is that Aitken found a situation and turned it to account. At the turn of the century, Canada was exploding outwards, literally so in the settling of the west, psychically so in its ambitions: "The twentieth century will belong to Canada," proclaimed Prime Minister Wilfrid Laurier. Yet its commercial and financial structures were turned backwards to a staid, conservative past. The stock markets were primitive. Most companies were family-owned, generating capital entirely out of profits or personal loans. An enterprising Toronto businessman, E. R. Wood, founder of Dominion Securities, introduced into the country the American idea of selling industrial bonds to raise capital for expanding companies. Aitken was a born salesman, not just because he could talk, but because he had a shrewd

---

* Before long, the two were once again close friends and business partners: in 1907, they put together the Calgary Power Company. In the late 1930s, when Bennett moved to England after the defeat of his government, Aitken was instrumental in having him made a viscount. In 1959, he celebrated their long association in a book titled *Friends*.

understanding of human nature. First in Halifax, then in Montreal, he became one of Canada's most successful bond salesmen, expanding later into the even more lucrative field of funding mergers and acquisitions: Canadian Car and Foundry as his first, the Steel Company of Canada as his most ambitious, the Canada Cement Company as his most controversial. In his biography, Taylor, who went through the records in detail, describes Aitken as "a man of fanatical integrity." Later investigators are more equivocal. "He . . . revealed a cunning desire to garner extra profits for himself by not telling certain people what they were entitled to know," write Armstrong and Nelles of Aitken's 1905 acquisition of the Demerara Electric Company in British Guiana. Certainly it is from this period that he acquired a reputation for sharp practice and shady dealing that he could never shake off. Perhaps he just made too much money too quickly. Perhaps, in those simpler times, people couldn't believe that money could be made out of money, other than illegally, rather than out of products or property. Perhaps he was just too smart and quick for the timid family compact that Canadian businessmen then amounted to. Most probably mud was thrown at him, much of it sticking permanently, because he angered and alarmed the corporate establishment: Sandford Fleming, the CPR patriarch, never forgave him for the Canada Cement merger, from which he came away a personal loser. Beyond any doubt, Aitken's life-long scorn for the establishment, unaltered by one iota when he crossed the Atlantic, dates from this period. Most relevant to our story, and no matter how, Aitken had by now amply equipped himself with the means to do what he really wanted – to pursue political power at the centre of Empire, London.

In later years, Aitken looked back on the events of Friday, July 17, 1910, as a watershed. At 5:00 PM, in his office in Montreal, the last documents were signed bringing the Steel Company of Canada into existence. An hour or so later, he swept out of the city, at the wheel of "a car as big as a house," bound for New York, there to embark for Britain aboard the *Lusitania*. "My success in making mergers had turned out so wonderfully well," he wrote. "Surely my gifts would be useful to the cause of the

United British Empire."* His initial plan was to market the first issue of Stelco bonds to investors, then to look round for other opportunities. Within a few months, he had acquired the controlling shares in Rolls-Royce and, cashing in politically on his success, had become a member of the House of Commons at Westminster.

Accompanying Aitken to London were a wife and two children. In a perfunctory kind of way, he'd become a family man. In January 1906, in St. Paul's Church in Halifax, he'd married nineteen-year-old Gladys Drury, daughter of the first Canadian-born officer to command the imperial garrison. She was beautiful, high-spirited, and intelligent – but he was not in love with her. "My wife had a livelier interest in me than I had in her," he informs in a candid, if cold-blooded passage that he eventually decided to delete from the published version of his memoir. "I had not married under any very compelling desire for marriage. It had been to some extent a matter of convenience to me. . . . If I were to have a permanent place in Montreal, I must have a family. And so I had made what I thought to be the best marriage." Not surprisingly, the union was not a success. While honeymooning in Cuba, he spent most of his time acquiring properties and electric tram companies. The following year, when he had his appendix out – in those days, a complicated affair that required several weeks in hospital – Gladys's solicitude irritated him so much that he instructed his doctor to send her away until he was fully recovered. Perhaps the key problem was that they were physically incompatible: all his life, Aitken was a compulsive womanizer, a man of rapacious sexual appetites, even though the writer Rebecca West, who loved him deeply, and with whom he had a disastrous affair in the early 1920s, confided to intimates that he was not always a brilliant

---

* There may have been an additional reason for the departure. As Peter Newman notes in his 1975 study, *The Canadian Establishment*, a rumour lingered for decades that Aitken's real motivation for quitting Canada so abruptly was that his application to join the Mount Royal Club, bastion of Montreal's Anglo-Scottish ascendancy, had recently been blackballed.

performer.* Those attributes of Aitken that made him so desirable as lover and as pursuer – lavish presents; the aphrodisiac aura of power; a certain quality of being "bad, mad, and dangerous to know" – were, of course, the obverse of those required of a successful husband and father. Of his three children, only Janet, the eldest and the only girl, born in Halifax in 1908, was close to him – largely because she too was both a sensualist and a risk-taker. "The boys are like you," he once wrote to Gladys, "Janet, I'm afraid, is like me."

Nothing is ever simple though. When the gentle, forbearing Gladys Drury Aitken died in 1927, of a brain tumour at thirty-nine, Max was devastated, not only by feelings of guilt that were far from misplaced – he was in a yacht at Biarritz with his current mistress and only just made it back in the nick of time on a chartered plane – but by an inchoate sense of loss. "My father looked stunned, as if for the first time in his life something had affected him too deeply for him to comprehend it," wrote Janet Aitken Kidd in her own memoir, *The Beaverbrook Girl*, published in 1987, the same year that she herself died. "'My harbour has gone,' he said. The tragedy of it seemed to mystify him. Then, 'I loved her so much, but she was too good for me.' He kept saying it over and over again." According to Janet, her father once again laid himself bare at the very end of his life, nearly four decades later. "We sat in front of the fire and he spoke to me about Mother, and the deep love he had felt for her. He spoke of nothing else, during which

---

* The story of this affair has been recounted by Victoria Glendinning in her 1987 biography, *Rebecca West*. Beaverbrook and West met in 1918, when he was British Minister of Information. She described him as "full of the real vitality – the genius kind that exists mystically apart from all physical conditions." In 1923, the two spent Christmas in New York together, "on the understanding that they were in love." But during the next fortnight it became apparent that "they were completely unsuited to be husband and wife. Rebecca meant that physical relations between them had been a failure."

In West's autobiographical novel, *Sunflower*, written in the late 1920s and published posthumously in 1986, Beaverbrook appears as the Australian millionaire Francis Pitt, "a little man with hair the colour of a fox and a very big mouth . . . the most self-possessed and male person [Sunflower] had ever met."

time he revealed his true feelings, so often suppressed behind an outward veneer of toughness and unpredictability. Although he talked only about Mother, the essence of what he said could be applied to all his relationships with people, both men and women, for whom he felt genuine affection – and there were many. Now at last, when the truth no longer made him feel vulnerable, he could speak from the heart."

The best description of the thirty-one-year-old Max Aitken as he set out to conquer London in the late summer of 1910 (the season of Halley's Comet, but, in Britain some things never change, the principal political problem was trouble in Ireland) has been provided by R. D. Blumenfeld. Almost forgotten now, "Blum," as he was always known, was one of the most zestful observers of the London scene; an American-born bon vivant who edited a lively but money-losing newspaper, the *Daily Express*. Within the context of this story, Blum's impressions of their first encounter, set down in his 1931 memoir, *All In a Lifetime*, matter in two ways. A few months later, the two having hit it off immediately, Aitken acquired a small interest in the *Express*, more or less as a personal favour to Blum, and thus was launched on the road to becoming a press lord. As much to the point, Blumenfeld had a country place in Essex, where one of his closest friends and neighbours was a rising star of the British army, Major-General Sir Julian Byng. As we shall discover, the connection between Blum and Byng would have a direct bearing on both Aitken's career and upon Canadian history. As Blum relates it, the occasion of their first meeting was a political luncheon in honour of Arthur Balfour, then the Conservative leader, to which Aitken had been invited by an acquaintance in the City. Blum, no doubt hoping to get an paragraph or two for next morning's paper, was probably not best pleased to find himself placed next to an unknown Colonial, "a comparative youth, carelessly dressed, with tousled hair, searching eyes, alternately hard and twinkling, and a large, full-lipped mouth which made him look cold and forbidding in repose and extraordinarily attractive when it spread itself in a smile over his colourless face."

Within five minutes, Blum was captivated. "Mr Aitken wasted no time in doing what appears to be his life's objective – namely, 'finding out.' He began at once, like Li Hung Chang, to stupefy me with a torrent of questions, flinging in a new one almost before I had answered the old. He lifted the top of my head, so to speak, and looked in, and having found there certain things that were strange to him, he proceeded to test and analyse them and weigh them. . . . I have never known a man who could assimilate information faster and adapt it to the purpose in hand with greater facility and conviction."

That same month of September, Aitken established a second relationship that would be of equal moment. He went round to a handsome South Kensington house to call on Bonar Law, a wealthy Glasgow iron merchant who was also a senior Conservative member. Then in his early fifties, a tall impressive figure with a flowing moustache and an ever-present pipe, Law was the only other man of affairs in London who was also a New Brunswick-born son of the manse – born in Kingston, later renamed Rexton, a small town on the Richibucto River, about twenty miles south of Newcastle. Their boyhoods aside, the two could scarcely have been more dissimilar. Law was ascetic and solitary, and had no interest whatever in reminiscing about New Brunswick. Indeed, when they'd first met two years earlier, when Aitken had dropped round while on a brief bond-selling mission to London, Law had found his bumptiousness tiresome and bought some bonds simply to get rid of him.

This time the chemistry worked and Aitken was invited to stay to lunch. "The food was not very good," he later recorded, "and I noticed with a little annoyance that I was given one glass of whiskey, whereas my host helped himself twice to what appeared to be a special whiskey out of his own bottle." Later, having discovered that Law was a teetotaller and that the bottle contained lime juice, he was covered with remorse. To the general surprise, the two became friends, and Law, known to the young Janet Aitken as "Mr. Smoke," often spent weekends at Aitken's country place, Cherkley Court. Certainly their relationship involved a large measure of mutual self-interest: Law became Aitken's political mentor, and soon helped him seek out a seat in Parliament. Aitken became Law's financial advisor, and quickly invited him to join a lucrative bond-selling syndicate. There was, however, much more to it than that. From Aitken, the languid Law – "intelligent, but no vitality," as

Talbot Papineau would shortly observe – absorbed life and energy by osmosis. Often, he would refer in public to the younger man as "my most intimate friend." For his part, Aitken found in Law many characteristics similar to those of William Aitken, his father. "I loved him more than any other human being," he wrote in 1922, when Law – ever "Mr. Smoke" – died of throat cancer.

During these first years in London, Aitken's most rewarding new friendship was with Rudyard Kipling, then in his mid-forties and at the peak of his fame. No record exists of their first meeting, but clearly what drew them together was a mutual passion for Empire. "I enclose a copy of *The Canadian Century*, a weekly magazine which I publish in Montreal," runs the first letter from Aitken in the voluminous file of their correspondence, dated November 14, 1910. "I am particularly anxious that you should read an article entitled 'The Reciprocity Investigation' by Mr. G. S. Foster, Finance Minister in the last Conservative administration." Three days later, Kipling responded politely and added a grace note, "How come I didn't catch you at the last Constitutional Club meeting?"

By mid-December, they had met several times, and Aitken was advising on Canadian investments. "The Westmount bonds at 4% are entirely satisfactory," he wrote. "I have taken the liberty of cabling Montreal Trust to say that any orders from you must be very carefully executed." But it would be to misjudge this relationship to assume that it was based only on money and hero-worship. Kipling, for all his celebrity, was essentially a lonely figure, "Mr. Sad," in Janet Aitken's description, a middle-class child from India, ill at ease in aristocratic society, a man with a difficult wife who lived in a grey stone pile in Sussex called Bateman's that nowadays, among literary shrines in England, is mostly notable for its cheerlessness. Like Law, he responded as moth to the flame of Aitken's energy, perhaps seeing in him the apotheosis of all the high-spirited young male animals he was so good at writing about – Kim, Stalky and Co. As befitted a man who was an icon, Kipling always made sure that he remained the senior partner in their friendship. "I think we will drop the 'mister,'" he wrote late in 1910, which, in the elaborate protocol of the times meant not yet "My Dear Max," but the intermediate "My Dear Aitken." "I would sooner not sit next to a man with an undigested speech in his system," he wrote the following year in response to Aitken's suggestion that the politician F. E. Smith (later Lord Birkenhead) be placed next to him at a political dinner. But when Aitken bought Cherkley Court in 1912 – a pseudo-French château that, except for its magnificent views of the Surrey Hills, was even gloomier than Bateman's – it was Kipling who not only gave him the present of a handsome guest book, bound in dark green leather, but inscribed it with a charming poem. Later that same year, he agreed to be godfather and namesake to the Aitken's third child, Peter Rudyard. In December 1913, when William Aitken died, no friend could have written a more tender or more appropriate letter of sympathy. "It isn't a matter on which men open up to each other very much, but I lost my father, who was a great deal of the world to me, a few years ago, and I know it hurts and what a change it makes inside one's mind forever after." Sadly, within a few years, Kipling and Aitken would fall out, over the very issue – imperial solidarity – that initially had brought them together; Kipling never forgave him for supporting the cause of Irish independence. By then – the captains and the kings depart – it was "Mr. Sad" who was in the subordinate position, the out-of-fashion troubadour of an Empire that was beginning to vanish.

"He is a young Canadian, not much over 30; he is a man of really exceptional ability, who, without any outside help, has made a large fortune; he is a keen Imperialist and for that reason, now wants to stand for Parliament." Signed by Bonar Law and dated November 14, 1910, this letter to the Conservative constituency association at Ashton-Under-Lyne, a textile town just outside Manchester, was Aitken's card of entry into British politics. While nowadays it seems quite astonishing that such an outsider could dare aspire to run for office, this was much less unusual at that time. Westminster was both centre of Empire and Mother of Parliaments: technically at least, all citizens of the Empire had equal rights there. In that pre-passport era, it was possible even for those without formal British citizenship to be MPs, witness one Baron de Forest, an Austrian subject, illegitimate son of Baron Hirsch, builder of the Orient Railway. Nor was it unusual for men active in the financial City to enter politics as a sideline, adding an additional club to their listing in *Who's Who*.

What *was* unusual was the whirlwind style of Aitken's political debut. The general election of December 1910 had come about unexpectedly, as a result of Asquith's controversial bill curbing the power of the House of Lords. In order to win his seat, this unknown Canadian – "Who is Mr. Aitken?" jibed his opponent – would have to defeat a sitting member who had the double advantage of being a Lancashire man. His answer was to turn the ten-day campaign into a theatrical event: brass bands, mass rallies, a special daily newspaper distributed free. "He advertised his personality as Barnum and Bailey might a new elephant," noted a contemporary journalist. To offset the liability of being struck almost dumb at the prospect of speaking in public, as is often the case with those who are uninhibited in private, he imported a galaxy of Conservative luminaries to perform on the platform, including Bonar Law, F. E. Smith, and, in absentia, Kipling, who, though unable to attend in person due to a death in the family, sent a supportive telegram. The real star turn turned out to be Gladys Aitken: in a splendid fur coat and hat overflowing with feathers, she dazzled everyone, and also charmed them with her easy and unaffected Canadian manner. On December 3, 1910, the Liberals were returned to office. But Aitken won Ashton-Under-Lyne by 196 votes. "His wonderful success is being discussed," pronounced the *Daily Mail*.

Success, though, was succeeded by nothing. Being an opposition backbencher was not at all Max Aitken's *métier*. "Waiting and listening were not occupations at which he ever excelled," A. J. P. Taylor notes drily. Giving speeches held no appeal, indeed, since it tended to trigger his asthma, it was something to be avoided. Save for Imperial Unity – upon which he'd centred his entire campaign – the concerns of the day concerned him little: when it came to home rule and the House of Lords, his instincts, if anything, were with the Opposition; on the subject of women's suffrage, he opted for an uncharacteristic neutrality. While gregarious, he was not clubbable and took little part in the camaraderie of the House. Much to Kipling's disapproval, the closest friendship he forged at Westminster – perhaps the closest friendship of his entire life – was with another outsider, the Irish Nationalist member, Tim Healy. (Much beloved by young Janet Aitken, Healy was a controversial figure, reviled by many Irishmen for having betrayed the great

Charles Stewart Parnell. He later became first Governor General of
the Irish Free State and died in 1931.)

Despite his 1911 knighthood, for "services to come" to the
Conservative Party (mostly in the form of subsidies to Conservative newspapers), real power eluded Aitken. For a time he thought
seriously of resigning from Westminster and returning to Canada
where the campaign against Laurier's Reciprocity Treaty was hot-
ting up. "I realize that you owe duty to your constituents in Great
Britain," wrote Sir Robert Borden in the spring of 1911, "but you
owe a closer duty to Canada at this juncture." The plan unfolding
in both their minds was that Aitken should run in New Brunswick
("a man of your driving force is especially needed in your native
province," Borden continued) and then, provided both he and the
Conservatives won, enter Borden's cabinet in a senior position,
perhaps even as Minister of Finance.

But Aitken had left too many enemies behind him. Sandford
Fleming chose precisely this moment to go public with the accusation that Aitken had pocketed $13 million out of the Canada
Cement merger by watering the stock. From Ottawa, Governor
General Earl Grey sent back word to Whitehall that Aitken's
appearance on the Coronation Honours list had evoked "a howl of
indignation and disgust throughout the Dominion." Thus he and
Borden regretfully reached the decision that his candidature
would be a distinct liability. As a substitute, he poured money into
the anti-reciprocity campaign; "I would hate to tell you how much
money I have spent," he wrote Kipling, and in September, on the
eve of the election, elicited from Kipling the famous telegram: "It
is her own soul that Canada risks today."

Frustrated, and more deeply hurt than he cared to admit by
the rebuff in Canada, Aitken mostly marked time during the years
that immediately preceded the outbreak of war. At the end of 1911,
operating for the first time as a backroom kingmaker, he played a
key part in the machinations that made Bonar Law successor to
Balfour as Conservative leader. Otherwise, he devoted most of his
time to his business interests, and to refurbishing Cherkley Court.
As always when insufficiently occupied, he was nervous and
depressed, and prey to hypochondriacal ailments. In the spring of
1914, he made up his mind to quit politics for good. "I have told my

constituents I am not going to stand for Parliament any more," he wrote Kipling. "I have been offered a partnership in one of the big houses and I am afraid I am yielding to the temptation." Again, events intervened. His next message to Kipling was of a quite different order. "If you want to see the real thing in the way of panic," he cabled on July 29, "Come to the City now."

Far earlier than most people, Aitken had seen that war was coming. As early as mid-July, he'd sensed strange vibrations in the City. As he wrote later, "It was clear to anyone with a real knowledge of markets that some obscure and colossal movement was on foot. . . . Someone, somewhere, knew of a definite intention." Aitken being Aitken, he also sniffed an opportunity. "The advantage to Canada and America will be enormous," he told Kipling. "The price of wheat will go up."

Incomparably more exciting, war promised political opportunity for those of unrecognized ability, perhaps even a chance at a cabinet seat. On Friday July 31, the start of the long holiday weekend that prefaced the actual declaration of war, Aitken dined in the country with Law and two other senior Conservatives, F. E. Smith and the flamboyant champion of Ulster, Sir Edward Carson. The discussion was tense and excited, for with Germany's intentions in regard to violating Belgian's neutrality not yet known, the Liberal government was sharply divided. The word was that if Britain declared war, as many as eight ministers might resign. Moreover, as Smith reported to the gathering, Winston Churchill, then First Lord of the Admiralty and the most hawkish member of cabinet, had already put to him the key question: if the government collapsed, would the Conservatives join a coalition?

For the cautious Bonar Law, the notion of negotiating through the hot-headed Churchill was out of the question. But Aitken was unable to resist getting in on the action. Brooking his mentor's disapproval, he tagged along with Smith to dine with Churchill at Admiralty House on the following evening. He provides a vivid account of what then transpired in his 1932 book, *Politicians and the War*. While not yet a close friend of Churchill, as he is careful to note, they were already more than acquaintances. "I had been dazzled by his brilliant powers," he recounts.

"I had dined at his house, had talked with him unreservedly – of course with plenty of display on his part of that kind of wit which contains the promise of coming intimacy."

The company were five: Smith, Aitken, and Churchill, and two other members of the Liberal government. In the opening stages of the evening, Aitken tells us, it seemed possible, even probable, that war might be averted. "While we were talking, a message was received announcing the postponement of the German ultimatum to Russia."

Of his own response to this news, Aitken is more than a bit disingenous. "I regarded it as an omen of peace and rejoiced in the prospect of escaping a European War." He's entirely faithful, though, in his reporting of Churchill's response. "He argued that the German menace had to be faced and fought out some time or another." While waiting for something more to happen – nowadays, they no doubt would have switched the television set to CNN – "a rubber of bridge was demanded." As the odd man out, Aitken doubtless paced around the room restlessly. All of a sudden, he continues, "an immense dispatch box was brought into the room." Churchill produced his skeleton key, opened the box, "and took out from it a single sheet of paper, which seemed singularly disproportionate to the size of the box, just as the paper seemed too big for the brief message typed on it. On that sheet was written the words, 'Germany has declared war on Russia.'"

Instantly, Churchill rang for his valet, stripped out of his dinner jacket and slipped into his lounge coat, and then strode out of the room, not to return. "He asked me to take over his partly-played bridge hand, leaving me, I must add, in an extremely unfavourable tactical position," Aitken recounts.

The political intrigue ended abruptly the next day. As Germany declared its intention of marching through Belgium, the Liberal government closed ranks, making a coalition redundant, at least for the time being. On August 4, when Britain declared war on Germany, only two ministers resigned.

As the bands played and the crowds cheered, Aitken was left searching for something to do. Enlistment was out of the question because of his asthma. The government made it clear that it could manage without his financial advice. During the six weeks of the

Race to the Sea, it was of all people his flamboyant Irish friend
Tim Healy who strengthened his resolve, Aitken tells us.

> It was the most critical moment of the Mons retreat. Healy
> and I left the House of Commons to walk along the Embank-
> ment to the Savoy and get a meal. As we walked, Healy was
> holding forth about the oppression of Ireland and the iniqui-
> ties of British rule. I paid scant attention to what he was
> saying. I had heard it all before. My mind was oppressed by a
> foreboding of disaster – for I had seen a dispatch which had
> just arrived from GHQ In France.
>   At last, we sat down at a teatable in the Embankment Gar-
> dens and I said, "I am tired of hearing about the grievances of
> the Irish – let me tell you something of the perils of the British
> Army."
>   I looked at my companion, and suddenly I saw the tears
> streaming down Healy's cheeks. In a passionate and vehe-
> ment flow of words, he dedicated himself, before God, to the
> service of the Allied cause, as though I was not even there as
> a spectator of his outburst.

In late September, Aitken embarked for Canada in the company of Healy. If an Irish Nationalist could swallow his pride, so
could he. He'd made up his mind what he should do – better yet
what he could do. The British army needed help, but there was no
way he would be allowed to help it. Every bit as much, though,
the Canadian Army needed help and he, with his connections in
London, his energy, his ambition, was in a position to help it –
and, in the process, to become a power in his own land.

15

The Eyewitness – and His Witness

The texture of the war has become ingrained in the whole fabric of national life, and the people are asking for news, not of some small, distant and almost alien army, but of themselves, and of events personal to their interest, comfort and happiness.
Sir Max Aitken. A report to Prime Minister Sir Robert Borden, 1916

During his quick visit to Canada in the early autumn of 1914 – he and Tim Healy left England just as the convoy carrying the First Canadian Contingent began heading the other way – Aitken obtained for himself a post best described as that of an unofficial overseas minister of information. As Taylor describes in his biography, he became "the voice of Canada in Great Britain . . . less official and more adroit than the High Commissioner." He was also, inevitably, a good deal more powerful than the luckless incumbent, Sir George Perley.

This time, Aitken didn't so much turn an existing situation to account as invent one for himself. Frustratingly, apart from the official Order-in-Council of January 6, 1915, announcing his appointment, the documentation available, both official and private, does

little to explain how he did this.* Certainly, he harboured a number
of handicaps. The alleged scandal over the Canada Cement merger
was too recent for Prime Minister Borden to have wanted to be
seen to be hand-in-glove with him; Borden, moreover, was a close
friend of Perley and would not have wanted to undermine him in
any way. Lastly, Aitken's most influential ally, Sam Hughes, was
away from Ottawa, having bullied Borden into allowing him to
follow the troops to England; indeed, by way of a fast liner from
New York, having arrived ahead of them. Thereafter Hughes spent
his time attending military reviews and lobbying for a commission
to lead the Canadians in the field, until an exasperated Kitchener
ordered him to return to his duties in Ottawa.

By whatever methods – guile, energy, and a judicious drop-
ping of the names of familiars, such as Kipling and Churchill, perhaps references to possible campaign contributions sprinkled in
as reinforcement – Aitken secured for himself a double appointment which possessed the singular advantage of seeming to be
quite modest while capable of being expanded exponentially. One
was as "Eyewitness" to the Canadian troops in the field. The other
was head of Canadian War Records.

"Eyewitness," in the immediate, mattered most. Hard as it is
now to credit, the Great War had begun with virtually no war correspondents present. Even at the time, this was difficult to credit:
more than half a century earlier, first in the Crimea and later
during the American Civil War, the legendary William Howard Russell of *The Times* had invented the profession, and made himself
famous in the process. At the turn of the century, the flamboyant

---

* While Taylor writes that "Aitken had long talks with Borden," the prime minister's
private diary for October and early November 1914 contains no reports of any meetings between them; indeed, during most of the time Aitken was in Canada, Borden
himself was out of the country, taking a brief respite from the war on a golfing holiday
in Virginia. As late as December 28, Aitken, having jumped the gun, was still scram-
bling. "Section of London Press agrees to give me opportunity to describe Canadian
mobilization in series of illustrated articles and Kipling has promised to help me. May
I have appointment now?" he wired Sam Hughes. On December 31, Nathaniel Curry, a
Canadian businessman in London, applied additional pressure to Sam Hughes. "Max
Aitken is in a bad hole because Bonar Law and F. E. Smith stated he had appointment
as Canadian Eyewitness and statement has been published in his constituency."

Richard Harding Davis, while in Havana, had helped William Randolph Hearst stampede the United States into the Spanish-American War; during the Boer War, the twenty-six-year-old Winston Churchill had managed the double feat of sending dispatches to the *Morning Post* while serving as a subaltern in the South Africa Light Horse. In 1914, though, "the war correspondent did not fit into the propaganda effort," as Phillip Knightley remarks in his definitive history of combat reporting, *The First Casualty*. In the opinion of Lord Kitchener, the Minister of War, reporters were "drunken swabs." He was determined to keep them away from the Front, and was aided, in a neat switching of roles, by Churchill, now First Lord of the Admiralty. "The war is going to be fought in a fog," Churchill pronounced. "The best place for correspondents . . . will be in London." Thus it was not until June 1915 that the first civilian correspondents were accredited, and only then largely because former American President Teddy Roosevelt advised Asquith that the British were losing the propaganda war for lack of realistic reporting from the Front. Almost the only printed reports of the climactic battles of August 1914, of the retreat to Mons, and of the race to the Channel, were those compiled by a British staff officer, one Colonel Ernest Swinton, and released to the press under the byline "Eyewitness." Mostly, Knightley notes, Swinton confined himself to describing the weather. "Fine, with less wind, although the nights now are much colder." As one editor is said to have remarked, "Eyewash would have been a better pseudonym."*

All but certainly, it was F. E. Smith and Bonar Law, with encouragement from Kipling, who put it to Aitken that he should become Canadian Eyewitness, very likely over port and cigars down at Cherkley. In Ottawa, this was translated into the honorary (unpaid) rank of Lieutenant-Colonel, together with the privilege of access to headquarters in France. As the sole source of published information about the doings of Canadian soldiers,

---

* To give Swinton his due, as a sometime writer of Jules Verne-style adventures, he came up with the idea for an armoured "landship" that led ultimately to the development of the tank.

Aitken thus became to the Canadian public (and with a conse-
quent effect upon his influence upon the government), *the* voice
of the war, much as as Edward R. Murrow, was the voice of the
Second World War for Americans.

Aitken's second invented position, as head of Canadian War
Records, was designed to address the gap created by the fact
that, as Taylor comments, while "the British authorities treated
the Canadian contingents merely as reinforcements of the British
army, Canadian ministers wished to maintain their soldiers as a
distinct force." His initial responsibilities were to keep a record of
Canadian casualties, reporting them back to Ottawa, for which no
system then existed independent of the British. Over time, Aitken
expanded the responsibilities involved into everything from the
collection and preservation of the war diaries of all units to engaging photographers and cinematographers and war artists to
record front-line scenes for the sake of eventual history, and,
more immediately, for use in contemporary propaganda.

A third wartime appointment that Aitken later secured for
himself takes us a little ahead of the story, but is best mentioned
here. In September 1915, he was appointed Sam Hughes's personal overseas representative, both in Britain and at the Front.
To all the influence Aitken already exercised as virtual minister of
information, he thus added the direct power of being the virtual
ambassador of Canada's most powerful politician. Since Hughes
was half-mad, it seems curious that so shrewd a judge of character as Aitken should have wanted to serve as his alter ego. The
chance to wield power – needs must when the devil drives –
drew them together. So also did the fact that they were both outsiders, each regarded with suspicion by the establishment, and
that Hughes had stood by Aitken during the Canada Cement
affair. Yet there was more to their relationship than expediency
and loyalty. Like Bonar Law, though in a quite different way,
Hughes was one of those individuals of whom, to the great baffle-
ment of others, Aitken would brook no criticism. The young Janet
Aitken dreaded Sir Sam's frequent visits to Cherkley. "He clanked
about, patronizing people in a loud voice, behaving as if trying to
maintain some popular image of himself," she relates. But long
after Hughes had been sacked by Borden and after Aitken himself

had become Lord Beaverbrook, and moved onto other things, their friendship continued undiminished. A few weeks before the war ended in 1918, Aitken wrote to Hughes, by then retired and in disgrace. "My admiration and affection for you is not disturbed by adversity."

Datelined "In a Flanders Town" – probably Poperinghe, mustering centre for the Ypres Salient – Aitken's first dispatch as "Eyewitness" appeared in papers all over the Dominion on March 27, 1915, three weeks before the Canadians went into action at Second Ypres.

> Picture to yourself a narrow street, the centre paved, the sides of tenacious mud. Line it on each side with houses, rather squalid, and with a few unimportant stores. . . . This town is like many other towns in this unattractive country. Its interest to us lies in the tenants of the moment. Walk down the street and you will, if you are a Canadian, feel at once something familiar and homelike in the atmosphere. One hears voices everywhere, and one does not need the brass shoulder badges "Canada" to know the race to which these voices belong. . . . And soon a company swings by, going perhaps to bath parade, that expeditious process by which in half an hour has cleansed the bathers and fumigated every rag they possess. And as they pass they sing carelessly but with a challenging catch, a song which, if by chance you come from Toronto, will perhaps stir some association, for these or many of them are boys from the college, and the song is a university song. . . .

Even when read today, the passage remains arresting, bristling with well-observed detail, the style forceful and cinematic, clearly the work of a natural reporter, if as yet of a rather cumbersome stylist. (By his own account, Aitken took some tips from Kipling but used mainly as models Robert Louis Stevenson and John Buchan.) In hindsight, it is clear that during his time in Flanders Aitken discovered his genius for popular journalism, foreshadowing all of his later success as a newspaper proprietor.

As was greatly to Aitken's advantage, his knowledge of soldiering – despite his friendship with Hughes, despite his having
married into a military family – could have been inscribed upon
the head of a pin. In the regalia of lieutenant-colonel he cut a
Chaplinesque figure: as a contemporary photograph reveals, his
tunic was too long, his hat far too small for his oversized head,
while his ludicrously large boots accentuated the shortness of his
legs. These deficiencies in appearance and expertise Aitken made
up for in bluff, touring the Front in one of his own Rolls-Royces,
screeching to a halt at regimental encampments, leaping out and
launching a torrent of questions at everyone he encountered,
much as he had once launched questions at Blumenfeld. Officers
with an eye to their own futures were delighted to take him in tow,
and pandering with their flattery. "My dear old fellow, you really

Sir Max Aitken, spring 1915.
He did not cut a splendid military figure, but as official
"Eyewitness" would soon discover his genius for popular
journalism.

are a brick and the way that you stood up to the fire when I took you around with me was splendid," wrote Lieutenant-Colonel David Watson, who later became commander of the Fourth Canadian Division. For many of those who were doing the actual fighting, though, he was a figure of derision. "I hear Max Aitken has been around again, pestering to be shown what a sap is," wrote Agar Adamson to Mabel. Where it counted, none of this mattered. All that mattered, as Aitken well knew, was being surrogate for his audience, asking the kinds of naive questions they would have asked, explaining the remote and alien business of war in language that ordinary Canadians could understand.

"You can picture our army in the field spread out like a fan," he wrote. "The long wavy edge of the fan is the line of men in the firing trenches, at the very forefront of affairs, often within a stone's throw of the opposing German line. Some hundreds of yards behind this firing line lie the support trenches, also filled with men. The men in the firing and support trenches exchange places every forty-eight hours. . . .

"Further back, along the ribs of the fan, one finds the headquarters of many brigades; behind these, headquarters of divisions; then headquarters of army corps, then of armies – the groups becoming fewer and fewer as you proceed – until at the end of the fan handle one reaches the general headquarters, where Field Marshal Sir John French stands, with his hand on the dynamo. . . ."

The dispatch that made Aitken's a household name was his vivid report of the Second Battle of Ypres, the terrible days in late April 1915, when the untried Canadian troops saved the situation by plugging a four-mile break in the allied line while under gas attack. This lengthy report, which appeared on May 1, was carried on front pages not just in Canada but all over the English-speaking world. Couched in the overblown "high diction" of the time, much of what he wrote doesn't stand up that well – "the battle which raged for so many days was bloody, even as men appraise battles in this callous and life-engulfing war. But as long as brave deeds retain the power to fire the blood of Anglo-Saxons, the stand made by the Canadians in those desperate days will be told by fathers to their sons," for example. Yet he retained his instinctive, journalistic appreciation of the power of the particular. He dared to tell at least some of the truth. "They suffered terrible casualties," he wrote. "For a short time, every other man seemed to fall. . . . The 4th Canadian Battalion at one moment came under a particularly withering fire. For a moment – not more – it wavered. Its most gallant Commanding Officer, Lieutenant-Colonel Birchall, carrying, after an old fashion, a light cane, coolly and cheerfully rallied his men and at the very moment when the example had infected them, fell dead." In this passage, Aitken set another precedent: this was the first occasion in which the name of an actual person had been given in a published dispatch from the Front. He not only created the precedent, he repeated it and amplified it into a kind of printed memorial to all the dead husbands and sons and lovers. "Lt.-Colonel Beecher was killed by a high explosive shell; Lt. C. A. James was killed by a mine; . . . Lt. Gordon was soon wounded and was afterwards killed; . . . Sergeant-Major Fraser was killed instantly by a bullet in the head."

Ironically, there is reason to suspect that this report was not all it appeared on the surface. The dateline, "Canadian Divisional Headquarters in Flanders, April 30, via London" does not scan with a report carried in the Ottawa *Journal* on May 7, noting that Aitken had been invalided home on April 24, suffering from "a severe attack of pneumonia." "As the battle began around that date," the *Journal* continued, "Sir Max Aitken was apparently not the author of the fight of the Canadian division." Perhaps – to give Aitken the benefit of the doubt – he really had been ill and Kipling had come to the rescue by constructing the report out of official War Office dispatches and first-hand accounts from survivors arriving in Britain. Or perhaps Aitken's pneumonia was psychosomatic, and he himself wrote the dispatch well away from the sound of the guns and the threat of a gas attack that for an asthmatic would have been all the more terrifying. It can be ventured that he realized at Ypres that although so daring in finance and politics, he was not gifted with physical courage. "Under his assertive exterior he was all nerves," writes Taylor, albeit in another context. "When the going got tough, Max often got sick," write Armstrong and Nelles. Telling also is that Aitken was painfully sensitive about wearing a uniform without taking part in the action. Indeed, on November 1, 1915, he wired Sam Hughes a request to be transferred to active service. "If recommended, I will gladly go to Canada and recruit my own battalion in New Brunswick." Within forty-eight hours, however, the request was withdrawn. "Please cancel my telegram as I am not suited to command a double company and Bonar Law and F. E. Smith have persuaded me to leave matters in abeyance."

What *is* certain is that shortly after Ypres, Aitken ceased writing "Eyewitness" reports, substituting instead a weekly press communiqué that was assembled by a succession of surrogates, among them Major R. F. Manly-Sims, a businessman from Port Arthur who was also a former British regular; Captain Theodore G. Roberts, younger brother of the New Brunswick writer, Charles G. D. Roberts; and later, Talbot Papineau. In London, he edited the dispatches into a book titled *Canada in Flanders* and published it at his own expense. (At 25¢ a copy it went through fourteen editions, the proceeds of $4,000 donated to the Canadian Red Cross.) Later, although Aitken made frequent short visits to Canadian headquarters as Hughes's representative, and maintained an establishment there, he seldom if ever returned to the front lines.*

Certain also is that from the summer of 1915 onwards, Aitken shifted the focus of his energies from Flanders to the corridors of power in London. His personal political base was the Hyde Park Hotel; his administrative nerve centre an eight-room suite of offices at Number 3 Lombard Street in the City, formerly his financial headquarters, provided rent-free to the Canadian government.

---

* During this period, Aitken frequently made his quarters available to Winston Churchill. Indeed, as Churchill's official biographer, Martin Gilbert has noted, their "lifelong intimacy" dates from this time. After the debacle of Gallipoli, for which he had been responsible as First Lord of the Admiralty, Churchill had seemingly thrown up his political future to command the 9th Battalion of the King's Royal Rifle Corps in the trenches. "At St. Omer, Aitken gave Churchill renewed hope in his future," Gilbert writes. "He never forgot how at that moment, when almost everyone else seemed against him, Aitken held out the hand of hospitality and hope."

As Hughes's overseas representative, he also had a room in the War Office. In the description of one observer, the sum of these parts "might almost have been a corps headquarters in the field. . . . It was as if Aitken had clandestinely built up a simulacrum of Sir Sam Hughes' office in Ottawa, where place-hunters, contractors, officials, politicians and pressmen came and went all day. What you had heard and saw at Ottawa, you heard and saw here. It was, in effect, the real centre and immediate source of authority of the Canadian Corps in Europe."

The observer in question was Henry Beckles Willson. Then in his middle forties, he was a tall, dapper honorary major who worked in the War Records Office as Aitken's second-in-command during the late winter and spring of 1916. No more than R. D. Blumenfeld is Willson remembered now, but at the time, to give him his due, he was a well-known popular historian and literary entrepreneur with a shelf-full of books to his credit, including a biography of Lord Strathcona and a Cartier-to-Riel tour through Canadian history titled *The Romance of Canada*. Willson was also a pioneer of what we now call the Heritage Movement. In the early years of the century, during the course of a long expatriate spell in England, he leased and refurbished Quebec House, the tall gabled red-brick manor at Westerham in Kent, where James Wolfe had spent part of his boyhood, collected much Wolfe memorabilia, still to be seen there to this day, and successfully conducted a subscription campaign to erect a statue of Wolfe on Westerham Green. Later, on his return to Canada, Beckles Willson bought Clifton, a handsome clapboard mansion at Windsor, Nova Scotia, once the home of Thomas Chandler Haliburton, creator of Sam Slick, and turned that into a literary shrine. Today, Quebec House is operated by Britain's National Trust; Clifton, which has been refurbished in recent years, is one of Nova Scotia's most popular historic sites.

It's as a compulsive diarist, though, that Beckles Willson merits his place in this story. As an historian, like most at that time, he was overblown and under-researched. But as a recorder of his own life, and of those who passed through it, he crackled with energy, frequently with gunpowder, occasionally with remarkable insight. The best example is a description of Sir Wilfrid Laurier that better than any other, reveals a central aspect of his character. The year was 1897; the Lauriers were in London for Queen Victoria's Diamond Jubilee celebrations; as a rising star in the Canadian community, Willson had been deputized to show them the sights:

> One day I accompanied them to the Tower of London, where the Premier rather surprised me by his utter unresponsiveness. In vain he was shown this and that memorial, relic and historic site; he seemed sufficiently familiar with the names of the characters and various deeds or events commemorated, but if he showed any emotion at all it was that of distaste, even repulsion . . .
>
> That evening, he said to me as we were going out to dinner, "That Tower of London was terrible. It brought back to my mind all that I have ever read of the terror, or the cruelty, the human suffering of past ages. That such tyranny, such bloody customs could ever have existed is painful to me. How could the world – which must have contained tens of thousands of sensible, right-thinking men, have tolerated all that bigotry and cruelty and abuse of power?"
>
> This conversation let a flood of light into the recesses of Laurier's mind. It convinced me of his utter aversion to all violence, to the martial pageantry of the past, to all conquests, however picturesque, or the triumphs of ambition and personal aggrandisment. His idea of fighting was with words; the fierce clash of principle, and the only heroism he really admired was moral heroism.

Like Agar Adamson, Beckles Willson belonged to the generation of Canadians who thought of themselves as "Overseas Englishmen." (In fact, Willson can be credited with coining that phrase: in 1924, he published a book titled *England: By an Overseas Englishman* that won praise from Kipling and Dean Inge of St. Paul's.) But he was also a nascent Canadian nationalist. Born in Montreal in 1869, the son of an official with the Allan Steamship Line, he was brought up there and in Port Colborne, Ontario, and, though skimpily educated, decided when still in his teens that he was destined to be a writer. In 1892, already the author of a novel, he crossed the Atlantic to try his luck as a free-lance journalist at the seat of Empire. "That was not the full extent of my audacity," he tells us in his 1929 memoir, *From Quebec to Piccadilly*. "I meant to treat only Canadian themes." No more a century ago than nowadays was such a plan viable – Canada was "remote, frozen, and dull," he was quickly informed by an editor – yet Willson achieved fair success, churning out a steady stream of features on such topics as the bookshops and markets of London, many of which he illustrated himself with pen-and-ink sketches, for publications that included the *Pall Mall Gazette* and the prestigious *Strand Magazine,* where his pieces sometimes shared the same issue with the latest instalment of

Henry Beckles Willson, a Canadian journalist and historian, worked at the War Records Office in 1916 as an honorary major. His good looks and suave manner had ensured his swift rise in society. Luckily for posterity, Beckles Willson was also a compulsive diarist.

Sherlock Holmes. He also produced a book nearly every year, including a romance titled *My Friend, the Little Cantatrice,* based on the career of the Canadian-born diva, Madame Albani, and a volume of verse titled *Drift.*

Equally impressive was Beckles Willson's success as a social operator. Propelled by a charming, if somewhat obsequious manner, and by exceptional good looks in the slender, smooth-featured, elegantly pompadoured style most admired during the 1890s, he moved onward and upward through London drawing rooms. In 1896, a full-length portrait of him by the fashionable painter Richard Jack adorned the Royal Academy exhibition. (By coincidence, a portrait of Mabel Cawthra by the Toronto artist Wyly Grier, was also featured in that year's Royal Academy.) That same year, Beckles Willson caught the eye of Alfred Harmsworth, the future Lord Northcliffe, who sent him on a five-month tour of Canada to produce a series of articles for the *Daily Mail.* Among other interesting footnotes to history, Willson noted privately that while Sir William Van Horne of the CPR "strikingly resembled Bismarck," he was "painfully embarrassed by women," and that Van Horne's second-in-command, the future Lord Shaughnessy, was "a plump, florid little man, wholly without culture, but possessing many social pretensions." The tour also included the independent colony of Newfoundland, where Willson's observation of St. John's as "a community divided into optimists and pessimists of the Hibernian type, than whom there are no more extravagant on earth," rings as true now as it did then. His fortnight in Newfoundland also produced enough material for an instant book, *The Tenth Island*; it may well have been Willson's description of "large areas of timber in the interior, suitable for woodpulp," that led a decade later, to Northcliffe's establishment of the paper-making town of Grand Falls.

For most of the next decade, Willson continued to flourish. At Laurier's suggestion, he wrote a two-part history of the Hudson's Bay Company that, by his account, the prime minister would have liked to have undertaken himself had he not been otherwise occupied. He also acquired an attractive and intelligent Canadian wife – the former Ethel Dudley of Port Colborne – and fathered three sons. Yet, sometime about 1909, the year he turned forty, both

Willson's career and his personal life began going awry. He fell out with Northcliffe. He fell out with his landlord at Quebec House. Indeed, for reasons not easily fathomed, it soon became Willson's destiny to fall out with everybody, including, eventually, much of his own family. Perhaps, as one of his grandsons suggests, "all the latent defects in his character began to overtake all his energy and ability." Perhaps the hard scrabble of making a living as a literary hack, constantly having to kow-tow to the rich and the famous, had exacerbated a natural tendency towards deviousness and resentfulness, and a capacity for taking umbrage that bordered on paranoia. In any event, Beckles Willson's return to Canada in the spring of 1913 was more in the nature of a retreat than a triumph, even though – "the thought of playing a part in the making of a new and vigorous school of Canadian letters had never left me" – he put a brave nationalistic face on it. Nor did his new life in Nova Scotia bring peace of mind. Inevitably, he got on none too well with his neighbours. Many of the expensive improvements he made to Clifton went up in smoke on the first cold night in October, when he was foolish enough to light "the great open fireplace in the library" without first checking the chimneys; only the last-minute arrival of the fire brigade saved the house from complete destruction. The following year his ambitious plan for a cross-country Canadian Club tour lecturing on "Canada's Undeveloped Literary Resources," foundered after a single appearance in Montreal. "The war intervened," he informs us. "National patriotism came to occupy itself with concerns of greater urgency and moment than literature."

Beckles Willson was now on his uppers. In sheer desperation, he set out for Ottawa, using the last of his savings to rent a suite in the Roxborough Apartments for the sake of appearances, and began a search for patriotic employment. One who befriended him but was in no position to help, was his next-door neighbour in the Roxborough, Mackenzie King. (In his own diary for 1915, King twice mentions spending the evening with Willson.) Others – when need be, Willson could still be as ingratiating as of old – were the Duke and, more particularly, the Duchess of Connaught. "She was very gracious and voluble," he noted on February 22, 1915, adding the interesting information, "She took whiskey at lunch." In the end, it was Sam Hughes, whom he had bombarded with a constant stream of memos, who came to the rescue. Out of the blue, on a sub-zero Sunday morning just after New Year's in 1916, came a summons to the office of the Minister of Militia. Willson's depiction of Hughes in action, scribbled in haste immediately after their meeting, takes us right into the presence of that astonishing figure.

> The man is five feet, eight inches high, of a square sturdy build, a thick neck, strong jaw and firm lipless mouth. His features suggest the Roman Caesars. His eyes are grey beneath beetling brows and his hair, which is cropped close, silver white. His voice is rough and imperious; when he smiles he shows small regular teeth. And with the smile, his expression undergoes a marked change, he grows benignant, even humorous, but at the same time more vulgar. His attitudes are ungainly and heavy, clapped into a black gown and tonsured, he might pass for a coarse but resolute Irish priest of the Middle Ages. . . .

The religious reference was clearly intended to be ironic, for, as Willson continued:

> He received me cordially, even boisterously . . . he began leaning back in his chair with one foot on the desk. "I have always been interested in history, especially the old religious wars of the middle ages. The bloody bigotry of the priests was appalling . . . Those goddamn priests were at the bottom of all those wars. They wanted to fix the human mind in a groove; I always taught that it should have free play. I taught school for twenty years and that was the secret of my success . . . I come on my mother's side of Huguenot stock; all Samuels are Huguenot – take Samuel de Champlain, they try to make out he was a bigoted Catholic . . . Champlain was no more papist than Henry of Navarre . . ."
>
> During the monologue he was occasionally interrupted by telephone messages, one from a member of his family. His face lit up and he chuckled fatuously. "Is that you Winnie, how is

my little grand-daughter this morning?" Then at last he informed me that he had heard from Sir Max Aitken. "He wants you," he said. "Pack up and get ready."

The rank of honorary major that Hughes had conferred was a good deal better than Beckles Willson had hoped for: better yet, it carried an annual salary of $4,000, more than enough to support him and his family comfortably. As second-in-command at the War Records Office, he would be privy to history in the making; with luck he would also have the opportunity to write it. Mackenzie King, by Willson's account, longed to be in his shoes, or said he did. "Bidding me farewell he said feelingly, 'How I envy you your good fortune.'" The Governor General, upon whom Willson called on the last day he was in Ottawa, was equally effusive. "The Duke spoke to me very kindly and paternally, saying that I now had a chance to distinguish myself in my own line, and perform a useful service to the country."

Then Connaught added a word of warning of considerable prescience, except that it applied equally to the person to whom he was saying it. "'I fear,' said His Royal Highness, 'Sir Max isn't quite a gentleman.'"

In the beginning, everything went swimmingly. On February 12, 1916, Willson's first day in London, "a damn fine martial figure" in his new major's uniform, he went round by appointment to the Hyde Park Hotel. "Punctually at ten, I presented myself and found Sir Max breakfasting in bed. He greeted me cordially, a bullet-headed, dull-skinned little man; his laughter and manner very boyish. Seeing that I was in the dark about my position, he proceeded to enlighten me. The collection and co-ordinating and précising of the War diaries of battalions, brigades and divisions had been neglected and this work would be entrusted to me." Despite Connaught's warning, Willson was charmed. "It appears he has purchased copies of several of my works, and having read them carefully decided I could be of use to him . . . I saw him in a fresh and far more favourable light."

On the following day, Aitken introduced Beckles Willson to the offices at Lombard Street. "I found he had converted his entire business staff into a military organization. The head clerk had metamorphosed into a uniformed sergeant-major, the book-keeper a sergeant, and there were two or three other sergeants, corporals and lance-corporals, all under the strictest military discipline." In charge of the staff was a former British journalist, Captain Wilfred Holt-White. An official photographer, Captain H. E. Knobel had already been appointed; plans were underway for engaging a cinematographer to take films of the troops in the trenches; an entire unit was engaged in producing a daily newspaper, the *Canadian Daily Record,* condensing military and home news for the troops in the trenches. "I confess I was little prepared for such a scene of activity," Willson relates. "The personnel were all working at high pressure, examining files, typing out documents, coding and decoding messages which were constantly brought in by dispatch-bearers."

Willson's own job was to set up the historical section. Mostly, this involved sorting out and classifying a huge mass of paper – everything from leave forms to medical records that had been piling up in confusion for well over a year. More importantly, it involved negotiating with the British War Office for release of the documents most crucial to history: the daily war diaries compiled by 112 individual Canadian units. Since the British refused at first to relinquish these, Willson had to find a way of getting them copied. With immense difficulty, he managed to persuade Harry Biggar, the Canadian archivist attached to the High Commission, to second his staff of female copyists, only to discover that the Public Records Office at Chancery Lane had no ladies' lavatories. That delicate problem resolved by having at last got the War Office to agree to letting the diaries be removed on loan to Lombard Street, he encountered another difficulty: none of the female copyists knew how to type. "All their transcribing work is written out, because forsooth, in Biggar's opinion, 'typewriting is not permanent writing!'"

Inevitably, there were moments of friction between these two super-egoists. Late in February, Willson relates, "an unpleasant quarter of an hour took place, when Sir Max suspected me of a desire to undermine him." Mostly, though, in these early days they warmed to each other, and even began to develop a mutual admiration. In a personal letter to Borden, Aitken went out of his way to to commend Willson's "zeal and knowledge." Willson, for his part, enjoyed being so close to someone so clearly in the know and in touch with the mighty. "I overheard today conversations between Sir Max and Bonar Law on the telephone," he reports with satisfaction early in March. "My new chief is certainly a most forceful personality." Perhaps some of their rapport derived from an occasional swapping of confidences about women: with his wife safely back in Nova Scotia, Willson had embarked upon a series of brief encounters, most notably with a co-operative divorcée named Narcissa.

In any event, on March 27, 1916, after a busy morning of précis-writing, and an afternoon spent revising proofs for a new edition of *Canada in Flanders*, Beckles Willson received a call from Aitken asking him to join him post-haste at the Marlborough Club. Going in, he was surprised to see Lieutenant-General Sir Edwin Alderson, Commander of the Canadian Corps, rushing out with a black look on his face. Clearly, something was up. "Confidentially, M. A. told me that Alderson had been with him for an hour, that the feud between him and Sir Sam Hughes cannot now be healed. 'I fear,' he continued, 'that Alderson must lose his command.'"

Perhaps the real bond that drew Aitken and Beckles Willson together, if only temporarily, was that both of them were addicted to conspiracy and intrigue. Now, after so many years of imagining and inventing conspiracies, Henry Beckles Willson was about to be eyewitness to a real one.

16

The Destruction of General Alderson

Canadian politics has been too strong for all of us.
Lieutenant-General Edwin Alderson, 1916

T he conspiracy that Beckles Willson watched hatching at the Marlborough Club in late March 1916 came to its dénouement less than a month later. On April 22 Aitken crossed the Channel to France. He motored to Château Beaurepaire, the handsome eighteenth-century mansion just outside Montreuil that General Haig had recently commandeered for his personal headquarters, for a private meeting with the Commander-in-Chief. By the time the meeting was over, Aitken had secured Haig's agreement to dismiss General Alderson as Canadian Corps Commander.

Even by Aitken's own standards, this was an act of extraordinary daring. "I was speaking on behalf of the civil power of the Dominion to a British commander in the field on a matter relating to generals directly under his command," he wrote later. In fact, Aitken was speaking on behalf of no one. Back in Ottawa, Prime Minister Borden knew nothing of what was happening until after it had happened. Indeed, unbelievably, except that we have Borden's own word for it, several months passed before the prime minister realized that Alderson had not agreed to resign, but had been summarily and brutally given the sack.*

---

* In his memoir, published posthumously in 1938, Borden records that on June 16, 1916, he had written to Alderson: "I am glad to know that the Canadian Army Corps had done so well under your command. We realize that at the time when you resigned the command the portion of the line was both difficult and important . . .

"In acknowledging my letter, General Alderson pointed out he had not resigned . . . I discovered that he was correct."

Aitken's destruction of Alderson sheds a good deal of light on his character: the cold-blooded mastery of destabilization techniques that would later lead him to admire the same aptitude in Stalin; the uninhibited pleasure he often took in being a bully; the implacable egocentricity with which he pursued his objectives. Yet it demonstrates also Aitken's brilliant grasp of *realpolitik* and the accuracy of his judgement. In dismissing Alderson he was acting, within the short run, for all the wrong reasons. In the long run, though, he was doing the right thing. By 1916, it had become evident that Edwin Alderson, for all his personal gallantry and devotion to duty, was no longer the right man to command the Canadians in the field.

Back in October 1914, assuming command of the First Contingent at dockside in Plymouth, Alderson had seemed the very model of a modern lieutenant-general. Certainly, from the point of view of both Borden and Kitchener, he was the best choice available, given that no Canadian generals had anything like the necessary experience, and anything was better than having to grant Sam Hughes his wish to lead "his boys" into battle. Then in his mid-fifties, a short dapper figure with a bushy moustache, Alderson had distinguished himself at Tel-el-Kebir, passed first in tactics at the Army Staff College, and had commanded mounted rifles in South Africa, some Canadians among them. Not yet apparent, though, was that Alderson was an archetypal officer of the old school, as evidenced by the fact that his patron and mentor was that military dinosaur, the Duke of Connaught, whose eye he had caught at Tel-el-Kebir. More to the immediate point, he lacked the nous and the political adroitness to accommodate himself to the specialized circumstances of his command: a senior British officer, he would be in charge of someone else's troops, not docile native soldiers as in the Sudan or India, who would never answer back, but chippy white Colonials. There was also, as Borden wrote later, "a distinctive difference between the spirit and outlook of the Canadian volunteer soldier and 'Tommy Atkins' of the regular army. General Alderson seemed quite incapable of appreciating this. He sometimes ordered the troops on parade an hour or so before he was ready

Lieutenant-General Edwin Alderson was Commander of the Canadian Corps from September 1914 to May 1916, but Canadian politics would soon prove "too strong" for him.

to review them. In the meantime, he would enjoy a nap. This was known and not appreciated." Above all, Alderson had the sheer bad luck to find himself plunked into the same small pool with a couple of sharks – Hughes and Aitken.

The trouble began on Salisbury Plain. Horrified by the Canadian equipment that Hughes had selected – hundreds of farm wagons with a turning circle far too wide for narrow country roads; boots that literally disintegrated in the mud; twenty-five thousand useless entrenching tools known as "MacAdam Shovels," an adaptation of a Swiss army invention for which Hughes's personal secretary Ena MacAdam had taken out the Canadian patent – Alderson ordered most of it scrapped. Even more, he was horrified by the officers. Many were incompetent and some had been "very drunk," he wrote Connaught. "They seem to have been pitchforked about, often by word of mouth, in many cases claims to seniority are merely, 'The Minister told me to go and take it up.'"

At Second Ypres six months later, Alderson performed competently if unimaginatively. "Rather than initiating action, he was usually to be found reacting, often belatedly, to enemy moves," writes the military historian, Daniel Dancocks, in his comprehensive study of the battle, *Welcome to Flanders Fields*. One reason for this was that Alderson was badly served by his subordinates – most particularly, as luck would have it, by two of Hughes's favourites: Brigadier-General Richard Turner, and Turner's brigade major, Garnet Hughes, the minister's eldest son and the apple of his eye. On the first day of battle, before the position of their brigade at Mouse Trap Farm near St. Julien had even been attacked, Garnet Hughes sent an urgent message to Alderson: "Our left driven back and apparently whole line forced back to St. Julien."

Alderson in fact held the line. But Hughes managed to convince himself that Turner and Garnet had been the heroes of the battle and Alderson the villain. "I can see no hope with Alderson in command of our boys," he wrote Borden. As the next best thing, he began lobbying ceaselessly for the promotion of both men, bombarding Aitken, now his official representative, with a daily barrage of cables demanding that Turner be given command of the new Second Canadian Division, and Garnet appointed to lead its Fourth Brigade. In the matter of Turner, a popular hero in Canada ever since winning the VC in South Africa, Alderson bowed to the inevitable. "I do not consider him really fit to command a Division but Canadian politics have been too strong for all of us and so he has got it," he wrote to a friend. But at Garnet, he drew the line, though, alas, not without wavering. First he indicated to Aitken that he was prepared to give Garnet the coveted brigade. He then changed his mind. "I am told that it has been published in the Canadian papers that I personally asked for (Garnet) Hughes to be made a Brigadier," he wrote Aitken. "I did not do so . . . I did not think that Hughes had the necessary experience." By this letter, the luckless Alderson managed to open up a second front against himself. It was Aitken who had leaked the information about Garnet's impending promotion. He was now severely embarrassed. "Unfortunately General Alderson was most inconsistent," he wrote Borden, "and afterwards talked indiscreetly."

The decisive confrontation between Alderson and Hughes was over the notorious Ross Rifle, Hughes's personal pride and joy. At Ypres, hundreds of soldiers had flung away these weapons, superb for target practice but far too delicate to be used in a war, and had picked up Lee Enfields from British corpses. As soon as the battle ended, Alderson asked his brigade and battalion commanders to report on their experience with the Ross. A few officers – mostly Hughes's friends – reacted favourably. Otherwise reaction was hostile. "The men have lost confidence in the Ross," one officer wrote. "It is nothing short of murder to send our men against the enemy with such a weapon," wrote another.

To get rid of the Ross, Alderson commissioned a series of tests matching it against the Lee Enfield and then sent the results to General Gwatkin, chief of staff in Ottawa. The Lee Enfield, the report stated, fired from 100 to 125 rounds as rapidly as possible. The Ross jammed from the twenty-fifth to the fiftieth round. In a strongly worded accompanying letter, Alderson pointed out that the official report had actually flattered the Ross. "It does not state, as was the case, that the hands of the men using the Ross were cut and bleeding, owing to the difficulty they had in knocking back the bolt."

When Hughes read the letter, he exploded with defensive outrage. He replied directly to Alderson with a volley of insults, and took the extraordinary step of sending copies to every Canadian unit commander, brigadier, and major-general overseas. He then took ship for England to settle the matter once and for all, if not of the Ross then of Alderson.

Such was the situation on March 27, 1916, when Beckles Willson was summoned to meet Aitken at the Marlborough Club, arriving just in time to see Alderson storming out. By then, Willson relates,

Sam Hughes and his staff arriving in London, *circa* 1916. He and Alderson had quarrelled bitterly over the notorious Ross Rifle, and Hughes had set out for London to have it out with him. By this time, however, Hughes's own days were numbered.

Hughes had advanced upon London and was ensconced in a suite at the Ritz, accompanied by an entourage that included his military aide, Captain John Bassett, and "2 or 3 extremely plain females, including the celebrated Miss Ena MacAdam, who apparently compose his travelling harem." To this point, the principal adversaries had yet to meet. "Alderson will not call upon Hughes unless he is sent for, and Sir Sam says he is damned if he will send for him," Willson reports. Aitken, meanwhile, was engaged in an uncharacteristic attempt at diplomacy. Knowing that an open row could damage army morale and upset public opinion, he'd scheduled a dinner in honour of Hughes at the Marlborough on the following evening, and had also invited Alderson to this neutral ground. To Aitken's great fury, the general refused to attend. Instead, he and Aitken had met privately for a conversation that had only made matters worse. "The general had called upon Max for his good offices, whereupon the latter had told him plainly, 'I am sorry General, but please understand I am first, last and all times with the Minister,'" Willson recounts.

Aitken had concluded his description of this stormy meeting with the ominous words, "I fear that Alderson must lose his command."

Deciding to get rid of the general was one thing; actually disposing of him quite another. Neither Kitchener nor Haig had any quarrel with Alderson, indeed, only a month previously, he'd been honoured with a knighthood. As a further complication, events conspired to remove Hughes himself from the scene. On March 31, he received an urgent cable from Borden, summoning him home immediately to face serious charges in the Commons related to the awarding of munitions contracts. "Owing to the minister's impending departure, everything at the office is in a turmoil," Beckles Willson noted in his diary. "Sir Sam very pale and worried." There was just time for the two co-conspirators, Hughes and Aitken, to hold a last council of war at Cherkley Court on Sunday, April 2. Luckily for posterity, Willson, now at the peak of his intimacy with Aitken, was also week-ending there and was privy to part of the conversation. "It was on this day that I first heard the name of General Sir Julian Byng mentioned," he relates. "Sir Sam asked me if I knew anything about him. I said I thought he was a competent cavalry officer with quite an unusual amount of character and initiative. The minister's only comment was, 'He's a lord's son, ain't he?'" Other imperial officers were mentioned, Willson added, "which made me certain that Alderson's supersession had been resolved upon."

Less than a week later, the fortunes of war played directly into Aitken's hands. Under General Turner's command, the Second Division got into terrible trouble at St. Eloi, just as Alderson had feared it would. Misreading the evidence of aerial photographs, Turner made a series of blunders, including misdirecting his

artillery fire. The result was the worst Canadian setback of the war
so far. Nearly 1,400 men were lost. Alderson made up his mind that
Turner had to go, and so advised his two superiors, Hughes and
Haig. Militarily, he was wholly correct; politically, he had signed
his own death warrant. "At issue was not competence but nationality," writes the historian Desmond Morton in his study of Canada's
overseas command, *A Peculiar Kind of Politics*.

From Turner in France, Aitken received an anguished cable
asking him to come post-haste and intervene. The moment he had
been waiting for was at hand. Arriving at Montreuil on April 22, he
first interviewed General Kiggell, Haig's chief of staff. "When I suggested that Alderson had been deeply prejudiced against Turner
since the battle of Ypres, Kiggell informed me that he would lay
the fact before the Commander-in-Chief," he later reported to
Hughes. Aware of the politics in play, Haig later recorded in his
diary that, "the danger of a serious feud between the Canadians
and the British" had to be weighed against "the retention of a
couple of incompetent commanders." (Haig's second reference
was to Brigadier H. D. B. Ketchen who, in fact, was even more
responsible than Turner for the debacle at St. Eloi.)

The next day Aitken saw Haig in person, the first time the two
had ever met. "After a long interview in which the ground was fully
covered, the CIC informed me . . . that in the circumstances it
would be impossible utterly to retain both Turner and Alderson,"
Aitken continued to Hughes. He and Haig had also arrived at the
conclusion: "General Alderson is incapable of holding the Canadian Division together." In this report, Aitken was being extremely
economical with the truth. In fact, he'd manipulated Haig into
making the decision he wanted while allowing Haig to believe that
he'd reached it entirely on his own. The best guide to what really
happened at Château Beaurepaire is provided by Haig's own diary.
"The Prime Minister of Canada made a personal request that General Turner should not be removed." Borden of course had made
no such request: it had sprung entirely from Aitken's mind and
mouth. As Haig's account further reveals, Aitken had imputed to
Borden thoughts that could not possibly have occurred to the
prime minister. "General Byng would be most acceptable to the
Canadians as successor to Alderson in the field," Haig recorded as

the official Canadian viewpoint expressed by his visitor. In truth, as Borden's own private diary is witness, he himself at that point was scarcely aware of Byng's existence. "Hughes reports that Byng will succeed Alderson, says he is a man of ability and great experience," runs the entry for April 29, 1916.

In later years, in an unaccountable squeamishness, Aitken would deny insistently that he'd had anything to do with Byng's appointment. Indeed, Byng himself, a straight-arrow and undevious soldier, never seems to have made the connection between his posting as commander of the Canadian Corps, announced officially at the end of May, and his close friendship with Aitken's own close friend, R. D. Blumenfeld. "Why am I sent to the Canadians? I don't know a Canadian. Why this stunt?" Byng wrote Blumenfeld on May 26, in a letter quoted by Jeffery Williams, in his definitive biography, *Byng of Vimy*. The answer, provided by Beckles Willson, thanks to his fortuitous presence at the Cherkley Court meeting in early April, was that Aitken had tossed out his name to Hughes as a possible successor to Alderson. In turn, the inspiration for that idea of Aitken's must surely have come from Blumenfeld.

For the luckless Alderson, nothing remained but humiliation. He fought a desperate rearguard action against the inevitable. On April 25, when Haig informed him that the decision had been taken not to fire Turner, he accepted it with good grace. "As a soldier and as a loyal subordinate, I will, as I told the CIC, do all in my power to make the best of the situation," he wrote Aitken. Not until early May, does it seem to have sunk in that he had no choice but to take up the post of Inspector-General of Canadian Troops in Europe that had been offered to him as a face-saver. "If it is really wished that I should do my best to co-ordinate things . . . and generally work for the good of the Canadian forces . . . I am prepared to accept the appointment," he wrote in a subsequent letter. As late as May 14, utterly unaware of the political motives behind his downfall, Alderson seems to have believed that he might yet hang in as commander in the field. He wrote again to Aitken: "I have just come back from seeing Turner, and am writing a line to tell you that he and I shook hands as cordially as we have ever done . . . I do not feel and do not think that Turner feels, that, should I not accept the other appointment offered me, the relationship between him and me would be at all strained." No record exists that Aitken answered any of these letters.

Once in England, Alderson quickly realized that to be Inspector-General of Canadian Troops in Europe was to be in command of nothing. In September 1916, he was given an appointment as an inspector of infantry. He never returned to the Front and died in 1927, a disappointed man. As may have been some consolation, in the summer of 1916, over Hughes's furious protests, the decision was taken to dispense with the Ross Rifle and to equip all four Canadian divisions with the Lee Enfield.

It was done brutally, but it was done well. From the instant of his appointment, Byng demonstrated both the easy rapport with the Canadians that had always eluded Alderson and the steely confidence needed to put Sam Hughes in his place. "The men are too good to be led by politicians," he wrote Blumenfeld. "I want to shove on the Canadians who have proved their worth and get rid of the Bumstunts." One of the first messages he received from Hughes – "Give Garnet the 3rd Division" – was promptly consigned to the wastebasket. Indeed, before much time passed, both Garnet Hughes and General Turner had been eased out of harm's way into desk jobs in London.

History, though, has a way of repeating itself. Alderson, at the very end of his life, could watch Byng, his successor as Canadian Corps commander, suffer much the same kind of political humiliation that he had once endured. In 1921, as the hero of Vimy, Byng was appointed Governor General of Canada. Five years later, having run afoul of Mackenzie King, he departed a broken man. The parallels between the two situations aren't exact, nevertheless, just as Alderson's fatal decision to fire General Turner had been perfectly correct, equally correct but equally lethal was Byng's decision to refuse King's demand for dissolution of a minority Parliament soon after an election, without the Leader of the Opposition having been given the chance to form a government. No matter the constitutional rights and wrongs of this affair, King managed to exploit it to give himself

Lieutenant-General Sir Julian Byng. His rising star crossed Alderson's on the way down. In June 1916, Byng became Commander of the Canadian Corps and the following spring led Canadians to victory at Vimy Ridge. In 1921, now Lord Byng of Vimy, he became Governor General of Canada. Eventually, though, he too would fall victim to "Canadian politics."

what he most wanted – an election-winning issue, and, as an incidental by-product of this accomplishment, to ensure that no future Governor General would ever again dare meddle in politics. Common to both situations was that, however self-interestedly, Aitken and King spoke for a new nation determined to be born, while Alderson and Byng, like the Duke of Connaught and Colonel Stanton before them, represented a dying imperial past.

A month after sacking Alderson, Aitken disposed of another victim. This time the axe fell on Henry Beckles Willson. "It is manifest now that Max and I cannot go on together," Willson wrote in his diary on May 26, 1916.

Given Willson's erratic temperament, something like this was bound to happen eventually. It's hard, therefore, to fault Aitken for getting rid of him. Yet, for all his self-destructiveness, this oddly engaging character deserves to be given a proper exit. In order to do so, it is necessary to introduce a new arrival at the War Records Office, who served as *deus-ex-machina* in the affair. He was Arthur George Doughty, like Willson an honorary major, but more importantly, the Dominion Archivist. Then in his mid-fifties, he was a donnish but imposing presence, with an awesome reputation for wheedling archival treasures, including Lord Durham's papers, out of the stately attics of England. Now, Doughty had wheedled his honorary commission directly from Borden in order to see for himself what Aitken was up to. Fiercely protective of his territory, and incensed about the denuding of his

Arthur Doughty, later Sir Arthur Doughty, Dominion Archivist. He was renowned for his ability to wheedle archival treasures out of the stately attics of England. During the war, he served as an honorary major and triggered the downfall of Henry Beckles Willson.

own London office – the dozen female copyists now working for Beckles Willson – he also intended to assert his control over war records. It was imperative to "save the material from which a true account of the share of Canada in the war could be written . . . so that we shall not depend on men such as Sir Max Aitken," he'd told a friend shortly before leaving Canada. On Monday, May 1, Doughty marched unannounced into the Lombard Street premises, "looking, with his CMG ribbon, like a weather-beaten, war-worn army veteran," in Willson's description. Straight away, Doughty announced that all Canadian records – civil, naval, and military – belonged to him by right of statute. "I shall never forget Aitken's face as we stared at one another," reports Willson. "I forget who burst into laughter first."

If Aitken laughed confidently, Willson should have done so uneasily. As fellow historians – Doughty too was an author, his most recent production a biography of the Quebec heroine, Madeleine de Verchères – they had known each other for years, but they'd never got on. To Willson, a maverick living by his wits, the archivist, with his rank and position and friends in high places, represented the establishment, both despised and intimidating. (Doughty's social network put even Aitken's in the shade. As recorded in his diary, his agenda for just that week included meetings with two former tenants of Rideau Hall, Earl Grey and the widowed Lady Minto, and an appointment with Lord Kitchener.) As for Doughty, he regarded Willson as an opportunist whose methods were dubious. Already, he had called upon Lady Strathcona, who was furious that two years previously Willson had written her late husband's biography without her permission and had had the gall to claim it was "authorized." "I do not wish to mention his name for fear I might say something I would regret," Lady Strathcona told Doughty.

Destabilized by Doughty's presence, as we would say now, Willson promptly proceeded to live up to his reputation. The following morning, he rushed around to the Hyde Park Hotel before Sir Max was even out of bed. Taking for granted that Doughty would be dealt with much as Alderson had been, Willson impetuously told his employer, as he later recorded in his diary: "Doughty utterly uninformed about Sir Max's position. Doughty

on secret mission to undermine him." But Willson had miscalculated grievously. Aitken always preferred a merger to a battle. He
was far too shrewd an operator not to know that the way to deal
with Doughty was to co-opt him. So he turned on the charm, and,
as always when he did so, he was irresistable. An hour-long conversation the next day ended with Aitken and the archivist the
best of friends. "He is the right man in the right place," Doughty
enthused in his diary. "It is surprising to find how keenly he looks
after the detail of the war records office. I cannot tell whether he
has any motive in view, but whether it is politics or pure patriotism he has evidently taken hold of the job and is determined to
make good." As shrewdly, Aitken had passed to Doughty his opinion that immediately after the war, all records should be transferred to the Public Archives.

Doughty's only quibble with Aitken was a small one. "Am surprised at his estimate of Beckles Willson," he recorded. "Thinks
he is reliable and energetic."

Within days, the most useful relationship that Willson had
forged since his days with Northcliffe had begun to disintegrate.
Suddenly it was Doughty rather than he who was invited down to
Cherkley for weekends, to admire the autographed editions of
Kipling and play tennis with Bonar Law. Feeling himself slipping
down a hole, Willson frantically dug down deeper. He stormed in
to Aitken to tell him that Doughty's great ambition was "to write a
history of the war and replace the name of Sir Max with his own."
He even tried to enlist Doughty as an ally, telling him, as Doughty
noted, "that he could not work under Sir Max as it was not playing
the game. His reputation as a writer was too great to permit him
to be gilding Sir Max's crown." So reckless was Willson's behaviour that it's impossible not to suspect that for a time he was
close to insanity. "Unhappy man," recorded Doughty of another
conversation. "Cannot explain what he really wants or what he is
doing. Seems suspicious of any person he meets." The last straw
was a disjointed memo to Aitken suggesting that in order "to rec-
tify errors and omissions," in Aitken's own *Canada in Flanders*, he
himself be commissioned to rewrite the entire book from scratch.
Two days later, Aitken called him in to tell him that his services
were no longer required.

Whether out of compassion or practicality – Willson's contract had some months to run – Aitken passed him along to Blumenfeld. He spent most of the summer in Flanders, writing articles for the *Daily Express*. Here, needless to say, there was more trouble. He infuriated Byng by intruding into a conference and demanding that the Corps Commander "paint him a word picture of the deeds of the Canadians." He infuriated Agar Adamson and Hamilton Gault by writing a piece about the Patricias that was riddled with errors. By September, Aitken had reached the limits of his patience. "I have gone out of my way to endeavour to find him suitable employment," he wrote Borden. "Mr. Willson, however, has defied my best efforts on his behalf."

Resilient and inventive as well as self-destructive, Beckles Willson managed somehow to survive. He cobbled his Flanders articles into a serviceable little book, *In the Ypres Salient*, that, no doubt to Aitken's annoyance, won praise from Kipling. He persuaded a London publisher to commission an anthology titled *O Canada*, a collection of light verse and humorous sketches supposedly written by men and officers at the Front, but in fact produced entirely by Willson himself. In 1917, he talked himself into a job with the War Office, collecting war trophies, many of which are now in the Imperial War Museum in London. The last year of the war found him in Jerusalem, where he scored a coup by acquiring the Turkish flag that had been lowered in surrender to General Allenby. Soon after the Armistice, he lunched with T. E. Lawrence in Paris and recorded, "He was almost impish in his behaviour and utterly careless whether his remarks were overheard or not. Indicating Premier Hughes of Australia who was sitting at an adjacent table, he said, 'There's a b———' loud enough to make me squirm," Lawrence also showed him his famous Turkish rifle, "a naked short fat weapon whose stock bore a series of minute notches. 'Each notch represents a dead Turk,' he remarked callously. He might have been a Sinn Fein gunman."

After the war, Willson settled in the South of France where, unlike Canada, living was cheap. He eked out a living as a writer, producing as his most notable achievement a 1924 novel titled *Redemption* in which, thinly disguised as its hero, Gregory Vant,

he attempted to get his own back at Aitken. As an intelligence officer at Canadian Corps headquarters, Vant discovers "the jeal-
ousies, the political interference against which some of the
bravest officers struggled in vain. He learned for the first time of
the deadly toadyism towards insufferable opportunists who were
turning the war to their own advantage and that of their own miserable clique." If Aitken – long since Lord Beaverbrook – read this,
he made no comment. Nor did he say anything about *From
Quebec to Piccadilly*, the 1929 memoir in which Willson took more
potshots at the "wire-pullers . . . centred at the Hyde Park Hotel . . .
who were exploiting the war for all it was worth to themselves."
Ironically, Willson's eldest son, Gordon, had by then started on a
long and rewarding career with the Beaverbrook newspapers. As
a further twist, in 1942, the year of Willson's death, Beaverbook,
by then Minister of Aircraft Production, personally selected his
old enemy's son as one of his chief propaganda writers.

After Beckles Willson's stormy departure, peace descended on
Lombard Street. Aitken devoted much of his time to completing
the second volume of *Canada in Flanders*, a process that involved
much difficulty with the War Office censors, who among many
attempts to prettify the truth, sought to change a sentence that
read, "The presence of wounded men in a crowded trench passes
the limits of horror," to "The presence of wounded men in the
trench makes it far worse."
    But Aitken's course as *de facto* representative of the Cana-
dian government in London was winding towards its natural conclusion. His friend and ally Sam Hughes, badly tarnished by the
scandals over munitions contracts, was clearly on his way out.
Byng, as new Canadian commander, had made it clear that he
would brook no interference from "Bumstunts." Increasingly,
Aitken's attention shifted back to British politics; indeed, in June
1916, Doughty, while weekending at Cherkley had witnessed a key
meeting between Bonar Law and Lloyd George that resulted in the
formation of the second wartime coalition. Yet, it was during this
transitional period that Aitken made perhaps his single most creative contribution to Canadian history. He established the Canadian War Memorials Fund, and thereby established Canada's first
official scheme for patronizing the arts.

The historian Maria Tippett gives a full account of this venture in her book, *Art at the Service of War*. Aitken's genius for popular journalism and for propaganda had always made him appreciate the value of documenting the war visually. "Before we can realize the patience, the exhaustion and the courage of the modern fighting man," he wrote, it was necessary "to see our men climbing out of the trenches." In 1916, a stills photographer and a cinematographer had been added to the War Records staff, a major exhibition of photographs at a London gallery would soon draw huge crowds and the first Canadian film of the war, *The Battle of Courcelette*, had been hugely popular.* Yet no visual record existed of what had happened at Second Ypres, the most important Canadian battle of the war so far. Not only were there no official photographs, there were not even any snapshots, since officers and men were forbidden to carry cameras in their kitbags. In order to illustrate *Canada in Flanders*, Aitken had had to commission after-the-fact drawings and sketches that were less than satisfactory. For a possible second edition, he spoke of purchasing a reconstruction of the PPCLI at Bellewaerde Ridge by the British artist R. B. Wollen. Himself no connoisseur – his own taste is exemplified by the Salvador Dali portrait of his friend James Dunn in the robes of Caesar now hanging in the Beaverbrook Gallery in Fredericton – Aitken, even so, had come to realize that even the best films and photographs could not capture the full truth about the war. As he wrote later, only paintings could provide "the most permanent and vital form in which the great deeds of the Canadian Nation in the war could be enshrined for posterity." So in the autumn of 1916, with the germ of an idea in mind, Aitken called in his close friend Lord Rothermere to help him find a way to report the war on canvas.

The scheme they came up with, a joint exercise in public and private patronage, was far ahead of its time. Out of it came several hundred works of art, including two of the best known icons of the Great War, *Canadian Gun Pit* by Wyndham Lewis and *Void* by

---

* A number of the photographs in this exhibition had, in fact, been faked, including the famous "Over the Top" shots by Ivor Castle, supposedly showing Canadian soldiers at Courcelette. As was noticed by men on leave, the soldiers were shown going into battle with canvas breeches over their rifles.

CANADIAN
WAR PHOTOGRAPHS

IN COLOR

DAILY
10-6

GRAFTON GALLERIES

ADMISSION 1/3.

This striking poster announced one of a number of exhibitions of war photographs organized by the Canadian War Records Office. The proceeds went to the Canadian War Memorials Fund to support Aitken's programme for war artists. The drooping cigarette by now had become almost part of the uniform. Steel helmets had been introduced in 1916.

Paul Nash. A quarter-century later, Sir Kenneth Clark, then Director of Britain's National Gallery, used it as inspiration for a similar program to document the Second World War for the British government. The Aitken–Rothermere scheme was amazingly simple. Artists who participated, piquantly designated "The King's Guests," were given honorary commissions in the Canadian Corps and salaries from the Canadian government. All other expenses – travel, materials, studio rental – were covered by the War Records Office through the sale of films, photographs, and publications. In the beginning, Aitken took for granted, as did Rothermere and all the others involved, that while the subjects would be Canadian, the painters themselves would all be British. He took for granted equally that there were no artists of any consequence in Canada. But realizing belatedly that the Dominion was producing some promising painters, Aitken moved quickly and, in the summer of 1917, invited A. Y. Jackson, then a corporal in the 60th Battalion, to become a "King's Guest." A good operator as well as a good painter, Jackson prepared himself for his interview by reading *Canada in Flanders*. In his 1958 autobiography, *A Painter's Country*, he recalled the occasion vividly:

> I awaited Lord Beaverbrook's arrival in his office where his little secretary, Sergeant Alexander, had his mail all arranged in piles of greater and lesser importance. He was poised with his notebook ready when His Lordship blew in like a cyclone. Beaverbrook read rapidly through the first letters, and began a running fire of instructions. "Tell Winston Churchill I will have lunch with him tomorrow at one. Tell Bonar Law I will see him at eight o'clock tonight. Tell Lloyd George to meet me on Thursday afternoon at four." He looked at me; for a moment he had forgotten who I was. Then, "Alexander," he said, "make this man a lieutenant." And he was gone as swiftly as he had come.

Soon, Jackson was joined by others, including Maurice Cullen, David Milne, and perhaps most significantly, F. H. Varley, whose painting titled *For What?*, a depiction of a wagonload of corpses about to be buried in a makeshift cemetery, is, if less well known, fully as powerful as the work of Wyndham Lewis and of Paul Nash.

For both Varley and Jackson, and later, Arthur Lismer, their experience as war artists was transformational. As Maria Tippett suggests, it catalysed the founding of the Group of Seven a few years later. "The stark, bleak, muddy-coloured landscape of the Front . . . had given a new appreciation for the irregular and barren wilderness of Northern Ontario." Back on the home front, Eric Brown, the visionary director of the National Gallery of Canada, pushed the scheme further by commissioning many artists, including a number of women – Mabel May, the sculptors Florence Wyle and Frances Loring – to document the Canadian war effort with depictions of shipbuilders and munitions workers and back-to-the-land volunteers. In Brown's opinion, it was imperative to encompass "every phase of the changed life of the people."

All of this Aitken had brought into being by his imagination and energy. Sad to say, and much to his own chagrin, the one

Arrival of Hospital Ship in Halifax, by Arthur Lismer. The Canadian War Memorials Fund was Aitken's most creative contribution to the war effort. While most of the original war artists were British, a number of Canadian painters were also commissioned. Lismer later became a founding member of the Group of Seven.

Private Brown Writes a Christmas Letter, by David Milne. Then in his mid-thirties, Milne joined the Canadian Army as a private in 1918 but did not see action. After the Armistice, he was commissioned to document the aftermath of war. This watercolour was painted on December 23, 1918, at Kinmel Park Camp in North Wales, where many Canadian soldiers were awaiting passage home.

Private Brown was a particular friend of Milne's; in the artist's description, "Brown is addressing his Christmas cards – a very serious business . . . He is trying to arrange the recipients to fit the ready-made mottos on the cards, and has them all spread out as if he were playing solitaire."

aspect of the war-art scheme that did not succeed was its ending. As he'd always intended, the entire collection was presented to the Canadian people after the war. But instead of building a new gallery modelled on the Pantheon in Paris, as Aitken had envisaged, politicians and public balked at any such expenditure, not least because by then, the war had come to be seen as divisive to national unity. Save for occasional resurrections, the paintings languished in the basement of the National Gallery for nearly half a century. (In the late 1950s, when Kenneth Clark visited Ottawa and asked to see them, he remarked that the "storeroom was very reluctantly unlocked" and "the dusty pictures hauled out of their racks.") In 1971, the National Gallery gave most of the works to the Canadian War Museum, in whose cramped premises this remarkable testament of artistic endeavour and of social history continues to moulder unseen. Perhaps, as Tippett remarks, what really mattered wasn't so much the end product as the process. If Aitken's inspired scheme turned out not to be the lasting memorial of the Great War that he had planned, it did give Canadian art and artists a kick-start into the brave new post-war world.

On December 18, 1916, William Maxwell Aitken was created Lord Beaverbrook. The title, taken from the name of a stream near Newcastle where he'd fished as a boy, was his reward for the role he'd played in partnership with his friend Bonar Law in displacing H. H. Asquith as prime minister and replacing him with Lloyd George. Beaverbrook's subsequent career in British politics and as a press lord belong to another story. Here, it's enough to say that shortly before gaining his title, he had acquired full ownership of the *Daily Express,* and that early in 1918 he was appointed Minister of Information, much the same position, but for the formal title, in which he had already served his native country. Thereafter, except in a sentimental and nostalgic way, he ceased to be a Canadian.

The country which had made him his fortune was just too small a stage to contain someone of Beaverbrook's talent and ambition and hubris. But before he left, he did repay the debt by giving us a "bedrock of history," in his own phrase, in the form of paintings and films and "Eyewitness" reports and scrupulously collected regimental records. Another part of that bedrock, Byng, Beaverbrook's choice as Canadian commander, engineered for Canadians at Vimy the greatest single military victory of their history. Beaverbrook took situations as he found them and, even if by ignoble means, he turned them to good account – for himself and for his country.

17

The Big Push

I believe that the climax of our troubles will be reached within the next few days, after which the day of peace will rapidly draw near. . . . This will be my last letter for a short while.

Lieutenant Owen Steele, Newfoundland Regiment.
A letter to his parents, June 30, 1916

Nineteen sixteen was the year when the war stopped being an aberration and turned into a constant, a nightmare of which people could no longer foresee the end even while still clinging to the assumption that surely, somehow, it must eventually end. Almost without exception, the headlines piled disaster upon disaster, their effect blunted only by the fact that the raw statistics of death had long since lost their power to shock. On February 21, the battle of Verdun had begun: by the time it was over, ten months later, half a million French and German troops had been killed and the French Army reduced to a condition of mutiny. In May, the naval battle of Jutland had ended indecisively at a cost of seven thousand British casualties. ("There seems to be something wrong with our bloody ships today," said Admiral David Beatty, as was not at the time reported in the newspapers.) Jutland's principal effect was to convince the Germans to wage future battles under the water. One of the victims of this new style of naval warfare was Lord Kitchener, Britain's War Minister, en route to a high-level meeting in Russia aboard the cruiser *Hampshire* when it was sunk by a mine off the Orkneys early in June. As for the Canadians, at the battle of Sanctuary Wood in the Ypres Salient, they'd come under a bombardment that in Agar

Adamson's description was "the most intense I have ever heard, even greater than at Bellewaerde Ridge." One Canadian general was killed and another badly wounded and taken prisoner; the Patricias themselves, now part of the 7th Brigade of the 3rd Canadian Division, lost their second commanding officer, Colonel Edward "Teta" Buller, shot while urging his men forward. Even more damaging to morale, Hamilton Gault, the regiment's founder and animating spirit, lost a leg and was never able to serve in the front lines again. "It is a wonder that any of us escaped," wrote Adamson to Mabel. "It is very hard to be cheerful."

The event that defined 1916, then and forever after, was the Battle of the Somme. In early summer, the centre of the action shifted away from the Salient into Picardy, a previously insignificant region of farmland in northern France. In the description of the historian A. J. P. Taylor, "The Somme set the picture by which future generations saw the First World War: brave, helpless soldiers; blustering obstinate generals; nothing achieved." Here, men would remember the dust as much as the mud; here, in his famous poem, "Break of Day in the Trenches," Isaac Rosenberg would address his "queer, sardonic rat,"

> *Now you have touched this English hand*
> *You will do the same to a German . . .*
> *What do you see in our eyes?*

From the Somme onwards, as Taylor writes, "the war ceased to have a purpose. It went on for its own sake, as a contest in endurance."

There were in fact eight separate battles on the Somme, beginning in July and ending in November. When the guns finally fell silent, the British armies had suffered some 420,000 casualties, the French close to 200,000, and the Germans about 450,000. At no place were the enemy lines pushed back more than five miles. The most that was achieved was to substitute British blood for the haemorrhaging that the French were suffering at Verdun.

Of those eight battles, it is the first that has been transmuted into myth. This was to be the ultimate Big Push. Haig brought up three divisions of cavalry to exploit the breakthrough that he would create by blasting the Germans into pieces or into the ground through a five-day artillery barrage (just under two million shells were fired) and then by smashing through what remained of the eighteen miles of German lines by the massed weight of thirteen British infantry divisions, some 150,000 men, as well as a smaller number of French troops.

They went over the top at 7:30 AM on July 1, amid a light mist that the rising sun would soon burn off, a flawless summer day. They then marched off, three deep in straight lines a few feet apart, through the tall grass and poppies of no man's land towards the German lands some five hundred to six hundred yards away. Each man carried sixty-six pounds of ammunition and supplies, apart from his rifle. Except when they had to go single file through the narrow and sparse gaps in the barbed wire, they maintained their lines except that, as they marched deeper into no man's land, more and more men would bow forward, as if leaning into a strong wind. By now the "creeping barrage" provided by the artillery, supposed to lay down a protective curtain of shells in front of them, had become ragged: either the shells were ranging too far ahead or had stopped moving, thus forcing the advancing men themselves to stop in the midst of open field – or else the gunners had begun misjudging the distance and were killing their own men by "friendly fire." As well, the Germans had come up from their dug-outs and their machine guns were spitting back across no man's land at a rate of six hundred rounds a minute.

The first wave faltered and then stopped. A second wave followed, then a third and a fourth. By early afternoon, virtually all British troops had retreated back into their own lines. In all, 20,000 had died and 40,000 had been wounded. This was the heaviest loss suffered by any army on any single day throughout the war.

After a pause of a day, the attack was resumed. The results were the same. On July 14, Haig ordered the cavalry in. They charged across the fields, swords flashing, lances glittering. For the German machine gunners, the horses and their riders made even easier targets than walking men. Perpetuated for another five months, the battles of the Somme amounted in Taylor's phrase to "the mindless apotheosis of the Great War."

No Canadian blood was spilled on that first day of the Somme. The turn of the Canadians would come later, in the autumn, at Courcelette and Regina Trench. But on July 1, blood was demanded, more of it proportionately than from any of the combatant countries, from the oldest of Britain's colonies, today the youngest of Canada's provinces. Among those who scrambled up the ladders in the furthest-forward line of British trenches and then formed themselves into a straight line amid the shouts and whistles and waving arms of their officers, were the 801 men and officers of the Newfoundland Regiment. One of them was Owen Steele, a stocky, sandy-haired, twenty-nine-year-old lieutenant, promoted from the ranks, in peacetime a promising salesman from St. John's being groomed for a top position in his family's long-established glass and china business, renowned both for his athletic ability and for singing a deep-chested bass in barbershop harmony. "I am surprised to see how happy and light-hearted everyone is," Steele wrote home to his parents on the eve of the battle. "Yet this is undoubtedly the last day for many."

Like the Patricias, though in a quite different way, the Newfound-landers were a regiment that stood apart from the others. They were a motley assortment of fishermen and loggers and trappers, with a sprinkling of St. John's merchant princelings on top, and since Newfoundland had no real militia to speak of, they'd set off for the war aboard the little steamer *Florizel* knowing not even the rudiments of drill. Yet they possessed an *esprit* and a sense of collectivity that would be denied to the Canadians as a whole until they won it in 1917 at Vimy. The Newfoundlanders, indeed, were more like an extended family than a fighting unit: virtually every man among them had been born on the island, which then had a population of less than a quarter of a million. Proudly, and making a virtue of necessity, they'd christened themselves "The Blue Put-tees," after the blue serge bindings they wrapped around their calves instead of the standard khaki, of which there'd been a shortage in St. John's. Their cap and collar badges bore the emblem of the self-governing colony, the head of a bull caribou. "They were not militaristic and they hated the ordinary routine of army life, but they wanted to do their share," wrote a remarkable late-comer to the regiment, Private Alonzo John Gallishaw. Generally known as Jack, he was a third-year student of literature at Harvard, a height he'd reached from a relatively humble St. John's "townie" background by his intellect and scholarship and the efforts of his sister, who kept a millinery shop on Cochrane Street. The outbreak of war had found him in Cambridge, and he'd crossed the border into Canada to enlist with the Canadians. Within days, though, he'd requested a discharge to return to Newfoundland to join his compatriots.

On Salisbury Plain, Gallishaw and the other Newfoundlanders kept themselves to themselves. "We are all very particular that we should not be classed as Canadians," Owen Steele wrote

Five members of the Newfoundland Regiment in their training camp just outside St. John's in September 1914. "They were not militaristic and they hated the ordinary routine of army life, but they wanted to do their share," wrote Private John Gallishaw who had rushed up from Harvard to join.

home. "Apart from the fact that we are much prouder of our distinctiveness as Newfoundlanders, the Canadians generally have been getting a bad name for themselves . . . especially in London." Indeed, much earlier, the Newfoundlanders had made it clear to all comers that they were a breed apart. On October 5, 1914, when the *Florizel* joined the trans-Atlantic convoy off Cape Race, one of the British escort ships, "evidently putting us down for Canadians," had saluted by playing "O Canada." "We responded with 'Rule Britannia,'" Steele reported.

Much to their fury, this proud little band did not get to take part in Second Ypres. Instead, they were shunted up to Scotland for further training. "From the day the Canadians left for Flanders, the Newfoundlanders had been obsessed by one idea, that they must get to the Front," wrote Gallishaw. At last, in the late summer of 1915, they were dispatched to the eastern Mediterranean to reinforce the battered British 29th Division at Gallipoli, the peninsula on the north side of the Dardanelles, the narrow strait dividing Europe from Asia Minor. To get himself there, Gallishaw put himself at risk of a court martial. Having been spotted as a literary type, he'd been seconded to the War Office to write up the regimental records, but he'd slipped aboard the troop train under cover of the blackout. "I blessed the name of Count Zeppelin, because it was fear of his invention that had caused it," he wrote later. With some help from his friends in Company C – "all you have to do is fall in with us," they told him, he later managed to stow away aboard the troopship and to remain, undetected and secretly fed, almost as far as Malta. When Gallishaw was at last found out, the adjutant bowed to the inevitable and issued him a rifle.

By the time the Newfoundlanders arrived at Gallipoli, it was evident that they were to be engaged only in a holding operation. Winston Churchill's bold strategy of opening up a second front had foundered several months earlier against well dug-in Turkish guns, at terrible cost both to British troops and to colonial forces from Australia and New Zealand. Gallipoli also turned out to be the end of Gallishaw's war, at least for the time being. He was wounded in November, in the unromantic circumstances of doing garbage duty, and invalided home. His recollections, though, provided the raw material for a remarkable book published in New

York the following year. Titled *Trenching at Gallipoli: A Personal Narrative of a Newfoundlander with the Ill-fated Dardanelles Expedition*, this was probably the first work to depict trench warfare from the point of view of the ordinary infantryman. Gallishaw was much less interested in describing military exploits than in the psychological dimension of warfare. "At first we dodged the sound of passing bullets," he writes, "but soon we came to believe the superstition that a bullet would not hit a man unless it had on it his regimental number and his name." Similarly, "it was strange to see week by week the psychological change that had come over the men. Most of all I noticed it in the songs they sang. At first these were songs of a boisterous character, but later, 'As We go Marching Through Germany' and the others gave place to

Newfoundlanders in their trenches at Gallipoli. Note the soldier on duty at the periscope. "At first we dodged the sound of passing bullets," wrote Gallishaw, "but soon we came to believe the superstition that a bullet would not hit a man unless it had on it his regimental number and his name."

songs that voice a longing for home, such as 'My Little Grey Home in the West.'"

Gallishaw was also one of the first to express publicly the fury produced in Colonials by the patronizing attitude of British officers towards anyone who in their terms was not a gentleman. On the hospital ship taking him away from Gallipoli, "the eyes of the man next to me were large with pain. I smiled at him, but instead of smiling back at me his lip curled resentfully, and he turned over on his side so that he could face away from me. As he did, the blanket skipped from his shoulder and I saw on his shoulder-strap the star of a second lieutenant. I had committed the unpardonable sin. I had smiled at an officer as if I had been an equal. . . . Once after that, when he turned his head, his eyes met mine disdainfully. That time I did not smile. I have often laughed at the incident since, but there on that boat I was boiling with rage. . . . I cursed him and the system that produced him and swore that never again would I put on a uniform."

Gallishaw did not abide by this promise. He returned to his studies at Harvard, but in 1917, after the United States entered the war, he enlisted in the U.S. Army, received a commission, and became an intelligence officer. In later years, he lectured at Harvard, established a school of creative writing at Cambridge, and during the 1930s worked as a scriptwriter in Hollywood, collaborating at one time with F. Scott Fitzgerald. He also wrote four more books, mostly on writing technique, none of which exhibited the power and originality of *Trenching at Gallipoli*. He rarely returned to Newfoundland, but in 1961 was an honoured guest at the ceremonies marking the official opening of the new campus of Memorial University, an institution founded in the early 1920s to commemorate Newfoundland's part in the Great War.

For Owen Steele, the three months that the Blue Puttees spent on Gallipoli were simply the curtain-raiser to a larger event. "This trench warfare is really very monotonous," he wrote home on November 1. "It cannot be compared to the Boer War, when one would get lots of excitement." Nor, as an eminently practical individual who had brought along all his warm clothes, was he discombobulated by the cold autumn gales. Even so, in early

Lieutenant Owen Steele. This photograph was probably taken behind the lines in France, shortly before he went over the top at Beaumont-Hamel. "We are all strangely thoughtful about the 'Great Push,'" Steele wrote home to his parents.

December, after a torrential rainstorm produced a flash flood that soon turned to solid ice, Steele couldn't help but be reminded of the devastating Newfoundland sealing-ship disaster of 1914, when scores of men from the steamer *Greenland* had been trapped on ice floes by a blizzard. "The men's faces were nearly all black as niggers, where they had been getting as close as possible to the smoking fires all night, and what with their eyes and woe-begone looks, they presented a really terrible sight." Still, while some regiments had suffered terribly – "One of the Worcester Officers told me that he had seen fully thirty men sitting up on the firing steps . . . frozen to death" – the Newfoundlanders had all survived. "Wonderful to relate, there was not a single fatality, which speaks well for the physique of our men," Steele remarked with much satisfaction.

Late in December, the Newfoundlanders formed part of the

rear guard that defended the retreat from Gallipoli. "I said, 'Looks like an evacuation, Sir.' He said, 'That's just what it is, absolutely,'" reported Steele of a conversation with his commanding officer. After a couple of thumb-twiddling months encamped near Suez, where the chief diversion was riding on camels and Steele kept himself in shape by twenty-five-mile walks across the desert, they arrived in northern France by way of Marseilles, to undertake what Steele described as "The Great Advance." Throughout May and June 1916, he reported "working parties day and night," as the Newfoundlanders dug trenches near the little hamlet of Beaumont-Hamel. They christened the forward trench that would be their jumping-off point, "St. John's Road." "No need to bother about us at all," Steele reassured his parents. "We shall soon finish off this blooming war. It is a wonderful sight to see all the immense preparations being made. Every road in every direction is clouded with dust, crowded with moving transport wagons, ration carts, timbered wagons, troops in large and small quantities. Everyone seems so cool about it all."

Yet Steele also reported "a strange pensiveness about everything. We are all strangely thoughtful about the 'Great Push.'" On June 22, having badly injured his knee in a riding accident, he had every excuse to go off to hospital. "But I would not go now, seeing that everything we have prepared for so long is about to come off. . . . I cannot help walking lame and only hope it will sufficiently improve by 'The Great Day' to enable me to do justice to my duties." By June 25, the leg had improved but censorship had tightened. "We have been specifically told to speak, or rather to write, of nothing but personal or family matters." On June 30, "the various battalions marched off whistling and singing and it was a great sight. Of course this is the best way to take things and hope for the best." Steele then advised his parents that he wouldn't be writing again for a while. "I believe that the climax of our troubles will be reached in the next few days, after which the day of peace will rapidly draw near."

On the morning of July 2, the day after the Big Push, the Newfoundland Regiment held its daily roll-call. Of the 801 who had gone over the top the day before, 68 remained to shout out their names. Owen Steele was not among them. He did survive the day itself, badly wounded, but died a few days later. We have no way of knowing how far he'd got before he was hit. Very likely he was somewhere in the vicinity of the landmark that the Newfoundlanders had titled the "Danger Tree," marking the beginning of no man's land. In his marvellous work of imagination of that title, David Macfarlane has described this as "an old apple tree, left from some orchard that had once been there. Somehow it had survived the barrages and rose like a skeleton from the lip of a shellhole." As the single landmark on that blighted field, the Danger Tree drew the Newfoundlanders towards it magnetically. By giving them something to aim at, it drew the German machine guns equally magnetically.

After Beaumont-Hamel, the Newfoundland Regiment was given the title, *Royal* Newfoundland Regiment. Lieutenant-General Sir Aylmer Hunter-Weston, the Corps Commander, described its contribution as "better than the best." All of which was too little too late. No unit among the Allies suffered more heavily. Their country paid a higher price proportionately than Britain itself or any other corner of its Empire. In 1914, Newfoundland, after more than three hundred years of colonial existence, had seemed poised on the brink of becoming a viable small nation, much like Iceland. New pulp and paper mills were working to capacity, so also were iron mines, above all, the fish were abundant and in demand. As soon as the war ended, fish prices collapsed. The leadership that might have carried the colony through had died in the war. By 1930, even before the Great Depression began to bite, interest on Newfoundland's public debt equalled half the entire annual revenue of the government. Of that $100 million debt, $40 million was accounted for by the unpaid bills of sending Newfoundlanders to the war. To avoid formal bankruptcy, Newfoundlanders abandoned self-rule to a committee of British-appointed bureaucrats, and some subsidies. Not until 1949, when Newfoundlanders chose a different kind of destiny and became part of Canada, did the society begin, slowly, to recover. Even today, amid an astonishing flowering of artistic creativity equalled, proportionately, only in Quebec, the sense of pride and self-respect of 1914, to which Gallishaw and Steele and the others bore witness, has not yet been fully regained. David Macfarlane, three of whose great-uncles perished in the Great War, has expressed this continuing sense of loss in *The Danger Tree*: "The century that carried on past their deaths was not what it might have been. It was largely a makeshift arrangement, cobbled round their constant and disastrous absence."

Today, of all the thousands of memorials to the Great War scattered over northern France and Flanders, the one at Beaumont-Hamel is the most eloquent. The ghosts here speak in the lilting Irish accent of St. John's and the Southern Shore, and the Elizabethan Devon and Dorset dialects of the northern bays. The outline of the St. John's Road trench that served the Newfoundlanders as jumping-off point is easy to find. From there, skirting the fragments of barbed-wire coils, it is a short stroll across a wide sloping meadow to the remains, dead and bare, of the Danger Tree, still there after all these years. Another short stroll leads to the German lines, still well dug in and intimidating. Here, visitors should halt and look backwards, and remember that where they are standing, not one Newfoundlander reached on that day. Then visitors should walk back past St. John's Road to the actual memorial. This is a mounded pyramid with a path circling upwards between wild juniper bushes transported across the Atlantic by citizens of Newfoundland who, in the immediate aftermath of war, raised the money to buy all of this land and to set it apart as hallowed ground. At the top is a stone base bearing the metal figure of a three-quarter-lifesize bull caribou. Head and antlers back, the caribou bays across the field where its sons fell.*

In early autumn, the Canadians marched south to the Somme. In mid-September, after a week of fighting and at a cost of more than seven thousand casualties, they captured the village of

---

* In July 1991, three veterans of the Newfoundland Regiment, all in their mid-nineties, returned to Beaumont-Hamel to take part in ceremonies marking the seventy-fifth anniversary of the Battle of the Somme. A documentary film of their pilgrimage, *Beaumont-Hamel: A Battle Remembered*, co-produced by Memorial University and by Ocean Pictures of St. John's, was shown on CBC St. John's on November 11, 1991, and deserves wider audience as a remarkable essay in oral and visual history.

The Caribou Memorial at Beaumont-Hamel. Proud but desolate, no other monument on the Western Front is as eloquent.

Courcelette, a few miles from Beaumont-Hamel. This was the first major engagement undertaken by the Royal 22nd Regiment. The "Van Doos," as this contingent of French Canadians, or *Canadiens,* was called, distinguished themselves by leading the attack. "If hell is as bad as what I have seen at Courcelette," wrote their commanding officer, Lieutenant-Colonel Thomas Tremblay, "I would not wish my worst enemy to go there."

Six weeks later, just before Haig called off the offensive, the new 4th Canadian Division won its spurs by capturing a couple of shallow ditches, littered with corpses, that they'd christened Regina Trench and Desire Trench. By then, the autumn rains had set in, transforming the dust of July into a sea of yellow mud. The military historian D. J. Goodspeed has written that when the Canadians were at last pulled out of the line, "they were so coated with half-frozen mud that a man's clothing, boots and puttees sometimes weighed 120 pounds."

Before the Somme offensive petered out, one change had

been made in British tactics which, if exploited properly, might
have justified some of the blood that had been spent by achieving
a clear breakthrough of the German lines. "The great surprise of
the attack yesterday was the appearance of Armoured Caterpillars," Agar Adamson wrote Mabel on September 16. "They can go
over any ground, over a 12-foot trench or a 6-foot wall. They
knock down anything in front of them, to knock down a tree they
rear up and put their weight on it, to knock down a parapet they
simply push it. They are very heavy and armed with quick-firing

Canadians cheering one of the first tanks. First used at the battle of Courcelette in September 1916, these new weapons astounded the Germans and also the Allies. In a report for the War Records Office dated September 14, 1916, Talbot Papineau noted, "Seven of these strange monsters had arrived at night, crossing open country and independent of all roads. Each one had its name: Cupid, Champagne, Cognac, Cordon Rouge, Chablis . . ."

guns. Machine-gun fire or a whizzbang has no effect on them, only a direct hit. Three of them last night went through a fortified village and returned. They are the wonder of the war. They are called tanks."

First used during the attack on Courcelette and its environs, these tanks astounded the Germans. But too few of them were used, no preparations had been made to follow up their initial success, and, as Lloyd George wrote later, "The great secret was sold for the battered ruin of a little hamlet." (It was not until more than a year later that General Byng, who by then had left the Canadians to command the British Third Army, used tanks properly for the first time in a famed attack on Cambrai. Despite breaking through the Hindenburg line and capturing thousands of prisoners and guns, Byng was not able to achieve decisive success because the reserves who could have been poured through the gap had been devastated at Passchendaele.)

When Adamson and the Patricias departed the Somme in mid-October 1916 to take up a new position near Vimy Ridge, he was in surprisingly good spirits. Along with the tanks, he'd been cheered by the sight of another advancement in technology. "Our aeroplanes seem to own the air," he wrote Mabel. "Not a single Boche is allowed to show himself. The time is now very close and I feel we are going to get a little of our own back." The Patricias themselves were coming away in relatively good shape. At Courcelette, they had taken all their objectives with relatively few casualties. For much of the battle, Adamson himself had been in command of the regiment (Colonel Pelley, a British officer who had succeeded Buller, was doing staff duty at brigade headquarters), and had been praised by the Corps Commander, General Byng, under whom he'd long ago served in South Africa. On October 31, Pelley was promoted brigadier and went off to another posting. To his surprise, indeed dismay, Adamson was gazetted lieutenant-colonel and appointed to command the Patricias. "The isolation of a commanding officer is necessary but most trying to one of my disposition," he wrote Mabel. "He is always Sir; on the smallest points and details he has to decide and be definite and not give his reason for doing so. One can never more than half-take even senior officers into your confidence. If things go wrong, it is your fault; if they go right, no matter how well thought out before, it is only considered the natural event of things."

Adamson no doubt was protesting too much. On Christmas Day, which was also his fifty-first birthday, he was deeply touched to receive "a very nicely worded message" from his sergeants. "We are always ready to work to our fullest capacity, but you must not expect us to keep up with you." A few weeks later, in the midst of a concert laid on by the Patricias' Regimental Comedy Company – a troupe that was forerunner to the famous Dumbells, and

Diaghilev's Ballet Russe, a seminal force in modern art, also influenced the Princess Patricia's Canadian Light Infantry's comedy team, a forerunner of the famous Dumbells. Officers encouraged such hi-jinks as a way of keeping up morale during the desolation of trench warfare.

that Agar had encouraged by enjoining Mabel to send over dis-
carded evening dresses and wigs scrounged from a theatrical
costumier – he was left at a loss for words when the Regimental
Pipe Major leapt to his feet, made a speech "in very broad Scotch,"
and then "asked to be allowed to play on the pipes a tune he had
been composing since June hoping for the occasion to play it to
me as CO."

"I had no idea that the great majority of men gave a damn
who commanded them," Agar signed off to Mabel.

Agar Adamson (*right*) and Charlie Stewart, 1916. On
October 31, Adamson was appointed Commanding Officer of the Patricias. He served in that post until early
1918, when he was succeeded by Stewart.

18

"The Soul of Canada"

*As I write, French and English Canadians are
fighting and dying side by side. Is their sacrifice to
go for nothing or will it not cement a foundation
for a true Canadian nation, a Canadian nation
independent in thought, independent in action?*

Talbot Papineau. Open letter to Henri Bourassa; July 1916

*I will not undertake to answer every point of the
dithyrambic plea of my gallant cousin . . . [but] his
long and diffuse piece of eloquence proves that the
excitement of warfare and the distance from home
have obliterated from his mind the fundamental
realities of his native country.*

Henri Bourassa. Open reply to Talbot Papineau; August 1916

For any officer, direct and artless praise coming up from the ranks of the kind Agar Adamson had received on becoming Commanding Officer of the Patricias, is the highest he can ever achieve. It was exactly the kind of praise that Talbot Papineau longed to hear, but so long as he was stuck in a staff job, could never hope to. Indeed, within months of accepting Max Aitken's offer it had begun to worry Talbot that he'd done the wrong thing. "Should I go back to the Regiment?" he wrote Beatrice Fox. "I cannot make up my mind. I should really be happier, but it is such a temptation to remain here and feel important and be comfortable. Sometimes it seems impossible that the war should ever end."

In the event, Papineau served on the staff for just under a year and a half. For the first few months, he was an aide-de-camp to General Alderson; after Alderson's dismissal, he was seconded to Aitken's War Records staff, based at Canadian Corps' headquarters in France, where, among other things he directed the cinematographers and wrote press communiqués. It was a time of introspection and confusion, when hope and high spirits alternated with frustration and self-anger. The work itself, while agreeable and even important, often left him feeling "simply looking pretty," as he wrote in a letter to Beatrice. There was also the gnawing awareness that this sort of work was not the work of a real soldier. Papineau could never shrug off a sense of guilt about leaving the Patricias nor a conviction that as soon as possible he should rejoin them. An additional worry was the unseen Beatrice: their correspondence was becoming ever more intense, bringing them ever closer to the stressful moment when they would have to decide whether to commit themselves to each other, or to accept tacitly that their romantic friendship was only a freak of the war. Above all, there was the fact that because he was now at headquarters, well behind the Front, Papineau could assume he would survive the war. Inevitably, his thoughts turned more and more to the future: to Canada's future and, more directly, to his own future. By his name, his education, his fluency in both French and English, his network of friends and kin, not to mention his vaulting ambition, he possessed all the credentials to reach for the top once the war was over, all the more because he now possessed the additional credentials of a distinguished war record and a Military Cross. That he alone among the original complement of the officers in the Patricias had survived without a scratch had to mean that he was being preserved for some higher purpose. Thus, while doing his staff-work, Papineau devoted much of his time and energy to figuring out how best to position himself for his post-war leap forward.

His old Oxford friend, Lionel Curtis, served as catalyst to Talbot's ambition. "You have proved your capacity as a soldier, but believe me, you will be judged by your insights as a statesman," wrote Curtis in February 1916, soon after his protegé was out of harm's way. "By reason of your courage, you have perhaps done more than anyone of your age to prove the reality of the British Commonwealth as a real state compounded of nations in which the British are but one element." Though his experiences in the trenches had not converted Talbot into a disciple of Curtis's creed of Imperial Federalism, the letter began to crystallize his thinking. "The problem which interests me particularly is as to whether the Imperialist or the Nationalist sentiment in Canada predominates," he wrote Beatrice. "My whole leaning is towards nationality, but I do not wish to oppose or destroy the value of an Imperial sentiment. Can I find a middle way?" A few days later, he returned to the same theme. "The issue in Canada after the war is going to be between Imperialism and Nationalism. . . . This controversy must result because we cannot continue as we are, and there is no longer any other alternative, though opponents of sovereignty threaten us with a third – namely, political absorption into the States. . . . My whole inclination is towards an independent Canada with all the attributes of sovereignty, including its responsibilities."

These musings were quite remarkable. At a time when Canada was still little more than a colony, with no responsibility for the conduct of its own foreign policy, Papineau was prefiguring – even outdistancing – such constitutional landmarks as the 1931 Statute of Westminster. If still only in private, he was preparing to nail his colours to the mast as a Canadian nationalist, even while, as then was common amongst others of his kind, wanting to anchor Canadian nationhood under the protective umbrella of a British Empire transformed into a federal Commonwealth.

This was visionary. Yet at the same time, an alternative vision of Canada's future was beginning to arise within the country he cared so deeply about. It was a vision, as Papineau was only too well aware, that threatened to move the ground from under his own political feet – indeed, had already begun to move it. This process had started in 1913, when the government of Ontario, dominated by Orangemen, responded in alarm to large-scale migration of French-Canadian workers (by that year, Francophones had come to number almost a tenth of Ontario's population) by adding a new, discriminatory provision to its Education Act. This was Regulation Seventeen. Effectively, it transformed hundreds of French-language schools, many of them run by religious orders, into English-language ones. A unilingual six-year-old could be taught in French only until he or she had finished the first grade. After that, all instruction had to be in English.

One of the first to take up the cause of "the wounded of Ontario," as he called them, was Henri Bourassa, editor of *Le Devoir*, and Talbot's first cousin once removed. Although a nationalist, Bourassa had initially supported the war effort, returning from a pilgrimage to Lourdes to write a long editorial arguing that "as an Anglo-French nation bound to England and France by a thousand ethnic, social intellectual and economic ties," Canada had "a national duty to contribute . . . to the triumph and above all to the *endurance* of France and England." At this point, Bourassa's attitudes reflected those of his fellow *Canadiens*. The first weeks of the war were a halcyon period for Anglo-French relations, when French-language newspapers began printing the Union Jack and the *tricolor* side by side on their mastheads, and when Archbishop Bruchesi of Montreal, blessing a contingent of volunteers bound for Valcartier, pronounced that "We have given England provisions and gold, and we will give her men. . . . We shall prove to England that we are loyal not only in words."

Soon, though, the patriotic euphoria began to yield to politics. Despite all the rhetoric, French-Canadians did not hasten to answer the call to the colours: only about twelve hundred enlisted in the initial contingent. English Canadians – Sam Hughes above all – did nothing to encourage them to believe they would be welcome. At Valcartier, as in Ontario schools, English was the only language of instruction. Senior French-Canadian regular officers were shunted off into meaningless administrative positions. Only because Laurier intervened personally with Borden were the Van Doos established as a distinct French-Canadian battalion. Later, Hughes appointed a Baptist minister as his chief recruiting officer in Quebec.

By Christmas 1914, Bourassa's opinion of the war had changed drastically. In general, he'd come to view it as a conflict between imperialisms, in which it made little difference who exactly was fighting who: French, British, and Russian imperialists versus the Prussians and Austro-Hungarians, or else vice versa, with a few partners changed. Increasingly, he began to draw parallels between the sufferings Franco-Ontarians were experiencing, and those being inflicted on helpless Belgians. "In the name of religion, liberty and faithfulness to the British flag, French Canadians are enjoined to go and fight the Prussians of Europe," he thundered from a Montreal platform in 1915. "Shall we let the Prussians of Ontario impose their domination like masters in the very heart of the Canadian confederation?" Early in 1916, the arrival of the Van Doos at the Front provoked another excoriating outburst.

By 1916, the gap between French and English Canada had become an open wound. Despite the valour of the Royal 22nd Regiment – the legendary "Van Doos," one of whose officers was a future Governor General, Captain Georges Vanier – French Canadians did not join up in large numbers. These recruiting posters, intended to spur enlistment by suggesting that at any moment *les Boches* might invade home territory, had little effect.

"This morning's dispatches announce the death on the field of honour of four soldiers of the French Canadian 22nd and the wounding of seven others," proclaimed the editorial in *Le Devoir*. "But does anyone believe that as a result of their sacrifice, the Boches of Ontario will suspend the war that they make against our language?"

Talbot's reaction was anger – perhaps also, a degree of embarrassment. He and his cousin had never been close; Bourassa, for one thing, was fourteen years older and belonged to another generation. Save for their common ancestor, their backgrounds were poles apart. As a passionate Catholic, and a *pur sang* (the expression then used rather than today's *pure laine*) it undoubtedly rankled Henri that it was Talbot, a Protestant whose lineage was three-quarters American, who bore the precious family name and was, with his brothers, heir to Montebello. (Talbot's grandfather, son of the Great Patriot and Bourassa's maternal uncle, had married Mary Eleanor Westcott of Saratoga Springs, New York, and their son had married Caroline Rogers of Philadelphia.) Yet they also had much in common, of which a considerable physical resemblance was only the beginning. Bourassa too, had spent his boyhood at Montebello, and they shared a passion for the Quebec landscape that was close to metaphysical. In an era that predated mass communications, when, as Ralph Allen has wonderfully expressed it, "the unaided tongue, the hurrying urgent pen, the white-hot printing press, were the sturdiest, almost the only vehicles of human communication," both were splendid writers and commanding orators. The beginnings of a promising friendship between them dated from the years leading up to the war, when Talbot, newly returned from Oxford, was setting up his law practice and Henri had just founded *Le Devoir*. At this time their political creeds were remarkably similar. Both believed in the development of an independent, bilingual Anglo-French Canada; indeed, as Bourassa noted later, Talbot was the more nationalistic of the two. "I gathered the impression that he was still more opposed than myself to any kind of Imperial solidarity. He even seemed much disposed to hasten the day of the Independence of Canada." Almost certainly, it was Bourassa who inspired Talbot's late-blooming interest in French-Canadian culture and folklore and inspired him to become an interlocutor between Quebec and the rest of the country as a Canadian Club speaker.

Thus Talbot never questioned Bourassa's passionate championship of Franco-Ontarians. In different circumstances, he might well have done the same himself. His law partner and virtual alter ego, Andrew McMaster, probably spoke for them both when he wrote, "One of the great factors of difficulty . . . is the race arrogance of the English-speaking Canadians – a spirit most highly developed in Ontario, in many ways the most provincial and least informed of our provinces." But this cause, however legitimate, was now in conflict with the greater cause of the war. At the Front, thousands were dying, French Canadians no differently from all the other combatants. For someone who had watched them die, the comparisons made between their sufferings and those of Franco-Ontarians, safe at home no matter how hard done by there, must have been intolerable. His outrage and contempt at a politician's exploitation of a domestic linguistic quarrel without regard to the consequences of this to the war effort, and therefore perhaps at an additional cost in lives, prompted Papineau to undertake the boldest act of his burgeoning political career. He made up his mind to challenge his cousin directly, on his own territory of French-English relations.

Papineau's challenge took the form of a long open letter to Bourassa. "What of the Soul of Canada?" he wrote in one of its most eloquent passages. "If you were truly a Nationalist – if you loved our great country and without smallness longed to see her become the home of a good and united people – surely you would have recognized this war as her moment of travail and tribulation. You would have felt that in the agony of her losses in Belgium and France, Canada was suffering the birthpangs of her national life. There, even more than in Canada herself, her citizens are being knit together into a new existence, because when men stand side by side and endure a soldier's life and face together a soldier's death, they are united in bonds almost as strong as the closest of blood ties."

The entire letter ran to nearly ten thousand words. Well aware that Bourassa's reply would be passionate and eloquent, equally keenly aware that by seeming to make common cause with "the Prussians of Ontario," he might be burning many of the political bridges upon which he counted to build his own political career, Papineau laboured long and hard over the missive. He wrote the first draft during his spell in hospital at the end of 1915. After many revisions and updatings – he read it aloud to his batman, but so far as we know, showed it to no one – he finished the final version at the end of March 1916 and then sent it to Andrew McMaster in Montreal to be typed and delivered. McMaster responded ambivalently and suggested much toning down. "I note what you say about the sacrifice we have made constituting for us a glorious history," he wrote. "At the Front, yes; in Canada no." Clearly, being more in touch with the local scene, he worried that Talbot could be destroying his political future in Quebec. But Talbot was obdurate – "I want it to stand as it is" – and on July 18, McMaster at last forwarded the letter to Bourassa. When no reply was forthcoming – Bourassa was in fact out of town – it was published in Montreal, Quebec, Toronto, and Ottawa newspapers, and shortly thereafter in papers across the country.

After the salutation, "My Dear Cousin Henri," Papineau's opening was amicable. "You and I have had some discussions in the past, and although we have not agreed on all points, yet I am happy to think that our pleasant friendship which indeed dates from the time of my birth, has hitherto continued uninjured by our differences of opinion." Yet, "I have nevertheless followed with intense feeling and deeply regret the course of action which you have pursued." This had been to criticize not merely the particular prosecution of the war but the war itself, and to argue that Canada should not have entered it. But, argued Papineau, "By the declaration of war by Great Britain upon Germany, Canada became 'ipso facto' a belligerent, subject to invasion and conquest, her property at sea subject to capture. This is not a matter of opinion – it is a matter of fact – a matter of international law." Given this reality, he continued, "Surely it was idle and pernicious to continue an academic discussion as to whether the situation was a just one or not, as to whether Canada should or should not have had a voice in ante bellum English diplomacy or in the actual declaration of war. Such a discussion may very properly arise upon a successful conclusion of the war . . . [but] if ever there was a time for action and not for theories, it was to be found in Canada upon the outbreak of war."

From the foundation of this somewhat academic analysis, Papineau vaulted to high rhetoric. Bourassa, he declared, had "arrogated" to himself "the high term of Nationalist." How then could he not understand that, "if without sacrifices of our own we profit from the sacrifices of the English soldiers, we can never hope to become a nation ourselves. How could we ever acquire that Soul or create that Pride without which a nation is a dead thing and doomed to speedy decay and disappearance?" The war, he declared, "was the great opportunity for the true Nationalist. There was the great issue, the great sacrifice which should have appealed equally to all true citizens of Canada and should have served to cement them with indissoluble strength. . . . What mattered the why and wherefore of the war, whether we owed anything to England or not, and whether we were Imperialist or not, or whether we were French or English? The one simple commanding fact was that Canada was at war and Canada and Canadian liberties had to be protected."

Then a personal aside, and an affecting one. "Could you have been here yourself to witness in all its horrible detail the cruelty of the war – to have seen your comrades suddenly struck down in death and lie mangled at your side, even you would have failed to wish to visit punishment on those responsible. You too would now wish to see every ounce of our united strength instantly and relentlessly directed to that end."

From this high ground, Papineau moved, as if across no man's land, but without a covering barrage, right into Bourassa's territory. "You and I are so-called French Canadians. We belong to the race that began the conquest of this country long before the days of Wolfe. That race was in its turn conquered, but their personal liberties were not restricted. . . . As a minority in a great English-speaking continent, we have preserved our racial identity and we have had the freedom to speak or to worship as we wished. . . . But if we are to preserve this liberty, we must recognize that we do not belong entirely to ourselves, but to a mixed population, we must rather seek to find points of contact and of common interest than points of friction and separation. We must make concessions and certain sacrifices of our distinct individuality if we mean to live on amicable terms with our fellow citizens or if we expect them to make similar concessions to us."

Then he opened his own barrage directly upon Bourassa. The war had provided the opportunity for the two races to find "points of contact and of common interest" and perhaps, amid blood, to make these ties indissoluble. Bourassa had "failed to grasp" this opportunity. "Despite the heroic and able manner in which French-Canadian battalions have distinguished themselves here . . . the fact remains that the French in Canada have not responded in the same proportion as have other Canadian citizens, and the unhappy impression has been created that French Canadians are not bearing their full share in this great Canadian enterprise. For this fact and this impression, you will be held largely responsible. . . . You will have brought them [French-Canadian nationalists] into a disrepute from which they may never recover. Already, you have made the fine term of *Nationalist* to stink in the nostrils of our English fellow-citizens. Have you caused them to respect your national views? Have you won their admiration or led them to consider with esteem and tolerance your ambitions for the French language? Have you shown yourself worthy of concessions or considerations? After this war, what influence will you enjoy – what good to your country will you be able to accomplish? Wherever you go, you will stir up strife and enmity – you will bring dishonour upon our race, so that whoever bears a French name in Canada will be an object of suspicion and possibly of hatred."

Papineau then delivered his prologue to his own future political career. "As I write, French and English Canadians are fighting and dying side by side. Is their sacrifice to go for nothing or will it not cement a foundation for a true Canadian nation, a Canadian nation independent in thought, independent in action, independent even in its political organization – but in spirit united for high international and humane purposes to the two Motherlands of England and France?"

Angry, eloquent, at times visionary, at times calculating, this was a new kind of voice to be heard in the distant, provincial colony – the voice of a pan-Canadian nationalist, one as eloquent as Laurier but more energetic and muscular. In answering echo came another voice, every bit as angry and as eloquent, and in its self-confidence also new of its kind – the voice of a *Canadien nationaliste*.

Bourassa's reply, addressed nominally to McMaster and thereby beginning with the formal "Dear Sir," appeared on August 2. He was barely into his first paragraph before he'd scored his first point. "Why should Captain Papineau, who writes and speaks French so eloquently, who claims so highly his French origin, and professes with such ardour his love for France, have written in English to his 'dear cousin Henri?'" (Near the end of the letter, he made the same point in a much cruder way, indeed in a manner that prefigured uncannily René Lévesque's famous challenge of Pierre *Elliott* Trudeau's right to call himself a *vrai Québécois* during the 1980 referendum campaign. "In spite of his name, Captain Papineau is utterly unqualified to judge the feelings of French Canadians. For the most part American, he has inherited, with a few drops of French blood, the most *denationalized* instincts of his French origins. He is separated by his religious beliefs and his maternal language. His higher studies he pursued in England. His elements of French culture he acquired in France.")

Next, some ground-clearing. At the war's start, Bourassa pointed out, he had "pronounced myself in favour of the intervention of Canada as a nation, for the defence of the superior interests uniting Canada with France and Britain." It was only later, "long after Capt. Papineau was gone, that my attitude was changed and brought me to condemn the participation of Canada – or rather, the political inspiration of that participation and the many abuses which have resulted therefrom."

Then to the heart of the matter. "The Government, the whole of Parliament, the press and politicians of both parties, all applied themselves systematically to obliterate the free and independent character of Canadian intervention. 'Free' enlistment is now carried on by means of blackmailing, intimidation, and threats of all sorts. Advantage has been taken of the emotion caused by the war to assert, with utmost intensity and intolerance, the doctrine of Imperial solidarity, triumphantly opposed in the past by our

Henri Bourassa, founder and editor of *Le Devoir*, *circa* 1912. On his mother's side – Azèlie Papineau, the daughter of *le grand patriote*, had married the Quebec painter, Napoleon Bourassa – he was Talbot's first cousin once removed. Whatever their differences over the war, they were both splendid orators and writers and shared a passion for the Quebec landscape. Perhaps a certain physical resemblance can also be detected.

Talbot Papineau, April 1916. This formal photograph, probably taken on leave in London at around the time he finished his long open letter to Henri Bourassa, shows him wearing the red tabs of a staff officer; the white ribbon denotes his Military Cross.

Between them, these cousins from Montebello defined with eloquence and urgency the terms of a debate about the character of Canada that continues today.

statesmen and the whole Canadian people." Far from being used as an opportunity to create an independent Canadian nation, "the war has achieved their enslavement; they [Laurier's Liberals], united with the Tory–Jingo–Imperialists of all shades to make of the participation of Canada in the war an immense political manouevre and thus assure the triumph of British Imperialism."

Here, Bourassa made clear that he was opposed not only to British imperialism, but also to "German Imperialism, French Militarism, and Russian Tsarism." He made the perceptive point that "the nations of Europe are the victims of their own mistakes, of the complacent servility with which they submitted to the dominance of all Imperialists." Canada itself, "a nation of America, has a nobler mission to fulfil than to bind herself to the fate of the nations of Europe or to any spoliating Empire." Bourassa then turned to the enemy, immediately confronting him – his own cousin. He admired "his silent courage in running to the front at the first call," but his "verbose political manifesto" added nothing to his merits.

Papineau, argued Bourassa, simply didn't know what he was talking about. "When he says that I am too far away from the trenches to judge the real meaning of the war, he may be right. On the other hand, his long and diffuse piece of eloquence proves that the excitement of warfare and the distance from home have obliterated in his mind the fundamental realities of his native country."

Specifically, declared Bourassa, Papineau "unhappily lends credit to the most mischievous of the many anti-national opinions circulated by the jingo press." He'd proclaimed that French Canadians were wanting in Canadian patriotism because their enlistment rate was less than that in the rest of the country. But he'd failed to notice that "the number of recruits in the various Provinces of Canada is in inverse ratio of the enrootment in the soil and the traditional patriotism arising therefrom." A disproportionate number of recruits from other provinces were recent British immigrants. "Under the sway of Imperialism, a fair number have not yet decided whether their allegiance is to Canada or to the Empire, whether the United Kingdom or the Canadian confederacy is their country." As much to the point, across the country, "the floating population of the cities, the students, the labourers and clerks, either unemployed or threatened with it, have supplied more soldiers than the farmers." Much more than the nationalists, it was Canadian reality that had discouraged recruitment. "There is among the French Canadians a larger proportion of farmers, fathers of large families, than among any other ethnical element in Canada." French Canadians, further, "are the only group exclusively Canadian, in its whole and by each of the individuals of which it is composed."

Bourassa now arrived at his central point. Above all, the reason for the low recruitment of French Canadians "related to deeper causes: hereditary instincts, social and economic conditions, a national tradition of three centuries." He was opposed to the war, Bourassa declared, because he was opposed to imperialism and its exploitation of people. There was also within Canada itself, "the bilingual question." In conclusion, he wove his two themes into a single, potent, political manifesto.

"The backward and essentially Prussian policy of the rulers of Ontario and Manitoba gives us an additional argument against the intervention of Canada in the European conflict. To speak of fighting for the preservation of French civilization in Europe while endeavouring to destroy it in America, appears to us as an absurd piece of inconsistency. To preach Holy War for the liberties of people overseas, and to oppress the national minorities within Canada is, in our opinion, nothing but odious hypocrisy."

In the immediate, Papineau won most of the honours. Overnight, he was transformed into a national hero. "Captain Papineau rises to rare heights of impassioned eloquence and rings true to the principles of Canadian nationality as he scourges the men who have brought Quebec into disrepute," eulogized the *Globe* of Toronto. He also gained a certain international reputation. On August 22, *The Times* of London reprinted his letter almost in full, under the heading, "The Soul of Canada," describing it as a "remarkable declaration, showing the effect of the war on one who by birth, tradition and opinion before the war, was closely allied to the High Priest of Canadian Nationalism."

Bourassa, though, spoke with the true voice of his people,*
as he would a year later during the Conscription Crisis and the
Khaki Election. Between them, these cousins from Montebello
defined with eloquence and urgency the terms of a debate about
the character of their country that, changed only its contemporary details, continues today, and that, it surely can be guessed
safely, will continue as long as Canada continues.

---

* The Conscription Crisis marked the peak of Bourassa's influence. Increasingly,
his advocacy of a quasi-mystical, pastoral Catholicism moved him to the political margins; even within Quebec, his nationalist credentials were challenged
shortly after the war by the *independentiste* preachings of Abbé Lionel Groulx.
Yet Bourassa's call for a bilingual, bicultural, Anglo–French Canada makes him
seem more a contemporary than an historical figure. He died in 1952.

19
Confusions and Frustrations

I am very glad you said in your last letter that our correspondence was now on a "different footing" and no longer merely for the entertainment of a "lonely soldier." I am glad you agree we are to become interested in each other as definite personalities.

Talbot Papineau. A letter to Beatrice Fox; March 7, 1916

B y the time the exchange of letters between him and Bourassa was published, events had moved on for Papineau. He liked basking in the applause – "very convincing," said General Byng. "You will undoubtedly go far" – and enjoyed reading his fan mail. "This will place you straight away in the position in public life which you ought to fill," wrote Lionel Curtis. From Montreal, Andrew McMaster reported that Laurier himself had thought the letter "splendid."

What seems to have been the single angry letter – "L. J. would turn in his grave to see how his descendant behaves" – was written in French and came from a Bourassa family connection, Cousin Henriette. Talbot answered in French and sent a copy to his mother. Roughly translated, it began, "I am before all Canadian, and I would have been happy to have been listed among his [Bourassa's] followers if his doctrine of nationalism could have envisaged our life as a nation in a manner *plus large*, can I say more . . . noble."

Quickly though, the personal took precedence over the

public on Talbot's agenda. His relationship with Beatrice was becoming increasingly complicated. Less intense, but equally problematic, was his relationship with his patron, Max Aitken, who, in a quite different way, promised to be every bit as critical to Talbot's own future as Henri Bourassa.

By now, Talbot had been writing to Beatrice for nearly a year. She was not the only young woman with whom he exchanged letters: fragments survive of a correspondence with a Montreal painter named Cecile Buller, and there were probably others. Also, by now numerous old flames from Canada had turned up in London with whom he could flirt and dance when on leave, including the glamorous Doris Aldous of Winnipeg, whom Talbot described as "the best dancer in Canada." Indeed, she had stopped off in Ottawa en route overseas to direct the Naughty Nine in the *Cabaret de Vogue*. But it was to the unseen Beatrice in Philadelphia that Talbot revealed himself as to no other woman but his mother Caroline. She'd become soulmate and safety valve; he'd told her of his childhood, his career as a lawyer, his hopes and ambitions for the future. In a manner that for the time was uncommonly frank, he'd confessed much about his sexual transgressions in London. Beatrice knew of his physical scars – "when I was ten, I was one of the first cases of appendicitis; two years previous to that I slid down an old board playing tag and drove an enormous splinter through my thigh" – and of the much deeper psychic scars inflicted by the war. "I cannot grow accustomed to these losses," he wrote just before leaving the trenches, moments after a man in his company had been shot by a sniper. "It is horrible, this killing in cold calculated blood, this deliberate lying in wait, as though we were hunting animals." Time and again, he told her of his yearning for Canada and for Montebello. "There is a place at home we call the Green Road," ran a letter from hospital at Christmas 1915, inspired by her gift of Walt Whitman's collection of poetry, *Song of the Open Road*. "Above it the trees meet in a lofty Gothic arch. In the autumn, the red leaves against the blue make me think always of the Sainte-Chapelle in Paris, with its many highly-coloured panes."

Since, alas, we cannot read Beatrice's letters, she remains for us a shadowy presence, illuminated only through the prism of

Talbot Papineau often sent sketches to Beatrice Fox. This pair, depicting the chapel at Montebello and the lodge gates, were done from memory and speak of his longing for home.

Talbot's responses. Yet she had revealed herself equally. At twenty-five, she was still a romantic innocent, in love with the idea of being in love with a gallant captain who had appeared in her life out of nowhere, and who wrote her such magical letters. "Your notion that we should meet at a Bal Masqué rather appeals to me," he told her in late 1915. "We must meet if we are going to meet in some more or less unusual manner." Another letter – "You threaten to make me read Cyrano to you aloud; I am fond of reading aloud, especially in French" – suggests that she had compared their situation to that of Cyrano de Bergerac and Roxanne. She sent him romantic presents, a heart-shaped silver box, a silver shoe, a tiny silver elephant to serve as a lucky charm. Yet Beatrice was also a young woman with a well-stocked mind of her own, who introduced Talbot not only to Walt Whitman but also to Rupert Brooke, and who peppered him with questions on all manner of subjects – What was Stephen Leacock really like? Why didn't Canada have its own homegrown Governor General? – and even sent him a disquisition on post-war world politics. "I did not a bit smile," Talbot assured her, "Your ideas are quite sound."

Talbot's letters, however, were not always magical. Quite often they must have left Beatrice bewildered. Even in peacetime, as many girls already knew to their cost, he was a complex figure, an elusive, solitary cat. The experiences of war had accentuated these qualities. Like Agar Adamson, Talbot was using a correspondence to exorcize the horrors of the trenches, but unlike Agar, whose method was simply to tell Mabel the facts, in their unvarnished horror, Talbot often escaped into fantasy. Sometimes he would sweep Beatrice off on a tide of high romance: "I should like nothing better than a honeymoon in cathedrals and libraries . . . I could show you Oxford and Touraine and Capri . . . Or how would you enjoy a canoe trip down the Danube, and then coming up the Rhine through Holland? By the way, do you bicycle?" On the very next page, though, he would hasten to explain that really, he'd only been fooling. "The strange thing is that whereas I have loved others and yet did not think them suitable, I think you suitable but do not love you . . . ."

Nor was Talbot at all times a master of tact. His sarcasm could be intimidating. "You have asked me to be 'honestly candid' in picking to pieces what you 'think and say,'" he told her on one occasion. "Even with my limited knowledge of your sex, I fully know the terrible risk of doing as you ask. I am quite willing to imagine you a pampered pet of society surrounded by social sycophants and flattered by much attention and many fulsome compliments. . . . But your object is insensibly dictated by vanity, for you would like to receive compliments whose hallmark of honesty you might trust. I doubt very much you would like to hear any uncomplimentary truths. . . . It is the artificial limitations of society which you tire of. You are like the Persian cat impelled by half-felt instincts to get out into a broader life. But you will not be able to escape and you would be unhappy if you did. You may be dissatisfied with dances and dinners and polo teas but you would be still more dissatisfied without them."

Even more hurtfully, Talbot went on. "You will never really be natural until you are deeply in love and it is quite probable that you will be denied even that remnant of Nature's creation, for you will choose to love not by instinct but by intelligence, choosing to mate with someone who is presentable at your house-parties, and who can supply you with the degree of comforts you are accustomed to. Personally, I hope the day will come when women will be sufficiently developed to create their own outlets and satisfy their own ambition, but as things stand today your best opportunity is to marry a successful man and through him achieve your purposes."

And yet, as Beatrice kept on discovering, nothing about Talbot was predictable. The next post would arrive with a letter full of apologies: "I am a miserable worm!! You may trample upon me and if I ever turn, it will only be to squirm under your foot. . . . You extend me a beautiful friendship and I rag you. I am contemptible. We do not seem to laugh together or cry, and it is I who am all out of tune with a poor warped heart that has fluttered too often ever to beat true . . . I am already bankrupt in your debt. What can I do in return? At least, if it were of value, I should like to give you my love." Another time, "Your letters are so loyal and good. You do not harbour all the doubts and skepticisms that assail me. You accept me in a generous and friendly spirit and I am a wretched fellow to be so unkind in return."

Talbot's appointment to the staff ushered in a new era in their relationship. Or so at least it appeared for a time. Now that he expected to have a long life ahead of him, he began to entertain the thought of spending it with Beatrice. "May I call you darling?" he wrote early in March, thanking her for a Valentine present of cigarettes and a heart-shaped box of candy. She too seems to have overcome her misgivings about becoming too deeply involved with someone who at times could be frightening, and had written far more expressively of her feelings than ever before. "I am very glad you said in your last letter that our correspondence was now on a different footing and no longer merely for the entertainment of a lonely soldier," Talbot's letter continued. "I am glad you agree we are to become interested in each other as definite personalities. I am proud of your work and your success and I want to remain connected no matter what may change in my own life." By now, they had both come to realize that matters between them were coming to a head. A correspondence of such intensity could not be sustained indefinitely. Either their romantic friendship would develop into a formal understanding – they would become "engaged to be engaged," as the saying went – or they would inevitably drift apart.

Exactly what happened next is uncertain. Some letters of Talbot's appear to be missing; another has some key words cut out of it, presumably by Beatrice. We do know, however, that Beatrice at one point wrote him beseechingly: "When I say I really love you, there isn't any comeback." We know further that early in May she took courage on the wing and sent him a coded telegram that told of her love. The first part of his response was all she could have wished for. "What an impulsive darling you are!" he replied. "We are engaged. We are lovers! I have hastened to the Signal Office and directed a cable to your address with the one word 'Congratulations' because it is the code word you suggested." Yet the rest of his letter was oddly equivocal: he looked forward to the "real love letters" she promised, and was "very happy at the rate of progress in Romance which we have made. . . . All the others I knew I did not love and would not. You were the unknown quantity – the romantic possibility, and everything I heard or saw or gathered from your letters confirmed me in that pleasing hope." Yet he continued to be evasive. He did not tell her he loved her. Instead, "I am a dangerous one to be serious with. . . . If you love me, I know the circumstances have much to do with it. Every woman has an instinct of affection for a soldier, just as a soldier wishes to have the love of a woman. . . . We cannot possibly tell, not until after the war. In the meantime, it is safer to play. I want you to love me and write me love letters for they will charm and amuse me, but I don't want you to really care. I want in return to charm and amuse you. I don't want to cause you any anxiety or sorrow. It is bad enough to have Mother thinking about me that way." He signed "Affectionately, Talbot," just as he might have to any other girl.

That Talbot did not feel as she felt was evident to Beatrice. Nor did it help that by the time she received this letter, she would also have received one written by him that pre-dated her cable, in which he'd seemed to have gone out of his way to make her unhappy. For months, as her own contribution to the war effort, and, even more, to please Talbot, she had been working on the maquette of a sculpture intended to serve as a memorial for the regimental cemetery at Voormezele. In April, she'd had the model photographed and sent the pictures to him by way of a mutual acquaintance, the American war correspondent, Frederick Palmer. Talbot dismissed her well-intended efforts quite brutally – perhaps the reminder of Voormezele accentuated his ever-present guilt about leaving the regiment – delivering the equivalent of a slap in the face. "If you intend to represent a soldier in uniform, you should have the real thing before you. In the model, there is not a single article of clothing or accoutrement that is correctly designated. The shape of the trousers and the way the puttees are rolled is of real importance. . . . And what is your figure doing? If he is to be perched up on top of a rock he will be dreadfully exposed and he must be charging or falling, otherwise he has no business there." Nothing more was ever heard of the sculpture, and several weeks passed before Beatrice wrote any more letters to Talbot. Their correspondence resumed in mid-summer: Talbot wrote more than a bit disingenuously, "I am worried lest you might have misunderstood my letter of criticism. I am afraid I have been horrid and discouraging." But it never quite recaptured its earliest freshness.

In that summer of 1916, Talbot had little enough time to write to anyone. In mid-June, he'd been seconded to Aitken's War Records Office staff, and, like everyone else in that remarkable empire, he embarked on a whirlwind of activity. "I am working night and day and I really am almost sick with fatigue," he told Beatrice in a short note, unembellished by romantic flourishes. "As well as being a staff officer, I am now Official Eyewitness. I have to write all official communications and descriptions, compile all historical records, write and edit the next books on the war. I visit the front line. I visit all the generals and colonels and I have to gather all the maps and documents etc. There is also an official photographer whom I am supposed to run. I write the weekly reports from the Corps to the Army and keep the diary. I have worked steadily an average of fourteen hours a day. Not complaining. I like it. But I can't do other things I like to do. No riding, no bridge, no reading, no letters, no sleep."

In the beginning, everything went swimmingly. For a natural writer, preparing the press communiqué was easy, and ego-boosting. "I have perhaps the widest audience I shall ever have in my life!" Talbot wrote Beatrice. "These accounts are published now in all the English papers as well as the Canadian and I believe the American also." His office at Canadian Headquarters in France was in the midst of a beautiful park with a château nearby that reminded him of Montebello. He was provided with a personal secretary, a Daimler with a chauffeur, and a splendid bay mare whom he promptly christened Queen Bee. His immediate superior, Lieutenant-Colonel R. F. Manly-Sims, Aitken's personal representative at the Front, was a sophisticated and intelligent officer with whom he soon formed a close friendship. Best of all, Talbot's relations with Aitken were excellent. "He is a curious man, very able and very free from intellectual shackles," he wrote Caroline who by now had herself moved to London to be closer to him and was filling in her time wrapping parcels at the Canadian Red Cross. "He speaks his mind and has no respect for mere position

Talbot Papineau riding his bay mare Queen Bee in the summer of 1916. He had named her in honour of Beatrice Fox.

or authority." Promotion to major seemed soon in the offing. "Sir Max has spoken in the highest terms of my work for him." Indeed, in late August, Aitken swept Talbot off to Paris in his Rolls-Royce to work on the proofs of the second volume of *Canada in Flanders*. There was even talk of his being appointed there as a liaison officer with the French Army. "I shall call myself Canadian Ambassador! Now will you marry me!" he wrote Beatrice in a letter that conveyed his high spirits, and endeavoured to convey also that so far as he was concerned, their relationship could now return to normal. "I have put your little photo in my wristwatch. It gives me the greatest pleasure to look at it. I am quite in love with it."

Before long, though, Talbot was restive again. As always, there was the nagging sense of guilt about leaving the Patricias.

It was one thing to swank around the Front in the Daimler, directing the cinematographers, posing himself in front of the ruined Cloth Hall at Ypres. But it was quite another to approach the trenches held by the Patricias, to be shooed away brusquely by Agar Adamson, and to read the disdain in his eyes. Talbot himself did not describe this encounter. But in a letter to Mabel, dated August 8, 1916, Adamson provided a full account:

> Papineau turned up two days ago with a cinematographic camera and wanted us to pose for him. I suggested he took photographs of the graves of the fallen and ordered him to get out of the lines as I did not think it fitting that in the present critical situation officers should be going about with a Punch and Judy Show.
>
> The general heard of it and quite approved, but my views are not shared by many Commanding Officers, who are only too anxious to advertise themselves and rehearsed all kinds of stunts when they heard they were coming, such as reading maps, giving orders, pretending to be shot and carried off on stretchers. I only hope the camera gets smashed. If Papineau returned to the Regiment and did his bit, it would be more to his credit than playing into Max Aitken's hands and driving about in motor cars and sleeping in a comfortable bed 16 miles behind the support lines.

Talbot's sense of being out of place revealed itself in a letter he later wrote to Beatrice. "More friends have gone. By what strange law am I still here? What right have I to selfish pleasure any longer? Should my living life not be consecrated just as their dead lives have been?"

To magnify his discomfort, he was becoming increasingly identified as a protegé of Aitken. By the early autumn of 1916, his Open Letter to Bourassa had made him a national hero. Never one to let an opportunity slip by, Sir Max suggested that Talbot return to Canada, under the auspices of the War Records Office, and make a speaking tour of every town and village. Talbot, naturally, was delighted. No better way could be envisaged to capitalize on his celebrity, and to secure his political future. He might even stay on, and run as a Liberal candidate in the coming election. Indeed,

Talbot Papineau on his rounds as an Eyewitness for the Canadian War Records Office in the summer of 1916. His sombre expression suggests a man out of sorts with himself. "By what strange law am I still here?" he wrote Beatrice Fox.

as Andrew McMaster reported, after a recent meeting of the Liberal Federation, "Sir Wilfrid called me aside to talk about you. He wants you to be our candidate, and asked me what constituency. I told him I had already thought of you running against Ames in St. Antoine or perhaps Argenteuil."*

In mid-October with the tour only six weeks away, a second letter from McMaster arrived as a thunderclap. He and another senior Liberal had discussed Talbot's plans for the speaking trip

---

* Sir Herbert Ames (1863-1954). A prominent Montreal businessman and civic reformer, best-known for his 1897 book, *The City Below the Hill*, describing the working-class districts of Montreal, he had been Conservative MP for the English Montreal riding of St. Antoine, and was re-elected there in 1917. The suburban riding of Argenteuil was represented by the Canadian High Commissioner in London, Sir George Perley, and he too was re-elected. McMaster himself had already decided to run in the Eastern Townships riding of Brome, and was successful.

and were gravely concerned. "We both feel it is unfortunate that you should be associated with Max Aitken," wrote McMaster. "Neither of us know him personally, but both of us regard him as an undesirable person for you to be identified with. I know you will do everything you can not to allow the Canadian public to imagine you are in any way affiliated with him."

Instantly, and to Aitken's great fury, Talbot cancelled the trip. "I am losing a great opportunity," he wrote his mother. "People might have thought more of what I had to say than of by whose orders I was sent out." To Beatrice, he was much more explicit. "My name was becoming associated with Sir Max. He is a power in the land. He has immense influence in both Canadian and English governments and consequently the greatest influence upon the Army. This is wholly pernicious. I am deeply opposed to political influences (especially Tory!). The Canadian government deserves defeat and disgrace. They have played politics with the lives of men. It has been damnable and I shall support any movement to destroy them. Consequently, I must be free from any connection with those influences." On November 10, in a letter to Andrew McMaster, which McMaster later passed on to Laurier, Talbot expressed his rage and frustration even more vividly. "I want to get to Canada not because I am quitting here or because my nerve is gone . . . I feel very deeply that my life having been spared in a miraculous manner, it is no longer my own . . ."

Simultaneously, by some adroit manoeuvring, Talbot severed his formal connection with the War Records Office, and reverted to being a General Staff Officer, although the switch was more cosmetic than substantive, since he continued to write the weekly communiqué. Any immediate need to decide what he next should do was solved by the intervention of Byng, by now a strong admirer of Talbot, who sent him on a two-month staff course. During it, he wrote a paper on "The Principles of Command," and impressed everyone by delivering a speech titled "The War and Its Influences Upon Canada," in which he further developed the ideas he had put forward in his letter to Bourassa. The war had made Canada a nation at last and given it a history, was his thesis, "a history that will form the firm foundation of a national construction," he declared, so that post-war Canada should become responsible for its own foreign policy, and "begin the development of a consular and even diplomatic service, with accredited representatives in France, Italy, Russia and the United States." Less presciently, he speculated on the effect that hundreds of thousands of returned veterans would have on political structures. "To a great extent the soldiers will have been freed from the shackles of purely party politics. We are likely to return to Canada sick to death of political intrigue and determined to exercise independent judgements. One thing which we will demand above all others is decency and honesty in our public men."

Talbot returned to his desk in mid-February 1917, to a job that was no longer rewarding. Despite his best efforts at distancing himself, the connection with Aitken – now Beaverbrook – continued to dog him. "For heaven's sake, please understand I am *not* doing Max Aitken's work," he wrote testily to Caroline. "As part of my duties, I am supposed to write each week the official communiqué. This takes a very very small part of my time, and for the rest I am busy with ordinary staff duties which are very exacting." As always, the thought of salving his conscience by returning to the regiment kept on recurring, yet, by now he was deterred not only by the effects this would have on Caroline, but also, as he talked out endlessly with his friend and mentor, Manly-Sims, by the prospect of death and mutilation, and even more acutely, by the fear that, having seen so much horror but then having put it behind him, the courage that had sustained him earlier would have left him. To compound Talbot's sour mood, his relationship with Beatrice had arrived at another crisis, and this time it was serious. Out of the blue, in late March, she sent him a cable that threatened to end it, once and for all.

COMPLETE CONFIDENCE IN YOU DESPITE IRISH LETTER. SITUATION ONLY FORCES GOODBYE ran Beatrice's telegram. To heighten the mystery, it arrived almost simultaneously with an exquisite miniature painting of herself that she'd sent Talbot for his thirty-fourth birthday. Their most recent exchanges of letters had been the most intimate in some time; once again it was beginning to seem possible that eventually they would meet and would marry. "Your last letter was the kindest and loveliest you have ever written me," he'd told her on New Year's Day. Six weeks later, on February 18, although it's unlikely he'd meant it in earnest, he'd almost proposed. "Let us be persuaded that we love and I can promise life in Canada to be full of fun and interest. Come over and marry me here and live in London. What sayest thou?"

Thus Talbot was totally baffled by Beatrice's cable. "What under the sun does it mean?" he wrote back. "What have the Irish to do with it?" A week later, when an explanatory letter from Beatrice arrived, the riddle was solved – or partially so. The "Irish letter," it developed, had originated at Kilmanaham Castle at Clonmel in Ireland. It had been written to Beatrice by Lady Donoughmore, the Anglo-Irish grand dame who had first introduced her to Talbot. Precisely what it contained is lost to history, but from subsequent correspondence it is clear that Lady Donoughmore had warned that during a recent leave in London, Talbot, and also Caroline Papineau, had talked out of turn about Beatrice, had suggested that she was flinging herself at his head. Specifically, the phrase "ulterior designs" had been used.

Talbot himself now fired off a telegram. YOUR CONFIDENCE ENTIRELY JUSTIFIED. ABSURD. FALSE SITUATION. PROFOUNDLY SORRY. WRITING FULLY. He followed it up with the most eloquent letter that he had ever sent Beatrice. "That in any thought or action I should have been ill-bred or inconsiderate towards you is utterly false, and I deny with all the emphasis in my power," he wrote. "There is not a word I have said or written of you that I would not have you know. I can lay bare my heart and mind without fear. I have always written to you with complete frankness. I have concealed no thought. I have had no reservations of mind. I have told you what I felt, what I liked and what I did not like. From the beginning, I wished our correspondence to be absolutely natural and free from the artificialities which surround so generally the intercourse between men and women. My letters have been written under considerable stress, and when each one might very conceivably have been my last. It is laughable that I should seek in any way to deceive you. . . . That this horrible, ugly cloud of suspicion should have come between us is unutterably sad. I suppose somebody said that we thought you wanted to marry me, or some silly thing like that."

Of particular distress to him, Talbot continued, was that Caroline should have been "dragged in." Much more likely, the real culprit had been his "well meaning but wholly irresponsible" friend Charlie Stewart, who was also a protégé of Lady Donoughmore. "He never stops talking. I am quite positive that he has given a description of our friendship and of our respective motives and actions which could very well lead to misconceptions. He is a constitutional story-teller and is regardless of consequences."

Talbot closed by thanking Beatrice for the miniature. "It was handed to me exactly on my birthday. It is the most precious

Beatrice Fox, *circa* 1917. This is a photograph of the miniature of herself that Beatrice had sent Talbot for his thirty-fourth birthday, and that he had described to her as "the most precious thing I have ever had. It seems to have a life, a soul of its own." He returned it to her, hoping that someday she would be able to give it to him in person.

thing I have ever had. It seems to have a life, a soul of its own. I am returning it to you. Will you keep it for me please, until someday when you may give it to me with the confidence with which you would entrust your own honour to me."

By his gravity and sincerity, Talbot restored Beatrice's confidence. Yet although the misunderstanding had been cleared up, somehow a worm of doubt had been introduced that this time could not be expunged. "We shall have to marry somehow, somewhere, just to confound the gossips," Talbot wrote a few weeks later. By then, though, he was writing as a friend and no longer as a putative lover.

Shortly after the contretemps with Beatrice, Talbot embarked upon his last, and his most important duty as Eyewitness. "I am quite safe," he wrote his mother on April 11. "I have slept 4 hours out of 48, and walked over the hardest ground more than 12 miles a day. I have been along our new front line and seen many Huns. I have to stay indoors now, and write our official account and pre- pare maps etc. It has been a splendid victory."

What Talbot did not tell Caroline was that never in his life had he felt more frustrated than during those forty-eight hours. While he looked on, scribbling notes and sketching out maps, the Canadians had scored, not just a splendid victory, but the most important British victory of the war thus far. For the first time, all four Canadian divisions had gone over the top together, com- bined into an army corps commanded by Byng. "We have pushed them back," wrote Agar Adamson to Mabel, of the performance of the Patricias. "Things have gone splendidly, and men awfully cheered."

The action described by Papineau and Adamson had hap- pened on Easter Monday, April 9, 1917. Attacking at dawn in a dri- ving rain, the Canadians had captured an escarpment seven miles long and shaped like a lozenge, rising out of the great sweep of the Douai Plain. This landmark was called Vimy Ridge.

20

Birth of a Nation

*No matter what the constitutional historians may say, it
was on Easter Monday, April 9, 1917, and not on any
other date, that Canada became a nation.*

D. J. Goodspeed. *The Road Past Vimy*

The character of the Canadian National Memorial at Vimy
Ridge is almost pharaonic. Twin pylons of Adriatic marble
tower upwards from the highest point of the ridge. At the
top of the pylons are figures carved in heroic scale representing
Peace and Justice; just below are Truth, Knowledge, Gallantry,
and Sympathy. The most compelling statue is the simplest: the
cloaked and hooded figure of a woman, standing alone overlooking the Douai Plain, its level expanse studded with heaps of coal
tailings that themselves resemble pyramidic tombs. This woman
represents the Spirit of Canada. Chin resting in her left hand, a
drooping spray of laurels clasped in her right, she is mourning her
dead sons. Yet the message conveyed by the statue, unlike that of
the desolate caribou at Beaumont-Hamel, speaks of defiance
rather than elegy. The Spirit of Canada seems to be saying that
somehow, what happened here was worth all the cost. Many sons
may have fallen but they won the day and thus were reborn.

Unlike any other monument that Canadians have erected to
commemorate their accomplishments, the Vimy memorial exhibits
not a trace of self-deprecation, of hesitancy, of ambiguity. In its
parts and in its whole it speaks of their certitude about what they
had accomplished by their performance in the Great War, above
all by their unprecedented victory on this hallowed ground.

Designed in the late 1920s by the Toronto sculptor Walter Allward, unveiled officially on July 29, 1936, by King Edward VIII, five months before he abdicated, the memorial is testament above all to the conviction Canadians held about themselves in the years between the wars. Despite the Depression, despite the increasing influence over them of their giant neighbour to the south, it still seemed possible that the twentieth century might belong to Canada. This attitude may have been naive and unrealistic. The fact remains that few of the 6,400 Canadians who, in the bleakest

This snapshot, taken on a visit to Vimy Ridge in October 1991, illustrates the pharaonic character of the monument. The scale is evident from the miniscule size of the human figures.

"The Spirit of Canada." She is mourning her dead sons, yet her message is as much of defiance as of sorrow.

year of the Depression, scrimped and saved their way across the Atlantic to be present at the memorial's unveiling, had any doubt that to be a Canadian was to be something special.

How much of that Canadian sense of selfhood still endures is a question that, mercifully for both writer and reader, lies far beyond the scope of this book. Nor, except in broad brush-stroke, is it the intention to describe the battle of Vimy itself. This has been done vividly and exhaustively by others, most notably by the military historian D. J. Goodspeed and by Pierre Berton in his 1986 *tour de force*, *Vimy*. Instead, we perceive the event itself, and its prelude and aftermath, through the view of a single Canadian soldier who was involved in it. He was twenty-three years old, a tall, gangling Ontario farmboy from southwestern Ontario. His name was Harold Adams Innis. Later, as a direct result of his experiences during the war, he would become the first major economic scholar that Canada has produced, author of those seminal works of Canadian economic history, *The Fur Trade in Canada* and *The Cod Fisheries*, and thereby the intellectual godfather of Canadian economic nationalism. Later still, as author of *Empire and Communications*, he would pioneer the exploration of the effects of modern media, unintended and often unrecognized, that Marshall McLuhan would transform into a universal vocabulary.

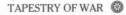

Nearly sixty-five hundred Canadians, many of them veterans and their families, attended the unveiling of the Vimy Memorial on July 29, 1936. This photograph shows the official fly-past. "The Spirit of Canada" can be seen in the left background.

The story must begin with the event itself. On April 9, 1917, Easter Monday, the four divisions of the Canadian Corps, operating as a unit for the first time, together with the 51st Highland Division (a British unit under Canadian command), in all, some 40,000 men, hurled themselves up the slopes of Vimy Ridge. This was a repeat of attempts made unsuccessfully the previous year and the year before that by French and British troops. By early afternoon, they had achieved most of their objectives, advancing some three miles, breaching through three successive lines of German defences and going on the following day to seize the ridge's commanding high point, Hill 145, where the memorial now stands. During their advance they captured 54 artillery pieces, 104 trench mortars and took more than 4,000 prisoners. In nearly three years of war, there had not been another allied victory like it on the Western Front, nor would there be anything comparable for more than another year, until the final allied advance of mid-1918.

The manner and execution of the operation was distinctively Canadian. No great flair or military inventiveness was involved. Indeed the commander, General Byng, demonstrated a lack of flair by failing to exploit his breakthrough, thereby allowing the Germans to re-form their line defending their stronghold of Lens in the centre of the Douai Plain. As commander, Byng amassed most of the credit for the success of the attack. The author of many of its most conspicuously commonsensical features, though, was his senior divisional commander, Major-General Arthur Currie, a former real estate operator from Victoria, B.C., whose motto was "Neglect Nothing." The deed was done by teamwork, by planning and, as *was* original, by the application of commonsense to problems that, until now, the military had regarded as insuperable, or at any rate had failed so bloodily to solve on the Somme and in the Ypres Salient.

Military doctrine required a prolonged artillery barrage to demoralize the enemy and to shatter his defence systems. This, however, warned the enemy that an attack was imminent. So instead, let's blast him without warning. At 5:30 AM, "a wall of sound, like ten thousand thunders," in Berton's description, burst out upon the ridge, some 983 artillery field pieces firing in unison, and, before they were done, hurling out six million shells, "at an average of three thousand a second." In most previous attacks, limited successes had turned into failures because troops had lost their way across the blighted, pitted moonscape. So, let's exploit the new technology of aerial photography, and let's use these photographs to build a large-scale replica of the three

German lines, and then rehearse and rehearse the attacking battalions until everyone knows where they are supposed to go and,
just as important, where those to the left and right are supposed
to go. ("We went over a large area of ground that had been
marked out with tapes, showing certain trenches that we will be
interested in," wrote Adamson to Mabel in late February. "This is
part of the new method of training and should be very helpful.")
To bring all of those thousands of troops to their jump-off positions in the manner of the Somme and the Salient would signal to
the enemy that an attack was coming, and also would expose the
waiting troops to German counter-barrage fire. So let's bring them
to the front lines by means of tunnels bored into the soft chalk,
blowing out the fronts of the tunnels at the last moment.

It didn't go as smoothly as on the practice dummy. The
German line was held by some elite units, including the Prussian
Guards. A storm, sleet mixed with rain, burst shortly before zero
hour, and later turned into a blizzard. The Fourth Division, on the
far left, fell well behind its schedule. The Highland Division, attacking in support on the right of the Canadian Corps, made almost no
progress at all. The casualties totalled 10,602, almost 2,600 of them
fatal. Yet far more ground had been won – the entire ridge – than
had ever been won before, and at far less cost. Prime Minister
Borden, attending meetings of the Imperial War Cabinet in London,
was exultant. "All newspapers ringing with praise of the Canadians," he wrote in his diary. Yet more exultant were Canadians back
home. CREST OF VIMY RIDGE TAKEN. CANADIANS LEAD IN TRIUMPH, read the
banner headline in the Toronto *Globe*, echoed in every paper
across the country. Henri Bourassa relegated the story to page 3 of
Le Devoir, yet even he bowed to the euphoria of the moment and
allowed an upbeat headline to slip past, "Les Canadiens sur La
Crète de Vimy." From the Patricias' commanding new position
overlooking the Douai Plain, Agar Adamson allowed himself a rare
moment of exultation. "The Corps Commander has specially noted
that we were the only regiment whose band played the men over
the top, as well as following up and acting as stretcher bearers off
their own bat," he wrote Mabel. He enclosed in his letter a prim-
rose and a violet picked in the woods in front of the ridge.

The part played by Harold Innis in this splendid affair was entirely unremarkable. As an artillery signalman in the 4th Field Battery attached to the First Division, his tasks were mostly the joe-jobs of tending the artillery horses and building plank roads over the mud so that the guns could be humped up to the new line. The terse, cryptic notes that he was making contain no insights into military tactics nor any profound musings about death and glory. His selected topics were almost always those of cold and hunger and exhaustion. "Got up at 4; dug in the trench, bombardment with large guns, 18 pounders, machine guns," he tells us on April 9, the day of the battle. On the following day, "Came up, built roads, found dead Fritzes, machine guns and trench mortars . . . nothing to eat, bully beef and biscuit, bury man in shell hole." Not until April 12 is there even a hint of relief. "Slept in German dug-out; comfortable; good view of country."

What *was* remarkable was that Innis was keeping this record at all. Private diaries were strictly forbidden by army regulations. All personal letters received, as we know from Adamson and Papineau, had to be destroyed immediately after they had been read, and all outgoing mail (except that of officers) was strictly censored. Had Innis's notes been discovered, he would have been punished severely, perhaps by a jail sentence, perhaps by the dreaded "Field Punishment No. 1," in which the culprit was lashed by the arms to a wagon wheel and left out for hours in all kinds of weather. Yet, displaying qualities of nerve and determination that would later reveal themselves in his scholarship, Innis somehow managed to write almost daily in a small pocket *aide-mémoire* that survives among his papers. Later in life, he would expand his compulsion for taking notes into scribbled observations about almost every imaginable subject and place, using these both in his scholarly works and his famous "Idea File."

Innis's streak of individualism was a product of his background and upbringing. He was Canadian Gothic in its purest form. Born on November 5, 1894, on a hundred-acre farm near Otterville, in southwestern Ontario, he belonged to careful, frugal, and quintessentially dour Scottish stock who had already been tilling the soil of Oxford County for three generations. The

Innises were also strict Baptists, with a reputation for hard work and sobriety. Not a background from which one would expect an internationally renowned economist to emerge except that it also produced an even more famous economist in the person of John Kenneth Galbraith.*

The dominant figure in Harold's childhood was his mother, Mary Adams Innis, regarded locally as "the wonder of Otterville" because, while still a girl, she'd invested a thousand-dollar legacy into a year's stay at a ladies' finishing school at Whitby, Ontario. Harold, the eldest of her four children, was her favourite. From the beginning she was ambitious for him. Indeed she had actually christened him "Herald" not "Harold" in the fond hope that he would have a career in the ministry; it was not until he'd joined the army that the spelling was changed on his birth certificate. Despite the finishing school, it was not a household in which music or laughter or poetry were given much encouragement. To the end of his days, Innis was famous for having no small talk and few social graces. But it was a close-knit and, in its own way, an affectionate family; apart from his mother, Harold was particularly close to his younger sister Lillian. Like most farm families during the lingering depression of the 1890s, the Innises were cash-poor – when Harold went to Otterville High School, he couldn't afford a hockey stick – but they were not penurious. The farmhouse itself, while spartan in appearance, was comfortable; perched high on a ridge, it offered a magnificent view of the surrounding countryside; houses and barns and orchards and fields, in those days still fenced by the interlocking roots of the original pine forests.

Even as a toddler, Harold was a noticer. According to his friend and biographer, the historian Donald Creighton, it was by observing the everyday activities that went on around him that the great idea that would inform his major works of scholarship began to take shape in his consciousness – that humble "staple products" like beaver pelts and salt cod were central to Canada's economic existence. "The rhythm of the farm danced slowly along

---

* Born in 1908 in the Dutton–Wallacetown area of southwestern Ontario, near Lake Erie, Galbraith described his childhood in a delightful memoir titled *The Scotch*, published in 1964.

his blood, echoed faintly in his memory ever afterwards," writes Creighton in a sweeping romantic passage that even though at odds with Innis's own terse and laconic personality, expresses the essence of his character. "He came to know the land, its contours, soils and vegetation, with a curiously intimate, even affectionate particularity. He could tell by a glance at a particular chestnut or hickory nut what tree it had come from; he could infallibly identify the source of a bucket of maple sap by its distinctive flavour." Child Harold noticed also how distant economic events could affect not just the economy of local farmers but the character of family farms themselves. As the Prairies opened up soon after the turn of the century, wheat ceased being an important cash-crop for Ontario farmers, and the Innises, like most of their neighbours, turned instead to dairy-farming and raising poultry. "On dark afternoons in late December, he sat at the table in the farmhouse kitchen, plucking the fowls that were to be carried in next day to the Christmas market at Brantford," Creighton continues; "he carried pitchers of cooling drinks to the men toiling away in the dried yellow fields under the scorching suns of August. . . . He noted similarities, he detected differences; he was conscious of both recurrence and change. And gradually the farm became known to him through an incredible mass of detail which was regarded, not in isolation but as part of a vast organic whole." Later, helping out an uncle who was a local storekeeper, the teen-aged Harold absorbed also the rudiments of business: "I learned something of the way goods were handled when brought in by freight-train and taken from various cars indicated on the way-bills," he tells us himself in the unvarnished prose of his own fragmentary, unpublished autobiography. "I learned something of the character of economical management, and the refusal to be badgered by travelling salesmen, and of the various devices by which farmers could be encouraged to buy more goods."

As a student, first at the local one-room school with its potbellied stove, later at Otterville High School, Innis was clever but not exceptional. By nature a packrat, he kept everything, and we note from a 1908 report card that his average that year of 77.8 per cent was far exceeded by the 89.3 per cent of one Leola Giles who vanishes thereafter from high school records, most likely, in the

way of most bright female students of that era, going on to become
a teacher. His composition book exhibits no gift for language –
"Innis as a scholar will forever be imprisoned in the dungeons of
unreadability" – another friend, the historian Arthur Lower,
lamented many years later – but does contain the occasional flash
of originality. "By 1950 there will be large airships manned with
soldiers and guns and war will be carried on entirely in airships . . .
There will be regular schedules of freight and of passenger carrying airships between the important cities of the world," he tells us
in 1909, only six years after the Wright Brothers. In the meantime,
there were the railroads, which in Innis's judgement would never
be superseded: having done on-the-spot research for an assign-
ment to describe a railway station by hanging over the Grand
Trunk Railway bridge at Otterville and peering down at the platform, his gift for observation transcended his syntax, so that all
of a sudden, we are there with him: "An oncoming passenger train
is approaching . . . the people rush out of the waiting rooms . . .
the baggagemen are hurrying through the crowd . . . the familiar
orders of the conductor are heard. . . . Now, the yells of the
cabmen are heard to attract the passenger's notice, or advertise
his hotel and business." Equally telling is the frequency with
which references to Mark Twain – "he has wrote [sic] many
humorous poems and stories which result in laughter from
most people" – pop up in the composition book. Unlike Galbraith,
Innis rarely allowed his own dry sardonic sense of humour to
enliven his scholarship, but it runs as a *leitmotiv* through his Idea
File, as in, "Most forward-looking people have their heads
screwed on sideways."

The next step in the inexorable progress towards the career
as a Baptist preacher ordained by Mary Innis was Woodstock Collegiate. This remarkable institution, as we learn from Alexander
John Watson (whose 1981 doctoral study of Innis, *Marginal Man*,
is the closest work yet to a full-scale intellectual biography), constituted a fundamentalist idea in the wilderness. Founded a generation earlier, it was a secular high school run by Baptists, "a
preparatory school which screened out promising rural students,
polished them and gave them the grounding which allowed them
to compete in the university milieu with students from far more

privileged backgrounds." In many respects, the ambience was narrow and ungenerous – among other prejudices that Innis was never able to shake off was a deep aversion towards Catholics, whom he invariably referred to as "Romans." Yet the curriculum was impressive, even by the demanding standards of the era. Innis was expected to become proficient not only in literature, grammar, history, and geography, but also in algebra, geometry, art, Latin, botany, geology, and physics. All of this had to be accomplished within a logistical framework that was challenging, even for a healthy and hardy teenager. The county seat of Woodstock was twenty miles distant from Otterville, and it was two miles on from there to the Innis farm. In order to get to school on time, Harold had to rise no later than six and walk into Otterville, so as to catch without fail the 7:00 AM train to Woodstock. After that, there was a mile-long walk to the collegiate. Small wonder that he made very few friends or had any fun. "During these years," writes Creighton, "he remained the country boy, poor, awkward, ill at ease, yet earnest and determined." By now, though, he was beginning to demonstrate an inexhaustible capacity for learning: in 1911–1912 he telescoped his final two years into one, even so, passing with honours.

In the autumn of 1913 he went on to McMaster University. This too was a Baptist institution, then located in Toronto, in a large red-brick building on Bloor Street that nowadays is the Royal Conservatory of Music. Here, Harold's first term was a disaster. Determined not to be a drain on the family resources, he'd taken the previous year off and spent it working as an interim teacher in the same one-room school where he'd learned his letters, supplementing this income by investing in a ferret to catch rabbits and woodchucks and muskrats, adding value to their pelts by tanning them "according to an Old Indian recipe," and selling them to furriers. But the high cost of living in Toronto – a humble room in a boarding house on Hazelton Avenue in Yorkville cost $1.50 weekly – almost defeated him. Cold, hungry and lonely, he was unable to concentrate on his studies. By Christmas, he'd decided to quit, and it took all of Mary Innis's talents of persuasion – she called in her brother, a successful doctor in London, Ontario, as an example of the value of higher education – to convince him to accept family help. Immediately thereafter, Innis started to flourish. "I am having the time of my life," he wrote his mother in January 1914. His marks, save in the Romanish subject of Latin, were excellent. He swallowed his shyness and joined the Debating Club. From yearbook photographs, we can see that he was maturing into an impressive-looking young man, who, but for jug ears and a preternaturally gloomy expression, might have been almost handsome. His intellectual horizons were beginning to broaden. "We are going to have Bourassa at the Literary Banquet," he wrote Mary later that winter. But he remained a devout and unquestioning Baptist, he reassured her, who took full advantage of all the opportunities afforded by the big city to sit at the feet of great preachers. "I heard Dr. Eaton of New York on Monday, and he's the foremost Baptist minister in America," he wrote her, "although I saw him later going down the street smoking." Then, as may not have reassured her, he added, "I have run across a lot of fellows in McMaster who tend towards Materialism or who believed there is no God, which was an astonishing fact to me."

The outbreak of war the following August impinged upon Innis scarcely at all. (Bourassa was correct in his observation that it was mostly recent British immigrants and "the floating population of the cities" who rushed to enlist.) For him, as for most of his contemporaries at McMaster, the British Empire was little more than an abstraction, a large section of the map coloured pink, rather than a cause worth fighting for, perhaps even dying for. In any event, he was becoming a Big Man on Campus, renowned for his debating skills and for winning top marks in both philosophy and political economy. Since he was a compulsive reader of the *Globe*, the baptism by fire of the Canadian troops at Second Ypres could not have escaped his attention, but it did not spur him to join up. Instead, during the summer of 1915, he further broadened his horizons, and earned the princely sum of $60 monthly, all found, teaching in a one-room school in the hamlet of Landonville in the wheat-growing district east of Edmonton, Alberta, much the same kind of sought-after summer job that John Diefenbaker had lucked into a year earlier in Saskatchewan. The expansive, invigorating style of the Last Best West, so different from that of Otterville, agreed with Innis: he wrote long enthusiastic letters home describing the crop yields of over a hundred bushels an acre, the duck-shooting expeditions, the picnics and rodeos, even a "Galician dance" that seems to have produced something remarkably close to a hangover. For Innis in later years, that long golden summer of 1915, when for the first time in his life he let go and behaved like a healthy young animal, took on the same halcyon glow that the last pre-war summer at Blue Sea Lake had for Ethel Chadwick. He seems even to have toyed briefly with the notion of settling down permanently. "There is a dandy 100-acre homestead, the best in the district, selling at $1,700," he told his sister Lillian.

Even in the frontier-land of Landonville, forty miles journey by stage from the nearest railway point at Vermilion, the war kept on intruding. "The war talk here is the same I guess as all over," Innis wrote to his mother, in mid-July. "Everybody knows what will happen next until it comes, and though unexpected, it was always expected." In August came the news that an Otterville acquaintance named Barney Ryder had been killed in action. This was the first wartime statistic to which Innis could attach a face and while his letter of condolence contained all the proper pieties – "Not only did Barney die for his country, but in a broader sense he died for civilization and the world" – it also suggests a new

Harold Innis at Landonville, Alberta, in the summer of 1915. Early in the century, in the Canadian west, school kept going in the summer. For university students, summer jobs as teachers were much sought after. Innis greatly enjoyed his summer in northern Alberta, especially the duck-shooting expeditions, as the rare smile in this photograph is witness.

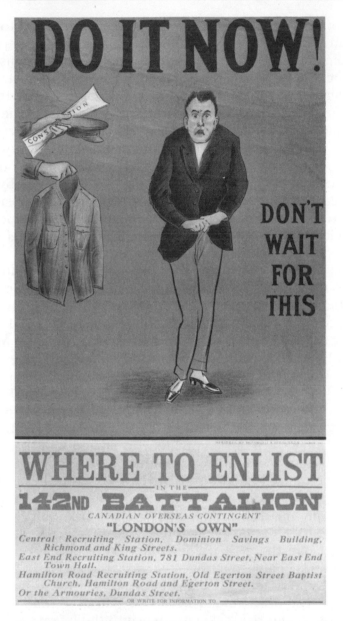

Enlistment poster, 1916. By mid-war, the threat of conscription was increasing. Such a poster would have influenced Harold Innis to join up.

sense of urgency. In the autumn, when Innis returned to Toronto to begin his last year at McMaster, the change in the campus mood was palpable. Suddenly, everyone was talking about conscription. Patriotic women could be seen roaming Bloor Street, handing white feathers to able-bodied men not in uniform. Even the Debating Society had changed: real questions had replaced the abstract and philosophical. On December 3, when McMaster faced Trinity College, the resolution was, "That commercial prosperity is necessarily a cause of war." This was the most important debate of Innis's college career; he won the day for McMaster by arguing the negative. The interrelations of commerce, he posited, had created an interdependent world. "Commercial prosperity," he concluded, "is not necessarily the cause of war; it is the only panacea for peace."

His moment of truth arrived inevitably in late winter. At the start of 1916, Prime Minister Borden had announced a major new recruiting drive; 500,000 men in uniform was now the government's objective. Like other universities, McMaster did its bit by waiving examinations for the graduating class; in early March, fifteen of Harold's friends left to join the artillery, leaving him in an agony of indecision. The countervailing pressure came from his family. Back in Otterville, frantic that he would enlist, Mary Innis was more determined than ever to steer him into a career in the ministry, and arranged for him to meet a group of Baptists in the Ottawa Valley town of Kemptville who offered him the chance to take charge of the South Gower Church as a lay preacher, even though he himself had not yet made a formal profession of faith by being baptized. Initially, Innis accepted. At the last moment, he changed his mind. "They pushed me too hard and I got suspicious," he told his son Donald, many years later. He decided that he would join the artillery. In a long, tortuous letter home, he explained his confused motives.

First, the practical: the artillery was known to be the safest branch of the army; much better to join now than to wait for conscription and risk being drafted into the infantry, which was "no place for a man if he wants to come back alive." Furthermore, "the man who doesn't go will have no chance after the war. The people will despise him and there will be no chance of

Harold Adams Innis in 1916. Born in rural Ontario of careful and frugal Scottish stock, he was Canadian Gothic in its purest form. This is his graduation photograph from the McMaster University yearbook. "Enlisted since graduation," reads the accompanying text.

his succeeding. Besides, I will have seen a great deal of country and will have seen life in no other way. It would be a profitable investment." Conspicuously absent from Innis's letter was any mention of imperial solidarity, nor for that matter, of Canadian patriotism. His ultimate motives were those of conscience, and there is no reason to doubt his sincerity. "It isn't so much because these other fellows went though that made me think. It is because if the Christian religion is worth anything to me [enlisting] is the only thing I can do. . . . Do you think I could conscientiously preach the truths of the New Testament and those eternal verities of the Bible, and stand by and sanction by my standing aside their wholesale violation as in the desecration of Belgian wives and mothers by heartless Germans? . . . It is as Sir Wilfrid Laurier has said, 'If Germany wins this war, nothing else in God's world matters.'"

By early April, Harold was Signaller Innis, with the serial number 339852. He assigned $20 monthly – almost two-thirds of his pay – to his mother to be put in the bank for his future education. The city of Toronto insured him for $1,000, free of charge, a service provided to all local recruits. After a few weeks of preliminary training at Camp Petawawa, he left for England in July. In mid-November 1916, Harold Adams Innis was in France.

21

A Lucky Man

. . . As we had imagined it:
afraid war would end
chasing Germans with bayonets
Pleasure of going over the top
Loaded down with German helmets (trophies)
As we found it:
Bully beef and hardtack
[railway] cars marked 8 horses or 40 men
bayonets used to toast bread and cut wood
Filling of sandbags
Helmets to wash in
damned dull, damned duty and
damned monotony of it . . .

Harold Innis. Notes for a reply to a toast
to returned veterans; 1918

As this mordant "found poetry" illustrates, Harold Innis would look back on his time in the trenches as a time of unmitigated horror. In later years, it was only with great difficulty that he could be persuaded to talk about it – and then, only to others who had shared the experience. Yet few other Canadians would benefit more considerably from the Great War. If Max Aitken exploited the war to invent his own greatness, the war thrust Innis's greatness upon him. "The war was his patron," writes John Watson in a key passage in *Marginal Man*. "It set his personality, imposed the great problematics which he would later tackle and forged the complex link between his sense of individualism and his nationalism." The war was also of immense practical benefit to Innis. It provided him with the seed money to make

Artillery enlistment poster.

the ultimate break with Otterville and to discover his true calling as a seminal economic thinker.

He'd started out little different from any other soldier. By mid-1916, the Canadian army had changed beyond recognition from the original Expeditionary Force that Adamson and Papineau had joined only two years earlier. Gone were the cockney

A view of some of the notorious boxcars designed for "8 horses or 40 men."

These contrasting images provide an eloquent gloss to Harold Innis's own description of the difference between the image of war and its reality.

accents and elongated upper-class vowels of the Overseas Englishmen; recruits now were mostly young callow farm boys and college students. Innis did set himself apart from the crowd by his determination to treat everything that happened as a learning experience. Thanks to his letters home – mostly addressed to his sister Lillian but intended for family consumption – and to the clandestine diary he began keeping on the train trip down to the embarkation point of Halifax, it's easy to visualize him in a series of cinematic vignettes. Here he is, on a scorcher of a day in July 1916, sweating in ill-fitting khaki, elbowing his way through a crowded railway car blue with smoke, making awkward excuses not to join in the card games, or to take a swig from the bottles on offer, finding his way eventually to the observation platform. He pulls out his notebook and scribbles down a series of observations. "Mustard in grain; sweet clover; also bluephlox. Peas mixed with oats," he writes of the landscape just east of Montreal Island that nowadays is suburbia but then was "lots of level ground, rolling land to the North." At Drummondville, he reports "large quantities of coal cars"; "Population 6000; Canada Chemical Company employs 2300 men." At Moncton, New Brunswick, then in its heyday as "Hub of the Maritimes," the whole contingent disembarked for a couple of hours and made a "brisk march through the city, with the band at its head." At dockside in Halifax, the security measures – unsurprising today – struck him as outlandish: "They inspected our kits again, for fear we had dynamite or anything, closed all the windows, would allow no-one to post a letter, and kept us locked up 'til after dinner when we marched down to the boat." Of the voyage across the Atlantic – so much for the future author of *The Fur Trade* and *The Cod Fisheries* – Innis's reports are prosaic. "It looks funny with water wherever you look and as far as you can see," he told Lillian, adding that he had earned an additional seven dollars "washing dishes and waiting on tables."

On arrival in England, Harold and the others were dispatched to Shorncliffe Camp on the Kentish coast near Dover, a vast agglomeration of Napoleonic-era stone barracks and new wooden huts and thousands of tents that had succeeded Salisbury Plain as the main training centre for Canadians. Here, he shared a tent with board floors ("by now we could sleep on bricks") with eight other signalmen. The food was unappetizing ("we get a lot of bread and butter") but the view of the Channel was magnificent ("on a bright day, they say that you can see France and even hear the sound of the guns"). For the next four months, he applied himself diligently to learning the mechanics of musketry drill, signalling, laying telephone wire, and of gun-drill with wagons and eighteen-pounders ("necessity of doubling and keeping under cover; rapid firing essential with a cool head"). More enjoyable for a farm boy were lessons in riding, and the care of the artillery horses. "I learned a lot more about horses than I ever knew before," he wrote home. "There are some here who hardly knew any more about a horse than a cow." His Baptist censoriousness kept breaking surface. "Some fellows spend terrible amount on booze," he wrote in his diary. "Sergeant-Major drunk most of the time." He himself, when off duty, haunted the local library – "not extra good for reference" – listened to local preachers, and hugely enjoyed the splendid teas laid on by a certain Miss Vickery, a "jolly old maid" who adopted him, and a couple of other of his more presentable fellow soldiers. "Well furnished house, bread very thin, chicken, fruit and custard, chocolates," he reports. In October, when granted a six-day embarkation leave with free transportation, he stretched the offer to the limit and went all the way north to Inverness in Scotland, where he noted "wild scenery, hairy sheep, abundance of turnips to feed sheep." At Edinburgh, he lucked into a comfortable bed at the YMCA for only threepence a night, and spent a whirlwind three days visiting not only the castle and Holyrood Palace, but also "John Knox's house; Adam Smith burial ground; Edinburgh University; Forth Bridge." Stopping off in London on the return journey, he fell in with a couple of Australian soldiers whose information about conditions down under ("many undercurrents in Australian politics; conscription failed in New Zealand") was carefully recorded in his notebook.

The most important thing that Innis learned during his four months in England was something much less tangible. He was beginning to realize, as were many of his colleagues, that he was not just a Colonial, but a Canadian. To this point, army life had agreed with him better than he'd expected. "I am enjoying myself," he wrote home to his mother. "I sometimes think I am the most enjoyable [*sic*] in the camp." Yet the spit-and-polish condescension of many of the British officers stuck in his craw. "Man given 14 days detention for saying to an officer when being asked to tighten girth on horse, 'Yes I'll do it,' instead of 'yes-sir,'" he noted in his diary. He was horrified when a sadistic sergeant insisted that untrained men gallop their horses, and then, when they fell off, referred to them as "falling maple leaves." Despite his affection for Miss Vickery, her effusive comments about Canadians coming over to help the mother country annoyed him. "We had felt that we were concerned with fighting for Canada, and Canada alone," he would write many years later. During his time in France, Innis's resentment towards the English presumption of superiority intensified. "It makes my blood boil when I think of Englishmen in Canada who have not the backbone to enlist," he wrote Lillian. "They are over in Canada making all kinds of money while our lads are out here suffering heaven knows what and for what is England's cause if it is anybody's." By the time he made this comment, Innis had become not simply a Canadian, but a Canadian nationalist.

On November 11, 1916, Innis sent a money order home and left his watch with Miss Vickery. Armed with his first pay in French currency – "25 francs; paper money much in evidence, even for 50 centimes" – he recorded in his diary, he and the rest of his artillery unit left for France, by way of Southampton and Le Havre, thence by a combination of "miserable wet box cars" and long muddy marches down to the Somme. Because of censorship, Innis's letters home during the succeeding eight months amount to little more than descriptions of the weather. Even then, he did slip in more information about life at the Front than the censors realized. "It is simply a case of walking in mud, sleeping in mud and eating mud if your grub happens to touch it," he wrote Lillian. "The only way this country could be muddier would be to be bigger." The elliptical notes he made nearly every day in his illicit diary are a good deal more revealing. About the drinking: "stopped in orchard, swiped apples, several drunk; Charly the cook decent when sober, bad when drunk." About the food: "jam, bread, beans and tea the favourite menu." About the dreary futility of much military activity: on December 12, he saw action for the first time at Bullay Grenay in the Lens sector, then relatively quiet. But it was "an awful bad trip; snowed heavily and melted, almost wet through all the way." About Christmas as a blessed relief. He was then in the village of Camblain Chatelain, known to everyone as "Charlie Chaplin," and lucky enough to be billetted in the barn of a "kind French lady" who not only laid on an excellent dinner – "boiled fat pork, cabbage salad, omelette" – but encouraged him to linger by the fire and "write at an acceptable table." The festivities, however, were marred by an army Christmas party in the village schoolhouse, where "everyone drunk from punch; some sick; school well decorated, used like pig pen." This was followed on Boxing Day by "route march to sober up the men. Some dropped out."

In January 1917, Innis became a small cog in the vast preparations being made for the attack on Vimy. Initially, this mostly involved "same old job of feeding and grooming horses morning

Soldiers load artillery at Vimy, 1917. As an artillery signalman, Innis's tasks involved spotting targets, and setting the range for these guns. He also looked after the
artillery horses and helped dig tunnels.

noon and night." By mid-February he was busy with pick and
shovel, digging gun and ammunition pits in the soft chalk, and
sometimes detailed to work on the tunnels. For the first time, the
horrors of war, rather than merely its discomforts, became manifest. "One of our airplanes came down," he notes on March 17.
"Awful crash; intestines all over the machine; head off the pilot."
A few days later, "brought dead man down on stretcher, badly hit
on face and head." On April 5, as the day of the attack grew
nearer, three men he knew well were killed by one shell. "Several
wounded, others with narrow escapes, buried in cemetery of
engineers . . . horse developed lockjaw from shrapnel wounds;
had to be shot; airplanes at night; dead horses by roadside." On

the day of battle itself, Innis was too tired and cold and hungry to gloat about victory; indeed, many years later, the fuller account he wrote in his own autobiography reads more like a description of defeat. "Our task . . . was that of bringing material to the front line so that a bridge could be thrown over the line immediately after the attack and that the guns would be moved over these bridges to a new front. This was of course, highly speculative and dependent on the weather and became a complete fiasco because of a heavy snowfall . . . and the impossibility of moving the guns forward in the mud." This curiously flat description of a great battle is in fact a faithful record of how any military triumph, or disaster, is seen at the time from the worm's-eye view of an ordinary private.

Harold Innis, early 1917. This photograph shows him behind the lines at Vimy. By now, the horrors of war were becoming manifest; the haversack around his neck contains a gas mask.

In 1979, nearly thirty years after Innis's own death, and more than sixty years after the battle, the best insight into what Innis really felt about what had happened was provided by his son Donald, in a comment quoted by Watson in his thesis. "What it meant to him I can only express in a word I have heard used by men when speaking about someone who has been at the Front or has escaped death, that they have been 'kissed,' and no other word that I know expresses it so well. The war was a test of his physical and mental resources such as he found nowhere else and could have found nowhere else. That he passed this test meant a great deal to him. . . . He had joined a fraternity that is unseen and unspoken but exists nevertheless." Donald Innis also remembered that in the late 1930s he. and his father had visited the memorial at Vimy. "His reactions were like those of someone visiting an old school, a place not liked but a part of his life."

Following the actual battle, fighting around the ridge continued for several weeks. Innis's battery was shunted around several times before it finally settled down just below the ridge, close to the village of Vimy itself. There were still periods of intense shelling but the worst seemed to be over. "The trees are nearly out in leaf," he wrote home on May 29, "and the fruit trees (what is left of them) are out in blossom. With the green grass, though shell holes are more prominent, we are reminded somewhat of home." In early June, with the weather now hot and fine, "baseball has become the mania. Everybody plays or is intensely interested. In last night's game we (the battery) came out ahead." Then on July 7, Innis and several other signallers set out to make their routine reconnaissance from old German gun-pits near the top of the ridge. Suddenly, he was hit in the thigh by a piece of shrapnel, and blood began pouring out of an artery. His companions stanched the flow, and humped him along on their shoulders to the dressing station. The following day, he was bundled on to a stretcher and shipped by train to the Canadian Army Hospital at Etaples. A week later, he was in Endell Street Military Hospital in central London.

Innis's leg wound turned out to be what was known, enviously, as a "Blighty" – neither life-threatening nor likely to be permanently incapacitating, but sufficient to remove a soldier

permanently from the army. For the first few weeks, he simply lux-
uriated in clean sheets and comfort. "This is some picnic to what
we have been accustomed to," he wrote his mother. "The grub is
jake* and there is nothing to do but write, rest and read." With the
censors no longer looking over his shoulder, he offered to answer
questions about what it had really been like in France. "I could
hand out a lot of dope but I hardly know where to start, so the
best way is for you just to trot out your questions, and I'll trot out
the answers." Perhaps because Harold was now safe, neither
Mary Innis nor anyone else in the family seems to have taken up
his offer to write truthfully about the war.

Innis began to consider his future. Gone now were all
thoughts of becoming a Baptist minister; his faith in formal religion had been dismembered in the trenches. In its place – as yet
inchoately – a different sense of mission was beginning to emerge.
In later years, he would speak of the "incommunicable bond" that
existed between men who had faced death when young. As one
who had survived the encounter, he owed an incalculable debt to
those who had not. This feeling of having been granted a second
life, of having been spared for a purpose, is common among all
veterans, and because of the peculiarly horrific circumstances of
the Great War, became central to the future lives of many who had
survived it. "Better men than I, abler men than I never came back.
I was just lucky," Innis's direct contemporary, Lester Pearson,
once commented. During his time in hospital, and whether consciously or unconsciously, Innis decided to live his own life as a
memorial to those who had died. He also promised himself, as he
later wrote, "never to have any part in letting men down who had
been in the Front lines." In the immediate, he was a strong sup-
porter of conscription, which he saw as a debt owed to those at
the Front. "No one questions the feeling of the soldiers in France,"
he wrote Lillian in November 1917 shortly before the Khaki Election. "They want conscription and they are not pleased with the

---

* "Jake" was a popular slang expression of the era, meaning "great" or "terrific."
According to the McMaster Yearbook for 1916, "That'll be jake" was Innis's signature expression.

attitude of what they call the young skunks, staying back. It could have been prevented by every man doing his bit, but since they would not do this, they will have to take the consequences."

By now, having moved on to a rehabilitation hospital in Surrey, and wearing a bright blue convalescent uniform, Innis had enrolled in the Khaki College. This was an innovative adult education programme for Canadian servicemen and through it he was able to make arrangements to begin work on his MA at McMaster. In fact – his wound had shattered an artery and took a long time to heal – he wrote most of his thesis while still in England. His subject was "The Returned Soldier," and it reveals both his gathering sense of mission and his burgeoning Canadian nationalism. First, he sketched a bleak portrait that might almost have been a self-portrait. "The

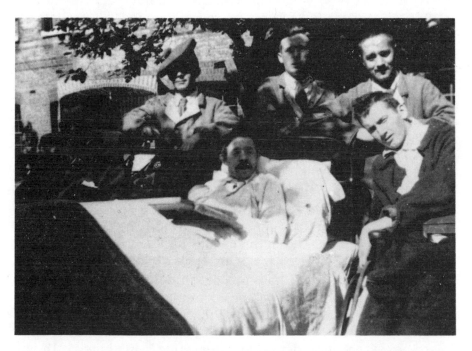

A group of convalescents at a Canadian military hospital in Surrey. Harold Innis is seated at right. Lucky enough to have received a "Blighty" wound, Innis wrote his master's thesis during his convalescence.

furnace of war has melted into a brotherhood in which the frills of humanity have disappeared. . . . A man who has been over the top taking chances with life and death has become carelessly indifferent to the mere happenings of everyday life . . . no one who has been wounded or no one for that matter who has seen a great deal of front line service, is physically or mentally better for the experience. . . . A long period in the trenches varying from six to 26 days without relief is usually followed by a reaction from which only the strongest survive." Almost as bad as fear was the sheer monotony of war. "The fact is always forced upon the soldier that he must obey orders. The result is more or less an indifference to what happens. . . . This cramping of individuality and the enforced idleness which usually accompanies it, have eradicated many of the characteristics which marked the ordinary civilian. It has introduced and created a lassitude, an indifference to surroundings which is not in his best interests." Then, clumsily but passionately, Innis put forward a remedy. "Work, work of brain and of brawn, co-operation, organization and determination to heal the sores . . . and to start again along the lines of sound national progress, is the hope of the Canadian people . . . that she may take her place among the nations of the world for the privilege of which her best blood had been shed."

In April 1918, still leaning heavily on a cane which he would not discard for another several years, Innis returned to Canada and received his formal discharge from the army and his MA from McMaster. He had settled on what he would do next, or so he thought, and planned to enter Osgoode Hall in the autumn to begin a career in the law. In the meantime there was the summer to put in, and, thanks to his army disability gratuities, he had money in his pocket. "I had an uneasy conscience that I knew very little about the subject of economics," Innis wrote many years later in his autobiography. "I decided therefore to take the summer school at the University of Chicago and thus to remedy to some extent my defective knowledge." In June 1918, he departed on the short journey southwards that would prove to be the most important of his life.

The years of achievement and fame that now lay ahead of Harold Innis belong to another story. Save for a few dutiful speeches in

Harold Innis in 1918. Back from the wars and looking appreciably older than in his graduation photograph, Innis was now considering his future. This photograph was taken around the time he enrolled at the University of Chicago.

Chicago supporting Liberty Bond Drives – Vimy had been won because of thorough preparation, was his message – his war was officially over. The decisive event was that, shortly after joining the University of Chicago summer school, all thoughts of the law had been abandoned. Instead, Innis decided to embark on a PhD in economics, making his first exploratory foray into Canadian economic history by selecting a history of the CPR as his thesis topic. It was also in Chicago that Innis met his future wife, an attractive and intelligent young woman named Mary Quayle, herself a student of economics. Their marriage, which took place in 1921 and produced four children, was famous for being happy and also for being ahead of its time. Not only did Mary Quayle Innis serve as her husband's amanuensis and after his death as keeper of his flame, she also became a successful writer in her own right, producing a short economic history of Canada, a steady stream of feature articles for B. K. Sandwell's *Saturday Night,* and a 1943 novel, *Stand on a Rainbow.*

Over the next three decades, Innis's star moved onwards and

Mary Quayle Innis. She too was a student of economics at the University of Chicago, where she and Harold Innis met.

Harold Adams Innis and Mary Quayle, *circa* 1919. This photograph was taken during their courtship. Innis was still using a cane, which he would not discard for another several years.

upwards: in 1930, *The Fur Trade in Canada* made his reputation as an economic historian; a decade later, *The Cod Fisheries* made him a scholar of world repute. As Chairman of the Department of Political Economy at the University of Toronto, he came to occupy one of the most influential positions in Canadian academe. "Innis was a lucky man, and he continued working in the way he had chosen to spend his life almost right up to the end," wrote William Christian in his 1980 introduction to the published edition of the *Idea File*. "I cannot help thinking that Innis had himself primarily in mind when he transcribed the following passage from Robert Louis Stevenson: 'If a man love the labour of any trade, apart from any question of success or fame, the gods have called him.'"

Yet for Innis, as for so many other survivors, the Great War remained a ghost that would never be laid. There was a driven quality to his endless, far-flung information-gathering journeys – dozens of trips by canoe all over northern Ontario and Quebec and Manitoba; down the Mackenzie River to Aklavik; journeys all around Newfoundland and Labrador by coastal steamer, indeed, in 1937, he suffered a nervous collapse from overwork. He had hated the war, and yet he kept religiously in touch with the members of his old battery, with the Frenchwoman who had been kind to him in 1916, and he used military terminology in his letters. "The fourth year occupies a peculiar position in the whole curriculum," he wrote to a colleague in a routine discussion of course structure. "The students are brought through their third, second and first line of trenches to the front line trench and to the outposts." The influence of the war was demonstrated most dramatically in Innis's behaviour early in 1940, in the course of a much-talked-about campus incident involving another eminent University of Toronto scholar who had become his anathema, the historian Frank Underhill.

A bit of background is in order here. As a scholar, even more as a university administrator, Innis believed passionately that the first principle of a university should be total detachment from politics. "With imperfect competition between concepts, the university is essentially an ivory tower in which courage can be mustered to attack any concept which threatens to become a monopoly," he wrote to a friend. This view brought him headlong into conflict with Underhill who, like some other academics of the 1930s, believed passionately that scholars should be *hommes engagés* and who had been a founder of the League for Social Reconstruction, forerunner of the CCF. In Innis's opinion, Underhill was "a traitor, ready to sell us [the university] out to any bidder." At the start of the Second World War, when Underhill was threatened with dismissal from the university because of his isolationist views, Innis was the last person who might have been expected to come to his defence. Quite the opposite. Innis wrote a furious letter to the university's president, pointing out that Underhill, like himself, had served on the Western Front and been wounded there, and that if the university dismissed Underhill, he would himself resign his professorship. Underhill was kept on, and continued to rile Innis with his progressive views, but Innis had kept the bargain he had made with himself long ago, "never to let down anyone who had served in the Front Lines."

Harold Innis died of cancer on November 8, 1952, three days after his fifty-eighth birthday. During the last weeks of his life, one who visited him often was a friend who had also seen service in the Great War, George V. Ferguson, then editor of the *Montreal Star*. To Ferguson's astonishment, for the first time in their long acquaintance Innis seemed actually anxious to talk about the war. "I said I had some of the old ordnance maps of the areas in which the corps had fought. I asked him if he would like to look at them . . . his face lit up and he said he would," Ferguson recounted. "He talked in those last months about the war. . . . All he could say about it was the horror of the performance. It was not that he himself had been wounded, that wasn't it. It was the more he thought about the thing, the more he thought of young men being destroyed who might have been so valuably useful. And he would speak with real bitterness . . . bitterness I've never seen in another man, about the stupidity of the whole performance which he had embarked on *himself*!"

22

Towards a Place of No Return

Talbot knew he was going into a place from which he was likely enough not to return but I never saw him happier or quieter in his mind.

John Archibald, a friend of Talbot Papineau's from McGill and Oxford. A letter to Beatrice Fox; November 1917

"I have made a decision which I am afraid may not entirely meet with your approval and which will no doubt cause you greater anxiety than you have recently been called upon to bear," Talbot Papineau wrote to his mother on May 22, 1917. "I have in short decided to return to the Regiment."

Opening this letter in her bed-sitting-room in South Kensington, Caroline would have been distressed but not surprised by its contents. She'd known this was going to happen ever since Vimy. For Talbot, that splendid Canadian victory justified all he had written to Bourassa; here indeed was "the foundation for a true Canadian nation, independent in thought, independent in action." As a junior officer on Byng's staff, Talbot had been deeply involved in the preparations for Vimy, particularly in the area of making improvements to wireless communications. He had also written the Eyewitness communiqué on the battle which had appeared in all the newspapers, along with a much more detailed top-secret report that even Adamson had praised. The fact remained though, that on this epochal day Talbot had been on the sidelines: he had not gone over the top with the Patricias and the rest of the Canadian Corps and thereby had not truly been present at the creation.

Thus, in the weeks after Vimy, despite Caroline's frantic urgings, he turned down opportunities that in other circumstances would have been tempting – the chance to go to America as a military instructor (On April 6, 1917, the United States had entered the war at last.), and also a chance to return to the War Records Staff, this time to write the third volume of *Canada in Flanders* under his own name. "Better to share in the making of history than in the writing of it," he told Caroline. "I shrink from the fresh discomforts, the physical fatigue and the narrowness of the existence, but I realize that if I have the necessary courage and character to see it through, I shall have proved myself much more of a man than I can ever do as a scribe." (In the event, Charles G. D. Roberts, the New Brunswick author and poet finished *Canada in Flanders*.)

As always with Talbot, idealism and patriotism were inseparable from ambition. Another reason for returning to the Patricias was that without further experience in the front lines, he could not hope for further advancement on the staff. Knowing that if anything, Caroline's expectations of his future greatness were greater even than his own, he was utterly candid. "Why oh Why am I so ambitious, my dear mother?" he wrote. "Could we not be happy with less honour and glory, more security and comfort?" All his life she had encouraged him to choose "the hardest of two alternatives, perhaps the one I dislike most." As they both knew full well, a tour of regimental duty would greatly enhance his chances for promotion to the key staff position of brigade major. There had been "almost revolutionary changes in the Regimental work since I was with them," and he needed the first-hand experience. Moreover, his mentor, General Byng, agreed "emphatically" that he was taking "the proper path," and had mentioned, once again, "my future career as a public man." Colonel Adamson, for his part, had professed himself delighted to have such an excellent officer back, or so Talbot informed his mother, and had remarked after their interview, "You have a very warm friend in the Corps Commander."

Here, as we know from Adamson's own report of this interview, Talbot was telling less than the full story. Their meeting had been a decidedly rocky half-hour, with Talbot acting as if he were doing the regiment a favour by returning, and presuming to make all sorts of impossible demands. "He wants to go to Oxford for five weeks to get fit rowing, playing tennis racquets and running, then two weeks with his mother in the country, then six weeks military training at some school in England," Agar wrote Mabel. "He said he intended to go into public life after the war, and thought that he would have a better chance of getting the support of the public if he could show he had been with the Regiment through some big push like the last one." Talbot had also been foolish enough to tell Adamson that he expected instant promotion to major and to be designated second-in-command. "I told him that if he came back he must do so as a Company Commander, and that he must make up his mind to stay as I did not propose to make the Battalion a training ground for the convenience of staff officers," Agar continued. "He can think of nothing but himself and annoyed me very much, although I did not comb him down as much as the self-seeking bounder deserved."

Undoubtedly, there was a certain bias in Adamson's attitude – ever since the embarrassing French lessons aboard the *Royal George* in 1914, Papineau had repeatedly rubbed him the wrong way. But his exasperation was justified. The flip side to Talbot's flair and panache was arrogance and conceit. His own opinion of himself was golden; he was more than ready to use his charm to curry favour in high places, and not above bullying those whom he considered to be his inferiors into doing what he wanted. This time he had miscalculated; Adamson was commanding officer of the Patricias, and Byng, even though Talbot's mentor, would never have dreamt of interfering with Adamson's decisions. Thus Talbot swallowed his pride and rejoined the Patricias on June 7, 1917, on Adamson's terms, as a captain with no special privileges, in charge of No. 3 Company.

Almost as soon as he was back with the regiment – the Canadian Corps was holding the line in the relatively quiescent Vimy sector – Talbot set aside all airs and pretensions. So far as we can judge from his letters, he sensed a vast weight lifting from his shoulders. His future was on hold for the time being. Once again, as at St. Eloi and Bellewaerde Ridge, he was living only in the present, part of the quasi-mystical brotherhood of which he had written to Bourassa, "when men stand side by side and endure together a soldier's life and face together a soldier's death, they are united in bonds almost as strong as the closest of blood ties." His new mood was reflected in his letters. "My world is very agreeable," he wrote Caroline. "My sides are hardened to the boards and I sleep like a top." To Beatrice, he was expansive. "I notice you do not speak of your work as much as you used to," he told her. "I am so afraid you think I am not interested . . . I *am*, very, and proud of your successes." It added to his cheerfulness that the nasty matter of the "Irish Letter" had been relegated to history and that he and Lady Donoughmore were now back to being good friends. "I had a long letter from her," he wrote Beatrice. "She tells me not to think anymore of what I termed her 'displeasure.'"

As mattered most of all to Talbot, his courage had not deserted him. During his first spell in the front lines, it became evident that the spirit that had won him his Military Cross was undimmed, indeed, that it shone all the more brightly for having been seasoned by the expertise gained from his study of warfare while on the staff. Adamson, far too good a soldier not to give credit where it was due, quickly revised his opinions. "Papineau is really very good," he wrote Mabel on June 15. "The other night, when his part of the trench was being very badly knocked about by shellfire, and his orders were to hold on at all costs, knowing that they must all be wiped out, he took the whole garrison out of the trench and put them in shell holes fifty yards in front. The Germans could not spot the range with any accuracy and kept on pounding the trench which they very badly damaged. Had his company remained there, most of them would have been knocked out for a certainty." Talbot, naturally, never knew about this letter. Instead, he no doubt received the highest compliment one fighting man can receive from another: a clap on the shoulders and a gruff "well done."

All through the summer of 1917, Talbot's astonishing luck continued to hold. Early in July, a brother officer and close friend from McGill, Percy Molson, was killed by the concussion of a trench mortar bomb. Talbot, by contrast, ventured out two days later on a daring daylight patrol and, as if in retaliation, captured a German trench mortar weighing over a hundred pounds. "I had several narrow escapes from shells etc. but it was all great fun," he reported to Caroline. When the regiment was out of the line, he threw himself into summer sports, playing "badminton, and tennis and basketball and even some lacrosse . . . time passes by very quickly and pleasantly . . . I have a big company concert to organize for tomorrow." He'd found another puppy to adopt, a black and white terrier called Tony. Sometimes, he whistled up Tony and wandered away from rough male pursuits to indulge his passion for nature. "Extraordinary how the flowers have sprung up over the beaten ground where I thought all seed or root must be permanently killed," he mused on to Caroline. "Yesterday, I counted twenty varieties. Tonight, I am having a dinner, and intend to have masses of these flowers to cover the interior of our little room." A few days later, now in the front lines, he recounted how he'd decorated his dugout with two German shell-cases filled with wildflowers, and turned a couple of rifle-grenades into candlesticks. He went on to describe the dugout in detail – "an old German one with four bunks and a skylight and a table, and in comparative safety, just to show my luck is still in." In mid-August, he received his coveted promotion. "I am a major and a real one," he told Caroline. "I have put up my crown and I feel very important indeed." The best accolade Talbot received though, was a sentence in a letter home written by one of his corporals, brought to his attention by a subaltern serving as censor. "Our company commander is Major Papineau, of whom you have no doubt read. He is a gentleman and a sport, and very popular."

In some of this, Talbot was undoubtedly keeping up a façade of insouciance so as not to trouble Caroline. He did not tell her that he'd lost the pearl-handled pen-knife that his brother Louis had given him and that, despite his professed disregard for superstition, had found himself strangely rattled by losing this lucky charm. He brushed off as "rather bad luck," an episode described in the regimental history as "the most trying since Vimy," when the Canadians, driving in on Lens through the slag-heaps, not only suffered heavy casualties but the Patricias lost twenty men to poisoning from shells containing the deadly new mustard gas, nearly all them from No. 3 Company. As for Beatrice, by summer's end Talbot's burst of enthusiasm about her work as a sculptor had dwindled: such letters as he did write, thanking her for gifts of bath soap and pine pillows and a hand-knitted sweater had about them a pro forma quality – "you really are a darling and extraordinarily good to me" – that she could not have failed to recognize. "Please dear B., don't think you mean any the less to me but I have rather felt strain recently and somehow have lost interest in everything except my work," he wrote on September 26. Evidence of just how far they had drifted apart, also the best measure of Talbot's own inner landscape, is contained in a letter to Caroline. "Sometimes, I feel I am not doing enough. I should be writing or speaking but I suppose that by just serving and waiting, and even by being killed I can accomplish far more in the long run . . . nearly 35 I am and very little or nothing done, and just as young as ever in some ways. Not a ghost of a chance of being married for instance. I am quite incapable of a grand passion. . . . Such pleasure as there may be in love and family, I am convinced I shall not know. It would have been rather interesting to have been in love during the war – so romantic. I could have written such letters."

The conjuncture of the worlds *killed* and *love* in that letter is telling. It's as if, facing the "great adventure of death," as late-Victorian romantics described it, Talbot found himself compelled to seek out life's other ultimate adventure, a perfect experience of sex.

Indeed, two years earlier, ruminating on his experiences in London, Talbot had written to Beatrice, "I intentionally sought enjoyment because I wished to experience the depths of experience." It is possible that this time he may have found it, although the true nature of this interlude is lost to history. All we know for sure is that early in October 1917, Talbot left northern France for a ten-day leave in England. His first duty, as always, was to Caroline. After devoting several days to her, he went up to Oxford, sought out old tutors, punted on the Cherwell. Towards the end of his leave – by now rumours were flying that the Canadian Corps was about to be shifted northwards once again, back into the Ypres Salient – Talbot spent a weekend down in Surrey with old friends from Montreal, one of whom was Martha Allan, eldest daughter of the shipping magnate Sir Montagu Allan, whose two younger daughters had drowned on the *Lusitania*, now working as a VAD (Voluntary Aid Detachment nurse).* Another member of

---

* Martha Allan (1895–1942). The eldest daughter of Sir Montagu Allan, she was an early patron of Canadian theatre, and founded the Montreal Repertory Theatre in 1930. Her own play, *All on a Summer's Day*, won the Jackson Trophy at the Dominion Drama Festival in the early 1930s.

the houseparty was a war widow named Sarah Shaughnessy. Then in her late twenties and the mother of three young children, she was a woman of exceptional beauty, with huge, limpid, dark eyes and raven-black hair, a southern belle from Nashville, Tennessee, who in 1912 had married Fred Shaughnessy, second son of the Baron Shaughnessy of CPR fame, an old friend of Talbot's from McGill. In Montreal, in the years leading up to the war, Sarah and Talbot had often encountered each other at balls and dinner parties, and in 1916, when Fred, by now a company commander with the 60th Battalion, was killed by a shrapnel bullet, he'd written an exquisite letter of condolence – the salutation, "My Dear Mrs. Shaughnessy" – indicating that as yet they were no more than pleasant acquaintances.

Amid the Surrey hills that mid-October weekend, acquaintanceship flared into passion, on Talbot's part certainly. Sarah Shaughnessy was by no means as intelligent or as challenging as Beatrice and scarcely any more beautiful, though of a completely different type. Rather, she was a gorgeous social butterfly who, like many war widows, had reacted to her husband's death by deciding to spend the duration living for pleasure – with the Duke of Connaught and Beaverbrook and later the Prince of Wales among her many admirers. Sarah was also vastly more sophisticated and worldly than Beatrice. The critical difference between Beatrice and Sarah was that Sarah was *there*. Precisely what happened between her and Talbot can be construed only from a single letter from him, dated October 15, 1917, written from London the night before he returned to the Front, but it hints strongly at a physical affair.*

---

* Nothing in Sarah Shaughnessy's papers survives to convey to us the nature of her own feelings for Talbot. In 1920, she married Captain the Honourable Piers "Joey" Legh, a former aide to the Duke of Connaught who later became an equerry to the Prince of Wales, and still later, Master of the Household to George VI. Her letters and diaries, collected and edited by her son, the playwright and screenwriter Alfred Shaughnessy (best known for writing numerous episodes of the popular 1970s television series *Upstairs, Downstairs*) were published in 1989 under the title *Sarah: The Letters and Diaries of a Courtier's Wife*, and provide an interesting portrait of social life in high circles in Canada and in England during the first half of the century. She died in 1955.

My Dear Sarah,
I have missed you. I miss you. I would like to hear you play
Bohème again tonight. I shall never forget how you played and
how you looked. No real sight of "craterland" will dull that
memory from my inward eye. I saw Martha [Allan] for tea and
we had a pleasant chat. Out of nothing, Martha said, "I didn't
know you were so fond of Sarah." I replied, "Of course I have
always been" . . . and left it at that. I shall not be responsible for
more than that publicly. So whatever gossip may carry to your
ears, hold me guiltless! Charlie [Stewart] already teases me and
I grow furious. He told me that Lord Beaverbrook was much
attracted to you and I fumed and stormed quite naturally and
sincerely until I calmed myself . . . I wish the future were not so
uncertain. I have nothing to depend on, not even you.
Affectionately,
Talbot

On the following day, October 16, 1917, Talbot caught the
leave train at Victoria Station and recrossed the channel. John
Archibald, an old friend from McGill and Oxford who saw him off,
remembered later that "Talbot knew he was going into a place
from which he was likely enough not to return but I never saw him
happier and quieter in his mind." Instead of returning to the section of the Front surrounding Vimy Ridge, he rejoined the Patricias in their new billets at Le Peuplier, a few kilometres south of
the Belgian frontier. Here, the regiment remained for another
week, engaging in strenuous physical training and practise in
map-reading. On October 23, the regiment moved up to the ruined
city of Ypres. Nobody needed to be told where they would be
going from there. Their destination, as everyone in the Patricias
and the rest of the Canadian Corps knew full well, was one where
many hundreds of thousands of British and allied troops had
already gone, and from which tens of thousands had not returned.
That destination was Passchendaele.

Sarah Shaughnessy. A beautiful war widow, she captivated Talbot Papineau on his last leave shortly before
Passchendaele. "I wish the future were not so uncertain," he wrote to her.

23

The Lost Leader

. . . I died in hell –
(They called it Passchendaele) . . .

Siegfried Sassoon, "Memorial Tablet"; 1918

Despite the doom-laden biblical resonance of its name and the large numbers of war cemeteries that encircle it, the pocket of southwest Belgium surrounding Passchendaele Ridge has long since reverted to its pre-1914 condition of pastoral somnolence. Unlike at Beaumont-Hamel and at Vimy, no attempt has been made to summon up old ghosts for the sake of visitors. The only notable feature is the ridge itself – a gentle rise rather than the distinctive hump at Vimy – that overlooks fields of damp pastureland a few kilometres northeast of Ypres. On the crest of this rise sprawls a small, unremarkable village, nowadays a bedroom suburb of Ypres, its single distinctive feature being that none of the red-brick houses date from earlier than the 1920s. Yet it was at Passchendaele that the Great War reached its nadir of horror. From here emerged the most famous and certainly the saddest quote of the war. When the battle was done, General Sir Launcelot Kiggell, Chief of Staff to the British Commander-in-Chief, toured the field for the first time. "Good God, did we really send men to fight in that?" Kiggell exclaimed.

Linger a little – rubber boots are advisable – and the ghosts will begin to emerge. This terrain is muddy at all times, because much of it is below sea-level, because of the heavy local rains, and because of the clay soil. In 1917, though, it was the battle itself that transformed Passchendaele into a malevolent swamp. The artillery barrages smashed the drainage systems, turning the terrain into "a grey, evil-smelling waste of stagnant, scum-coated water and mud," in the phrase of historian D. J. Goodspeed. Away from the "roads" of wooden duckboards, not only men, but also horses, trucks, artillery pieces, and entire sections of light railway were swallowed up. "The ground beggars description," Agar Adamson wrote Mabel on October 23. "The strongest and youngest cannot navigate without falling down." A British survivor recalled "that dreaded suction," and added, "It was worse when the mud didn't suck you down. When it yielded under your feet you knew that it was a body you were treading on." The actual numbers of casualties – approximately 350,000 – suffered by the British, the Canadians, the Australians, the New Zealanders and the French were not larger, proportionately, than those caused by Verdun or by the Somme. What made Passchendaele unique and has embedded it forever in our consciousness as a symbol of meaningless horror was that in no other battle did so many of the wounded die. They didn't all succumb to exposure or to loss of blood. They weren't all gassed. Many died by drowning. Siegfried Sassoon, in the succeeding lines of the poem quoted above was simply providing a factual description.

> . . . *my wound was slight,*
> *And I was hobbling back, and then a shell*
> *Burst slick upon the duck-boards; so I fell*
> *Into the bottomless mud, and lost the light.*

Many of the bodies were not recovered until the spring thaw of 1918 pushed them back to the surface.

Because it is the source of the strongest of our images of the whole of the Great War, because the Canadians were fed belatedly into the battle, achieving their objective but at a horrendous cost, and, most directly, because it was here that the hero of this book was cut down, as futilely as the rest, it is worth trying to probe into some of the causes of this greatest single act, among so many during the Great War, of unmitigated military madness.

Strictly in terms of grand strategy, the battle in fact did make a few grains of sense. Haig needed badly to do something that year.

As these photographs illustrate, Passchendaele was the most hideous of all Great War battlefields, a sea of mud in which drowning was as great a risk as were enemy bullets and shells. Wooden duckboards were the only means of passage.

The Germans had just launched unrestricted submarine warfare, inflicting great damage to British shipping if at the cost to themselves of bringing America into the war; in March, a revolution at Petrograd had swept Tsar Nicholas II from power, creating the possibility that Russia might sue for a separate peace; the French army, riven by mutinies which reached a peak in the spring of 1917, was incapable of any more offensives. Even tactically, the choice of Passchendaele had some merit: a break-through there could deprive Germany and its submarines of the Belgian channel ports; even a serious breaching of the German line, creating "opportunities for the employment of cavalry in masses," in Haig's phrase, would restore the morale of the French.

These, in any event, were the arguments Haig used to convince the doubting new prime minister, Lloyd George. In fact, it's difficult to believe that Haig himself believed in them: no break-through of the kind he envisaged had been achieved anywhere in three years; no worse place to attempt one could be imagined than amid the mud of Flanders.

No breakthrough, needless to say, was ever achieved. Yet Haig poured more and more men into the swamp for four months. The generals beneath him and the politicians above him pleaded for a halt. He persisted. Why? Haig's objective was attrition. The attacks, he was convinced (in defiance of the logic that defenders are always better protected) would kill more Germans than the British, French, Canadians, Australians that they killed. "By this means and this means only can we find victory by wearing down the enemy's resistance," he told one of his generals who argued for the attacks to be called off.

In fact, Haig never came even close to achieving his goal. The historian Denis Winter, in his authoritative work, *Haig's Command,* estimates that German casualties, at some 250,000, were only two-thirds of those of the Allies. All of the effort produced only one purely tactical victory. In the first week of November, the Canadian Corps stormed Passchendaele Ridge successfully. Five months later, when the Germans launched their last, *Kaiserschlat,* offensive, the ridge was quietly surrendered without a shot being fired.

So why did Haig press on? Part of the answer, surely, is the brutalizing effect of war. Haig's judgement, always rigid and unimaginative, had been coarsened by three years of fighting during which he had won for the Allies, at a cost of hundreds of thousands of young men, a handful of miles of ruined French and Belgian landscape. There was also Haig's vanity. "I do beg of you to do your utmost to prevent our Government delaying to take action until the American army is in the field," he wrote to a cabinet ally a month before Passchendaele. (In his diary, he contemptuously dismissed the far-larger French army as "a broken reed.") Lloyd George may have came closest to answering the fateful question. After a failed attempt to bring the slaughter to a stop in mid-October, he commented to a colleague that Haig was "completely unbalanced."

The attack upon Passchendaele was launched at 3:50 AM, on July 31, 1917, preceded by two weeks of one of the heaviest barrages of the war. Some 5,600 prisoners were taken, and long lines of trenches were captured. But none of the objectives outlined on the staff officer's maps was reached. The real enemy turned out to be the weather. On the first afternoon of that first day, it started to pour down in torrents. The rain fell as heavily the next day, and on into the following week. Again and again, through to mid-August, the British attacked. Again and again, they were halted in the middle of the quagmire, unable to penetrate the cunning new German defence system of lozenge-shaped pillboxes nested deep in the mud, with concrete walls five feet thick. To Lloyd George, it had become a "ghastly hecatomb of slaughter." He tried to stop it. Haig responded by declaring that just one more push would achieve his objective. This, he now ordered, would be the capture of Passchendaele Ridge.

On September 20, the attack resumed. At a cost of 20,000 casualties, an outcrop of the ridge was captured. A fortnight later, another British attack pushed further up. "The enemy is teetering," Haig declared. On October 12, the Australians went in. Within a day, they had suffered 60 per cent casualties and were back in their own lines. For his last fresh reinforcements, Haig turned now to the Canadians.

Their triumph at Vimy had invested the Canadian Corps with a reputation as elite troops, even if at times they could be recalcitrant and raucous. Equally remarkable was the reputation of its new commander, Lieutenant-General Arthur Currie – now Sir Arthur Currie – who had succeeded Byng the previous June, the latter having been promoted to command the Third Army after Vimy. Just turned forty-two, Currie, as Haig well understood, was now one of the most capable commanders within the entire British army.

War churns up improbable heroes. Prior to 1914, Currie's military experience included nothing more demanding than having been colonel of a militia unit, the Gordon Highlanders of Victoria, B.C., a position to which he'd aspired mostly for reasons of business and social advancement, in the way of most summer soldiers. He was the antithesis of spit-and-polish, a large, paunchy, and profane man who lacked entirely the sense of flair and of theatre that turns generals into popular heroes. Far more disadvantageous to Currie were the rumours that buzzed about his personal integrity – and not without reason. He was not just a failed real estate speculator but an outright embezzler. In 1914, just before going overseas, he'd diverted nearly $10,000 of regimental funds, earmarked for the purchase of uniforms, to cover the debts of his bankrupt real estate business: not until 1917, when two wealthy brother officers came to the rescue, was this embarrassing matter resolved. On the battlefield, though – cometh the hour, cometh the man – Currie became a quite different kind of being. The qualities that set him apart from the conventional British professional – Byng included – were his scrupulous attention to detail and his insistence on keeping casualties low. Shortly before the attack on Vimy, Currie, then commander of the First Division, had argued ferociously with Byng against the need for making raids into the enemy trenches in advance of the battle. "I'm not sacrificing one man unnecessarily," he had said. His vindication came when his First Division achieved all its objectives quickly, while the Fourth Division, weakened by the loss of too many good men in a disastrous trench raid a few weeks earlier, got into serious trouble.

"Passchendaele! What's the good of it?" Currie raged to his

staff when he first learned, in early October, that the Canadian Corps might be sent there. "Let the Germans have it, keep it – rot in it. There's a mistake somewhere. It must be a mistake. It isn't worth a drop of blood." A few days later, when Haig took the unprecedented step of visiting Canadian headquarters to deliver his orders in person, Currie did his best to dissuade him. For the best part of an hour, the two paced up and down the parade square. Another Canadian officer, Major-General Archie Mac-Donell, watched the scene from the window. "It was apparent that Haig was putting a proposition to Currie he was not for," Mac-Donell wrote later. "Haig was very earnest and very animated and after a halt during which he had failed to convince Currie, would take him by the arm and walk up and down with him in a very animated way and evidently full of argument." Currie's own memoirs provide the gist of the conversation. "I carried my protest to the extreme limit . . . which I believe would have resulted in my being sent home had I been other than Canadian Corps Commander . . . I pointed out what the casualties were bound to be, and asked if a success would justify the sacrifice." Haig said in reply, "Someday I will tell you why, but Passchendaele must be taken." (Haig's later explanation to Currie was that "to help the morale of the French army and of the French people and the British people, he was determined to finish the fighting of 1917 with a victory.")*

The best Currie could do was to wring a concession: instead of serving with the Fifth Army under General Gough, whom he had distrusted since the Somme, the Canadians would replace the Australian Corps in General Herbert Plumer's Second Army. On October 13, the day after the disastrous attack by the Australians, he made one last appeal to Plumer. "My orders are clear," Plumer replied with a shrug. Two days later, in cold rain, the Canadians began moving northwards. On Monday, October 15, Currie set up

---

* Currie's protest did have an effect eventually. During the Second World War, as Goodspeed notes, the Commander of the Canadian Army Overseas, General A. G. L. MacNaughton, was authorized in an extreme emergency to withdraw Canadian forces from their role of acting in combination with British forces. (MacNaughton had fought at Passchendaele.)

Lieutenant-General Sir Arthur Currie (*left*) with Field Marshal Sir Douglas Haig. Unlike his dapper superior, Currie did not look the part of a professional soldier. But he was probably the best military commander that Canada has produced. He and Haig argued over Passchendaele.

his headquarters at Poperinghe; on October 17, he toured the front lines. "Battlefield looks bad," he wrote in his diary. "No salvage has been done and very few of the dead buried."

The Patricias, on that date, were still encamped at Le Peuplier. There, Talbot Papineau, just back from leave, was setting his own house in order. "I am on the eve of grave events," he wrote Beatrice on October 21, "I have only a short minute in which to write but I wished to make sure you heard from me."

Talbot began his letter light-heartedly. In one of war's strange incongruities, the Christmas present he'd requested from Beatrice, a pair of running boots for regimental sports, had just been delivered to him, along with a long funny enclosure describing her search for precisely the right kind and the right size. "Your 'Quest of the Boots' was so diverting that it seemed a real shame all the fun should be for my own personal enjoyment only," he told her. "As for the boots, they are the most wonderful things I have ever seen. But my dear B., how could you think I would ever ask for anything so expensive. I only meant a pair of the canvas running boots with a rubber sole." In return, he explained that he was making arrangements to send her a sofa cushion bearing the regimental crest. He referred briefly to his London leave, and, perhaps feeling a bit guilty about his fling with Sarah Shaughnessy and no doubt worried that Beatrice might hear about it through another "Irish letter," made a casual reference to Sarah. "She was from Nashville, married Fred Shaughnessy . . . both very old friends of mine."

Then Talbot, in effect, said goodbye. Being Talbot, he did so with grace. "You are really the only clever girl I think I have ever known. . . . Whatever happens, you must realize that I have thought of you and been happy and grateful for you now and to the end. I am in excellent health and spirits . . . I am sorry this has to be such a short letter and that I have to be so reticent . . . Better wait for my next letter before replying. Then I trust we can have a real resumption of correspondence." He signed off more intimately than he had ever done before. "Believe me always affectionately and gratefully, Your Talbot."

On that same day, Talbot wrote also to Caroline. This letter contains intimations of his mortality, but it was not yet farewell. "I never felt better in my life," he assured her. "This morning we had a church service and sang 'Nearer my God to Thee,' familiar of how we used to sing as kids at Montebello. I would gladly listen to you playing them again. No one ever played the piano as well as you." Then, referring to his leave, he added. "Dear little mother, how pitifully little I seem to have seen of you. Too bad – my restless soul. One hesitates to allow emotion to come out – my whole policy is one of suppression and control. . . . We will find a fund of buried affection after the war."

On October 23, the Patricias moved up to Ypres, remaining there in improvised billets for another five days. "I shoved the men into what cellars could be found," Adamson wrote Mabel. "The shelling on both sides is most intense. . . . The ground is just one mass of shell holes all full of water." Writing to Caroline, Talbot was sparing in his descriptions. "It has been very rainy and wet but we managed to build a little open fire and were jolly and happy," he told her. "After all, what does the outside world matter. Our own events are too absorbing."

On Friday, October 26, the Canadian Corps opened its offensive. The Patricias were kept in reserve. This first phase of the battle lasted for two days and ended with the line advanced some eight hundred yards, but with the final objectives not taken. The Canadian losses so far were 2,481 men, about a third of whom had been killed. The second attack was scheduled for October 30. "Just a hurried line, my last I am afraid for a few days," Talbot wrote Caroline on the twenty-seventh. "We are all in fine spirits. Never did I less regret my decision than at this moment. Always know that if I do get killed I was completely happy and content to the last moment and that my only regret is due to the sorrow it will cause you and the boys. Remember dearest that if I can my spirit will be with you to comfort you and my only unhappiness will be yours. I say this just in case in order that you may know what my last thoughts were. My mind is concentrated in the effort here, but my heart is always full of love and gratitude for you, dearest and sweetest of mothers."

On October 28, in mid-afternoon, the Patricias began moving up towards the Front, advancing in single file along the duckboard. Shortly after 1:00 AM, they moved into their support trenches near the hamlet of Gravenstafel. In advance of the main attack, No. 4 Company advanced five hundred yards and captured an enemy pillbox. At mid-morning on the twenty-ninth, Adamson held a conference of all his company commanders; zero hour was set for 5:50 AM the following day. The objective would be first Duck Lodge, and then Meetcheele, a slight rise of ground just in front of Passchendaele itself, both positions heavily defended by pillboxes. Sometime during that afternoon, Talbot seized a few moments and wrote one last letter to Caroline. "We have been fortunate so far and all things are cheerful. I have even shaved this morning in a little dirty water. . . . There seems so little to say, when if I only knew what was going to happen I might want to say so much. These would be poor letters to have as the last ones but you must know with what a world of love they are written." He then quoted Robert Herrick, as best he could remember. "Always remember I could not love thee so well, or you love me, did I not love honour more. You have given me the courage and strength to go very happily and cheerfully into the good fight." This was the happy warrior's last farewell.

During the late evening of October 29, the four companies of the Patricias moved forwards to their jump-off positions. The moon was up, and they were spotted by the Germans; men and officers in all companies were killed by snipers. At 11:05 PM, Talbot, as the senior company commander, sent a message to Battalion Headquarters. "All four companies are now reported to be in their assembly positions . . . Germans reported to be wiring [laying barbed wire] in road across our immediate frontage." The small hours were filled with confusion: the jumping-off trench turned out to be too close to the artillery barrage-line and was pulled back a hundred yards, a complicated manoeuvre completed barely ten minutes before zero hour. To add to the stress, strong winds had grounded the aeroplanes so that no up-to-date information about new German positions was available. As one last morale dampener, it had been decided that the conditions were too chaotic to allow the pipers to play. So the actual attack was launched in unaccustomed and ominous silence.

In the last moments before he and his company went over the top, Talbot spoke his last recorded words. He turned to Major Hugh Niven, another Old Original who was second-in-command of the Patricias and who had just come up to direct the attack. "You know, Hughie," he said. "This is suicide."

Talbot Mercer Papineau died about three minutes later, just before 6:00 AM on Tuesday, October 30, 1917. He and two other officers appeared to have been hit by a shell as soon as the enemy counter-barrage came down. (The German machine guns were not yet in range.) No one saw him fall. No one knew whether he'd been killed instantly, or had succumbed to shock or loss of blood, or whether he had drowned. His loss wasn't confirmed until the attack had been completed. His body was never recorded as having been found.

Throughout the Patricias, the casualties were terrible. By the time Papineau's No. 3 Company reached its intermediate objective at Duck Lodge, it was being commanded by its wounded sergeant-major. By the time it closed in on Meetcheele, a corporal was in command. Yet by afternoon, they had reached their principal objective, Meetcheele, clinging on there for thirty-six hours despite the ferocious counter-attacks. During these protracted engagements, Lieutenant Hugh Mackenzie and Sergeant G. M. Mullin won the regiment's first Victoria Crosses, capturing a pillbox that was holding up the entire advance. "The ground we gained is of some importance," Agar Adamson wrote Mabel. "But I cannot help wondering if the position was worth the awful sacrifice of life."

On November 6, the First and Second Canadian divisions took Passchendaele itself. Six days after that, on November 12, Haig issued the order, "We must stop the offensive in Flanders." Less than a week later, on the dry terrain of northern France, General Byng's Third Army launched a surprise attack with massed tanks at Cambrai. He pushed forward four miles, stormed through the Hindenburg Line, and captured thousands of prisoners. But since the reserves that might have been poured through the gap had been destroyed at Passchendaele, it was purely a symbolic victory.

Canadian casualty figures were 15,634, uncannily close to Currie's pre-battle forecast of 16,000. Once again, with 750 dead and wounded, the Patricias had suffered more heavily than any other regiment. "Less men are left than on the historic 8th of May," Adamson wrote Mabel on October 31.

To a degree that was extraordinary, Talbot Papineau became for Canadians the symbol not only of Passchendaele, but of all the golden promise cut down by the Great War. All over the Dominion, the tributes poured in. "Without doubt, he was destined to fill a high place in public life," eulogized the Ottawa *Citizen*. "Many people who had no personal acquaintance with him regarded him as the one man specially fitted to lead in the task of reconciling the two races." "The only consolation for a loss like this is the hope that by the very nobility of his sacrifice, the late Major Papineau's memory may in years to come effect more for the unification of his country and the triumph of his principles than his own living effort could ever have accomplished," wrote the editorialist of the *Financial Times* of Montreal.

British editorialists were equally lavish. *The Times* described Papineau as "a shining example of French-Canadian patriotism, under unusually difficult conditions." The *Daily Mail* saluted him as "A Lost Leader" and remarked, "May Canada learn from his death the lesson he would have taught had he lived."

The "What Ifs?" persist. Even now Papineau remains a vivid and tantalizing presence. The easiest description of the loss Canada experienced by his death is that he was the Pierre Elliott Trudeau who never was. Had he survived Passchendaele, Papineau would almost certainly have survived the war as a staff officer. Afterwards, as a war hero, the highest political posts would have been within his reach even though it has to be guessed that at the Liberal convention of 1919 Mackenzie King, himself, ironically, the grandson of an 1837 rebel, William Lyon Mackenzie, would still have come away with the leadership within his grasp. Even so, as a French Canadian and as the bearer of that people's proudest name, Papineau would have had a significant, perhaps a decisive effect upon the unfolding of Canadian history. Just possibly, the *Daily Mail* had it right in its encomium of him as "A Lost Leader." On November 3, 1917, King wrote in his diary, "I saw notice of Talbot Papineau having been killed in action. One of the finest and best and bravest of men, a great loss to Canada, the British Empire and the world." Some years later, King had a chance conversation on a train with Talbot's Philadelphian uncle, Jay Rogers, who, having heard that the Prime Minister was aboard, asked for an introduction. According to family legend, King's first remark was that but for the war, Rogers would have been asking to meet his own nephew because "Talbot Papineau would have been in my shoes." Later still, while attending the founding convention of the United Nations in San Francisco in April 1945, King encountered an acquaintance of Caroline's, a prominent Montrealer named Joseph Bech, active in the United Nations Association. According to a note found in Caroline's papers, King told Bech that Talbot "was the most brilliant man of Canada, and that he would have been proud to be in a Cabinet with Talbot Papineau as Prime Minister." Perhaps among all of the tributes, the one that comes closest to capturing the essence of Papineau as he came to be remembered by all those who had crossed his path is contained in a private letter to Beatrice from John Archibald, Talbot's old friend from McGill and Oxford, in whose digs he had frequently lodged when in London on leave, and to whom he had confided something of the nature of his relationship with Beatrice. "He lived life so keenly, it was no tired, blunted life that he gave up . . . I never knew anyone like him, and never expect to find another."

On November 15, 1917, a memorial service was held in London for Talbot and for all the other officers and men of the Patricias who had perished at Passchendaele. The venue was Holy Trinity Brompton, a fashionable church in South Kensington, a short distance away from Caroline's lodgings in Queen's Gate Gardens. As we know from the black-bordered programme preserved among Caroline's papers, the service began with "Lead, Kindly Light" and included Chopin's "*Marche Funèbre*." These days, curates at Holy Trinity Brompton wear jeans and pullovers and the services feature electric guitars. Yet, when the church empties, it's possible to slip back in time to that grim November Thursday. As Colonel-in-Chief, Princess Patricia was there as chief mourner, occupying the place of honour in the front pew, along with her father, the Duke of Connaught (the duchess had died five months earlier), and Lady Evelyn Farquhar, widow of the regiment's first commanding officer. Probably, although we don't know for certain, the princess had invited Caroline Papineau to join them. (Mabel Adamson was at Furnes in Belgium). The altar was draped with the Canadian ensign.

The side pews were occupied by women wearing mourning and by a few men wearing black armbands. The centre pews were a solid block of officers and men wearing khaki, many on crutches and leaning on canes. "There could have been no-one there who did not feel the beauty of the closing part," read the account that appeared in the *Daily Mail.* "From inside the church in the stillness could be heard the commands of the sergeant-bugler outside, followed by 'The Last Post.'"

Slipped into Caroline's programme of the memorial service is a poem sent to her by a friend the following Christmas. Titled, *From the Trenches: There Is No Death*, it was silly and sentimental, yet in a curious way moving in its attempt to reassure a mourning mother that her pain encompassed some higher purpose:

> *. . . Hark, ye can hear us calling*
> *From each to each a greeting*
> *As we meet – comrades and erstwhile foe*
> *Friend! Is this all to death?*
> *Why should we ever fear*
> *This passing through a shadow*
> *Which seems but a moment's shock,*
> *As though we had but bowed our heads*
> *To pass beneath a narrow doorway*
> *From some dugout small, and found*
> *Ourselves a little blinded by the light*
> *Which shines from Heaven's eternal day*
> *You here! You Too! – and you!*
> *How glad we are to find*
> *Each other, and to prove,*
> There is no death!!

Agar Adamson's letter of condolence to Caroline is missing from her papers. But Caroline's anguished reply, dated November 25, 1917, and written from a country retreat in Sussex, exists among his own. "Every word you said of Talbot I read and re-read and in the expressions of admiration and esteem in which he was held, I find my almost only solace. The courage and readiness with which he faced what I am told was a desperate attack, fills my heart with pride, but also with great bitterness. I've nothing. Nothing can console me for the loss of my boy who had been the joy and comfort of my life."

She lived on and on, until 1951, in an apartment on Sherbrooke

Caroline Rogers Papineau, *circa* 1917. She lived to be ninety-three, but never recovered from Talbot's death.

Street in Montreal. None of her other three sons had matched Talbot in her affections, nor could they fill the gap left by his absence.* In 1929 they sold Montebello to an American developer, H. M. Saddlemire, for $75,000, and the Papineaus departed from land they had held for nearly two centuries. Saddlemire built a 228-bedroom "log palace" next to the manor house and turned the property into a luxurious resort known as Lucerne-in-Quebec. When this scheme foundered, the CPR acquired Montebello and it

---

* Of Talbot's three brothers, Louis-Joseph, the eldest, was employed by the Bell Telephone Company and died in 1971 at the age of ninety. Westcott served in the artillery for three years and after the Armistice went to Russia with the Canadian Military Expedition. On his return to Montreal, he became an executive with Canadian Industries Limited (CIL) and died in 1946. Philip, who was too delicate to enlist, served with the Red Cross in the south of France during the war, and later lived with Caroline at Montebello. He died unmarried in 1932.

Nowadays, the ranks of this proud family have grown sparse. No direct descendant of *le grand patriote* bears the name, Louis-Joseph. But Westcott's two daughters, Jacqueline DesBaillets of Montreal and Renée Christie of North Hatley, Quebec, both now in their seventies, remain dedicated keepers of the flame.

became the Seigniory Club, an exclusive ashram for the Canadian elite.* In 1970, it was rechristened Château Montebello and opened to the public, and in recent years has become a popular hotel for weekend breaks, frequently used for seminars and conferences. Perhaps Talbot would have been pleased to know that in 1981, the G7 summit of Western world leaders was held on the grounds where he had once played at being Dollard at the Long Sault and Hereward the Wake, and of which he had written to Beatrice, "there I was born and there my heart is."

Beatrice for her part seems to have lived a full and rewarding life. Her career as a sculptor was successful; she was best known for her portraits in marble and bronze, including a striking bust of Sir Wilfrid Grenfell, the great medical missionary of Labrador, that can still be seen in the chapel of the International Grenfell Association Hospital in St. Anthony, Newfoundland. She was known equally well for her illuminated manuscripts, among them a book of congratulations sent by the Colonial Dames of America to King George V on the occasion of his Silver Jubilee in 1935. In later years she also became a writer, publishing four books, including a study of arts and crafts in the British Isles titled *Treasures Under Glass* and a biography of her father, *Country Doctor*.

Sometime during the 1920s Beatrice married a Philadelphia businessman named Charles F. Griffith, and moved to a house called Lynhurst in the fashionable Main Line suburb of Ardmore. In 1934, apparently at Caroline's behest, although relations between them do not seem to have been intimate (Beatrice's signature is not among those in the guest book at Montebello in the years that led up to its sale) she parcelled up all the letters that Talbot had written her and, through the intermediary of Philip Mackenzie, an executive at Fidelity Trust in Montreal, and also an old friend of Talbot's who had served with him in the Patricias, sent them to Canada as a gift to the Army Historical Section. In the early 1960s, along with the letters Talbot wrote to

---

* In September 1945, when the cipher clerk Igor Gouzenko defected from the Soviet Embassy in Ottawa, RCMP agents spirited him away to the manor house at Montebello for safekeeping and interrogation.

Caroline and copies of his reports for the Canadian War Records Office, these were transferred to the National Archives. In later years, the National Archives has acquired additional memorabilia, including the Montebello guest book, and an album of family photographs.

Beatrice also included in her gift the miniature of herself that she had sent Talbot in 1917, and that he had returned to her, hoping that someday she would be able to give it to him in person. "It seemed to belong so with the letters," she explained in her covering letter to Philip Mackenzie. Here, for the first time, by then in her mid-forties, Beatrice reveals something of herself to us directly. "This week – March 25th – is the birthday anniversary. [Talbot would have been fifty-one.] I am grateful indeed that I can mark it by a feeling of great serenity – and that this whole story is in safe hands. And home again to Canada . . . If you think it is best to simply do nothing but place the whole in the 'Vaults' that has been my first thought. But if you think that as a bit of dream-stuff which has outlasted the war, it is precious and joins some of the other lovely 'Supergifts' to the world, let it be delicately used – to quote Peter Ibbetson, we 'dreamed true.'"

Peter Ibbetson was a popular novel of the 1890s by George DuMaurier. More likely, given the conjointure of dates, Beatrice had more immediately in mind the film version of 1934 that starred Ann Harding and the young Gary Cooper. An odd, moody period piece, occasionally screened nowadays on late-night television and in repertory cinemas, it reflects the between-the-wars preoccupation with the supernatural and with juxtapositions of time and space. Knowing what we do of the story of Beatrice and Talbot, it's easy to understand the film's appeal. The plot concerns a pair of star-crossed lovers who, though separated by fate, find fulfilment in long dream sequences. The romantic conceit of *Peter Ibbetson* is that the separated lovers dream exactly the same dream and embrace within it, as they had never been able to do in real life. The delicacy of her imagery – "we dreamed true" – and her evocative request, "let it be delicately used," suggest that Beatrice never, really, got over Talbot. She died in Haverford Pennsylvania on December 4, 1968, leaving no children.

When Beatrice parcelled up Talbot's letters in 1934, and sent them home to Canada from her "little local post-office" at Ardmore, she typed out and used as epigraph a poem that he had sent her in October 1915, a few months after their correspondence had begun. "I know something about French Canadian folklore and our Canadian poetry," he had told her. "How do you like this bit which is specially appealing to me now? It was written by a poor devil in Quebec who afterwards died in exile."

> *J'ai vu le ciel de l'Italie*
> *Rome et ses palais enchantés*
> *J'ai vu notre mère patrie*
> *La noble France et ses beautés*
> *Mais en saluant chaque contrée*
> *Je me disais au fond du coeur*
> *Chez nous la vie est moins dorée*
> *Mais on y trouve le bonheur.*

> *O. Canada quand sur ta rive*
> *Ton heureux son est de retour*
> *Rempli d'une ivresse plus vive*
> *Son coeur répète avec amour*
> *Heureux qui peut passer sa vie*
> *Toujours fidèle à te servir*
> *Et dans tes bras, mère cherie,*
> *Peut rendre son dernier soupir.*

"I wonder if I shall be more fortunate than the unhappy author," Talbot had added. "He loved his Canada, but he did not love it more than I do."

24

The Worst of Times

In the early days of the war we had strength to endure it.
But in this, the fourth year, when we had hoped for
victory, it is very hard to bear.

Lucy Maud Montgomery. Diary entry; November 1, 1917

The months after Passchendaele were dark months of bereavement, a time of "black, annihilating despair," as Lloyd George later described his own feelings. Britain, racked by food and fuel shortages and by growing industrial strife, and threatened also by increasingly severe daylight air-raids from the new Gotha bombers that had succeeded the Zeppelins, was approaching psychological burn-out. In London, the dance of death continued unabated, becoming ever more macabre and ever more dependent on drugs, particularly cocaine which was obtainable in West End hotels in half-crown packets. The fashionable novelist Stephen McKenna wrote later of "a spectacle of debauchery which would have swelled the record of scandal if it had been made public but which is mercifully forgotten because it is incredible."* The news from Flanders was the immediate cause, of course. The news was equally bad on every front.

---

* Canadian authorities were equally disturbed by the widespread use of cocaine among men on leave, known to some by the code expression, "hooking up the reindeers." Early in 1918, *Canadians in Khaki*, a publication produced by the War Records Office, featured a cautionary short story, "The Saving of Tom McKay," about the attempt of a glamorous "drug fiend" named Isabelle to entice an upstanding Canadian sergeant to purchase "a packet labelled innocently 'rice powder,'" and how this was foiled by the deft intervention of an army nurse.

On October 31, the day that the Canadians advanced upon Pass-chendaele Ridge, the Italian army was routed at Caporetto. On November 7, the Bolsheviks seized power in Petrograd; a few months later, Leon Trotsky withdrew Russia from the war by sign-ing the peace treaty of Brest-Litovsk. Far worse was the gathering sense of futility about the war itself. On November 29, Lord Lans-downe, a former foreign secretary and former Governor General of Canada, who had lost a son at the Front, wrote to the *Daily Tele-graph* urging a negotiated peace. His plea was ignored, and he was ostracised socially. But, if only in private, people now speculated freely that the war would continue until well into the 1920s, might only be ended when one side had only one soldier left. Coming home on leave after Passchendaele, the poet Edmund Blunden noted "the large decay of lively bright love of country, the crystal-lization of dull civilian hatred on the basis of 'the last drop of blood.'"

The mood in Canada was almost as bleak. Here too, there was food rationing (caused in part by shortages of farm labour) and fuel shortages – in February 1918, all factories in Quebec and Ontario, save war plants, shut down for two days. There was a more immediate cause for the pessimism. Added to the long lists of war casualties, there was now a long list of civilian casualties. On December 6, two freighters, one of them the *Mont Blanc*, a French munitions ship loaded with picric acid and TNT, collided in Halifax harbour. "By a single stroke of evil magic, the whole place had been transformed," wrote the Dalhousie English pro-fessor Archibald MacMechan in his official report. The massive explosion, the greatest man-made blast to that time, destroyed the entire north end of the city, killed 1,630 people, and left thou-sands maimed and blinded by jagged pieces of flying glass. In his report, MacMechan described: "Here was a man with his side torn open and his entrails exposed. There was a woman cut in two and gasping her last. One woman was seen . . . naked and bathed in blood. Her left breast had been cut off but for a shred of flesh and as she walked unconscious, she held it up with her hand." This was the only time, in the First or the Second World War, that Canadians experienced directly the reality behind all those distant, grainy photographs and optimistic dispatches of the war correspondents. The experience de-stabilized them. As the novelist L. M. Montgomery recorded in her diary, while in Toronto on a shopping trip she'd come out of Eaton's loaded with parcels, bought from a passing newsboy a *Star* bearing "the big black headline, HALIFAX CITY WRECKED," and glanced at the story while waiting for her streetcar. "I was not alarmed," she informs. "I concluded that some steamer named *Halifax City* was wrecked, and although this would have been a sensation in the *Lusitania*'s day, it is a mere commonplace now." Twenty minutes later, Montgomery continues, "I came to my senses aboard an uptown car without any recollection of how I got there . . . while my brain was trying to take in the magnitude of the disaster."*

As painful for Canadians, their home front was dividing against itself. Since the start of 1917, casualties in the Canadian Corps, incomparably worsened now by Passchendaele, had outnumbered voluntary enlistments by two to one. The only remedy – given that the war, as everyone said, had three or more years yet to run – was conscription, or "compulsory enlistment" as Prime Minister Borden preferred to call it. On June 11, Borden introduced a bill in the House calling for "compulsory military enlistment on a selective basis . . . to provide such reinforcement as may be necessary to maintain the Canadian army in the field." He asked Laurier to help him implement it without injuring national unity, by joining the government in a national coalition. Laurier, aware that French Canadians would regard him as having left them unprotected and voiceless, refused. But he pledged to make one last effort to try to tie together the minority and the majority. His alternative was a national referendum. "Have an appeal to the people," he wrote to a friend, "If they decide in favour of conscription, as it seems to me that they will . . . whatever influence I may have will be employed in pleading to the Quebec people that the question is settled by the verdict of the majority."

---

* By coincidence, the sons of two of our characters experienced the Halifax disaster. Rodney Adamson and Gordon Beckles Willson, each aged sixteen, were both cadets at the new Canadian Naval College, which was ripped apart by the blast. Neither was injured, although Rodney was blown out a window, but since news was hard to come by, both families had an anxious few days.

Nearly seventy-seven now, Laurier was no longer master in his own political house. Across English Canada, prominent Liberals, Manitoba's Clifford Sifton perhaps the most prominent, were passionate advocates of total war, and thus of conscription. "Yesterday it was Pardee and today it will be Graham! Graham and Pardee as dear to me as my own brothers," wrote Laurier in anguish of two Liberal defectors. Even the Toronto *Globe*, Clear Grit to the core since the days of George Brown, deserted him. If alone, and aged, Laurier's eloquence and his vision had not left him. On July 19, just before the final vote in the Commons, he delivered a prophetic warning, "This bill has in it the seeds of discord and disunion. . . . It is an obstacle and a bar to that union of heart and soul without which it is impossible to hope that this Confederation will attain the aims and ends that were in view when Confederation was effected." The bill passed by 102 votes to 44. In October, Borden announced that an election would be held on December 17. A week later, he introduced a new "Union"

Sir Wilfrid and Lady Laurier on their golden wedding anniversary in 1918. He had lost none of his eloquence and vision, but was no longer master in his own political house.

government; it included nine leading Liberals as ministers, not one of them French Canadian. Eight of the nine provincial premiers announced their support for the new government, and for conscription. The exception was Lomer Gouin of Quebec.

The Khaki Election, as it came to be known, was the most divisive in all of Canadian history. It was more like a civil war than an electoral contest. Back in June, Bourassa had warned that forcible military service would turn French Canadians, "the most peaceable, perhaps the most orderly population of the two Americas into a revolutionary people." Through the summer and into the fall, riots broke out in Montreal, with crowds marching through the streets, shouting *"A bas Borden!"* and *"Vive la revolution!,"* breaking windows and shooting off blank cartridges. In August, the summer home of the publisher of the *Montreal Star*, Lord Atholstan, was dynamited. Bourassa took to warning against "sterile violence." But his chief lieutenant, Armand Lavergne, the son of Laurier's inamorata, Emilie Lavergne, perhaps, indeed, Laurier's own son, mounted a platform in Quebec City to declare that he was ready to be "hanged or shot" before he would accept conscription, and that, "If you are still descendants of those who were sent to the scaffold crying *'Vive la liberte! Vive l'independance!'* you should take a pledge to disobey it." (Tens of thousands of young Québecois would do this in effect, by fleeing into the woods to escape conscription.)

Once the election began in earnest, Unionist supporters responded in kind. "Make every ballot a bullet," urged the *Manitoba Free Press*. "A vote for Laurier is a vote for the Kaiser." Among some, a belief began to take hold that Canada's real enemy lay within. The *Toronto News* expressed that attitude by printing a map of Canada on its front page; eight provinces were in red, Quebec was in black. Attitudes toward other internal "enemies" were as harsh. Jingoism had manifested itself throughout the war; in 1916, the Ontario town of Berlin changed its name to Kitchener; in some quarters it was even considered disloyal to admit a liking for the works of Bach and Beethoven. On the advice of Solicitor General Arthur Meighen, Borden now disenfranchised all immigrants from Germany or Austria-Hungary who had arrived less than fifteen years previously. He also widened the vote to suit his

The Khaki Election of December 17, 1917, was the most
divisive in Canadian history. More than any other single
event, it split Canada into two nations. This poster is
typical of many.

own purposes, extending the franchise to all women over twenty-one who had sons, husbands, or brothers at the Front. Nellie McClung, feminist and previous pacifist, but who now had a son overseas, applauded the measure. Those few who did not paid the price. Francis Marion Beynon, women's editor of the influential *Grain Grower's Guide* in Winnipeg and once a close confidante of McClung's, was forced to resign from her job because of her opposition to conscription, moving soon afterwards to New York where she poured out her feelings of betrayal in an autobiographical novel *Aleta Dey*.*

None of the people we have met in these pages was directly involved in the election. Ethel Chadwick canvassed – for conscription naturally – with the Ottawa May Court Club. Harold Innis's pro-conscription views have been recorded already; although once a hero-worshipper of Laurier, he now urged his sister to vote for Borden. All of the soldiers, like Adamson, had the right to vote, and all undoubtedly cast their ballots for conscription, as, assuredly, Talbot Papineau would have done had he lived.

The election results were a foregone conclusion. On December 17, the Unionists won 153 seats, the Liberals 82, all but 20 of them in Quebec. Mackenzie King, who had remained loyal to Laurier, was defeated in his grandfather's old constituency of North York. Bourassa, ironically, declared for Laurier as the lesser of two evils, a decision that played into the government's hands. Few others stood by the old leader. "It is really too bad that I should have to cast my first vote against Wilfrid Laurier, whom at one time I thought little lower than the angels," wrote L. M. Montgomery. "But he is an old man now and he has outlived his glory and betrayed his country."

Because the effects of that Khaki Election continue to haunt us today, it is easy to forget that with luck things might have turned out differently, or at least not as badly. In hindsight, Borden is often seen as the villain of the piece; in fact, he performed most of the time like a gentleman, and, as we shall soon

---

* The conflict between Beynon and McClung was dramatized by Wendy Lill in her 1984 play, *The Fighting Days*.

see, very much like a Canadian. His offer to Laurier to join in a true national government was a genuine attempt to safeguard national unity. Borden may well have been right, as he wrote years later, that "If he [Laurier] had been ten or fifteen years younger, I am confident he would have entered the proposed coalition. . . . [But] he held an unrivalled position in the affection and reverence of the French Canadians; and he was convinced he would lose this pre-eminence." English Canada's jingoistic anger has to be set in the context of the terrible losses so many families had suffered and, almost worse, the widespread presumption that these losses would continue. If the news, equally at the Front and at home, hadn't been so bleak at that particular time, the patriotic fury of most English Canadians might have been tempered – as happened in both Australia and New Zealand where similiar attempts to introduce conscription were defeated.

Yet conscription happened and it split Canada into two nations. Each came out of the war convinced that the other had let it down, could never again entirely be trusted. The following March, a riot broke out in Quebec City when police tried to arrest conscription defaulters. The crowd burned the Military Service Registry office and attacked English-Canadian establishments. Martial law had to be declared and troops sent in from Toronto. On April 1, soldiers fired on a mob that had trapped them in Quebec City's narrow streets; four civilians were killed. Appeals from the clergy and from political leaders led to a cooling of at least the public expressions of French-Canadian outrage. It helped

(Opposite above)
Soldiers overseas took part in the Khaki Election and could vote in any constituency they chose. Many were directed by their officers to choose constituencies where votes for conscription were most needed.

(Opposite below)
Canadian nursing sisters casting their votes. To ensure the outcome, all women over twenty-one who had sons, husbands, or brothers in uniform were given the franchise, as were women serving overseas.

that the tribunals in Quebec, in contrast to those in the other provinces, were exceptionally lenient to claims for exemption from conscription. (Those most severely treated by the tribunals and police were the minorities in English Canada, like the Jehovah's Witnesses, who claimed exemption as conscientous objectors.) It helped even more that the war should have ended so unexpectedly, so quickly. But the damage still was done; and for so little. The final Conscription Bill contained so many loopholes – along with farmers and farmers' sons, seminarians and "legitimate" conscientious objectors were excused – that out of 401,882 single men and widowers forced to register, over 90 per cent claimed to be exempt. In the end, 100,000 conscripts were enlisted, given uniforms, and sent off to be trained. When the guns finally fell silent, only about 25,000 of these had even made it as far as France.

The special poignacy about the conscription crisis is that it nullified the effects of the exercise in national conciousness-raising that was taking place simultaneously. By the winter of 1917–18, Canadians had proven themselves, first at Vimy, then at Passchendaele, as front-line soldiers of equal calibre to the best in Europe. They had proven, to themselves above all, that they were something more than Colonials. Harold Innis was by no means the only Canadian who had begun to think of himself as a soldier and citizen of an emerging new nation that could take its place alongside all the others in the world. The heavyweight – literally so – among this new self-aware breed was that extraordinary ex-realtor, General Sir Arthur Currie. In March 1918, Haig, in anticipation of a German offensive, set out to re-organize his armies and directed that the independent status of the Canadian Corps should be ended and its four divisions transferred to direct British command. Currie refused to accept the order and, by appealing to Lloyd George through the intermediary of Borden's new overseas minister in London, Sir Edward Kemp, managed to get it rescinded. By contrast the Australians, for all their fire and spirit, accepted the same order when it was applied to them.

What Currie had done, Borden himself now proceeded to do. His conversion to Canadian nationalism traversed even greater territory. An unassuming, phlegmatic lawyer from Nova Scotia, by now sixty-three years old, he had while opposition leader ridiculed Laurier's 1909 plan to create a "tin-pot" Canadian navy; his own naval policy called for a direct contribution of three Canadian-built dreadnaughts to the Royal Navy. As prime minister, Borden, at the start of the war had carried deference to the extreme of inviting the Governor General, the Duke of Connaught, to sit in on cabinet meetings. But as the war progressed, Borden came increasingly to feel that he and his people were being taken for granted. "The Canadian Government have had just what is in the daily press and no more," wrote the prime minister to his High Commissioner in London, Sir George Perley, early in 1916. "It can hardly be expected that we shall put *400,000 or 500,000 men in the field* and willingly accept the position of having no more voice and receiving no more consideration than if we were toy automata." Passed on by Perley to Colonial Secretary Bonar Law, this letter resulted in top-secret documents being dispatched regularly across the Atlantic (in a canvas bag loaded with lead, to be thrown overboard if the ship were captured). Far more substantively, an Imperial War Cabinet was established in 1917 of which Borden and other Dominion leaders were members. When this body assembled in London for its second formal meeting in June 1918, Canada's soldiers had won their laurels at Vimy and Passchendaele, while Borden had won his own political laurels as the only Dominion leader to extend his war contribution to the limit of conscription. (Britain itself had introduced conscription in June 1916.)

Immediately upon his arrival in London, Borden was briefed by Currie. "He gave an awful picture of the war situation among the British," the prime minister recorded in his diary. "Says incompetent officers not removed, too casual, too cocksure, no foresight." On June 12, the eve of the conference, where, besides some friendly faces like Jan Smuts of South Africa with whom he'd struck up rapport, and Hughes of Australia, and Lloyd George, and Bonar Law, there would also be stern arch-imperialists of the old school like Lord Curzon, former Viceroy of India, and Lord Milner, former Governor General of South Africa, Borden recorded in his diary, he "slept badly . . . rose early." Just when he decided to do what he did, and what finally nerved him to do it, we do not

Sir Robert Borden opening a Victory Bond Drive in
Ottawa in 1918. Union Station is in the background.
Union Jacks remain prominent, but by now Borden him-
self was becoming a Canadian nationalist.

know. His diary only hints at the strain he was under: "Began
speech at 11:30; spoke nearly an hour; gave a full summary of
Canada's position; throughout spoke without hesitation and more
rapidly than usual."

What Borden did at that Imperial War Cabinet had never
been done before. He told his peers and superiors the truth about
Passchendaele, and therefore about how the entire war was actually being waged. "I sent for General Currie and ordered him to tell
me the truth," Borden informed the Imperial War Cabinet as
recorded in its own minutes. He then told them what Currie had
told him: "Whenever the Canadian Corps was called upon to

attack, Currie always had his attacking troops in the trenches at least thirty-six hours before the time fixed for the attack. . . . On one of his flanks, a British battalion came into the trenches the night before the attack. Four companies wandered over to the Canadians in the morning and asked if the Canadians knew where they should go. Two of these companies stationed themselves at a point which proved to be about a hundred yards ahead of the barrage. When the barrage lifted, these two companies became non-existent. The two supporting companies, in their confusion, attacked the Canadians. Currie was informed he was supported by 364 guns but he found only 220. When he asked for more guns, he was asked to send indents [official requisitions]. He said he could not fight the Germans with indents."

After he had finished expressing Currie's opinions, Borden expressed his own, doing so in a way that has probably never been equalled at any war cabinet meeting before or since. As he reached his concluding lines, Borden strode across the floor to the British prime minister. He seized Lloyd George by the lapels of his frock coat and shook him. "Mr. Prime Minister," he said. "I want to tell you that if there is ever a repetition of Passchendaele, not a Canadian soldier will leave the shore of Canada so long as the Canadian people entrust the Government of my country to my hands."

The brave win the laurels. Curzon, of all people, applauded and came up to shake Borden's hand. Lloyd George, far from being outraged, was delighted. As part of his own attempt to prevent any more Passchendaeles, he arranged for Borden, the next day, to repeat his speech virtually word for word to an audience of Britain's most senior generals. Borden was never deferential again. When peace came five months later, he insisted that Canada sign the Treaty of Versailles in her own right, and insisted also, over the objections of the American delegation, that Canada be given its own seat at the new League of Nations and at the International Labour Organization. None of this would have happened but for the war, but Borden himself had now become one of its casualties. Harrowed throughout the war by painful attacks of boils that signalled a deeper disability, he yielded to his doctor's advice and resigned the prime ministership in July 1920, slipping away to tend his beloved wildflower garden and to read the classics in the original Greek and Latin. Yet he kept up an active interest in public affairs, wrote numerous essays on national and international subjects later published as *Letters to Limbo* as well as his own political memoirs and during the 1920s and early 1930s, as might have surprised Henri Bourassa, made a point of writing much of his own private diary in French. Borden died in 1937, less well remembered as an architect of nationhood than he deserves to be.

25
Casualty of War

*I once told you that the only thing in the world worth
living for was love. . . . To this, I have since added a
duty to one's country . . . added to which the good luck
of finding the opportunity to make other people happy.*

Agar Adamson. A letter to Mabel Cawthra Adamson; 1918

As 1918 approaches, the threads begin to draw in on this
tapestry. Time now to bring to conclusion the story of Agar
Adamson.

For Agar, as for Currie and Borden and also for Harold Innis,
the war had been transformational, although it had not made of
him a Canadian nationalist. Meditating on his father's motivation
for going to war, Anthony Adamson has written: "If he had asked
himself seriously and intellectually what he fought for, he would
probably have fallen back on the trite phrase, 'King and Country.' A meaningless mystic phrase? Perhaps, but underlying it
was an ideal. . . . It was that great WASP achievement, the British
Empire." The real transformation within Agar had been private
and personal. In 1914, when we first met him at Lansdowne Park
in the company of Ethel Chadwick, he was no more than a
middle-aging failure, albeit a most charming one. He had done
well out on the veldt in South Africa, but had squandered away
the intervening years living a self-indulgent life on Mabel's

money. Now, he was Lieutenant-Colonel Agar Adamson, DSO, known affectionately by his men as "Ack-Ack," Commanding Officer of a regiment legendary for its bravery, and also, almost as important to him, for smartness and *esprit-de-corps*. "You will be as much pleased as I am to know that the GOC [General Currie] considers that during the year past the PPCLI have made the best showing in fighting, discipline, drill and dress in the Canadian Corps, and he wishes us to be quoted as an example," he wrote Mabel in January 1918. So bucked was Agar by this message that, on the next day, he rounded up a group of new officers recently promoted from the ranks, and set out to teach them the rudiments of horsemanship.

Agar, however, was now fifty-two. He had to have been one of the oldest battalion commanders at the Front, in any army. The strain of more than thirty consecutive months in the trenches – six weeks, as the war poet Robert Graves reckoned later in *Goodbye to All That,* was enough to turn most men into physical and nervous wrecks – was starting to show. The previous summer, he'd spent a week in hospital with trench fever. Later, he'd been hospitalized by a dose of mustard gas. So poor was his vision, even in his good eye, that he was helpless without the monocle that was now enshrined in regimental folklore, and, even with it screwed in, continually fell into holes and bumped into obstacles when inspecting the trenches at night. He was also beginning to be jumpy. "I met him coming out of Knightsbridge underground station," recalls Anthony Adamson, then ten years old, of a home-coming on leave in mid-1917. "He was still covered with mud. I asked him if he had killed many Germans. His face went gray."

There were other, more personal reasons for Adamson's jumpiness. Despite their daily exchange of letters, the relationship between him and Mabel was under a strain that became progressively more severe. Their problem wasn't the classic wartime one of infidelity – so far as we know, neither of them thought for an instant of looking elsewhere, indeed, in his letters, Agar frequently joked about officers and other ranks needing "to get their hair cut," by which he meant their need to seek out a prostitute in

Poperinghe or Boulogne.* Rather, it had to do with an incompatibility of temperament that had always troubled their marriage, and that the later stages of the war had begun to accentuate. For the first year or so they'd been happier than at any time since their very beginning, she hugely enjoying being a co-conspirator in the bureaucratic battle against Colonel James's attempt to dismember the regiment and, when he first went across the Channel, impulsively boarding a troop-train so as to kiss him good-bye on the jetty.

Since those early days of togetherness, Mabel had become increasingly wrapped up in her own war. She too had been transformed by it. Her Belgian Canal Boat Fund, based at Furnes, a medieval market town just behind allied lines, had been from the outset a serious project rather than one of the many charity endeavours engaged in by society women so long as 'gallant little Belgium' happened to be in fashion. It kept on growing until it was

---

* Liberated from the stern morality of small-town Canada, the sexual energy of many members of the Canadian Corps was legendary – as demonstrated by a letter back home to a trusted friend written by a battalion commander from the Prairies.

> It was too rough to cross the channel and they held us up a day in Boulogne, and that gave us time to check things up a little and I sure did after being five months at the front and never a chance to shake a loose leg (enough said). Well to start with the other officers and myself managed to get fixed (capital F) up for the night, and we got a couple of very good ones and had a swell time (hope they didn't swell) took them to dinner etc. etc. and left the next morning for London. . . . Put up at the Regent Palace Hotel and then got busy on the line for some of my steadies. . . . I sure had a time. . . . London is the place, I can tell you. I used to put in all day with one of my steadies, and then at night, after the theatre at 12:30 used to start out again and go home to some girls flat for the night. . . . Kept my room at the Regents Palace but never slept there at all. . . . Now I am back at the same old job none the worse for wear, getting ready for the next leave . . . but mums the word.

Similarly, the account of an anonymous soldier of a certain mademoiselle at a notorious estaminet called *The Black Cat* in Armentières: "She told me she had just saved a battalion from dying of sexual starvation. 'You know,' she said, 'I just put it between my legs, give it a squeeze and say 'next.'"

Mabel Adamson at Furnes in Belgium *circa* 1917. The huts housed the relief workers of the Belgian Canal Boat Fund. Mabel wears a uniform with a head-dress adapted from that of Flemish nuns.

responsible not only for the care and feeding of 370 children in a refugee school at Furnes, but for providing food and clothing to an additional 300 refugee families while simultaneously operating a medical clinic and pharmaceutical dispensary. From 1916 onwards, Mabel spent much of her time at Furnes itself, frequently under air-raid, and within shelling-range of enemy guns. She too became a commanding officer, turning a cadre of post-debutantes with sobriquets like "Winkie" into a disciplined team of relief workers. As stressful for one of Mabel's stern Cawthra ethic was learning to deal tactfully with the values of those who were being helped. On one occasion, she was horrified to discover that a useful gift of six dozen girls' underpants sent by Eaton's in Toronto was about to be consigned to the scrapheap. Nicely bred girls, said the nuns in charge of the refugee school, could not wear such outrageous garments. (Not that the nuns needed much training in how to act with worldly skill. "We pray daily for God to bless you, dear Benefactress, and to return you a thousand-fold all that you are doing," wrote their mother superior to Mabel at Christmas 1916. The next paragraph contained a request for a waterproof coat for the parish *Aumonier*, plus "three large umbrellas," and several yards of black serge "to mend our habits which are very much worn.")

Agar was genuinely supportive of Mabel's work. Every so often, he slipped up to Furnes for a couple of days, occasionally commandeering a presentable subaltern to entertain "Winkie" and the others. Shortly after Vimy, he and Mabel even managed to spend a full week together in Paris that was almost a second honeymoon. "It was great fun wandering around together," Agar wrote his son Anthony. "Your mother showed me all sorts of places she used to know when studying painting."

Increasingly, though, as each of them was absorbed in what he or she was doing, the doings of the other became an intrusion. It was Agar, who after all was risking his life in the line, who had a better claim to feeling neglected. Mabel, during her increasingly infrequent sojourns in London, became more and more irritated by his ever-lengthening shopping lists: requests for flashlight batteries, pâté from Fortnum and Mason, *real* clotted cream from Devonshire; silk underwear from the Army and Navy; wigs and costumes for the regimental comedy company. Once, he sent her a broken wristwatch belonging to a "little orphan girl" in a house where he was billetted and asked her to get it fixed. She delayed dealing with the matter. "I do not see why you should neglect my little girl's bracelet watch when your entire time is taken up by doing similar work for other Belgians," Agar wrote her. This provoked action, but his letter of thanks was deliberately calculated to annoy: "I do hope the Belgian child will be sufficiently grateful for your superhuman efforts at having her watch wound up and the tremendous financial undertaking it involved, each and both of which you have so thoroughly reported to me on oft and several occasions." In another letter he referred, teasingly but also tauntingly, to "the woman I know better than she knows herself."

The moment when the widening distance between Agar and Mabel turned into a gulf happened in May 1917. Agar travelled to London as one of the men of the hour: at a special outdoor presentation at Buckingham Palace, he, along with several dozen other officers, was to be personally invested by the King with his Distinguished Service Order medal. This above all was an occasion on which he expected to have Mabel at his side. Instead, he went to the ceremony accompanied only by his ten-year-old son Anthony. Mabel had sent word from Furnes that business there was too pressing for her to join him. (Agar equipped Anthony with a top hat and cane and afterwards took him to a full-course dinner at the Ritz.) For two full weeks afterwards, Agar was too resentful to write Mabel at all. By June 6, he'd cooled down sufficiently to write plaintively, but with uncommon perception for so stolid an old soldier, "I am very much in love with you and like to tell you so, which is more than you ever do to me, and if the Belgian Barge Fund has taken your affections, even if this dear old gallant Regiment is more sacred to me than even you . . . I still love dear old Mabel best of all."

Mabel's own side of this sad affair deserves a hearing. Much of the time she was not only physically exhausted – a difficult menopause, we can suspect, may have been part of the problem – but seriously ill. As early as 1916, she'd begun suffering severely from iritis, an inflammation of the eyes that affected her appearance and made reading and writing difficult; sometime in mid-1917, she began having severe internal pain that she said nothing about until, in mid-September, she collapsed at Furnes and had to be sent home by ambulance. When Agar rushed home on compassionate leave, she did her best to make light of it, insisting that he return to France in time to command the regiment at Passchendaele, even though her doctors, and Mabel herself, suspected that she was suffering from cancer. In February 1918, knowing that the Patricias were out of the line and unlikely to be in action for some time to come, she wrote beseechingly, for perhaps the first and only time in their marriage. "I would rather do anything than worry you . . . I want you more than any words can say, but I would rather you never came than feel I had taken you away from what you consider your first duty . . . I try to keep going and not think, and also to pretend that I feel well." That Agar understood what it had taken for her to write in this way is signified by the fact that this is one of the very few of Mabel's letters that survives from their wartime correspondence.

Agar rushed back to England. Knowing his stay might be indefinite, he resigned his command of his beloved Patricias. Later that month, she had a serious operation, and while the real source of the trouble is unclear, it proved not to be cancer. Indeed, save for the persistent iritis, Mabel recovered quite quickly, later returning to Furnes while Agar, in the middle of March 1918, returned to France.

By then, though, Charlie Stewart had become Commanding Officer of the Patricias, and on a permanent basis. "The Brigadier was very nice about it," Agar wrote to Mabel. "Whoever is in command should be full of health and youth. My blind eye and age were against me and if I returned to the Regiment it would only be a short time before I crocked up." It's easy to guess that Agar, when he'd resigned, had done so partly to provide the brigadier – and himself – with a graceful out. In September 1918, when Stewart was killed during the last great allied advance, Major A. G. Pearson, an officer who had joined originally as a private, was appointed to command.

For all practical purposes, Agar Adamson's war was over. A staff job was found for him, at Divisional Headquarters well behind the line. He remained there until the end of the war, just eight months later, and then served briefly with the new military government in Bonn, in occupied Germany, filling the post of a summary court officer, or magistrate. "I know how happy you will be at the end of the war," he wrote Mabel on Armistice Day, November 11. "I shall always regret that I was not in at the finish." (On that day, to the skirl of the pipes, the Patricias had marched triumphantly through the city of Mons, where the British had first gone into action four years earlier.) As one who had written hundreds of letters of condolence to widows and mothers, he closed with a note of extraordinary perception. "I doubt very much if all the real rejoicing will not always be dampened by the memory of the tremendous list of killed during the last four years, especially among women who have lost their husbands and sons and have been carrying on with war work to help forget it. The quiet of peace and want of excitement will make them realize their loss as they have never done before."

Agar and Mabel Adamson, *circa* 1918. In its early stages,
the war had brought them together, but toward its end
they had drawn apart.

Shortly before the Armistice, Agar sent Mabel a love letter that
was perhaps his most expressive. "I told you once that the only
thing in the world worth living for was love," he wrote. "To this, I
have since added a sense of duty to one's country . . . added to
which the good luck of finding the opportunity to make other
people happy." It would be nice to report that after four years of
tragedy and turmoil, these admirable people should have been
able to find happiness at last amid the peace they both had done
so much to earn. From Canada, where he was briefly dispatched
in the spring of 1919 to take part in ceremonies surrounding the
formal demobilization of the Patricias, Agar wrote letters filled
with love and longing. "I don't think I can possibly live much
longer without being with you for keeps," he told Mabel. "During
the war it was a necessary evil that had to be but now that peace
is with us, I long for peace conditions."

But this alas, was not to be. Their post-war contentment was
quite brief. In the summer of that year, they took lodgings at

Bruges, the beautiful, medieval city in northern Belgium unscathed by the fighting, and showed twelve-year-old Anthony the scenes of both their wars: the huts and Flemish nuns at Furnes; St. Eloi and Passchendaele and the regimental cemetery at Voormezele. In the autumn, they returned to Canada and moved into a magnificent new house on the Port Credit property that Mabel had ordered built, with curly Flemish gables to remind them of their war, and windows that overlooked Lake Ontario. Here, Mabel was able to pick up her old life as a patron of the arts, and she also cultivated a new interest – breeding chow dogs.

But Agar had become one of the war's casualties. His ailment was not physical but a delayed form of shell shock that nowadays would have been recognized and possibly remedied. All the accumulated stress he'd bottled up for so long soured his judgement and his temperament. He became impatient and irritable. Cars made him jumpy and he got into quarrels with taxi drivers. He blew up at waiters in restaurants and at his own servants for constantly serving the breakfast toast in the British style, cold and in a rack, instead of hot and already buttered, the way he liked it. He often so far forgot himself as to treat his own sons as batmen, rapping out orders and berating them if their fulfillment of them was slack.

The most persistent source of discord between him and Mabel was his refusal to sort himself out and find useful employment. "She was not niggardly with money," recalls Anthony. "She knew he had no professional or commercial skills. If he had only done volunteer work at a veterans' hospital, or gone in for growing a special kind of tomato, or become a church warden, or even cleaned his own shoes and put up with cold toast, they might have been happy." By the early 1920s, their marriage had ceased to exist in all but the social pretences, and increasingly less and less even there. Agar spent much of his time in Ottawa visiting old friends like Minnie Scott, or else in England where he became semi-addicted to the roulette wheel, selling off pieces of family silver to cover his debts, including a silver snuff box that according to family legend had been a wedding present from Robbie Burns to his great-grandmother. A letter written to him by Mabel in the spring of 1929 makes painful reading. "If you care to come out to Canada and spend a couple of months as my guest, I will try to be amiable. If you do come, you must accept my conditions. *I am not your wife*. You are not the master of this house."

That summer of 1929 was the last Agar would spend in Canada. In October of that year, having developed a keen interest in flying, he went up in an experimental plane with a British aviator to fly over to Ireland. They crashed into the Irish Sea, and while both survived to be picked up by a trawler, the two hours spent clinging to the wreckage was too much even for his exceptional constitution. Two months later, Anthony, who was by now studying architecture at Cambridge, found him in dire condition in a private hotel in Bayswater and cabled Mabel. "I sat with him and was astonished when this man whom I so admired, who had defeated Germany, should in gasping breath say, 'Tony, I have been a failure.'"

Mabel arrived only hours before Agar died. "When we got to his room he was already breathing stertorously," Anthony continues, "his private nurse for these last days burst into tears. I placed the oxygen mask over his face. He soon stopped breathing. My mother said simply, and without tears, "That's it! Will you go downstairs and deal with it."

On the following day, at the undertakers, Mabel looked for the last time on Agar. She regarded him silently, and then said, "It is a beautiful face, isn't it?" His body was cremated; with a panache that father had passed onto son, and that Agar would greatly have relished, Anthony carried his father's ashes back to Canada in his own leather top-hat box. Even more would Agar have enjoyed, indeed would have been deeply moved by, the magnificent funeral that Mabel had arranged as her last gift to him. At Toronto, his ashes were set in a light coffin and, with a company of the Royal Canadian Regiment serving as honour guard, placed aboard a special train to Port Credit. There, the coffin was transferred to a gun carriage, and joined by a cortège that included three pipers, a company of the local militia regiment, the Peel and Dufferin, and a riderless horse with empty boots reversed in the stirrups. Many of the mourners were veterans of the PPCLI who had known Agar as "Ack-Ack"; the current Commanding Officer of the regiment, Lieutenant-Colonel Ten Broek, who had served under him as a Company Commander, came in from Winnipeg

Lieutenant-Colonel Agar Adamson, DSO. "It is a beautiful face, isn't it?" Mabel said as farewell.

where the Patricias were now headquartered to serve as a pall-bearer, wearing his resplendent winter uniform, fur hat slashed with blue. When "The Last Post" had sounded, the old sweats adjourned to the basement of the church, where Mabel, no matter that Peel County was officially dry, had ordered in large quantities of beer. The chief mourners adjourned to Grove Farm for sherry and whiskey. "My father would have loved it," recalls Anthony. "My mother knew that and had done it for his sake."

Mabel lived on at Port Credit, always active in promoting the arts and in community activities. She died there in 1943. Of their two sons, Rodney, the elder, became a mining engineer and celebrated mountaineer, and, from 1940 until his death in 1954 in the crash of a Trans-Canada Airlines North Star, he was Conservative MP for York West and a member of George Drew's shadow cabinet. Anthony became a noted architect and town planner, best known for his achievements in the field of architectural preservation, including the establishment of Upper Canada Village and the saving of Toronto's Union Station. His remarkable family memoir, *Wasps in the Attic*, and his extraordinary powers of recall have made it possible to write this account of his parents' war.

For Agar and Mabel Adamson, the years of the Great War were more than simply the central event of their lives: these years *were* their lives. By the winter of 1917–18, though, Canadians of their cut – overseas English, or British North Americans – belonged to yesterday's generation. For the coming new generation, the Great War would mark the start of their lives, and they would fit easily into the different kind of Canada that would emerge from out of the war. Harold Innis is the exemplar of the breed. Two new characters, whose lives afterwards extended almost down to our own, take us through to the end of the war and to the last twist in this tapestry.

26

The Education of
Grace MacPherson

*It was glorious to think that at last I was actually driving
an ambulance. It was a dream hatched out, and has
meant more to me than anything has meant yet.*
    Grace MacPherson. Diary entry; April 9, 1917

In late July 1917, the Canadian War Records Office staged a large
exhibition of photographs from the Front at the fashionable
Grafton Galleries in central London. Crowds flocked to the
show, and once they'd oohed and aahed at the pictures showing
tanks in action and soldiers going over the top, they lingered at
the section that featured half a dozen photos of a young woman
identified only as a "Canadian Ambulance Driver." She was shown
at the wheel of her vehicle, cranking it up, pouring water into the
radiator, crawling underneath to change a tire. (So beguiling was
this last shot that it also turned up on the front page of *The Canadian Daily Record*, a round-up of news from home and abroad
issued by the War Records Office.)

Looking over these images today, it's easy to see why those
war-weary crowds lingered. The girl in the pictures wasn't a stunning beauty – her teeth were irregular, and her nose rather prominent. There was nothing about her of the ethereal, idealized
"angel of mercy," so popular with propaganda illustrators. Yet she
possessed unmistakable star quality. Her smile was cheeky and
infectious and it was impossible not to smile back at her. She was
youth, energy, and hope personified; a good deed in a wicked

An exhibition of Canadian War Photographs at the
Grafton Galleries in London, 1917. The large photograph
showing Canadian troops going over the top had in fact
been faked.

world; a perfect metaphor of the emerging, self-confident new
Canada. Even now, unlike most of the other characters in this
story, who seem in their photographs like figures frozen in history, this anonymous young woman strikes us immediately as
being our contemporary.

Her name was Grace Evelyn MacPherson. She was twenty-
three years old, and she came from Vancouver. The uniform she
wore was that of a VAD (Voluntary Aid Detachment) driver with
the British Red Cross. Based at Etaples, the huge military hospital
complex ten miles south of the port of Boulogne, she was one of
about a hundred young women – three others were also Canadian, and there were two Newfoundlanders – who ferried
wounded soldiers back and forth between trains and hospitals

These photographs of the Canadian ambulance driver Grace MacPherson were also featured in the War Records Office exhibition. Her diary tells us that they were taken on June 8, 1917, just as she was completing a difficult probationary period.

and ships bound for England. On June 8, the day the photographs were taken, Grace was just completing a difficult two-months' probationary period. As she recorded in her diary, her immediate thought, on being summoned to the commandant's office after "the busiest day we have *ever* had; five trains and an evacuation," was that she was about to be sacked. "I said to the Commandant's secretary, 'this is where I get the Devil, eh?' She said, 'No, there are two Canadian officers here who want to take your picture.' I thought she was having some fun – but quite right. Wanted me as representing Canada. . . . It was an awful ordeal posing, and the Commandant, when she saw me, laughed and said 'Poor Dear.' "

Grace was protesting too much. Clearly, she charmed the photographers – Captains Ivor Castle and F. O. Boville of the War Records Office – and they her. "They asked me to go up the line with them anytime I could get off. Would surely love to, but have an idea OC would not approve. However, ask anything once."

Despite their semi-cloistered image as "the angel in the house," Canadian women had always worked – on farms and in fish plants, in shops, schools, libraries, and churches. From the turn of the century, as typewriters and telephones became standard equipment in offices, an advance guard, of which Grace MacPherson was a member, had begun "going out to business," as the phrase went. The difference the Great War made was to give many women the opportunity – in many cases also the necessity – to move out of a familiar environment that, even when typing and shorthand were involved, was essentially an extension of their homes. In tens of thousands, they moved into the kind of strange, intimidating, work-places to which men were accustomed, removed from their homes and neighbourhoods, often removed from their towns and cities, removed in many instances from their country itself, not just the overseas volunteer workers like Grace but also the 30,000 women who, as we've noted earlier, followed husbands and lovers to live in Britain for most of the duration of the war. Early in 1918, soon after the Khaki Election, the new Union government extended to all Canadian women over twenty-one the right to vote. The more significant sociological and psychic change had already taken place: the war had liberated many women from their own hearth.

Not until about half-way through the war did the nature of this change become apparent. For the first couple of years, most women had done what came naturally to them. Like Ethel Chadwick, and L. M. Montgomery's heroine, *Rilla of Ingleside*, they knitted socks and rolled bandages, sold tags in aid of gallant Belgians and Smokes for Soldiers, staged patriotic entertainments, distributed largesse to the needy families of soldiers (who frequently regarded them as Nosy Parkers, checking up to ensure that money had not been squandered on needless luxuries, like buying a gramophone). Save for a handful of wealthy and strong-minded women, like Mabel Adamson and Lady Drummond of the Canadian Red Cross in London, the only significant exceptions were army nurses, of whom a small cadre had existed within the Canadian Army Medical Corps since the Boer War. At the outbreak of war, their numbers began to grow exponentially: 105 nursing sisters, already nicknamed the "Bluebirds," because of their smart blue uniforms, sailed overseas with the First Canadian Contingent. (Unlike British army nurses, who were considered non-commissioned officers, all the Canadians held commissioned rank, probably because at that time nursing had higher social status in Canada than in England.) In early November, a senior matron and thirty-four sisters crossed the Channel to find a suitable site for the first overseas Canadian hospital, settling on a large hotel near the golf course at Le Touquet, a seaside resort adjacent to Etaples already staked out by the British as a medical receiving centre. Simultaneously, several Canadian hospitals were established in Britain, most notably at Cliveden, the magnificent mansion overlooking the Thames at Taplow in Buckinghamshire, lent for the duration by the flamboyant American-born Lady Astor. Other Canadian nurses served much further afield: More than a hundred went out to the eastern Mediterranean with a Canadian medical unit attached to the ill-fated Gallipoli expedition: so bad were conditions at their base hospital at Mudros on the Greek Island of Lemnos that more than half came down with amoebic dysentery, and two died there. (After Gallipoli was evacuated, these nurses went on to Salonika, in northern Greece. In later years some remembered with affection the boyish charm and hi-jinks of a young private named Mike Pearson, a medical orderly with the University of Toronto Hospital Unit.) Of all the 2,504 Canadian nurses who eventually served overseas, the most adventurous time was had by four who travelled to Russia in 1916 to help set up an Anglo-Russian hospital in Petrograd. The following year, from the windows of the nurses' residence overlooking the Nevsky Prospect, they had a spectacular view of the March Revolution. "Several times we had to stop while on the way to the hospital, the firing was so heavy," Sister Edith Hegan of Saint John, New Brunswick, wrote later. "We were worried lest the shots might strike some of our already badly injured patients. And we were interested enough to wish to get back to our windows too, for it is not often that one can watch the death of a monarchy and the birth of a new republic."

For women on the home front, the pivotal year was 1916. "Farmerettes," who dressed outlandishly in boots and breeches, began being recruited to help with the harvest and to pick the fruit crop. The real pattern-breakers, though, were the 35,000 Canadian women who took jobs in munitions factories. The experience of one speaks for many: nearly sixty years later, interviewed for a remarkable oral history project organized through the Opportunities for Youth programme, an upper-middle-class woman described pseudonymously as "Elaine Nelson," recalled in vivid detail her days as a shell-filler at Fairbanks-Morse in Toronto, wearing an ugly grey smock, and a "ghastly yellow mob-cap."

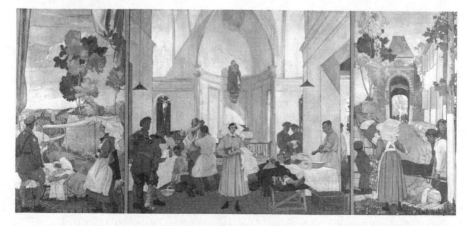

No. 3 Canadian Stationary Hospital at Doullens. By Gerald Moira.

Canadian women working on the land. By Manly Macdonald.

Women Making Shells. By Mabel May.

Acetylene Welder. By C. R. W. Nevinson.

During the war, the lives of many Canadian women were transformed as they moved into the strange, intimidating workplaces to which men were accustomed. Their activities were documented by war artists, including a number of women, commissioned through Beaverbrook's Canadian War Memorials Fund.

"Elaine Nelson" continued: "My first experience was when they said, 'We'll allot you the first set of howitzer shells.' The foreman met me at the door and he just beckoned to me. The reason why he couldn't say anything was because you couldn't have heard him! I just had to follow him. I went through all these avenues and avenues of clanking, grinding, crashing machines. Some of them were so close together that in order to get to the machines, they'd built a kind of stile – several steps up and then you walked across and went down again. . . . The foreman led me in behind one of the machines, and I stood by the wall and watched. He demonstrated how to do *one* shell, and then he stood aside and pointed to me. And so I very gingerly walked up to the machine and did what he had done. Then he stood there and said, 'Again!' and I did another one. Then he just waved me goodbye and off he went. I was *panic-stricken*. But I got used to it."

The work was dirty and monotonous and dangerous. "The shell was turning all the time and you had to *quickly* knock off these jagged long pieces before they got as far as your face," Elaine recounted. She was constantly splashed by corrosive chemicals that penetrated the protective smock. "When I first started, I just wore the crêpe de Chine underclothes that I would wear ordinarily. Of course they rotted in a week. So I smartened up pretty quickly and wore my brother's long johns." Later, when she was promoted to inspector, there was the constant worry of making a mistake. "I had nightmares that I passed a shell that had been imperfect and might kill our own boys." Yet for Elaine, as for most of her co-workers, doing a man's job at Fairbanks-Morse, rubbing shoulders with women she would never have encountered otherwise, was an experience she wouldn't have missed for the world. "There was a kind of *esprit de corps* . . . There was everybody, every single class from squire's lady to Judy O'Grady and some a few shades lower than Judy. . . . In finding they were just the same as we were, just hadn't had the chances we had for education, we began to realize that we were all sisters under the skin. . . . Another thing too: there's nothing that draws people together more than mutual trouble. The war went so much against us so often, that we felt, 'the boys are doing that for us, what are we doing for them?' You just rolled up your sleeves and you didn't care how tired you were or anything else."

No job to which a woman could aspire was more glamorous than driving an ambulance. In the early stages of the war, as with munitions making, this gruelling and sometimes dangerous work, often conducted at dead of night along roads greasy with mud, had been deemed unsuitable for women, and in any event, few of them had yet learned to drive. But after the Somme, as the need for men at the Front grew more and more pressing, VADs had taken over the ambulance convoy at Etaples and by the following year, young women like Grace MacPherson had captured the public imagination. Unlike nurses, whose starched uniforms and veils harked back to Florence Nightingale, ambulance drivers in their goggles and gauntlets and the dashing black leather trench-coats and aviator helmets they wore in the winter, seemed to belong to the future. "I received an impression of extraordinary beauty," wrote the journalist F. Tennyson Jesse, early in 1918, describing a night with the convoy in a piece for British *Vogue*.* "The girls looked like splendid young airmen, their clear, bold faces coming out from between the leather flaps. They were not pretty, they were touched with something finer, some quality of radiance. I could have wished them there forever, like some sculptured frieze, so lovely was the rightness and the inspiration of it."

Grace herself would have hooted at this hyperbole. Her own accounts of her war, scribbled hastily in a small pocket diary, were short, breezy descriptions of the daily routine. "Lent to night shift last night . . . today could not find J Depot. . . . Pouring rain. CO says I must get into breakfast earlier." Unlike her direct contemporary, the VAD nurse Vera Brittain, who, by coincidence, was also in Etaples in 1917–18, keeping the journals that later produced the classic wartime memoir, *Testament of Youth*, Grace rarely attempted to be insightful or reflective. It is the very immediacy of her diaries that makes them compelling. Like Ethel Chadwick, though in far more challenging circumstances, she was *there* and she *saw*. She too left behind a testament of youth.

Born in Winnipeg in 1895, the youngest of six children of a Scottish-born civil engineer, Grace moved to Vancouver with her family as a child. Her father died shortly afterwards, and when the diaries begin, in 1912, she was a skittish eighteen-year-old, "spoiled rotten," as the phrase went, living with her mother in a pleasant house on Hornby Street, in what is now downtown Vancouver. Their circumstances were comfortable though not wealthy, and as might not have been the case in staider cities like Ottawa or neighbouring Victoria, where most girls in her situation

---

* Fryniwyd Tennyson Jesse (1888–1958) was one of the few women journalists to report from the Front. Later, she became one of the most popular novelists of her day, best known for her riveting crime novel, *A Pin to See the Peepshow*, recently re-issued by Virago Press.

stayed home and did the flowers, she was completing a course in shorthand and typing at Sprott-Shaw business college, looking forward to finding a job. Grace was one of the most popular girls in the city, with a bubbly personality, a great line in small talk and an endless supply of beaux on the string. Her exuberant, go-ahead style matched that of Vancouver itself. The city was only a few years older than she was, transformed in 1886 from a sleepy lumber village into the west-coast terminal of the CPR, and from there into a boomtown, its population at 100,000 having quadrupled since the turn of the century. Like Vancouver, known for its many strikes, Grace had a strong streak of rebelliousness. "Ma keeps trying to impress on me the idea that I have very little sense," she informs. But she was also a nice girl who taught Sunday school at St. Andrew's Presbyterian Church and was a pillar of its youth group. In the style of the period, she enjoyed making walnut fudge and date cake, going for picnics at English Bay and long rambles round Stanley Park, watching the moving pictures at the Rex Theatre and vaudeville shows at the Pantages, and dancing the one-step at *thé dansants* at the fashionable new Hotel Vancouver.

A year or two later, by now a secretary at the Pennington Typewriter Company, Grace startled Vancouver and prefigured her future. Thanks to her doting but long-suffering mother, who doubtless was looking for a way of channelling Grace's irrepressible energies, she became one of the first women in the city to own her own car. It was a sporty Paige Detroit, with the licence number 7827 and she was enormously proud of her ability to drive it with flair – sometimes a bit recklessly. "I got a blow-out, jacked it all up and changed it *myself*," she tells us. "Later, on the way out to Kerrisdale, a big Winton Six ran me into the curb, so I got even, went very slowly and kept him behind."

So far as we can judge from the diaries, the first year of the war impinged surprisingly little upon Grace. Accounts of knitting and rolling bandages do not feature; she was much more absorbed in chronicling an on-again, off-again romance with a certain Gordon B. Proctor whose proposal she eventually turned down. The presence of officers in uniform, most of whom belonged to the local 72nd Battalion, added fizz to the social scene, but even when boyfriends and her elder brother Alex went off to the Front, it didn't yet seem possible that some might never return. "There were about 25,000 out to see off the 72nd," she informs. "My hand was swollen from so much shaking." In the manner of Ottawa's Naughty Nine, she also flung her arms around a number of special favourites – "Leo and Stan and Allan" – and kissed them goodbye.

Inevitably, reality intruded. Instead of joining a Canadian regiment, Alex had gone directly to England, and enlisted as a lieutenant in the Highland Light Infantry. His letters were frequent, Grace tells us; then, on September 2, 1915, a telegram arrived from the War Office, informing his family that he had died of wounds at Gallipoli. "Oh this terrible war," she wrote in her diary. "I never dreamed that Alex would be killed. He was *so lucky* always." Soon afterwards – troubles never come singly – she herself was involved in a near-tragedy. On January 13, 1916, ("Why oh why was I ever born?") she ran over a teenage boy who ran in front of her car at a downtown intersection. "I tooted, he stopped, then started quickly and stopped again. The radiator hit him and the whole car went over him, but thank God not the wheels." In the event, the boy was not killed, though he suffered a badly broken arm and severe concussion, and the police decided that, while Grace might have been going a bit too fast, the accident was probably unavoidable. But her feelings of guilt, coupled with her grief over Alex, and, by now over Boy Templeton, the first of her beaux to die in action, put an end to her giddiness. A new and much more serious Grace was beginning to emerge. As decisively, the accident had given her an insight into her character. Her nerve had been tested and not been found wanting. She hadn't screamed or gone into hysterics. Even the police had praised her quick-thinking. "A man came up and wanted to phone for an ambulance. But I grabbed him and said, 'No, every minute counts, *help me*, get him into the car. . . . Went up 12th and then Granville at about 50 miles per. I met Dr. McEachern at the door, and he and another Dr. rushed out the stretcher." A few weeks later, Grace wrote to the War Office and to the British Red Cross, offering her services as an ambulance driver. The replies were not encouraging – everything seemed to depend on being on the spot – but she decided to go anyway, on spec. "I certainly hope for sufficient willpower and courage," she wrote in her diary.

Grace arrived in London early in August 1916. It was a measure of her spunk that in order to get there, she had spent every lunch hour for two months besieging the Canadian Pacific Steamship Office in Vancouver, with a request for free passage. "The boys get it. Why not me. I'm volunteering too," she said over and over. According to family folklore – the diaries for this period are missing – the steamship officials eventually gave in, just to get rid of her. Save for an elderly Vancouver couple who'd chaperoned her aboard ship, she knew no one. In great expectations, she rushed round to VAD Headquarters at Devonshire House in Piccadilly only to be bitterly disappointed. "By *one day*, I just missed a job in France."

Grace, being Grace, refused to be fazed. She found herself a room in a boarding house in Bloomsbury, 34 Bedford Place. She talked her way into a job at the Canadian Pay Office. Before long, she ceased being lonely. Far from being vast and threatening, London turned out to be nearly as cosy as Vancouver. It was impossible to walk down the Strand or through Piccadilly Circus without running into half a dozen old boyfriends on leave, and they in turn introduced her to others. Naturally, as a nice girl, she behaved with propriety, never drinking anything stronger than lemonade, never – well, hardly ever – dancing til dawn. But like thousands of other nice girls liberated by the war, Grace couldn't help but be swept up in the febrile gaiety of wartime London, that "strange mix of hedonism and danger," as Vera Brittain has described it. She rode down to picnic at Richmond in the sidecar of a motorbike, danced at the Savoy and the Trocadero and the Carlton, marvelled at the gorgeous slave market scene in the spectacular musical, *Chu Chin Chow*, and knew all the words to its signature tune, *Any Time's Kissing Time*.

All of this, however enjoyable, was only a stopgap. Grace continued to call weekly at Devonshire House. In the autumn, she took courage on the wing, marched down to Canadian Headquarters at Argyll House near Oxford Circus, and got an appointment with Sam Hughes himself, then on his last ministerial mission to

Britain. He wasn't particularly helpful – "Said France was no place for me, but I might do good work in England and would give me a letter to Colonel Hodgetts of the Red Cross" – but at last, on March 28, 1917, "my marching orders came." Grace would be one of a draft of twenty girls, dispatched to reinforce the convoy at Etaples. A beau named George MacLaren gave her a pair of goggles, and for good luck, his Motor Machine Gun Brigade insignia. Not to be outdone, another beau provided the badge of his regiment, the Little Black Devils of Winnipeg. In a great state of excitement, she dashed around London assembling her kit: high-laced boots, plenty of warm underwear. Everything, including the leather coat and helmet, Grace paid for herself. Within the Voluntary Aid Detachment, *voluntary* was the operative word. She would have the honorary rank of lieutenant, but would receive no salary, only four shillings weekly for laundry, and ten shillings for mess expenses. On April 7, 1917, two days before the Canadians took Vimy Ridge, she crossed the Channel to Boulogne and, after "filling out many forms," arrived at Etaples the next day, in a snowstorm.

Nowadays, driving south down the coast road from Boulogne, past the gaudy *hypermarchés* that cater to British tourists, and, just beyond Etaples, the glitzy resort of Le Touquet, it's difficult to imagine how it all would have appeared to Grace so long ago. Only the sea and the sand dunes and the pine woods remain the same. In 1917, as we know from Vera Brittain, the railway line ran past a sprawling and ugly metropolis of army camps, "in which at one time or another, every soldier in the British army was dumped to await orders for a still less agreeable destination." The roads were rutted and muddy, peasant women trudged along them carrying bundles of faggots on their backs. Clotheslines in dooryards were hung with rows and rows of khaki shirts, since such women frequently eked out their living doing laundry for soldiers. Etaples itself, a small fishing port, had been transformed into a whole town of hospitals, each one a little town in itself. "I was reminded of nothing so much as the great temporary townships in the canal zone at Panama," wrote F. Tennyson Jesse of her own flying visit. "I almost expected to see a negro slouch along with his tools slung over his back, or to catch sight of the dark film of a mosquito-proof screen over doors and windows."

Despite its ambience of grunginess and impermanence, the hospital city of Etaples was a masterpiece of organization. Much might have gone awry in the British Army, but by 1917 few criticized its treatment of the wounded. "The whole system works like an endless chain propelled by an unseen power," one Canadian padre wrote to his wife. "There is no confusion under the most severe stress." Each battalion at the Front had its own Field Dressing Station; patients were then transported to a Casualty Clearing Station, usually equipped with an emergency operating room and always located on a railway line, and then on to Etaples. Here, there were more than forty thousand beds and a score or more of hospitals – including several operated by the Canadian Army Medical Corps, the original quarters in *Hotel de Golfe* having long since overflowed into huts. The task of the ambulance drivers was to meet the incoming hospital trains, in which the wounded lay on rows of shelves, in carriages with white-painted interiors, and deliver them to the designated hospital. These were "convoys." In the reverse process, "evacuations," they took patients returning to "Blighty" to the trains, sometimes directly to a hospital ship at Boulogne. They worked twelve-hour shifts, 8:00 PM to 8:00 AM, or vice versa; one convoy and one evacuation, which took about three hours each, was the day's average, although, as Grace tells us, when there was a "show" on, such as Vimy or Passchendaele, there were many more, and drivers might be on duty for forty-eight hours running, with only a few hours snatched for sleep. On top of all this, each VAD was responsible for the maintenance of two or three ambulances, which meant much labour in the repair shops; each day at noon, every vehicle was inspected by the Commandant and, in Grace's words, "there was not much she ever missed." The ambulances themselves were cumbersome, awkward McLaughlin Buicks donated by patriotic organizations throughout the Empire. In Grace's opinion, "it was a marvel they ran at all considering the earlier treatment they got (or did not get) from the men from whom we took over." Drivers were identified by the numbers of their vehicles, Grace usually drove RA660.

She took up her duties in the highest of spirits. Greatly to her surprise, her room in the dormitory hut was far more comfortable than her boarding-house room in Bloomsbury. "Nice bed, sheets, pillows and blankets galore; lovely hot baths any time of the day and things nice and clean," she wrote home to her mother. "Our mess has long tables and benches, and we eat from tin plates and mugs, just as I like things." The food was plain but well cooked with hot soup and cocoa available at any hour. The recreation hut somehow managed to be warm and cosy, with wicker furniture and chintz cushions plus "a beautiful big gramophone, dandy records and a lovely piano." Her first tour of duty was a night-time evacuation to the railway station at Camiers, seven miles away, and except for some difficulty finding the right entrance to the 7th Canadian Hospital – "I asked a 'uniform,' 'where do I stop, old top?' and it turned out to be a captain!!" – it went like clockwork. Her cargo of patients were all convalescent "sitters" who did not require stretchers. No matter that 660 had "a nasty slipping clutch," she drove it splendidly, and the section leader, Miss Chambers, appeared to be "quite pleased." Driving back to the

No. 7 Canadian Field Hospital at Etaples. On her first night on duty as an ambulance driver, Grace MacPherson drove patients from this hospital to an evacuation train bound for "Blighty."

compound, Grace was exalted. "It was glorious to think that at last I was actually driving an ambulance. It was a dream hatched out and means more to me than anything has meant to me yet," she wrote in her diary.

Within twenty-four hours, Grace's mood had changed radically. "What a terrible day," she wrote. That she'd dared call a captain "Old Top" had been reported. So had other indiscretions, including being "too free" with the stretcher-bearers. "The Commandant sent for me and told me that she did not think I was taking my work seriously enough." Next day – "woe is me" – she was caught with her engine running while waiting at a siding. "I tried to explain that it was a cranker and that I was only trying to get it warmed up to be easy to start." From then on, Grace was in hot water almost daily. "The Commandant is absolutely *fiendish* to me," she wrote on April 19. "She is such a cat and has the means of making me absolutely miserable." One bone of contention was a bright red sweater that Grace wore over her tunic. "She said I must not wear 'that sweater' ever again." Another was the Little Black Devil badge she wore as a lucky charm. "She wanted to know all about it and then ordered it off." To make matters worse, most of her fellow drivers were stand-offish and chilly, and she strongly suspected that some of them liked nothing better than pouncing on her every slip and reporting it. None of the other Canadian girls were in her particular section, and except for Armine Gosling – "a Newfoundlander and *lovely*" – she had no one to talk to. So she poured out her heart in her diary. "I'm the talk of the whole convoy. I've developed into the most awkward, ungainly, self-conscious lump alive. I have gone through Hell on earth, and nobody will ever know how I have felt. How I envy the boys in the trenches and the game of chance they play compared to the Sneak-Spy System of Cats that goes on here. In all hundred-odd girls here, about 25 can play the game, and the others are not fit to wipe one's boots on, and I thought such girls as there would be in this kind of work would be topping."

In hindsight, it's easy to see that both sides were suffering from culture shock. Never before had Grace experienced at close quarters the phenomenon best descibed as "the Englishness of the English." VADs were recruited almost exclusively from the

British upper classes, in whom a conviction of their own superiority was inborn, and for whom it was a first principle that "rowdy Colonials" belonged to the lower orders. To be fair to the Commandant, leaving aside her own prejudices, she too was new to the game. Outside of hospitals, few precedents then existed for women working together, and even there all authority figures were male. Other than upper-class girls' schools, the OC had no models to go by, no matter that most drivers were in their mid to late twenties (twenty-three was the minimum age). There was also the fact – one that would also pertain during the Second World War – that public opinion was deeply skeptical about the private morals of women in uniform. Thus discipline was excessively strict. VADs were forbidden to speak to NCOs or other ranks – except for stretcher-bearers and orderlies, with whom a degree of discourse was unavoidable. They were not allowed to dine out with officers, only occasionally to go out to tea with them, and only then with prior permission and another VAD along to act as chaperone. Any girl suspected of dancing with men was instantly sacked. Thus Grace, with her breezy west-coast style and her independent ways, presented a considerable problem. It was easy to mistake her insouciance for insolence.

Matters came to a head towards the end of May, shortly before the photographers arrived. "The Commandant called me in and told me dreadful things," wrote Grace. "My whole attitude was wrong. I would not accept discipline. How can any human being, especially a woman be so damn brutal!" She then had a talk with her section leader, Doris Chambers, who was more sympathetic. "She said she would recommend that I be transferred to Boulogne to drive a lorry, where I would be more free from discipline and more independent." The offer was tempting – but Grace rejected it. "I said I would rather stay here – and for some reason I would, even if I *am* miserable – just to *stick it* and show them I can!"

Grace did stick it out. She swallowed her pride and dyed her red sweater black. Things began to improve a few days later, when she came in from a convoy and found a big box of her favourite Pascall chocolates in her room. On top was a note from a fellow driver who up to now had not been notable for friendliness. "Eat these and don't worry. I'm your chum when you want one." Even the Commandant – though Grace never really warmed to her – began to seem like a human being. "Thunder and *awful* lightning all last night," she reports on June 5, 1917. "The Commandant hates it. But she was out in it all, looking after the girls on the night shift. She is a sport there all right." A few days later, summoned to change the wheel on the OC's car, Grace actually struck a chord of response. "For some unknown reason, I amused her very much."

By now, as the OC could not have failed to recognize, Grace was on her way to becoming one of the best drivers in the convoy. Thanks to experience with her Paige, she was not only streets ahead of most at changing and mending tires, she could cope with the most balky of the ambulances, even No. 680, known as "The Kangaroo." She was utterly fearless, whatever the weather or the condition of the roads. Far from funking out in her first air-raid, Grace found it thrilling. "There were all kinds of guns firing. We could scarcely see the plane but could see shells bursting in the air. One bomb fell on the beach about a quarter of a mile from us." She also began to develop a new maturity, learning how to handle badly wounded men with the right mixture of tenderness and dispassion. "Some very bad cases tonight," she reports on one occasion. "One man had most of his ear and nose off. Another had his arm off just below shoulder, and stump was hanging out. I just *steeled* myself to look at them while strapping them in, and did not let myself feel sorry for them, for if I did what would happen? I drive as carefully as I can. I went over a bump very slowly, and one man said, 'For God's sake go easy.' The others told me I was as careful as could be considering the roads." One night, "in a very small, smoky and stuffy orderly room," she dealt with a patient in the throes of an epileptic fit. "There were about 12 men standing around and sitting on him. I suggested that we get him outside where the air was a little better, and a man said, 'Why Miss, but it's raining.' I told them it didn't matter if it was raining aerial torpedoes, out he must go." Yet she never really got used to the horrors. "Tonight, at the Canadian hospital, a poor old man was sobbing his heart out and wailing, 'My son, my dear dear son.' As long as I live, I will never forget that sobbing. He had wired the mother saying there was a fighting chance."

Her letters home reflected her sense of urgency, her growing

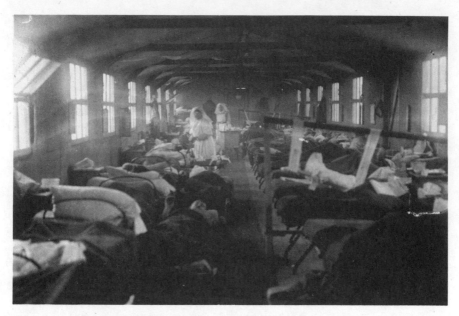

Interior of No. 7 Canadian Field Hospital. Grace MacPherson learned how to treat the wounded with the right mixture of tenderness and dispassion.

awareness of what war really meant. "I wonder if it would stir the souls of our hardened slackers back in Canada to see some of the sights over here as we see them," she wrote to her old Sunday-school teacher. "Men in all stages of their misery and suffering, simply pouring out of trains and being taken to hospitals already packed and too full to receive them; lying on their stretchers in the reception tents, or hut floored with straw – and the most cheerful beings alive they are too."

In the midst of all this, Grace managed also to have a good time. Nowadays, after a half-century of peace and amid the solemnities of political correctness, it seems almost heretical to suggest that the conditions of war also provide the circumstances in which it is possible to live with an intensity that otherwise is out of reach. In 1917–18, this was as true for Grace MacPherson as it would be for those who, closer to our own memory, lived through the Second World War dodging torpedoes on the North Atlantic or buzz-bombs in London, recalling it later, in Charles Ritchie's marvellous phrase, as the "Siren Years," evocative of a witches' brew of allure and terror. As in London, Grace's old boyfriends from Vancouver kept on popping up out of nowhere. Once, out on convoy, she found herself driving right through the ranks of the 72nd Battalion. "Hello Vancouver," "Hello Grace," they called to her. Some even remembered her old licence number. "How's 7827?" they shouted. "How's the old Paige getting on?" By now, she'd become "dear true friends" with most of the other drivers; off duty, they discussed the pros and cons of bobbing their hair – many were doing so, but Grace decided not to – and danced with each other in the recreation hut. The resort of Le Touquet and its adjacent beach, *Paris-Plage*, were only a ten-minute tram-ride away; always careful to ask permission, and always with another VAD to play "gooseberry," she sometimes went to grab a quick swim followed by a "slap-up tea" with officers at the Franco-British Hotel or the *Chat bleu* café. Ever resourceful, Grace once managed a tête-a-tête dinner with a beau named Gordon MacPherson by claiming that he was her brother. The greatest adventure was a ride in a tank. After much wheedling, the Commandant allowed her and three other drivers to visit an unnamed boyfriend "with a wonderful big tank badge on his shoulder." "The four of us walked five miles," she wrote home. "He showed us around, and then we got in and drove in it. Over ditches, swamps and young hills! Oh! it was a wonderful experience! There is lots of room inside them, but one can't stand straight – I can just manage to at 5'6". It was interesting to hear about them too. There are two types – the male and the female – the male carried a 6-pound gun, and the female a machine gun. I think we are the first and last girls ever to get a ride in one."

Grace's most harrowing days in France began in the early spring of 1918. "Paris is being shelled by long-range guns!" she wrote in her diary on March 22, 1918. "Awful rumours that Amiens is taken." On March 24, "the worst train in the World's History came in tonight. Cattle truck train, 350 aboard lying on stretchers and then on the floor for 38 hours. Nothing to eat or drink. No dressings. Fractures only with bandages on, splints unheard of. We were driving from 7 until 4:30 AM. In once for 5 minutes."

She was describing the receiving end of the last great German offensive. First on the Somme, and a fortnight later in Flanders, General Ludendorff's armies smashed through the allied lines. "Nothing had ever equalled the tension of those crushing days," wrote Vera Brittain. "Into our minds had crept for the first time the secret, incredible fear that we might lose the war."

Grace's own accounts became more and more attenuated. "Oh so rushed," she wrote on April 11. "5 trains and 4 evacuations. We are still losing ground." On April 15. "4 convoys and 4 evacuations. 6 or 7 of us fell asleep at the wheel last night. Courtenay ran over a rockpile and woke up." All the time now, a ceaseless and deafening roar filled the air. Motor lorries and ammunition wagons crashed endlessly along the roads; trains full of reinforcements thundered up the line. In Vera Brittain's description, "Etaples resembled a Gustave Doré illustration to Dante's *Inferno*. Sisters flying from the captured Casualty Clearing Stations crowded into our quarters; often completely without belongings they took possession of our rooms, our beds and all our spare uniforms. By day a thudding crescendo in the distance, by night sharp flashes of fire in the sky told us that the War was already close upon their heels."

Soon, war was directly overhead. Up to now, the hospitals at Etaples had served to protect the main railway line from Boulogne to Paris. Everyone had taken for granted that even the Hun would spare the wounded. But early in May, air-raids began in earnest. A total blackout was strictly enforced; no matter how foggy or rainy, the ambulance drivers were forbidden to turn on their headlights. The final entry in Grace's diary is dated May 20. "Last night biggest raid on record. Appalling damage and loss of life."

In 1919, back in Vancouver, she described the events of that terrible night to an audience of local women:

It was a beautiful moonlit night. No warning was given. There were sixty machines in the raid, coming over in relays of twenty each. The Men's staff quarters of the No. 1 Canadian General Hospital were the first to be hit, suffering about 115 casualties, seventy or more killed, among whom was Sergeant

Brown, a charming Vancouver boy. The nurses' quarters suffered as well: three nurses were killed instantly, and many severely wounded. Many of the other camps also had hundreds of casualties, the total list approximately 750. The Huns dropped aerial torpedoes and incendiaries, and while the huts were in flames, they swept down and peppered the dead and wounded with machine-gun bullets.

As she recounted in her speech, Grace and the other drivers had a miraculous escape:

We had no protection whatever and were ordered to remain in our huts. With each bomb or burst of anti-aircraft fire, shelves and dishes came tumbling down. But no bombs struck our Convoy and none of us were hit by the shrapnel which was falling like hail all around us. [After the raid was over], We drove and faced the music. There were ghastly gruesome sights indeed, but it was much nicer to be driving than sitting idle. None of us had "the wind up" in the least degree, but the men seemed terrified, probably they realized what had happened as we did not. The amount of damage was sickening. One captured German pilot said that he was very sorry to have hit hospitals, that they had tried to get the railways and ammunition and supply trains. Instead they had hit two ambulance trains. Fortunately they were not loaded, but three or four coaches of each were wrecked, and many orderlies killed and wounded.

Save for remarking that RA660 had behaved beautifully, Grace did not describe her own role on the night of the raid. Indeed, she made light of it. "Let it not be repeated erroneously that my worst experience was the raid. I think my really and truly worst experiences were being strafed by our Commandant." But a letter in the Vancouver *Province* that survives among her papers tells us that she performed with great courage and resourcefulness during that terrible night. "She is a very gritty woman," wrote Captain Donald Martyn, MC and Bar. "She was the first on the scene with her machine and she worked all night without a quiver, and let me

say, there were not a few men panic stricken on that awful night of horror. . . . In the estimation of officers here, and of her own corps, Miss MacPherson is described as 'the bravest of them all,' to quote one high official's words."

Perhaps the official Martyn quoted was indeed the dreaded Commandant. If so, Grace must have been amazed by the rest of her comment. "Miss MacPherson keeps her machine the cleanest, always."

In the late summer of 1918, Grace left Etaples and returned to London. By now, even her celebrated nerve was beginning to wear thin, and so were her financial resources. She worked briefly as secretary to Lady Perley, wife of the Canadian High Commissioner, and then as head driver at an American military hospital in London, a job that paid a proper salary.

In the winter of 1919, Grace MacPherson came home to Vancouver and took a job with the newly set up Department of Soldiers' Civil Re-establishment. It is good to be able to report that within weeks, at a dance for returned veterans, she met the great love of her life. According to family folklore, not only did the handsome and dashing Major David Livingston make a beeline for her across the floor, he quite literally swept her up in his arms and announced that she was the woman he was going to marry, leaving Grace for once at a loss for words. After an equally whirlwind romance, they were married in the spring.

(Opposite above)
On May 19, 1918, during the last great German offensive, the Canadian hospital complex at Etaples was bombed and severely damaged. Three nurses were killed instantly and several severely wounded. This photograph shows the nurses' quarters.

(Opposite below)
The funeral of one of the Canadian nurses killed in the raid of May 1918. In military fashion, her coffin is carried on a gun carriage.

   Like most women whose lives had been turned upside down by the war, Grace returned to her hearth, devoting herself to her husband and son and daughter. Also good to report, though, is that she did not retreat to a genteel merry-go-round of bridge and tea parties, but spent much of her early married life in the roustabout surroundings of the northern British Columbia wilderness, where David Livingston, a civil engineer like her father, was in charge of building branch lines for the CPR. Later on, growing ever more outspoken, she remained at heart the cheeky ambulance driver, more than once embarrassing her children ("Hey, that's your mum!") by insisting on marching with the men in Armistice Day parades. Always active in community affairs and taking a particular interest in veterans' hospitals, Grace encouraged her daughter Diana Livingston Filer to seek a career, first as a CBC producer and later as a senior CBC executive. "That I was expected to make something of myself was quite simply taken for granted," Diana Filer recalls. Grace MacPherson Livingston died in Vancouver in 1979. Of all the characters in this book, she is the one who could as easily have lived in our own times.

27

The Hundred Days

*. . . Somehow, all of us sensed that we were on the edge
of great events . . .*

Brooke Claxton. Unpublished memoir; *c.* 1958

"We started moving on August 3. We knew we were in for something big. Secrecy was the order of the day; our battery was under sealed orders." Drafting his memoirs more than forty years later, Brooke Claxton could remember the prelude to the great allied victory at Amiens as vividly as if it had been yesterday. How the armies moved only at night; how the road was clogged with four columns of wheeled vehicles – guns, lorries, ambulances, and everything else, with horse-drawn vehicles and caterpillars and tanks advancing in parallel along the roadsides. "At the only crossroads, an accident occurred of dinosaurian proportions. A caterpillar drawing an 8-inch gun locked horns with another large vehicle. The traffic was jam-packed for miles. Soon there was a big crowd around the crossroads, not knowing what to do. Then a general arrived. Clambering onto the caterpillar's canvas top he told everyone who could do so to grab hold of the vehicles and when he told them to 'heave,' they were to tear the vehicles apart and throw them off the road. And so it happened."

With the blockage at the crossroads unsnarled, Claxton's unit, and all the other units that had been brought to a halt there, surged forward to join the rest of the Canadian Corps near the village of Villers-Brettoneux. On Thursday, August 8, with the French to their right and the Australians and British to the left, they smashed into and through the German lines, advancing more than eight miles. After nearly four years of stalemate, the impossible was happening. Movement, advance, victory. This transformation in the character of the war had been set in motion four months earlier by the Germans themselves, who on March 21 had launched their *Kaiserschlat*, or Emperor's Offensive, under General Ludendorff. Reinforced by divisions hurried west from the now-peaceful Russian Front, their armies virtually destroyed Gough's British Fifth Army, badly battered the French, and thrust the Allies back toward the Channel ports, bringing even the hospital complex at Etaples where Grace MacPherson worked, within reach of their planes. To stop this brilliant, desperate offensive, Haig issued his famous "backs to the wall," no-retreat order. It worked, if not so much because of the legendary British stubbornness in defence (the Canadians happened to be out of the action in the rear), than because Ludendorff did too well for his own good. His soldiers out-ran their supplies, they became exhausted, and, above all, they became demoralized as, once behind the allied lines, they were able to compare the abundance of the food and equipment there – that of the newly arrived Americans being by far the most abundant – with their own near-starvation rations after four years of blockade. Against these over-extended German forces, the vast allied armies, led for the first time by a single commander, Marshal Ferdinand Foch, now began to move, first tentatively and then with growing confidence and skill and speed as they realized that the impossible really was happening.

In its closing nine months, the First World War thus became at last the kind of war that everyone had taken for granted it would be when it had started. Suddenly, trenches and barbed wire and minefields and even nests of machine guns ceased to be an impenetrable wall and became obstacles that still delayed but no longer could immobilize armies from moving forwards or backwards. If only briefly, and still at the cost of heavy losses, war once again became exhilarating, swashbuckling. For all who took part in the great allied offence that began at Amiens, those celebrated "Hundred Days" that raced on until early November, when abruptly the Kaiser abdicated and Germany surrendered, were the source of their proudest memories. Since Brooke Claxton arrived in France only a few months before the Allies began their headlong advance and was not involved in their precipitous retreat, his war was not just a "good war," as the saying went, but one of the best wars in which any Canadian took part.

This last of our characters, whom some readers will remember as a senior cabinet minister during the late 1940s and early 1950s, and afterwards as the first Chairman of the Canada Council, is also the youngest of them. Just coming up to twenty, lanky and lean and bursting with energy, Claxton still resembled an overgrown schoolboy. Born in Montreal in 1898, he was a scion of the Anglo-Scottish ascendancy. His grandfather, T. J. Claxton, had been a leading dry-goods merchant, and later Vice-President of Sun Life Assurance. His father, A. G. B. Claxton, was a prosperous lawyer and keen sportsman, chief counsel for the Metropolitan Life, a director of the Montreal Amateur Athletic association. Brooke's mother, Blanche Simpson, came from much the same background; her father had been one of the first physicians to

Brian Brooke Claxton, *circa* 1910. Like most youngsters of his generation, he worried that the war would end before he was old enough to enlist.

graduate from McGill; her mother had been society editor of the *Montreal Gazette*. The world he'd grown up in, first at Lower Canada College and later at McGill, resembled the privileged and pleasurable world that Talbot Papineau had known some years earlier: picnics and sailing out at the Lakeshore, skiing and bob-sledding on the Mountain; hockey games at the Arena; long golden summers at Métis Beach, a resort on the south shore of the lower St. Lawrence, in those days almost as popular as Murray Bay. Like Papineau, Claxton had been a student of Stephen Leacock. "His ideas were as dog-eared as his notes," he wrote later. "But this really did not matter because he had a wonderful voice, a great heart and was a remarkably brilliant teacher." More unusually, Claxton also listened to lectures given by Harold Laski, later to become the great left-wing guru of the London School of Economics, who in 1915–16 taught for a year at McGill. "He was so erudite a scholar and so brilliant a talker that he seemed to come out of some book," Claxton remembered. "The trouble was that in listening to him one could not see the wood for the trees or hear the tune for the sound."

Like most teenagers of his upbringing, Claxton was wildly excited by the outbreak of war. "My prayer was that it would last long enough for me to get into it," he recalled in his memoir. There was also a hidden agenda. "My boyhood had not been particularly happy, and while my work at school had been consistently good, I was not outstanding among my fellows. War would, I felt, give me my chance." Indeed, for all its apparent security, Claxton's boyhood had been traumatic. His parents' marriage had been troubled and turbulent – bridge was one of the few things they had in common, a predilection they passed on to their son – and in 1911, Blanche Claxton had decamped to England, leaving twelve-year-old Brooke alone with his father, an object of curiosity as much as of pity in an era when most people kept up appearances no matter how miserable their private circumstances.

The first step towards the war was to join the McGill branch of the COTC (Canadian Officers' Training Corps). This involved, among other things, drill practice on campus and in the Montreal Armouries, route marches on the Mountain, lessons in map-reading and military engineering and military law and discipline. More important was the satisfaction of male camaraderie. "To be one of a thousand men who were young and keen, working together to approach perfection was a thrilling experience," Claxton recalled. "After drill, a group of us would have coffee or cocoa and toast at Childs' restaurant, or the basement of Bryson's drug store at the corner of Peel and St. Catherine." In the spring of 1916, he left McGill midway through his Arts course, and became a subaltern in a local militia regiment, the Victoria Rifles, expecting that as soon as he turned eighteen he would proceed overseas. In the meantime, he was put in charge of a picquet guarding the Victoria railway bridge. From the mixed bag of old sweats and ex-convicts who made up this unit, Claxton learned much about soldiering. "So refined had been our associations in the COTC, I don't think I had heard before this of the expression 'to soldier,'" he tells us. "What it meant was to have the know-how to behave on all occasions like a tried and experienced man. It meant knowing who and how to salute, laying out your kit, getting your rations, having enough coal, getting leaves, escaping extra duty, digging a trench, getting 'your rights' – all by fair means or foul, but with a minimum of effort." What soldiering with the Victoria Rifles did *not* mean however, was actually going to the wars. It soon became evident that an overseas draft was unlikely to be raised in the near future. So, the following year, Claxton gave up his commission and joined an artillery unit, the 13th Siege Battery, being raised at McGill. "I don't think I had ever been as happy as when this step, definite and final, brought to an end to months of uncertain hopes. I was a number, 2341302 in the Canadian army, a rear-rank gunner, and I was bound for overseas."

In June 1917, he sailed from Halifax, aboard the troopship ss *Justicia*. Arriving at Liverpool on July 4, the first thing Claxton noticed was that all the ships and civic buildings were flying the Stars and Stripes. The Yanks were coming. That same day, one of the first American troopships had completed its trans-Atlantic journey by entering the harbour. "Quite a few of them were with us as we boarded what seemed to us the toy trains that would take us that night across England."

Claxton spent nearly eight months in England. Much of the time he was bored and frustrated. By this late stage of the war,

Brooke Claxton in 1917, shortly before going overseas
with the 10th Siege Battery. He had resigned a commission in order to get to the Front.

such *esprit de corps* as had ever existed within the vast, sham-
bling Canadian training establishments had dissolved into
malaise. Shunted purposelessly from Otterpool to Shorncliffe
and then on to Witley, he and the rest of the Battery absorbed
much about "soldiering" and "scrimshanking," little about warfare. "At Otterpool, we were exposed to graft of every kind: the

Brooke Claxton's army paybook. Soldiers usually carried the same paybook throughout the war; the various insertions and crossings-out served as a kind of diary.

sergeant-major, otherwise a very decent chap, received it by overcharging for watches and jewellery he sold to the troops; the quartermaster sergeant sold the rations on such a scale that we were consistently underfed." At Shorncliffe, one of the chores was cleaning out a set of barracks shortly to be turned back to British troops. "The worst part was handling the blankets. There were tens and thousands of them of every size, and colour and cloth. They had only one thing in common and that was that they were filthy." There were some compensations. Thanks to his mother's connections – their relations had resumed on a friendly, but not a warm, basis – the callow young Claxton sometimes found himself moving in glamorous company. On one of his leaves, she took him to lunch at the Ritz, where Winston Churchill was at the next table. "Presuming on having met him before, my mother presented me. At least I had the distinction of being the only 'other rank' in the room. He said something nice about Canadian troops." Thanks again to his mother, he once played bridge at a private club with the famous writer of thrillers, E. Phillips Oppenheim. "At that time, I had read more of his books than of Churchill's. The stakes were a pound a hundred with side-bets, and a 'double' here and there, all made in the most off-hand fashion." Other diversions included four visits to *Chu Chin Chow* – a life-long lover of showtunes, himself possessed of a loud and enthusiastic if decidedly untuneful voice, Claxton apparently enjoyed this even more than Grace MacPherson had; long bicycle rides in the English countryside, and in December, casting the first vote of his life in the Khaki Election. In his memoirs, Claxton was too cagey to say how he'd voted – most probably, like all others overseas, for the Union government. At least in hindsight, he took umbrage at the Unionists' tactics. "It was a shocking affair," he informs. "The dates had been staggered so that word could be sent from Canada of the places where the Union candidates needed votes, soldiers overseas having the right to vote anywhere. Many of our battery were told to vote in Brome County in the Province of Quebec, where I don't suppose any of us had ever been." (Despite the crude efforts to stuff the ballot-boxes, the Liberal candidate here was handily elected. He was Andrew McMaster, Talbot Papineau's law partner, who had remained loyal to Laurier.)

At long last, prospects for actually getting to the war were beginning to look up. In mid-autumn, at Deepcut in Hampshire, an artillery training camp run by the British Army, instruction had started in earnest. "Despite the fact that we had only one modern gun on which to train, in no time at all we were exceedingly keen about our work." There, the unit was also re-organized and renamed the 10th Siege Battery, with a complement of six how-itzers, seven officers, one warrant officer and seven non-comis-sioned officers, under the command of Major Lewis Ord, a former supervisor of CPR machine-shops. Claxton himself was promoted to sergeant. In mid-March 1918, he and the others received their orders to proceed to the Arras sector, by way of Southampton and Le Havre. "As our train dawdled along I read *The Thirty-Nine Steps* by John Buchan," Claxton tells us.

"We found the front in a high state of excitement and appre-hension," was Claxton's first impression of his arrival. "The Ger-mans had just broken through at Cambrai. We were to go into action at once. About as well as anyone can do with newly worn six-inch howitzers, we entered the battle with guns firing in all directions." In fact, the Canadian Corps did not play a key role in stalling the Ludendorff offensive, and before long the Battery moved into a "wonderful position on top of Vimy Ridge," not far from where Harold Innis had been a year earlier, with comfortable quarters in old German dugouts. Here, no matter that the Front was still "windy," with heavy harassing fire, Claxton hugely enjoyed himself. "Even in the line, we played bridge or poker sev-eral times a week. Bridge was at a franc (sixteen cents) a hundred. The big game of poker was jack and ace pots with franc bets. In a night, it was easy to lose fifty or even a hundred francs, more than a month's pay." The responsibilities of command came to him easily – as sergeant in charge of two gun crews, he had thirty-five men under him – indeed, at the age of nineteen, he sometimes found himself acting as a kind of father confessor not only to his subordinates, but also to the officers. The difficulty here was essentially one of class. Major Ord, the Battery commander, a self-made man with much practical experience in gunnery, had usurped the position formerly held by Stopford Brunton, a gradu-ate of McGill who had originally raised the Battery, and who, to exacerbate the tension between them, was also Sir Stopford Brun-ton, holder of a British baronetcy, one of a number of titled aristo-crats who had emigrated to Montreal in the years before the war. "Ord was complicated and clever and he had the special kind of sensitivity which some self-made men have," Claxton tells us.

"Brunton was almost childlike in his naive simplicity. He had been to college and final, fatal mistake, he had a title. That he was one of the most humble and decent people living could not offset all of this in the feelings of Ord. Nights when I was 'on duty' at the guns, Brunton would come down and talk for hours. One night he was trapped with us when we got a pasting and he and I sat on the bunks in my shelter and he continued to pour out his soul while the bursts were bouncing around." Eventually, Claxton helped resolve the situation by encouraging Brunton to apply for a transfer to an imperial battery. As for Ord, in Claxton's opinion, "one of his deficiencies was to our advantage. He was a poor figure of a soldier, and did not know or have any feeling for drill. Consequently, we had no unnecessary parades, in fact, in the line, hardly any parades. Ord had only one rule and it was a good rule. All the men must be kept busy all the time – at something useful. Until we got to the end rush, we were always kept at work, improving gunpits, trenches, dugouts, roads, communications and everything else. The guns had to be spotless. Laboriously, we scraped the camouflage paint off the bronze breech-blocks and filed and smoothed them to mirror brightness."

Late in June, events began to quicken. The Battery was ordered out of the line for intensive training in "open warfare." "This was the first indication that we were really winning the war," Claxton relates. "Until this time, a favourite topic of talk had been the best way to demolish our own guns!" The fortnight of training "was designed to give formations the will to move and to get into action fast, and also I think to shake us loose from some of the habits and thinking that went along with static warfare." The next move, in mid-July, was to a suburb of Arras. "Now, the front had become remarkably quiet. An order – KEEP YOUR MOUTH SHUT – came down that rumours were to stop, and surprisingly that is what they did. Somehow, all of us could sense that we were on the edge of big events."

So great was the secrecy surrounding the advance upon the enemy salient at Amiens, that General Currie only informed his divisional commanders of his battle plans on July 29. It was only on August 3, when Claxton's unit received its orders to begin moving forward, that he himself realized that the vast array of gunpits and battery workings they'd been constructing in front of Arras had been only a clever decoy: the "big events" were to take place thirty miles to the south. On the long march forward, no fires were allowed. The initial objective, marked by a green line on staff officers' maps, was to penetrate two miles into German lines; the red line marked the intermediate objective two miles further on. The dotted blue line marked an objective that seemed almost impossible, eight miles distant from the original Front. If all went impossibly well, the cavalry would be sent through the gap.

Claxton's own role in all this was small, but critical. The position selected for the 10th Battery was an exceedingly tough one. "This was the country of the Somme; it had been raining heavily for several days and the fields off the roads were old battlefields, porous as blotting paper. Off the roads, there was no traction for the wheels [of the trucks and caterpillars]. We had to forge our way across these broken fields more than half a mile." In Innis's day, only a year previously, horses had been used to haul the guns, and, under the circumstances, animals might have been more appropriate. Axles bogged down in the mud, Claxton tells us, "instead of them [the vehicles] pulling us, we had to pull them one by one." It's easy to imagine the grunting and sweating. Each gun weighed a ton and a half. "At one time I had more than fifty men on the dragropes. But somehow we got them in, and then there were the shells, each one had to be carried in on some man's shoulders more than half a mile. We had four hundred shells per gun and each one weighed a hundred pounds."

Zero hour was 4:20 AM, on August 8. "In addition to taking part in the creeping barrage, every few minutes we would switch to another target. The success of the battle depended on the enemy's surprise and this was almost complete. Some Germans were captured before they had come out of their dugouts. As the dawn came up, we could see over to our right the glorious spectacle of a cavalry division in motion, moving to the attack. Our troop-strafing aircraft stunted, cavorting in the air to show their joy. This was it!! We were on our way! We had started at last!"

What had been started at Amiens would end in a victory so decisive that Ludendorff would describe August 8, 1918, as "the black

The 10th Canadian Siege Battery in France, and one of its howitzers, painted with camouflage. Each gun weighed a ton and a half. At the Battle of Amiens it took fifty men on drag-ropes to get each one in position.

day of the German Army." The Canadians, attacking in the centre of the line, had liberated ten villages, taken 5,033 prisoners and captured 161 guns. "From the depths of a very full heart I wish to congratulate you all on the wonderful success achieved," Currie wired to his troops. While he himself had not been the principal planner of the victory – that honour belonged to his fellow Colonial, Lieutenant-General John Monash of the Anzac Division – Currie's troops had pushed the full eight miles, further than the British, French, and Australians to their right and their left.

By mid-August, the progress at Amiens had petered out. Gains still were made, but the German resistance had stiffened, and in the space of just four days, casualties mounted to 9,000. Currie ordered the attacks to cease. Victory at Amiens and elsewhere, though, had made Foch and Haig realize that they might actually have the Huns on the run. *"Tout le monde à la bataille,"* decreed Foch. All of the armies – French, British, American – now would drive continuously against the Germans, giving them no chance to rest and reorganize. The next target assigned for Currie and the Canadian Corps was Drocourt-Quéant, a formidable defence line. Beyond it, eastwards, lay open flat country where no trenches had been dug nor fields of mines and barbed wire laid. If the Canadians broke through here, they really would be through.

So began the famous "Hundred Days" that encompassed the apogee of Canada's military effort during the First World War. The casualties would be terrible: 42,000 Canadians dead and wounded over a span of just three months; among them at Bourlon Wood, on September 26, Charlie Stewart, the last one of the "Old Originals" to be Commanding Officer of the Patricias, hit by a shell shortly before the attack. But the achievements would be magnificent: a string of victories continuing without interruption until the Armistice. Much of the credit must be given to the Canadian troops and officers. They were now rated as an elite contingent, rated higher by Haig than even the Australians, the ultimate compliment. But a large share of the personal credit is due to Currie. Today, he is scarcely remembered. Yet he may well have been the best military commander Canada has ever produced.

In Denis Winter's memorable phrase, Arthur Currie possessed "the appearance of a company cook with his characteristic dress of shirtsleeves and braces." Yet he possessed also, Winter adds, "a great capacity for war." This resided in an intuitive understanding – he was no professional soldier – of what modern technology could do, and thus what had to be done to minimize its lethal effects and to capitalize on the unfamiliar possibilities that it opened up. There was nothing flashy or original about his tactics. Their defining style was the application of common sense. Currie won his battles by combining all available armaments, artillery, tanks, bombers, machine guns, infantry, and cavalry, by scrupulously plotting out the territory by aerial reconnaissance, and by launching his actual attacks amid conditions that were as near as possible to complete surprise. (One of Currie's innovations, recalled by the journalist Gregory Clark, was to insist that maps be issued, not just to officers, as was the norm, but all the way down

Lieutenant-General Sir Arthur Currie, GCMG, KCB. This official portrait by the British artist Sir William Orpen was painted shortly after the war. A contemporary British military historian describes Currie's victory at Drocourt-Quéant in September 1918 as "the British Army's single greatest achievement on the Western Front." Yet today, Currie is scarcely remembered.

the ranks to lance-corporal.) His achievements, from Vimy through Passchendaele, at Amiens and on to the end through Drocourt-Quéant and Canal du Nord, were equalled by few other generals. Winter describes his victory at Drocourt-Quéant as "the British Army's single greatest achievement on the Western Front." Winter is convinced that had the war continued into 1919, if not even into 1920 as everyone assumed, Lloyd George would have appointed Currie Commander-in-Chief in place of Haig, with the Australian Monash as his Number Two.

Few Canadians today are aware of any of this. No university has been named in Currie's honour, as has one for Monash, nor any major public building. One reason is the style of the man himself. Unlike Byng, with his burly manliness, or for that matter Haig, the icy imperialist, Currie lacked charisma. He had no aptitude for public speaking, indeed, in private possessed a jarring propensity to use foul language. The ordinary troops never warmed to him. "Often he seemed to have a talent for picking just the wrong phrase," remarks his biographer, A. M. J. Hyatt. "On one occasion he told survivors returning from the line, 'That is the way I like to see you, mud and blood.'" That he was a Colonial made it harder for him to gain recognition, not just in the Mother Country but also in the colony. He was also a poor political operator, lacking "the gift for stroking fur the right way," in the expressive phrase of one of his colleagues.

The worst blow to Currie's future reputation was struck by two powerful and vindictive enemies behind the scenes: Sam Hughes and his overweeningly ambitious son Garnet. At the war's start, relations between them all could not have been more cordial. Garnet, a junior major in Currie's militia regiment, had convinced his father to appoint him to command the 2nd Infantry Brigade. By mid-war, though, relations had deteriorated. In 1915, unimpressed by Garnet's performance at Second Ypres, Currie did not recommend him for promotion to brigadier, a post created by his own appointment as Commander of the First Division. Thanks to his father, Garnet got the appointment anyway. In 1916, Currie further infuriated Sam by refusing to replace British staff officers with Canadians, and by his determination to keep the Canadian

Corps lean and mean, at four divisions, using new recruits as rein-
forcements, instead of expanding it.* The last straw came in the
summer of 1917 when Currie, having just been appointed Corps
Commander over Hughes's protests at the insistence of General
Byng, refused to appoint Garnet to fill his old slot as Divisional
Commander. A three-hour shouting match between them in a
London hotel – "I was told that his father wanted him to get the
position and God help the man who fell out with his father,"
Currie wrote later – led to a vendetta that encompassed Beaverbrook, Hughes's old ally. Reports appeared in Canadian papers
and also in the official War Records Office publication, *Canadian
Daily Record,* that Currie was in ill health, and that he did not get
on with his British commanders. One story even had it that he
was to be relieved of his command because of the terrible Canadian losses at Passchendaele.

    Later, after the war, when Currie had become Principal and
Vice-Chancellor of McGill, and Claxton had returned there to
finish his studies, the two became friends: Claxton's account of
one of their conversations amplifies even further the extent of
Hughes's vendetta and how deeply the general had been
wounded by it. "Currie described to me the intrigues carried on
by a clique to undermine his position as Corps Commander. When
his duty required him to make a brief visit to England, friends
there told him of rumours being spread that he had been and in
fact still was in hospital with venereal disease, that he had been
stoned by the troops at various places and so on. On this visit,
one officers' mess in the south of England had treated him with
what was pretty close to silent contempt. After dinner he told
them to stay where they were, he wanted to talk to them. He faced
them with their action and got them telling him what they had
heard about him. Needless to say, the way Currie handled this
won the group over . . . But the intrigues continued. The climax

_____

* Hughes wanted the Canadian Corps expanded to seven or eight divisions.
Currie's decision improved the Corps' efficiency at the political cost of leaving
many Canadian officers with no troops to command. At one point in 1917, Agar
Adamson found himself having to deal with "five awful majors," sent to the Patricias by direct order of Hughes.

Sir Sam Hughes and his son, Garnet Hughes. These two
conducted a vicious vendetta against General Currie.

was reached, and the crisis was passed when the Government
sent Sir Clifford Sifton to tell him that he had the full backing of
the Borden Government. Currie came over to London specially
from France, met Sifton at the Carlton Hotel and there Sir Clifford
told him that he was to carry on his job."

Currie's accomplishments in 1918 ought to have ended the

squabble. Their very magnitude magnified it. After the war, in March 1919, Sam Hughes launched an astonishing attack upon him in the House of Commons, accusing Currie of "butchery," of "needlessly sacrificing the lives of Canadian soldiers." He was further, "a coward, unworthy of association with his fellow men and women." Borden, away at the Paris Peace Conference, was not there to defend his general. Perhaps still intimidated by Hughes, the rest of the cabinet was silent. By the time Borden returned to give Currie a warm vote of confidence – "No general at the front more fully realized the solemn duty . . . to avoid needless sacrifice" – the damage had been done.

In 1920, after a brief, unhappy term as Inspector-General of Militia, Currie received the McGill appointment. Despite his own lack of formal education, he was a great success, an excellent administrator and fund-raiser, known also for his friendliness to students. But in 1927, Hughes struck again, this time from beyond the grave. A small newspaper in Port Hope used the occasion of the unveiling of a plaque in Mons, where the war had ended, to repeat one of Hughes's charges – that Currie had needlessly sent troops to their deaths by launching attacks on the eve of the Armistice. This time, Currie could fight back. He sued for libel, and he won his case. When he returned to Montreal, crowds of students met him at the station and pulled him through the streets in an open carriage. But Currie never really recovered from the ordeal of a two-week trial that made headlines across the country, over which hung the cloud of his old financial embarrassments, and which was prefaced by a gruelling examination for discovery in which he was grilled about his every movement during the war, including 200 separate questions about his conduct at Second Ypres. There was also the fact that although he had claimed $50,000 in damages he was awarded only $500, not nearly enough to cover his legal costs. (In the event, these were paid by McGill.) After a long period of ill health, Currie died of pneumonia in 1933, still only fifty-eight. A few weeks earlier, he had written his own last notes on the war. "I wish I had the power to make all Canadians see clearly one day of the gas battle in April 1915, or of the Passchendaele battle in 1917." In the context of the manuscript, notes his biographer, Hyatt, "the reason he longed for such an opportunity is quite clear. Anyone, he assumed, who could share the experience of Ypres and Passchendaele would never advocate another war. Anyone who truly understood the nature of battle would never propose its repetition."

Drocourt-Quéant, also known as the Second Battle of Arras, involved an attack upon a defensive line as formidable as that of Passchendaele Ridge save only for the mud. The attack began on August 26 and hard fighting continued for a week, with the Canadians suffering some 8,000 casualties, until the Germans had been pushed back across the Canal du Nord. One of Currie's most effective tactics, defying the wishes of Haig, was to use his Motor Machine Gun Brigade instead of cavalry, and, in another adroit use of modern technology, to combine these with troops riding bicycles. Sergeant Claxton himself missed out on this action, the 10th Battery having briefly been attached to the French artillery.

By now, though, the action was continuous. While not a true defensive line, Canal du Nord was an almost impassable obstacle, made yet more forbidding because the Germans had flooded the marshes on either side. At a conference, Byng heard out Currie's plan of attack and asked, "Old man, do you think you can do it?" Currie said nothing, only nodded. He had chosen, at great risk but with great daring, to send his troops across through a dry, but almost impossibly narrow, strip of the canal to the south. Again, his reconnaissance was painstaking, this time done mostly from balloons. Again, he achieved almost complete surprise. The attack began at 5:20 AM on September 27. "We fired 1,616 rounds with twenty changes at numerous different targets," recounts Claxton, who by now had rejoined the Canadians. Soon after noon, despite ferocious counter-fire by concentrated machine guns, the Germans were retreating all along the Front. Never before had so many prisoners been taken. As always, the Germans re-grouped and counter-attacked fiercely, bringing the general advance to a halt in the first days of October. On October 3, Currie issued a special message. "In the short period of two months the Canadian Corps (supported at different times by four British divisions) has encountered and defeated decisively forty-seven German divisions – that is nearly a quarter of the total

German forces on the Western Front." They had gained twenty-three miles, and, on October 10, as a capstone to their achievements, they entered and liberated the town of Cambrai.

Now began the war's endgame. "Some hard fighting lay ahead, but the Allies were now pursuing a thoroughly beaten enemy," writes D. J. Goodspeed in *The Road Past Vimy*, adding that, "as it turned out, the Canadians proved to be instinctively good at a war of movement, where individual initiative and resourcefulness counted for much." This description could almost have been written with the daring and self-confident Claxton in mind. By now, he'd been promoted to Battery sergeant-major. Indeed, with the erratic Major Ord "gone down the line for a rest," and with only one other officer remaining, Claxton was virtually in command of the Battery.

He'd become a seasoned warrior and in some ways a sombre one. He marked his twentieth birthday, August 23, by attending the funerals of three comrades killed by a shellburst. A few days later, he had a 4.2 "whizbang" land at his feet. "Fortunately, it was a gas shell and fortunately I had been a gas instructor. Even so I was badly shaken and almost blinded for a time." At Canal du Nord, another shell "dropped a few feet from six of us, killing one outright. Three others were badly wounded, two of them dying later of their wounds. The only other man with me who was not hit was a staff sergeant considerably older than most of us. He and I had to combine what we could by way of first aid, and getting the wounded away as the shelling was still going on. Even before this, I had been on the spot for so many casualties that I had got in the habit of carrying a pretty elaborate first aid kit and of sleeping on a spare stretcher." Right after Cambrai came the severest test of Claxton's nerve. "A big shell, probably from a 7.7 'Jack Johnson' detonated about fifty of our one-hundred-pound shells. This *was* an explosion and it created an inferno. Boxes of the cartridges for our guns were going up like Roman candles in a dozen different pyres. Through the smoke and dust and fire I heard one of our men screaming. It was Bill Reid of my crew. He was buried up to his neck in brick and his head was bleeding all over from small cuts. He said, 'Don't bother about me, Wattie and Gordie are underneath.' Frantically, we tore at the bricks with our hands. We first got Bill out and then the other two underneath him. For me, it has always seemed a miracle of morale, of spirit of fellow-feeling – call it what you will – that these two should have been buried alive and crushed and somehow evoked, dug-out, saved, evacuated by the will of their friend." Reticent by nature and upbringing, Claxton understated his own role. Yet reading between the lines of his stilted descriptions, it's impossible not to sense the mood of high exaltation, and sheer animal high spirits, with which he and the rest of the Canadian Corps raced through the fields of October, advancing through farmland and villages untouched by the war. "During these days, the battery started leap-frogging guns, sometimes making five moves in a day. It was not unusual to have the battery in three or four places, scattered over a distance of ten to fifteen miles. Sometimes we had to send back twenty-five miles or more for shells, rations and mail, all three of which miraculously always arrived. The pressure was such that once I got left behind with a small party and for more than a day we lived off a hundred-pound bag of fine oatmeal which someone had jettisoned."

In the hamlet of Villers-en-Canchies, Claxton, at twenty, found himself having to make a life-or-death decision. A corporal sent to the Battery as reinforcement stopped off at the village and refused to go any further. "He had been four years in France, mostly with the infantry, and he had 'had enough.' This kind of thing could not be allowed to pass unnoticed. So I gave him a going-over and paraded him before our only officer. I suppose that in the infantry he might have been shot for desertion, but the officer took the same view as I did and after the talking was over, we had no more trouble."* On from there to Valenciennes, an industrial town a few miles south of the Belgian border where, in the last days of October, the Canadian Corps made its last setpiece attack. "We were close up on the infantry, nearer than we had ever been before," recounts Claxton. "The range was not much more

---

* During the war, twenty-five Canadians were executed by firing squad under the disciplinary provisions of the British Army Act. The Australians, by contrast, refused to be subject to these provisions.

than a thousand yards. Our targets were in plain view. What was the war coming to? Soon they would have us up with the machine guns! For some reason, probably to check the route and the bridges I went into the city ahead of the Battery. A crazy scene stands out in memory. A shop full of musical instruments had got messed up by a shell adding greatly to the gaiety of some troops who had found something to drink."

In the first week of November, the first wave of Canadians crossed into Belgium. On November 10, though, Claxton and his Battery were still in France, "in a wretched village called Rombies." It was cold and pouring rain. "The enemy was still fighting hard. As we entered the village German infantry were moving out at the other side, and for the first time we were subjected to machine gun fire by infantry. We fired that night for the last time."

That same night, came word of the Armistice, a strange word few really understood, with many wondering if it only meant a cease-fire (as, technically, it could have done). "But pressure was to be continued. We were to move forward again on the eleventh." Claxton's war ended as if it were a scene in a film. "As we got to the main road, a lorry driver landed one of our guns up to its muzzle in a mine crater. We had just got men on the ropes and I was saying 'Together, heave,' when a truck of another unit drove by on its way back from the front. 'Leave your blankety-blank gun there, you blankety-blanks. The blankety-blank war is over.'"

The last shots actually fired by any Canadian soldiers were those exchanged with die-hard German troops holding out in the town of Mons in the last few hours before the 11:00 AM Armistice went into effect on November 11. The liberation of Mons, which had no military value, and which resulted in several Canadian casualties and one fatality, was the source of the accusation that Currie had needlessly sought "glory"; his defence was that Foch had decreed that the advance should continue until a specific cease-fire order was issued.

28

Ave Atque Vale

The Great War is over – the world's agony has ended.
What has been born? The next generation may be able
to answer.

Lucy Maud Montgomery. Diary entry; November 11, 1918

I n the capitals of the Allies, the surge of joy and of wild hi-jinks unleashed by the Armistice has not been equalled to this day. In London, the revelry went on for three days: hundreds of thousands crammed Trafalgar Square, dancing round and round it and singing, "Knees Up, Mother Brown." Canadian and Australian soldiers pelted each other with Brussels sprouts liberated from Covent Garden market, and lit a huge bonfire that scorched the base of Nelson's column so badly that the scars remained visible until the monument was sandblasted in the late 1980s. In Paris, led by the famous soprano, Marthe Chenal, vast crowds in Place de l'Opèra bellowed out the "Marseillaise," over and over again. In Ottawa, where the news arrived just before dawn, a huge electric sign on the pinnacle of the Château Laurier, erected a few weeks earlier to urge everyone to BUY VICTORY BONDS was hastily converted to flash out the single word, VICTORY. Spontaneously, every band in the city headed for Parliament Hill, followed by crowds armed with flags and tin whistles. "'The Maple Leaf Forever' was played," reported the *Citizen*, "and a chorus of hundreds of thousands joined in the refrain. It is not to be wondered that women cried and that strong men were not ashamed of the tears that trickled down their cheeks. The celebration will be handed down

November 11, 1918, in Toronto. Shortly after 3:00 AM, Eaton's big "wildcat" siren woke up the whole city. Women munitions workers left the night shift and paraded up Yonge Street, beating tin pans and blowing whistles.

to the generations to come as the most momentous event in the history of the city."

At the Front, the atmosphere was curiously muted. "There was little jollification; everyone was too tired," Claxton remembered. "I found no one who took any joy in the victory." Instead, arriving in Boussu, a village about eight miles from Mons, it was business as usual for him and the Battery. "The guns were parked in the square. I saw most of the men billetted down in a convent overlooking the Place de Ville, and went to bed." In any event, Claxton personally was in no state to celebrate. The great pandemic of Spanish influenza that during the winter of 1918–19 killed more than had died in the war, had caught up with him, and he had a temperature of 102 degrees.

Young, strong, and healthy as a horse, Claxton recovered quickly. Soon, like all the other soldiers of all the armies, robbed suddenly of their purpose, he found himself milling around in the querulous aftermath of war, a condition that in some ways was harder on the nerves than war itself. Everyone wanted desperately to get home, to reunite with their families and to re-start their careers and lives; no one any longer gave a "blankety-blank" about discipline. Indeed, within a week of the Armistice, Claxton, as Battery sergeant-major, was in the alarming position of having to defuse a small but potentially dangerous mutiny provoked by a tactless order from brigade to resume gun-drill for four hours daily "to correct the faulty drill caused by service conditions." *Force majeure*, knowing that there was no way his exhausted crews would obey the order, Claxton counselled passive resistance. "It was my guess that the orderly officers would confer and then one of them would go off to get the colonel commanding the brigade. The latter would soon arrive on the scene and after a certain amount of talk he would probably express his willingness to see the men. He would give a patriotic oration referring to Bolshevik influence. I said no one must say anything throughout. There must be no catcalls, not even a sound. We would have to play it by ear, but he might be persuaded to leave the parade ground. . . . This was all very improper, but if it had not been handled some way, there would have been a stubborn refusal, the calling in of other troops and even possibly bloodshed." Luckily for all concerned, Claxton's strategy worked. During the next several months, though, there were several far more serious disturbances among Canadian troops, the worst of these a riot in which five were killed and twenty-five injured at Kinmel Park, a crowded camp in North Wales, where men awaiting passage home had been cooped up for months. (One factor was a shortage of transport ships and also of railway capacity in Canada. Another was that through bureaucratic insensitivity many of those first demobilized were newly arrived conscripts rather than tired veterans.)

Claxton and the rest of the Battery came home in May 1919, aboard the *Mauretania*. By now, he had been awarded the Distinguished Conduct Medal; as he'd discovered when sorting out the unit's records, he would also have ended the war as an officer had the disorganized Major Ord remembered to send in a recommendation that already bore his signature. (Ord *had* remembered to send the warmest of letters to Claxton's father: "Your son's work is an example to all . . . his courage and fearlessness are very conspicuous.") He arrived at Place Viger Station in Montreal on May 11, six months to the day after the Armistice. "Like the June day we left, the sun was shining brilliantly as we marched proudly between crowds of cheering Montrealers. Before long we were at Peel Street barracks. It was our last parade. The senior artillery officer present made a one-sentence speech, saying that we would always remember that we had done our job, the friends we had made and lost, the country we had served. There were no heroics, no glamour and no glory, which was just as it should be. Our relatives and friends were waiting. We stepped into civvy street."

Claxton's subsequent career can serve as a metaphor for all those Canadians who had gone to war as blithely and innocently as he had done – Lester Pearson as the best-known fellow member of the breed, Harold Innis as another – and who returned wiser, broader, far more mature. It can serve also as a metaphor for the maturing nation that had emerged from the war on the brink of its coming of age and that then went on growing up on the foundation created by that hard-earned experience all the way up to the end of the 1950s. For the rest of his life, Claxton was fired by a deep sense of urgency, a conviction that he owed to those who had died and to the country that had given him the opportunity to serve, a commitment that had to be fulfilled by public service. "We came back with a new-won pride in being Canadian, a sentiment which was to do much to impel us forwards," he wrote, in his rather flat way, in his memoirs.

Far more revealing of Claxton's true feelings is a short article signed only with his initials, and contained within his scrapbooks. Presumably written for a McGill publication, it was titled *The Unreturning Army that was Youth*, and describes the death of a close friend killed randomly by a shell-burst: ". . . A sunlit summer's day, as he, forgetting war, was bathing in a petrol tin, sporting and splashing in joy of life, a shell arrived and smeared the smooth brown skin with blood . . . an arm was carelessly left hanging at the stump. . . . He is dead now. The world and I have lost a gallant soul. . . . The cynic says it is better for the good to die young – why? With the joy of life just discovered, with friends to make, with work to do and love to know – Why is he dead? And why, when he is dead, do I remain alive? Why?"

Naturally – he was never a rebel – Claxton first finished his arts course at McGill in record time, then studied law and went into partnership with his father. In 1925, again doing as was expected, he married Helen Savage, daughter of a prominent Montreal businessman and sister of the Montreal painter Annie Savage, a union that would be exceptionally happy and would produce two sons and a daughter. Montreal society, however, was somewhat taken aback when instead of moving into fashionable Westmount, the newlyweds found themselves a crumbling seventeenth-century Québecois farmhouse on the fringes of Notre-Dame-de-Grace, restored it, and painted it pink. Here, they became known for the gregarious, unstuffy style of their entertainments: Sunday night suppers, "three or four evening parties a year with dances and singing," as Claxton recalled; always, on Christmas Eve a huge open house to which "people did not wait to be asked and brought their friends." The man at the piano was always Claxton's brother-in-law, Terry MacDermot, himself a former gunner and later to become a diplomat (whose son Galt MacDermot went on to fame and fortune as the composer of that iconic musical of the 1960s, *Hair*). To Claxton's great pride (and perhaps due to the influence of his sister-in-law, Annie Savage), the first Montreal exhibition of paintings by the Group of Seven was held in the pink farmhouse in 1927.

Claxton's real post-war passion through the twenties and thirties, though, was the phenomenon that he describes as "The Canadian Movement." This was shorthand for a bevy of idealistic new organizations that had sprung up post-war, among them the revitalized Association of Canadian Clubs; the Canadian League; the Canadian Institute for International Affairs; the League of Nations Society. While their constitutions varied widely, their organizing principle was a non-stop pan-Canadian talkfest. The movement networked together an ever-growing number of high-minded, idealistic, and ambitious young men—in those days, few women could join such clubs – who, in between speech-making and pamphleteering, all had a wonderful time. "Memberships overlapped," Claxton explains. "Everyone kept changing their hats. But we all played the same tune, and that was 'O Canada.'" He joined everything going, also founded his own "Montreal Group," with a particular bent towards defining Canada's role in the world, and on trips out to Winnipeg headed straight for Childs restaurant to mingle with the most influential group of all, the cel-ebrated "Sanhedrin," a cluster of politicians and journalists that included the young journalist Grant Dexter and that was presided over by the great guru of the *Manitoba Free Press*, John W. Dafoe. They all thrived amid an oxygenic atmosphere in which all things seemed possible, no peak unclimbable. "The war itself had broken down the barriers of mountain, lake and sea," Claxton recalled. "Right across Canada were associations and individuals concerned about the same kind of things and working to the same goals, though they might take different ways to get there." Through the Association of Canadian Clubs, he got to know its new national secretary Graham Spry, idealist *par excellence*, also a moral manipulator of consummate grace and élan, who himself, while wearing another hat as founder of the Canadian Radio League, lobbied ceaselessly for a publicly owned national broad-casting system. Spry enlisted Claxton into the cause so that, as the League's unpaid legal counsel, he became with Spry one of the founding fathers of the CBC.*

There was another and a darker aspect to the Canadian Movement, and specifically to the Canadian League. In many countries post-war, there were people who demanded law and order and discipline, the advent of Bolshevism coupled with the permissiveness of the Jazz Age quickening the urge, of which the darkest manifestations were Fascism and National Socialism. Canada's echo, inevitably, was much milder. As Claxton relates, the League's spiritual godfather was Lord Byng of Vimy, who on arriving as Governor General in 1921 had suggested that "the ability of and patriotic devotion of the officers he had got to know in France was going to waste." As a result, some of Byng's closest associates, in particular Colonel W. D. Herridge, later to become R. B. Bennett's brother-in-law and Canada's Minister to Washington, decided to reconstruct the remnants of Lionel Curtis's prewar Round Table network into an organization dedicated to fostering "The National Spirit." "It is difficult to say whether Byng had anything else in mind," Claxton continues. "But similar associations in Australia at almost the same time led to a semi-fascist movement which is described in D. H. Lawrence's *Kangaroo*." In the event, Claxton and others managed to divert the League's energies away from Byng and Herridge's interests; most productively, they successfully lobbied the government of Ontario into repealing the iniquitous Regulation Seventeen that had disallowed French-language instruction in the schools.

Inevitably, Brooke Claxton's interest turned to politics. A lifelong Liberal, he was elected to the House of Commons in 1940, and soon became Parliamentary Secretary to Mackenzie King. Although never a socialist, he was on the left wing of the party –

---

* Graham Spry (1900–1983). The son of an army officer, Spry himself was just too young to have been in combat, although he did serve as a private in the Canadian Army Service Corps at Shorncliffe. A good account of his own involvement with "The Canadian Movement" and of the brilliant exercise in political lobbying that produced the CBC is contained in *Passion and Conviction*, a collection of his letters and diaries edited by Rose Potvin (University of Regina, 1992).

perhaps those long-ago lectures from Harold Laski had had their effect – and in 1943, when the CCF became the Official Opposition in Ontario and also topped the Liberals nationally in the new-fangled Gallup Poll, he seized the moment to persuade King and other more recalcitrant members of cabinet to adopt a sweeping new set of social policies modelled along the lines of the Beveridge Report in Britain; these included universal old-age pensions, floor prices for farm products and, most radically, but also most astute politically, family allowances. The following year, Claxton entered the cabinet as Minister of National Health and Welfare; in 1946, he became Minister of National Defence, remaining in this position until he retired in 1954 to become president of Metropolitan Life. Although one of the most innovative members of Louis St. Laurent's government, he is remembered by some as an austere martinet who held letters up to the light before reading them to make sure that the margins on each side were precisely even. Others recall that he was as energetic and as tireless as the Sergeant Claxton of old. In a 1952 profile in *Maclean's* magazine, Blair Fraser wrote that few of his executive assistants, all young men and ex-veterans, "can keep up with the minister for more than a few days at a time." Once, when visiting Canadian troops in Korea, Claxton asked one of the artillery batteries to put on a demonstration. When the interval between the determination of target and firing the first round turned out to be exactly fifty-five seconds, Claxton clapped his hands and told the gunners with a grin that they'd matched exactly his own best time, long ago at Amiens with the 10th Siege Battery.

Claxton's most important contribution to Canada came right at the end of his career. In the late 1940s, he became seized with the idea, again borrowed from Britain, that arts and scholarship should be subsidized by the government. Claxton sold his idea to J. W. Pickersgill, then Louis St. Laurent's chief aide. "We talked it over," Pickersgill has recalled, "and together we sold the idea to Mr. St. Laurent." The resulting Massey Commission recommended the creation of the Canada Council. To reassure St. Laurent, who considered the arts a frivolity and was particularly suspicious of ballet, Claxton agreed to become the Council's first chairman in 1957. From the beginning, through a judicious selection of staff (most notably the quirky choice of the former British intelligence agent Peter Dwyer as the first Arts Supervisor), and by establishing and defending fiercely the principles of independence from government and of a commitment to excellence, Claxton created the conditions by which the Council became perhaps the most creative institution that Canada has ever produced.

Yet amid all Brooke Claxton's achievements, as with those of so many others of his generation and mindset, there was forever a blind spot. In an era when, aside from a few exceptional individuals like St. Laurent and Georges Vanier, French Canadians were virtually non-persons in Ottawa, Claxton was probably more sympathetic to the French Fact than most. He had, after all, campaigned against Regulation Seventeen. Yet he was a man of his time and place: on the eve of Quebec's Quiet Revolution, he was scarcely more aware of what was actually happening there than John Diefenbaker was. For the ceremonies surrounding the opening meeting of the Canada Council on April 30, 1957, Claxton had left no room on the agenda for his vice-chairman, the legendary Georges-Henri Lévesque of Laval, one of the Revolution's progenitors, to make an address in French. "I knew that unless I was seen to be a presence, the Council would have no credibility in Quebec," Lévesque has recalled. Discreet approaches were made, but to no effect. Finally, a few moments before the actual ceremonies began, Lévesque drew Claxton aside. "I told him that if I was not going to be able to speak in French, I would not attend," he said later. "I would tell the newspapers why."

Claxton immediately created space for Lévesque to speak. Before the day was out he had decreed, then unique in Official Ottawa, that all telephone calls received by the Council would be answered in both French and English. From then on, he asked Lévesque's advice on any Council matter. A close friendship developed between these two individuals of such utterly different backgrounds. Claxton took to having all his letters to Lévesque translated into French and signing them "Brooke." One that Lévesque particularly treasured was written shortly before Claxton's death from cancer in 1960. It was an invitation to baptize Claxton's first grandchild. In his own stiff, Waspish way, this last of our characters had done what he could to bridge the two solitudes.

On Tuesday, February 21, 1919, at Bramshott Camp in Surrey, the Princess Patricia's Canadian Light Infantry held a farewell parade for their Commander-in-Chief, Princess Patricia. Elegant as always, in a wide-brimmed felt hat and a stole and muff of ermine tails, she was escorted jointly, as seemed to be most fitting, by Hamilton Gault, the regiment's founder, and by Agar Adamson, the only surviving commanding officer among the "Old Originals." "She made a very nice speech but seemed very nervous," Agar reported to Mabel, who was in Furnes, winding up the affairs of the Belgian Canal Boat Fund. "She gave me a muffler knitted by her mother of which she had only four left." Later, there was a lunch to which officers' wives were invited; whether or not Agar was hurt by Mabel's not being there, he made light of it in his description. "I had my room togged up for the women to powder their noses in. Lady Evelyn [Farquhar] told me I had saved the situation since they had motored fifty miles from London. She was in great spirits and said there ought to be a 'chair' at all the Universities to teach men a great many things they don't know about entertaining womankind."

The following week, Princess Patricia ended her own war happily by marrying Commander Alexander Ramsay, RN, the former naval ADC with whom she'd fallen in love in Ottawa in the winter of 1912, the same season of Ethel Chadwick's romance with Lord John Hamilton.* At the wedding in Westminster Abbey, the regiment mounted a guard of honour. Agar was one of the

---

* On her marriage, Princess Patricia relinquished her royal title and lived happily ever after as Lady Patricia Ramsay, peripatetic naval wife and mother of a son who served with the Grenadier Guards in the Second World War. She continued to serve as Colonel-in-Chief of the Patricias throughout their service in the Second World War and in Korea, and in 1964 travelled to Edmonton to review her troops on the fiftieth anniversary of the regiment's founding. She also kept up her interest in painting, and towards the end of her life, experimented with abstract compositions. Lady Patricia Ramsay died in 1974. Her successor, and the present honorary colonel of the regiment was (probably not entirely by coincidence) another Patricia, Lady Patricia Brabourne, elder daughter of Earl Mountbatten of Burma, who has since succeeded to the title Countess Mountbatten. As must surely be unique among regiments, the PPCLI, now approaching its eightieth anniversary, has had only two honorary colonels-in-chief.

On February 21, 1919, Princess Patricia, Colonel-in-Chief of the PPCLI reviewed her regiment for the last time before it returned to Canada. Agar Adamson is on her right in both photographs. Princess Patricia married the following week and renounced her royal title. As Lady Patricia Ramsay she remained Colonel-in-Chief until her death in 1974.

guests, accompanied in Mabel's absence, by his mother-in-law, Mrs. Cawthra. To his amazement, as he reported to Mabel, for an evening reception that preceded the wedding, he was able to squeeze into the same set of dress blues that he had had made by an Ottawa tailor at the time of the South African War. A few days later, he was deeply touched to receive a personal letter from Patricia, written on her honeymoon. "If I am ever near you, may I hunt you up, and if you find yourself near me, and don't do so, I shall always feel there are things lacking in friendship that should not be."

Shortly afterwards, Agar and Hamilton Gault embarked aboard ship to bring the Patricias back home to Ottawa. On Wednesday, March 19, the day they arrived in the capital, the weather was mild as May. They were met by the mayor, in all his robes, at the station and given a formal civic welcome. They then marched to Parliament Hill and presented arms to the Governor General, the Duke of Devonshire. Adamson himself was not in command: by common consent, that honour belonged to Gault, "the getter-up of the Regiment," as Ethel Chadwick had written in 1914, a lifetime ago. "They had provided horses for us," Agar wrote Mabel, "but Gault preferred to walk." For the second time in a month (Laurier had died on February 17), Ottawans turned out in their thousands to say hail and farewell. The entire city was decorated with flags; three hundred old Patricias had come in from Montreal and Toronto.

Ethel herself, by dint of arriving early, had managed to get a good vantage point. "I saw them very well," she relates. "But it was sad to see them, only 39 of the Originals. They wore their steel helmets and carried their bayonets also and looked as if they were going into action. The flag made and presented by Princess Patricia was carried, a shabby-looking rag now, but O how glorious."

"The sun shone on their helmets," Ethel continued. "Hamilton Gault walked, or rather limped with one leg gone. It's so sad. 'Then they came back but not the six hundred.' Instead, they are lying on battlefields of France – not lost though, but living in imperishable time, in Canada's story. Ideals for the generation to come."

The Princess Patricia's Canadian Light Infantry marching through Ottawa on March 19, 1919. Only thirty-nine
of the Originals who had left in 1914 had returned with
them. Agar Adamson and Hamilton Gault were among
them and can be seen wearing steel helmets in the left
foreground. Despite his wooden leg, Gault insisted on
marching. "The sun shone on their helmets," wrote
Ethel Chadwick in her diary. "The flag made and presented by Princess Patricia was carried, a shabby-looking rag now, but O how glorious."

The official ceremonies over, the Patricias marched through
the city to the Exhibition Grounds at Lansdowne Park. Here,
where everything had begun four and a half years earlier, they
were formally demobilized. "By 10 PM, every man had his railway
ticket, his pay and a suit of civilian clothes," Agar wrote Mabel. "It
was very sad to see them all go, but it had to come." A few days
later, he gave a tea party for old Ottawa friends in his rooms at the

Victoria Chambers. Among them, as if to complete this tapestry neatly, was Ethel, who had tagged along with Agar's old friend Minnie Scott. "Colonel Adamson is one of the very few remaining officers of the regiment," she noted in her diary. "I gushed a bit to him on purpose. He was very merry, brought us in to see his orange pyjamas hung on the door of his room. Nice to have seen a celebrated PPCLI once again. When last I saw him, it was out at Lansdowne Park, just before they left for France."

One last thread remains. The names of many thousands of British and overseas soldiers whose bodies were never found, and who therefore could not be laid to rest beneath a white headstone with a regimental crest in one of the cemeteries tended with loving care by the Commonwealth War Graves Commission, are inscribed upon the Menin Gate at Ypres. There, every evening at sunset, "The Last Post" is sounded.

Because of his rank of major, Talbot Papineau's name heads the list of unburied Patricias. But in his case, the inscription is incorrect. Three weeks after Papineau fell at Passchendaele, a reconnaissance party led by his close friend Charlie Stewart went out across the sodden, blasted territory. "A pair of feet with reversed puttees was seen sticking out of a shellhole full of water" Agar wrote to Mabel on November 20, 1917. "Stewart said Major Papineau always wore his puttees that way. They pulled the body out, and by examining the contents of the pockets, found it to be Papineau. He had been hit by a shell in the stomach, blowing everything else away."

Stewart and the others buried Talbot and put up a rough wooden cross. It's long since gone. They never told Caroline. Tread softly at Passchendaele, because you tread upon a dream of what we might have become.

finis

Picture Credits

Principal sources are credited under these abbreviations: National Archives of Canada (NA), Canadian War Museum (CWM), Memorial University Library (MUL), University of Toronto Archives (UTA).

1   Up at Blue Sea Lake

p.3, NA PA110878; p.5, NA PA178417; p.7, NA PA178430; p.8, (left) NA C21314, (right) NA C15568

2   "An Irish Cinderella"

p.23, NA PA178425; p.26, NA PA178427; p.29, NA PA178432; p.34, (left) NA PA29975, (right) NA C19273; p.35, NA PA178424; p.38, NA PA164606; p.42, NA C23432

3   Bugles in the Distance

p.49, NA C95742; p.51, NA C20240; p.52, NA PA107278; p.58, NA PA27006; p.60, NA C18586; p.63, NA PA22759; p.66, NA PA7218 (also courtesy CWM); p.67, NA C6925

4   The Captain Returns

p.78, p.80, courtesy, Anthony Adamson

5   The Unlikely Lieutenant

p.86, Rideau Hall; p.87, NA PA34032; p.88-89 NA C11574; p.92, NA PA115905; p.93, NA PA117292; p.97, (upper) NA PA185547, (middle left) NA PA185546, (middle right) NA PA185548, (lower)

17 The Big Push

p.299, MUL, Centre for Newfoundland Studies, Joseph R. Smallwood Collection, 075; p.301, MUL, Centre for Newfoundland
Studies; p.303, MUL, Centre for Newfoundland Studies; p.307,
courtesy, Frances Innes Baird, Private Collection, St. John's;
p.308-309, NA PA1481; p.311, NA C5638; p.312, NA PA2095

18 "The Soul of Canada"

p.317, (left) NA C95269, (right) NA C93228; p.324, NA C27360;
p.325, NA PA13222

19 Confusions and Frustrations

p.331, (upper) NA C137033, (lower) NA C137035; p.337, NA PA13223;
p.339, NA PA434; p.343, NA C137034

20 Birth of a Nation

p.346-347, Sandra Gwyn; p.348-349, NA PA148872; p.358, UTA
B72-0003/034 [02]; p.359, NA C95736; p.361, UTA B72-0003/034 [06]

21 A Lucky Man

p.364, NA C95377; p.365, UTA B72-0003/034 [09]; p.369, NA PA1083;
p.370, UTA B72-0003/034 [08]; p.373, UTA B72-0003/034 [09]; p.375,
UTA B72-0003/034 [14]; p.376, (upper) UTA B72-0003/034 [15],
(lower) UTA B772-0003/034 [13]

22 Towards a Place of No Return

p.387, courtesy, Alfred Shaughnessy

23 The Lost Leader

p.391, (upper left) NA PA1229, (upper right) NA PA2165, (lower)
NA PA2084; p.396, NA PA2497; p.404, NA C977

24 The Worst of Times

p.412, NA PA65B; p.414, NA C93222; p.416, (upper) NA PA8158,
(lower) NA PA2279; p.420, NA PA24963

25 Casualty of War

p.426, p.430, courtesy, Anthony Adamson; p.433, NA PA135073

26 *The Education of Grace MacPherson*

p.436, NA PA18848; p.437 (upper) NA PA1315 (lower) NA PA1249; p.440, CWM, 8555; p.441 (upper) CWM, 8390, (lower) CWM 8409; p.442, CWM, 8667; p.450, NA PA2438; p.454, NA C80026; p.458, (upper) NA PA3747, (lower) NA PA2562

27 *The Hundred Days*

p.463, NA PA185538; p.466, NA PA185539; p.467, NA PA185536; p.472, NA PA185535; p.474, CWM, 8685; p.477, NA PA698

28 *Ave Atque Vale*

p.484, CWM, 8685; p.493, (upper) NA PA5997, (lower) courtesy, Anthony Adamson; p.495, NA PA39713

Sources

This book is based principally on primary sources: letters, diaries, personal memoirs, and scrapbooks. But I have also drawn from scores of published works. As I did in *The Private Capital*, I have listed both primary and secondary sources under the headings of the chapters in which they have been mainly used. At the outset, though, I would like to single out four books that have guided me all the way through and from which I have quoted frequently. At the top of this list is *Ordeal by Fire: Canada 1910–1945* (Doubleday, 1961) by Ralph Allen. In some ways, this popular history has been overtaken by both scholarship and sociology – nowadays it would be impossible to sketch a portrait of of pre-1914 Canada without mentioning Nellie McClung. Nevertheless, Allen summons up the temper of the times leading up to the Great War, and the reality of trench warfare as it was experienced by Canadians with an empathy and a wealth of vivid detail that has not been surpassed. I, for one, would have liked to have invented his image of Canada on the eve of the war: "For all it knew of what lay ahead, it might have been a happy child swinging a five-cent scribbler in one hand and a shiny new pencil-box in the other on the way to the first day of school." Among military histories, *The Road Past Vimy*, by D. J. Goodspeed (Macmillan of Canada, 1969) is concise, lucid, and written with great elegance. *Marching to Armageddon* by J. L. Granatstein and Desmond Morton (Lester & Orpen Dennys, 1989) is comprehensive, authoritative, and richly illustrated. And, like all writers nowadays who take the Great War as their subject, I must acknowledge a great debt owed to Paul Fussell for his masterpiece, *The Great War and Modern Memory* (Oxford University Press, 1975).

Prologue: These Years Were Their Lives

The poem by W. D. Woodhead quoted here was found in *Harold A. Innis: A Memoir,* by Eric A. Havelock, a monograph published by the Harold Innis Foundation at the University of Toronto in 1982. The substance of this work was delivered in two lectures sponsored by the Innis Foundation, given at Innis College on October 14, 1978. According to Havelock, the poem first appeared in the *Dalhousie Review* in the late 1920s. The original version was longer; the stanzas that I have quoted were quoted by Havelock from memory. As he notes, "On the whole, such words as these were more responsive to the sentiments of the returned veterans than the more familiar lines about the Flanders poppies composed by Colonel John McCrae." I am grateful to Robert Fulford for bringing Havelock's monograph to my attention and for lending me his own copy.

1: Up at Blue Sea Lake

The prime source for this chapter, and for a number of others, is a major manuscript collection in the National Archives, the papers of Ethel Chadwick (NA MG30 D258). This collection includes diaries written almost daily for more than three-quarters of a century (1895–1971) – comprising a great mass of scribblers and account books, here and there a leather-covered volume that was obviously a Christmas present – and voluminous scrapbooks covering the same period. Those contemplating taking a plunge into Ethel's diaries are well advised to take warning: while the journals of her childhood and girlhood make charming reading – all the more because they are frequently illustrated with charming water-colour sketches – the older Ethel grew, the more self-absorbed she became, and the more indecipherable her handwriting. Nevertheless, this collection is a goldmine of information about social life and customs in a post-colonial society, and about everyday life as it was lived by conventional, upper-middle-class women. Additional information about the ambience of Blue Sea Lake as an unofficial summer capital of Ottawa has been taken from an article written by Ethel Chadwick for the July 1935 issue of the Canadian society magazine, *Mayfair,* and from memories provided by Eileen Scott Morley, of London, England, formerly of Ottawa, who knew Blue Sea Lake as a child in the 1920s when the pre-war aura was preserved almost intact, and who well remembers Silver Birches and Fairview Point, and, indeed, Ethel Chadwick herself. The biographical note on the Ottawa-born actress, Margaret Anglin was drawn from *The Canadian Encyclopedia* (Hurtig Publishers Ltd., 1985); J. A. Ritchie's lines carved over the main entrance to the Parliament Buildings are quoted by John Robert Colombo in *Colombo's Canadian Quotations* (Hurtig Publishers Ltd., 1974).

Because this was a scene-setting chapter, I delved into a wide range of sources in search of period detail. Borrowings have been made from the principal academic studies of the era, *Canada: A Nation Transformed, 1896–1921,* by Robert Craig Brown and Ramsay Cook (McClelland and Stewart Ltd., 1974) and *Canada 1900–1945* by Robert Bothwell, Ian Drummond, and John English (University of Toronto Press, 1987). More specifically, the whereabouts of Prime Minister Borden at the outbreak of war were established from Borden's private diary, available on microfilm at the National Archives (NA MG26 H Vol. 449, reels C1864–C1867); of Sir Wilfrid Laurier, from *Laurier, The First Canadian* by Joseph Schull (Macmillan of Canada, 1965); of the Duke of Connaught and the militia review at Petawawa from contemporary Ottawa newspapers; of John Diefenbaker from his autobiography, *One Canada* (Macmillan of Canada, 1975); and of Lester Pearson from *Shadow of Heaven,* the recent definitive biography by John English (Lester & Orpen Dennys, 1989). English's book is also the source for the quote from the *Chatham Daily Planet:* "Many a young Leander spent the whole afternoon in the water or else lying in the sun and basking on the sand." In his engaging autobiography, *When I Was Young* (McClelland and Stewart Ltd., 1976), Raymond Massey provides an amusing account of his trip through France with his elder brother Vincent. Sir Max Aitken's astute comment about the gathering storm is found in his biography, *Beaverbrook,* by A. J. P. Taylor (Hamish Hamilton, 1972). For the description of the contents of the Ontario Fourth Reader, I am indebted to Ralph Allen's *Ordeal by Fire,* also for information about contemporary consumer products, and about those controversial railway buccaneers, Mackenzie and Mann. Notes on the *Empress of Ireland* disaster, about the *Komagata Maru,* and about the Ontario provincial election of June 1914 were mostly compiled from contemporary newspapers. *Home,* by Witold Rybczynski (Viking Penguin, 1986), provided many of the details about the increasing modernization of urban life; the information that "pregnant women rarely appeared on the streets," is taken from *The Great War and Canadian Society* (New Hogtown Press, 1978), an excellent compilation of oral history edited by Daphne Read, based upon a research project sponsored by the Opportunities for Youth programme. Sir Arthur Conan Doyle's comments on Canada appeared in the Ottawa *Citizen* for August 1, 1914. For Rupert Brooke's descriptions of Canada in 1913, I am indebted to *Rupert Brooke in Canada,* a collection of his letters and articles about Canada edited by Sandra Martin and Roger Hall (Peter Martin Associates, 1978).

2: "An Irish Cinderella"

The epigraph for this chapter comes from *A Book of One's Own: People and Their Diaries* by Thomas Mallon (Ticknor & Fields, 1984). Any reader who, like me, is intrigued by the reasons why men and women become compulsive diarists, will find answers in this idiosyncratic and beguiling anthology. Biographical material about the Duke and Duchess of Connaught is drawn mainly from the *Dictionary of National Biography.* Cynthia Asquith's remark about Connaught being "the only gentleman royalty with manners and presence" is from *Lady Cynthia Asquith; Diaries 1915–1918* (Hutchinson, 1968). Information about the Duke's long relationship with Leonie Leslie came from *Edwardians in Love,* by Anita Leslie (Hutchinson, 1972). Edward VII's acerbic comment about his younger brother – "It was all the fault of the women" – is taken from *The Enigmatic Edwardian,* a biography of the king's trusted courtier, Lord Esher, by James Lees-Milne (Sidgwick and Jackson, 1986). Katharine Villiers's recollections of pre-war Rideau Hall are contained in her autobiography, *Memoirs of a Maid of Honour* (Ivor Nicholson and Watson, 1931). *Rideau Hall*, by R. H. Hubbard (Ministry of Supply and Services, 1977), provides an excellent, if reverential, account of Connaught's term as Governor General. Otherwise, this chapter is drawn from Ethel Chadwick's diaries from 1895 to 1914, and from clippings in her scrapbooks, amplified by a childhood memoir, *Social Memories of Montreal,* that she published privately in 1967 and that exists among her papers.

3: Bugles in the Distance

Once again, Ethel Chadwick's diaries are a key source. Information about the first stages of the war comes from *The Guns of August* by Barbara Tuchman (Macmillan, 1962). C. P. "Coly" Meredith's account of his attempts to enlist is contained in his unpublished memoir at the National Archives (MG29 E62, file 12). The brief biographical sketch of the Minister of Militia, Sam Hughes, is drawn mainly from the authoritative biography, *Sam Hughes*, by Ronald G. Haycock (Wilfrid Laurier University Press, 1986). This is also the source for the description of Hughes's eccentric behaviour on the eve of the declaration of war and for the comment of Hughes's aide, John Bassett, "Contracts are sent to a great extent to those firms who have political pull . . ."

The account of Joachim Ribbentrop's time in Ottawa is derived from two sources: his own autobiography, *The Ribbentrop Memoirs,* written while awaiting execution at Nuremberg in 1946 and published some years later with an introduction by the historian Alan Bullock (Weidenfeld & Nicolson, 1954), and *This Man Ribbentrop* (Julian Messner, 1943), a biography written during the Second World War by Paul Schwarz, a former member of the German diplomatic service who had defected the Nazi regime and was then living in the United States; Schwarz's informants included a number of Ottawans who remembered Ribbentrop well. Coly Meredith notes in his memoir the story about Princess Patricia warning Ribbentrop to leave Ottawa; Meredith's theory is also noted dismissively by R. H. Hubbard in the footnotes to *Rideau Hall.*

Mackenzie King's accounts of his and Laurier's movements and conversations on the eve of the war are taken directly from King's diaries for 1914 (NA MG26 J13); so also is King's account of his reactions to watching the first Ottawa contingents marching to Ottawa's Union Station. The description of Sir Wilfrid Laurier's reaction to visiting the Tower of London in 1897 – "History has always made too much of kings and criminals" – is provided by the Canadian-born journalist who served as his guide, Henry Beckles Willson, in his memoir, *From Quebec to Piccadilly* (Jonathan Cape Ltd., 1929). This book served also as a principal source for a number of later chapters.

Accounts of the first church parade of the Princess Patricia's Canadian Light Infantry are taken from Ottawa newspapers; the account of the regiment's beginnings comes from an abbreviated history, *Princess Patricia's Canadian Light Infantry* (Leo Cooper, 1984), by Jeffery Williams, written to commemorate the seventieth anniversary of the regiment.

4: The Captain Returns

The principal source for this chapter is *Wasps in the Attic*, a wonderful, richly detailed family memoir written by Agar Adamson's younger son, the noted architect and preservationist Anthony Adamson, published privately in 1988, but available in a number of research repositories, including the National Archives, the Archives of Ontario, and the Metropolitan Toronto Reference Library. An additional source, used minimally in this chapter, but which will become increasingly important further along, is the massive collection of Adamson's letters from the Great War held at the National Archives (MG30 E149). This superbly well-organized collection contains both the originals and typed copies of all the letters that Adamson wrote daily to his wife Mabel from the Front, and a number of letters written by Mabel Adamson to her mother Mrs. John Cawthra of Toronto. The account of Adamson's time in South Africa is adapted from a longer account that appears in my own earlier book, *The Private Capital: Ambition and Love in the Age of Macdonald and Laurier* (McClelland and Stewart Ltd., 1984); this in turn was based on the letters Adamson wrote Mabel during the Boer War, also contained in the Adamson collection at the National Archives. Eileen Scott Morley's recollections of Adamson's charm were related in a conversation in London in 1989.

5: *The Unlikely Lieutenant*

I am not the first nor will I likely be the last to find Talbot Papineau an irresistable figure to write about. In 1977, Heather Robertson incorporated a number of his letters to his mother and to Beatrice Fox into the text for her book on war art, *A Terrible Beauty* (James Lorimer and Company, Ltd., 1977); a few years later, Robertson made extensive use of the letters in her remarkable novel, *Willie* (James Lorimer and Company, Ltd., 1983), in which Papineau appeared in semi-fictionalized form as a romantic hero, the great love of the book's fictional heroine, the delightful Lily Coolican, herself a kind of metaphor for Canada. In 1988, an actor playing Papineau was a central figure in Brian and Terence McKenna's film about the Great War, *The Killing Ground*.

All the letters to Caroline Papineau and to Beatrice Fox (typed copies exist of the latter, as well as the originals) are contained in the Talbot Papineau papers at the National Archives (MG30 E52, Vol. 1 and 2). This magnificent collection also includes much other documentation of Papineau's brief life, including the exchange of letters between him and Henri Bourassa. Other relevant material can be found in another Papineau family collection (MG24 B2), which includes the Montebello guest book with Laurier's signature. A pre-war album of family photographs, mostly taken at Montebello and illustrating the style of Papineau's house parties, has recently been added to the collection of the National Archives Photo Division.

The biographical sketch of Papineau has been drawn mainly from his letters and from other family material, also from a eulogy written after the war by a boyhood friend and brother officer, Major George Macdonald, and contained among Papineau's papers. (Macdonald provides the description of Papineau's speech at the Canadian Club meeting in Vancouver just as war broke out, from which he rushed back to Ottawa to enlist.) Information about his scholastic and rowing career at Oxford was kindly provided by the archivist at Brasenose College, Mrs. Elizabeth Boardman. Additional background information about the Papineau family was provided by Mme. Jacqueline DesBaillets of Montreal, daughter of Talbot's younger brother, Westcott. Notes on Lionel Curtis (1872–1955) were drawn from the *Dictionary of National Biography*. Another young Canadian targeted by this indefatigable Imperial Federalist and who proved more receptive than Papineau was Vincent Massey, as recounted in his own autobiography, *What's Past is Prologue* (Macmillan of Canada, 1963).

The description of the Princess Patricia's Canadian Light Infantry contained in this chapter is drawn from Jeffery William's brief history of the regiment, and, more importantly, from the original two-volume official history, *Princess Patricia's Canadian Light Infantry,* by Ralph Hodder-Williams (Toronto, 1921). The description of Captain Charlie Stewart was provided by Stewart's nephew, Charles Ritchie, in his memoir, *My Grandfather's House* (Macmillan of Canada, 1987), in which Stewart is the central figure in two essays, "On Leave," and "My Uncle's Medals." Agar Adamson's descriptions of training at Lévis, and the passage across the Atlantic aboard the *Royal George* are drawn from his 1914 letters.

6: The View from Basil Mansions

This chapter has been assembled from *Wasps in the Attic*, from Agar Adamson's letters, and from letters to Mrs. John Cawthra written from London by Mabel Adamson. (Most of these are contained in the Adamson collection at the National Archives; a few remain in the keeping of Anthony Adamson.) The descriptions of life in wartime London are drawn from contemporary British newspapers and magazines, most notably *The Times* and *The Lady*, and from two richly detailed social histories: *Dear Old Blighty*, by E. S. Turner (Michael Joseph, 1980), and *How We Lived Then*, by Mrs. C. S. Peel (John Lane, 1929). (The latter is the

source of the quote, "We danced every night. . . .") The astonishing information that by 1917 about 30,000 Canadian women had
travelled to London is contained in the *Canadian Annual Review*
for 1917 (p. 518). Captain Ambrose's poem about mud was found
in a commemorative volume titled *With the First Canadian Contingent*, published to raise funds for the Canadian Field Comforts
Commission (Hodder & Stoughton, 1915).

Last but not least, for much of the textural detail in this chapter
I am indebted to Anthony Adamson's exceptional memory. When,
despite persistent efforts, I was unable to gain access to Number 16
Basil Mansions, the flat in which the Adamsons lived during the war,
in order to soak up its ambience, he came to the rescue by sketching a detailed floor plan, and described in detail its furnishings,
many of which can still be seen in his own house in Toronto.

7: The Belgian Canal Boat Fund

This chapter is drawn mainly from Mabel Adamson's letters to
Mrs. Cawthra, and from *Wasps in the Attic*. Biographical information about Lady Drummond and the quotes from Lady Aberdeen
come from *Types of Canadian Women*, a useful collection of short
biographies by Henry J. Morgan (W. Briggs, 1903). Information
about the Canadian Red Cross Society in London is drawn from an
article, "Canadian Women War Workers Overseas," by Mary
Macleod Moore in *The Canadian* magazine, November 1917.
Descriptions of the suffrage society march of July 1915, and of the
rumours that pervaded London were provided by Mrs. Peel in
How We Lived Then. H. F. Gadsby's profile of Sir George Perley
appeared in *Maclean's* magazine in March 1915; further information about Perley comes from *Canada in London: An Unofficial
Glimpse of Canada's Sixteen High Commissioners*, a publication
produced by Canada House in London in 1980 to mark the centennial of Canada's first official overseas establishment, and also
from *A Peculiar Kind of Politics* by Desmond Morton (University of
Toronto Press, 1982), an interesting study of the Canadian political and military community in Britain during the Great War. The
Saturday Night editorial critical of Perley appeared in the issue for

March 29, 1919. A clipping is contained in the collection of Perley papers held at the Archives of Ontario (MU 4113).

Copies of the John Hassall poster commissioned by Mabel Adamson are still extant. I was lucky enough to acquire one at an auction of Great War ephemera held in London in 1989.

8: Fortunes of War

For the scene-setting descriptions of trench life, I am greatly indebted to *The Great War and Modern Memory*, by Paul Fussell; equally as much, in terms of the Canadian context, to *Ordeal by Fire* by Ralph Allen. Helpful also, have been the remarkable evocations of the trenches contained in *Rites of Spring: The Great War and the Birth of the Modern Age* by Modris Eksteins (Lester & Orpen Dennys, 1989). My own personal observations of the PPCLI regimental cemetery at Voormezele and other landmarks were made in the course of a pilgrimage made to the Ypres Salient in September, 1988. At one time or other, during my research, I visited all the places where my characters had been during the war, except for Gallipoli; it may be useful to note that the guidebooks I found most helpful were *A Guide to the Western Front* by Victor Neuberg (Penguin, 1988), and *Before the Colours Fade* by Rose E. B. Coombs (Plaistow Press, 1983). Otherwise this chapter is drawn from the letters of Agar Adamson and Talbot Papineau, and from the official regimental history by Ralph Hodder-Williams.

9: Pluck Against Science

The descriptions of the Battle of Bellewaerde Ridge are taken mainly from Agar Adamson's letters to Mabel, from Mabel Adamson's letters to Mrs. Cawthra, and from Hodder-Williams's regimental history. Talbot Papineau's letter describing his rescue of the regimental colours was written on July 30, 1916, to the American war correspondent, Frederick Palmer, in order to correct Palmer's erroneous report, in a book titled *My Year of the Great War,* that it was the Patricias normal practice to carry their colours into battle. "The colours are never taken into the front line, nor would they be carried into action. They have always remained in Battalion headquarters which are, however, sometimes not more than 50 to 100 yards behind the front line. The unusual situation which has led to the misunderstanding was created on May 8th, 1915 . . ." (Palmer's chapter on the Patricias was titled "The Maple Leaf Folk"; Papineau made on it a number of annotations in pencil, including the fact that "Sergeant-Major Frazer was hit while I was talking to him. I wore his cap with hole through it afterwards for 3 weeks," and sent the pages to Beatrice Fox.) Anthony Adamson's memories of Folkestone in the summer of 1915 are contained in *Wasps in the Attic*.

10: *Home Fires Burning*

Much of the textural detail about life on the home front contained in this chapter, including information about recruiting gimmicks, about the display of model trenches at the 1915 Canadian National Exhibition, and about the patriotic efforts of Muriel K. Bruce and Jessie McNab, is drawn from *Ontario and the First World War: 1914–1918*, a collection of documents edited and with an excellent introduction by Barbara M. Wilson, published by the Champlain Society (University of Toronto Press, 1977). Other information – about the post-Ypres memorial service on Parliament Hill, about the advertisements concerning mourning placed by the Ottawa department store, Murphy-Gamble, was gleaned from contemporary Ottawa newspapers. Notes on the Women's Peace Conference at The Hague and about the Canadian pacifists Laura Hughes and Alice Chown, come from Diana Chown's introduction to a new edition of *The Stairway* (University of Toronto Press, 1988), an autobiography written by her great-great aunt and published originally in 1921. The account of Laura Hughes's speech to the conference appeared in the Ottawa *Citizen* on May 1, 1915. The quote from Nellie McClung – "By the time we have emerged from the furnace of war, the clear sacrificial fire may have purified us . . ." is from *In Times Like These*, a collection of McClung's writings and speeches about the war published in 1915.

The excerpts from the diary of L. M. Montgomery used here and in other chapters are taken from *The Selected Journals of L. M. Montgomery,* Volume II, 1910–21, edited by Mary Rubio and Elizabeth Waterston (Oxford University Press, 1987). Montgomery's novel of the Great War, *Rilla of Ingleside,* is currently available in a Seal paperback edition. An excellent new study of Montgomery's work, *The Fragrance of Sweet Grass; L. M. Montgomery's Heroines and the Pursuit of Romance* by Elizabeth Rollins Epperly (University of Toronto Press, 1992) was published just as this book was being completed. In a chapter titled "Womanhood and War," Epperly discusses *Rilla of Ingleside* at length and in a preceding chapter, "Heroism's Childhood," notes that Montgomery's 1919 novel, *Rainbow Valley,* was also a response to the war. "This is a novel about the children who were to mature into the soldiers and the workers of the war."

Mackenzie King's comment about wartime skating parties at Rideau Hall was made in his diary on January 4, 1917; Coly Meredith's descriptions of Camp Petawawa and of his relations with the Russian ballistic experts come from his unpublished memoir at the National Archives (MG29 E62 File 12). Otherwise this chapter is based on the 1914–15 diaries of Ethel Chadwick.

11: The Naughty Nine

Madge Macbeth's *roman à clef* about Ottawa, *The Land of Afternoon,* was published in 1924 by Ottawa Graphic. Copies occasionally turn up in second-hand bookstores; my own copy, like many others, has been annotated in pencil by its original owner, indicating who most of the main characters "really were." Ethel Chadwick's bowdlerized account of the *Cabaret de Vogue* appeared in the Ottawa *Journal* in February 1963. Contemporary accounts were found in the *Journal* and in the *Citizen* on January 27 and 28, 1916. The social pages of these newspapers also list the names of those socially prominent citizens who attended the cabaret. The fact that Major-General Sir Willoughby Gwatkin, Chief of Staff in Ottawa during the Great War, was an amateur ornithologist who also enjoyed writing light verse is noted by Desmond Morton in *A Peculiar Kind of Politics.*

The account of the Duke of Connaught's quarrels with Sam Hughes and later with Sir Robert Borden, and the part that Colonel Edward Stanton played in them, has been pieced together from a number of sources, including Borden's 1938 autobiography and his private diary entries for March 1916. (A particular bone of contention between Connaught and Borden was the duke's opposition to United States citizens being recruited for the Canadian forces; the Prime Minister, in exasperation, instructed his principal aide, Loring Christie, who later became a diplomat of note, to draft a stiff memo outlining the constitutional position of the Governor General.) The anecdote about Hughes forcing his way into the viceregal box at the Russell Theatre is contained in *Sam Hughes*, by Russell Haycock; this is also the source for additional biographical information about Hughes and for the comment by a Canadian officer, "The mad mullah of Canada has been deposed." Hughes's remarks about the Duchess of Connaught being a spy are reported in *As the World Wags On*, a gossipy memoir by the contemporary journalist Arthur Ford, published by Ryerson Press in 1950. Borden's remark to Sir George Perley about the possibility of Sir Wilfrid Laurier being appointed Governor General is noted by Robert Craig Brown in his biography, *Robert Laird Borden* (Macmillan of Canada, 1980); the Prime Minister's annoyance at not being consulted about the Duke of Devonshire's appointment is recorded in his own private diary for June 25, 1916. Connaught's bitter comment to Sir Wilfrid Laurier – "I am chased out of the country" – was recorded on October 14, 1916, by the diarist M. O. Hammond, an editor on the staff of the Toronto *Globe*, whose papers are held at the Archives of Ontario. Hammond was quoting J. F. Mackay, business manager of the *Globe* and a close confidante of Laurier. Further evidence of the bad feeling between Connaught and Borden – which Sir Robert in later life always went out of his way to disclaim – is contained in a memorandum written by John Bassett, former aide to Sam Hughes, included as an appendix to *Men and Power*, Lord Beaverbrook's 1956 account of political machinations during the Great War. "On the Duke of Connaught's return to England, writes Bassett, "he sent Sir Wilfrid and Lady Laurier a loving-cup of remembrance, but gave no recognition whatever to Borden or his wife." It is also interesting to note that while Borden, ever-cautious, makes no mention of Connaught's impending departure until June 3, 1916, ("HRH a few days ago told me that he is taking his leave early in October") he had, in fact, been informed of Connaught's recall considerably earlier by Sir Max Aitken. ("No doubt you have been informed that Duke . . . will retire in August, but if not you can rely on this information from me," Aitken had cabled Borden on April 27. Undoubtedly Aitken's information had been provided by his close friend, Bonar Law, then Colonial Secretary (HLRO BBK/E/1/10).

The balance of this chapter is drawn from the 1916–17 diaries of Ethel Chadwick, from her entries in later years, and from the 1966 newspaper profile written by the Canadian Press reporter, Marilyn Argue.

12: Letters to an Unknown Woman

Except for a few details about the sinking of the *Lusitania* taken from contemporary newspapers, this chapter is drawn entirely from Talbot Papineau's letters to Caroline Papineau and to Beatrice Fox.

13: The City of Earthly Delights

Information about the hedonistic ambience of wartime London is provided once again by the invaluable Mrs. C. S. Peel in *How We Lived Then*, and by E. S. Turner in *Dear Old Blighty*. (Turner provides the information that Rosa Lewis of the Cavendish Hotel furnished lonely officers with everything they needed including "a nice clean tart.") Lady Diana Cooper's evocative description of "these nightmare years of tragic hysteria" is contained in the first volume of her autobiography, *The Rainbow Comes and Goes* (Rupert Hart-Davis, 1958). The Bishop of Durham's remark about drinking champagne "despite the King's example," comes from the chapter titled "Home Affairs" in *The Myriad Faces of War*, an encyclopedic account of Britain during the war years by Trevor Wilson (Polity Press, 1988). Impressions of London as it appeared to the young Canadian airmen Don Brophy and Harold Price were found in *A Rattle of Pebbles: The First World War Diaries of Two Canadian Airmen*, edited and introduced by Brereton Greenhous (Ministry of Supply and Services, 1987). Information about the Gault divorce case is drawn from Sir Robert Borden's diary for March 10, 1916, and the letters of Talbot Papineau and Agar Adamson. (In *Wasps in the Attic*, Anthony Adamson notes that at the age of ten, he too became involved in the controversy over changing the design on the regimental cap and collar badges. "My father sent me a sketch [of the new design] and I wrote back that I thought the vp on the collar badge was too big for the crown and ought to be reduced in size.")

Otherwise, this chapter is drawn from Talbot Papineau's letters to Beatrice Fox and to Caroline Papineau.

14: "An Odour of Genius"

The comments about Beaverbrook made by Malcolm Muggeridge, Michael Foot, and Clement Attlee come from *The Beaverbrook I Knew*, an anthology of personal recollections edited by Logan Gourlay (Quartet Books, 1984). Lady Diana Cooper's remark, "a strange attractive gnome with an odour of genius about him," comes from her autobiography, *The Rainbow Comes and Goes*; her recollections of hymn-singing from *The Beaverbrook I Knew*. The biographical sketch has been compiled from a number of sources, principally the biography, *Beaverbrook*, by his close friend, the historian A. J. P. Taylor, and Beaverbrook's own memoir *My Early Life* (Brunswick Press, 1965). (A comprehensive biography by the British journalists Anne Chisholm and Michael Davie, to be published in 1992, was not available at the time of writing.) Notes on the making of Beaverbrook's fortune come from *The Elements Combined*, William Kilbourn's history of the Steel Company of Canada (Clarke Irwin, 1960) and from a more recent study, *Southern Exposure: Canadian Promoters in Latin America and the Caribbean 1896–1930* by Christopher Armstrong and H. V. Nelles (University of Toronto Press, 1988). A good recent account of his time in Calgary with R. B. Bennett is contained in *R. B. Bennett, The Calgary Years*, by James Gray (University of Toronto Press, 1991). The suggestion that

Aitken had been blackballed at Montreal's Mount Royal Club is contained in *The Canadian Establishment* by Peter C. Newman (McClelland and Stewart Ltd., 1975). A private source informs that earlier he had been blackballed by the Saint John Club, not because of suspected financial chicanery but because of his treatment of Gladys Aitken. Aitken's own comment on his marriage, "My wife had a livelier interest in me than I had in her," is quoted by Taylor in his biography. Additional information about Aitken's marriage and his relations with his children is contained in *The Beaverbrook Girl,* a lively, if perhaps not entirely reliable, memoir written by his daughter, Janet Aitken Kidd, shortly before her own death (Collins, 1987). His affair with Rebecca West is recounted by Victoria Glendinning in her excellent biography, *Rebecca West* (Weidenfeld & Nicolson, 1987); West's own impressions of Aitken, thinly disguised as the Australian millionaire, Francis Pitt, are contained in her posthumously published novel, *Sunflower* (Weidenfeld & Nicolson, 1986), with an introduction by Glendinning.

A vivid account of Aitken's appearance and manner during his first days in London is given by R. D. Blumenfeld in his memoir, *All in a Lifetime* (London, 1931). Aitken himself describes the beginnings of his friendship with Bonar Law in *Politicians and the War* (Thornton-Butterworth, 1928). The letter from Law introducing him to British politics is quoted by Taylor in *Beaverbrook*; the account of his whirlwind campaign at Ashton-under-Lyne is also drawn from Taylor, and from contemporary newspaper accounts in the vast file of clippings covering every aspect of Beaverbrook's career held at the House of Lords Record Office in London. The account of his friendship with Rudyard Kipling is drawn from the file of correspondence between them, held at the House of Lords Record Office (BBK/C/197). The letter of April 1911 from Sir Robert Borden inviting Aitken to return to Canada and enter politics is contained in the file of their correspondence at the House of Lords Record Office (BBK/C/50). The description of Aitken's movements on the outbreak of war and the dinner with Winston Churchill, comes from *Politicians and the War*. This is also the source for the account of his pivotal conversation with the Irish Nationalist Member of Parliament, Tim Healy.

15: The Eyewitness – and His Witness

As remarked in the text, information as to how, exactly, Aitken secured his double appointment as "Official Eyewitness" and as head of Canadian War Records is sketchy. His telegram to Hughes of December 28, 1914, and that of Nathaniel Curry are contained in the Hughes–Aitken file at the House of Lords Record Office (HLRO BBK E/l/7).

Background information about war correspondents is drawn from Phillip Knightley's comprehensive history of combat reporting, *The First Casualty* (Harcourt, Brace, Jovanovich, 1975). Janet Aitken's impressions of Sam Hughes are contained in *The Beaverbrook Girl*. Aitken's letter to Hughes,"my admiration and affection for you is not . . . disturbed by adversity," is dated September 9, 1918 (HLRO BBK E/1/7). Lieutenant-Colonel David Watson's letter, "My Dear Old Fellow, you really are a brick," is dated August 8, 1915 (HLRO BBK E/1/12). Early reports as Official Eyewitness are contained in the large file of newspaper clippings at the House of Lords Record Office. Specifically: "Picture a narrow street . . ." is taken from the *Montreal Star* for March 27, 1915; "You can picture our army in the field spread out like a fan," from the Halifax *Herald* for April 3, 1915; the description of the Second Battle of Ypres from the Ottawa *Citizen* for May 1, 1915. Martin Gilbert's account of Aitken's deepening friendship with Winston Churchill is on page 620 of *The Challenge of War, Winston S. Churchill 1914–1916* (Heinemann, 1971).

Needless to say, nothing in the official Beaverbrook record exists to suggest that this boldest of financiers may have been lacking in physical courage. This supposition, however, does not come out of thin air. The report in the Ottawa *Journal* noting that "Sir Max Aitken was apparently not the author of the fight of the Canadian division," appeared on the editorial page on May 7, 1915, in a column titled "Notes and Comment." The item was based on information contained in the April 24 edition of a London publication titled *Canada* – presumably a newsletter for the overseas Canadian community – which ran as follows: "Sir Max Aitken, MP, has been invalided home owing to a severe attack of pneumonia. Since his arrival in England, he has made good progress and hopes to return to the front soon." That Aitken was ill with pneumonia during May 1915 is noted also by Alan Wood in a short biography, *The True History of Lord Beaverbrook* (Heineman,1965). Wood also remarks on "a matter of psychological curiosity," that Aitken, "twenty-five years later, on the outbreak of the Second World War, was to be particularly harsh in his gibing at brass-hats and staff officers. He was especially scathing in attacking, again and again, those who wore uniforms without taking part in actual combat." Clearly, the inference is that Aitken himself belonged to this category. In 1914–15, this anomaly was undoubtedly a matter of some embarrassment, all the more because Aitken, still in his mid-thirties and crackling with energy, was undeniably of military age. Thus Wood quotes also a report from the Ashton *Reporter* in Aitken's constituency, quoting Sam Hughes to the effect that "Aitken was anxious to engage in actual service but if no place could be found for him at the front he was desirous of being allowed to organize a regiment in Canada." The telegrams of November 1915 quoted in the text requesting command of a battalion and then cancelling this almost immediately are held at the House of Lords Record Office (BBK E/1/7). For reasons both of physical health and of psychic temperament, Aitken was certainly unsuited to be a front-line soldier; his hypochondria and endless pursuit of rest cures is well-documented in his papers.

The description of the Canadian War Records Office at Lombard Street as "the real centre and immediate source of authority of the Canadian Corps in Europe," appears in *From Quebec to Piccadilly* by Henry Beckles Willson (Jonathan Cape Ltd., 1929). Aitken's own official reports of the operations of the office are held at the House of Lords Record Office (BBK E/1/20). The account of Beckles Willson's life and career is drawn from this memoir, and also from the original diaries on which it was based, and which are in the keeping of his grandson, Anthony Beckles Willson of Twickenham, England. (The riveting pen portrait of Sam Hughes, and the amusing account of the "lady copyists" appears only in the diaries.) Beckles Willson's account of the meeting between Aitken and General Alderson at the Marlborough Club on March 27, 1916, is taken directly from his diary; a broadly similar account drawn from the diary appears also in *From Quebec to Piccadilly*.

16: The Destruction of General Alderson

My conviction that Aitken, acting single-handedly rather than on behalf of the Canadian government, and with instructions from no one, not only secured the removal of General Sir Edwin Alderson as Canadian Corps Commander, but selected General Sir Julian Byng to replace him, is based on a number of sources: Sir Robert Borden's 1938 autobiography and personal diary; the diaries of the British Commander-in-Chief, Sir Douglas Haig; Aitken's report of his April 23, 1916, meeting with Haig to Sam Hughes (HLRO BBK E/1/7); Beckles Willson's book, *From Quebec to Piccadilly*, and Willson's original diaries. Yet another indication that Borden himself was entirely in the dark about events is a telegram from Aitken to Haig dated April 27, 1916. "I have received a telegram from Sir Robert Borden advising me that Cabinet has approved of my proposal [to offer Alderson the post of Inspector General of Canadian troops in England] and I will deliver communication to War Office today. Sir Robert Borden asks for information about Major-General Byng and I hope you will not find it necessary to action in this connection until I communicate Sir Robert's views to you." (HLRO BBK E/1/7). The most comprehensive published account of the affair is provided by Russell Haycock in *Sam Hughes*. Haycock too is convinced that "it was Aitken's pressure on Haig that decided the outcome" (p. 298), although he does not specifically suggest that it was also Aitken who had promoted Byng as Hughes's replacement. A few anomalies remain: Haig's own diary account of the conversation between him and Aitken is dated April 21, 1916, when in fact their meeting took place on April 23. However, as the British military historian Denis Winter points out in his recent authoritative study, *Haig's Command* (Viking, 1991), Haig rewrote and amended his diaries after the war.

Alderson's *curriculum vitae* prior to the war is contained in the file of correspondence between him and Aitken at the House of Lords Record Office. (BBK E/1/11). His dismay at the Canadian equipment selected by Hughes is recorded by Desmond Morton in *A Peculiar Kind of Politics*; this is also the source for Alderson's letter to Connaught about the poor quality of Canadian officers.

Daniel Dancocks, in his authoritative study of Second Ypres, *Welcome to Flanders Fields* (McClelland and Stewart Ltd., 1988), provides a good account of Alderson's performance during that battle, also that of General Richard Turner and Garnet Hughes; this is also the source for Alderson's comment, "Canadian politics have been too strong for all of us." Alderson's letter to Aitken regarding Garnet Hughes's promotion, "I did not think that Hughes had the necessary experience," is dated October 18, 1915 (HLRO BBK E/1/11); Aitken's subsequent letter to Sir Robert Borden, "Unfortunately General Alderson was most inconsistent . . ." is dated December 3, 1915 (HLRO BBK C/50). The account of the confrontation between Alderson and Hughes over the Ross Rifle is drawn mainly from *Sam Hughes* by Russell Haycock and from *A Peculiar Kind of Politics*. Alderson's letters to Aitken after his dismissal are contained in his file in the Beaverbrook papers (HLRO BBK E/1/11). Byng's letter to Blumenfeld about his own appointment as Commander of the Canadian Corps is quoted by Jeffery Williams in his biography *Byng of Vimy* (Leo Cooper/Secker and Warburg, 1983). Williams also notes that Byng, immediately upon taking over command of the Canadian Corps was concerned about political interference, and that "Blumenfeld asked Byng to take Max Aitken into his confidence, suggesting that he should be able to help." That Aitken was co-operative and, bowing to the inevitable, had recognized that the price of Alderson's dismissal would be a diminution of his and Hughes's influence, is demonstrated by a letter written by Byng to Blumenfeld on June 18, 1916, also quoted by Williams: "He seemed to realize that the state of affairs was impossible and I hope he also realized that I would resign if present state of affairs continued. There is nothing else for it, to officer these splendid men with political protegés is nothing short of criminal." (That Aitken, on at least one occasion, was forced to eat humble pie is demonstrated by a communication sent to him on June 8, 1916, by his personal representative at Canadian Corps Headquarters, the unflappable Lieutenant-Colonel R. F. Manly-Sims. "General Byng impressed upon me that he . . . proposed to make his own appointments. . . . On my return, I received your wire relating to the 2nd Brigade and can clearly see a clash coming.")

The account of Beckles Willson's downfall at the War Records Office is taken from his own diaries, and also from the war diaries of Sir Arthur Doughty held at the National Archives (MG30 D226 Vol. 8). Willson's demand that Byng "paint him a word picture of the deeds of the Canadians" is contained in a letter about the incident written to Aitken by his personal representative at the front, Lieutenant-Colonel R. F. Manly-Sims. This, and Aitken's subsequent letter to Borden, ". . . Mr. Willson has defied my best efforts on his behalf . . . ," are contained in Willson's file in the Beaverbrook papers (HLRO BBK/E/1/15). Notes on Beckles Willson's future career are taken from *From Quebec to Piccadilly*, and from his diaries. Willson's postwar novel, *Redemption,* was published by Putnam's in 1924. Information about the career of his son, Gordon Beckles Willson, was provided by Anthony Beckles Willson.

Aitken's difficulties with military censors over the second volume of *Canada in Flanders* are recorded in *The Great War of Words: British, American and Canadian Propaganda and Fiction, 1914–33* by Peter Buitenhuis (University of British Columbia Press, 1987). For the account of the Canadian War Memorials Fund, I am greatly indebted to *Art at the Service of War*, an excellent study by Maria Tippett (University of Toronto Press, 1984). A. Y. Jackson's account of his meeting with Beaverbrook is taken from Jackson's autobiography, *A Painter's Country* (Clarke Irwin, 1958). An intriguing scholarly deconstruction of the faked "Over the Top" photographs taken by Ivor Castle of the Canadian War Records Office is provided in a paper titled *Reading the Unwritten Record: How to Dissect Photographs as a Primary Source for Historical Research*, by Lilly Koltun, Director of the Documentary Art and Photography Division of the National Archives. This paper was presented at a symposium on social history and photography held at the Art Gallery of Mount Saint Vincent University in 1985, of which the proceedings have been published.

17: The Big Push

Notes on the bleak mood that prevailed in 1916 – "the year when the war stopped being aberration and turned into a nightmare" – are drawn mainly from *The First World War: An Illustrated History*, by A. J. P. Tayor (Hamish Hamilton, 1963, currently available in a Penguin edition). This is also the source for the broad-brush-stroke descriptions of the Battle of the Somme. Admiral David Beatty's quote about Jutland was found in the anthology, *Voices from the Great War*, compiled and edited by Peter Vansittart (Jonathan Cape Ltd., 1981). In the matter of Kitchener's death at sea, the Dominion Archivist Arthur Doughty, who had called upon Kitchener a month earlier and presented him with a copy of his biography of Madeleine de Verchères, provides an interesting footnote, more revealing of the author than of the War Minister. "His loss is felt to be a national one," Doughty wrote on June 6, 1916. "It is a source of gratification to me to have had such an interesting conversation with him just before his fatal trip. I am glad that I delivered to him the first copy of *A Daughter of New France*. He told Sir George Arthur, his secretary, that it was the most charming book he had ever seen."

Background detail on the Royal Newfoundland Regiment is drawn from *The Fighting Newfoundlander*, the official history by Colonel G. W. L. Nicholson (Government of Newfoundland, 1964), from *What Became of Corporal Pitman?* by Joy B. Cave (Breakwater Books, 1978), and from the account written by Captain Leo C. Murphy, contained in the *Book of Newfoundland*, edited and published by Joseph Roberts Smallwood (Vol. 2, 1937). (Borrowing Aitken's title, Murphy is described as "Official Eyewitness.") The book that best describes the nature of Newfoundland's tragedy during the Great War and its effect upon future generations is *The Danger Tree: Memory, War and the Search for a Family's Past* by David Macfarlane (Macfarlane, Walter & Ross, 1991).

John Gallishaw's book, *Trenching at Gallipoli* was published in New York in 1916. Copies nowadays are collector's items: two that I know of and have consulted are held respectively at the Centre for Newfoundland Studies at Memorial University Library in St. John's and at the Imperial War Museum in London. Unfortunately – time and distance were factors here – I was unable to find out as much about Gallishaw as I would have liked. Unusually for St. John's, he and the entire Gallishaw family seem to have faded out of living memory. An article in the *Newfoundland Quarterly* for December 1910 suggests that his forebears, and perhaps his father, had been employed as harbour pilots for the port of St. John's. From St. John's city directories, I was able to establish that in 1909, he and three sisters, Agnes, Kate and Henrietta lived with their widowed mother, Anastasia, at 16 Bannerman Street in St. John's. By 1913, "Alonzo John" no longer appears in the directory, but Anastasia, Agnes (described now as a "milliner"), and Kate (a saleslady at Ayre and Sons department store) were still listed as living at their previous address. Thus, it's reasonable to guess that Gallishaw's sisters had helped pay for his education. (A few members of the elder generation still recall Agnes Gallishaw's hat shop on Cochrane Street.) One who did know Gallishaw well and assigned him a place in history was J. R. "Joey" Smallwood: since Gallishaw was a full decade older than Smallwood, it is most likely they became friends during the early 1920s, when Joey was working in New York as a newspaper reporter and Gallishaw was lecturing at Harvard. In any event, apart from *Trenching at Gallipoli*, the brief biographical sketch of Gallishaw is drawn from the account written by Smallwood in the *Encyclopedia of Newfoundland* (Vol. 1, 1983). From this, it is evident that Gallishaw, who was born in 1890, lived to a ripe old age, since the citation notes an interview between them conducted (presumably over the telephone) in June 1982.

As to Owen Steele, typed copies of his letters home are preserved in a blue leather album held in the archives of the Centre for Newfoundland Studies at Memorial University Library. Notes on the Canadian role at Courcelette and Regina Trench, and about the first appearance of tanks, are drawn mainly from *The Road Past Vimy* by D. J. Goodspeed, and from Agar Adamson's letters. (In a report for the War Records Office, dated September 14, 1916, Talbot Papineau notes: "This AM I visited the section of Heavy Section Motor Machine Gun Corps attached to the Canadian Corps for the offensive of September 15. . . . Seven of these strange monsters had arrived at night, crossing open country and independent of all roads. They had parked outside Albert. Although rumours had spread like wildfire, their secret had been well-kept. Each one had its name: Cupid, Champagne, Cognac, Cordon Rouge, Chablis.")

18: *"The Soul of Canada"*

Thanks to the public-spirited/entrepreneurial efforts of Arthur Hawkes, a British-born journalist then employed by the Toronto *Star*, the exchange of letters between Talbot Papineau and Henri Bourassa was published in pamphlet form in 1916, under the title *Canadian Nationalism and the War,* and sold for 10 cents a copy. The copy that I used was found among Talbot Papineau's papers. A copy of the report of Papineau's letter in *The Times* was subsequently reprinted under the heading, *The Soul of Canada,* in *The Brazen Nose*, the magazine of Brasenose College, and was provided to me by the college archivist. Copies of numerous congratulatory letters written to Papineau, including the letter from Andrew McMaster reporting Laurier's comments, and the note from Lionel Curtis, are contained among his papers.

In *Ordeal by Fire*, Ralph Allen provides an excellent background account of Regulation Seventeen and its tragic effects. My principal guide to Henri Bourassa's attitudes towards the war, and to his speeches and writings, was *The French Canadians* by Mason Wade (Vol. 2, 1911–67, Macmillan of Canada, 1968). Unremarkable for insight and overtaken by more recent scholarship, this work remains invaluable for its encyclopedic day-by-day chronicling of events. The balance of this chapter is drawn from Papineau's letters to his mother and to Beatrice Fox.

19: *Confusions and Frustrations*

Except for Agar Adamson's letter of August 8, 1916 – "Papineau turned up two days ago with a cinematographic camera" – and his subsequent letters about the Battle of Vimy Ridge, which are contained among his papers, this chapter is drawn mainly from Talbot Papineau's letters to Beatrice Fox and Caroline Papineau. A copy of *The War and Its Influences Upon Canada*, the speech delivered by Papineau to the Canadian Corps school at Pernes, France, in February 1917, is contained among his papers. (After the war, on January 26, 1920, this speech was read aloud to the members of the Canadian Club of Montreal by E. Languedoc, KC, prefaced by a short eulogy written and delivered by Major George Macdonald, from which, as noted earlier, some biographical detail about Papineau was drawn.)

20: Birth of a Nation
21: A Lucky Man

My entry point and principal source for both of these chapters in which Harold Adams Innis is the central figure, is a superb doctoral thesis, *Marginal Man* by Alexander John Watson submitted to the University of Toronto in 1981. As noted in the text, this is the closest work yet to a full-scale intellectual biography of Canada's first major scholar, and I am greatly indebted to John Watson, now Executive Director of CARE Canada, for his generosity in allowing me to quote from it extensively and to adopt his own organizing principle – "The war was Innis's patron . . ." – as my own. I should also note here that it was John Watson and not me who first identified Innis's notes for a reply to a toast to returned veterans as the piece of "found poetry" that appears as epigraph to chapter twenty-one. I also owe a debt to Professor Mel Watkins of the University of Toronto for bringing *Marginal Man* to my attention and for lending me his own copy. Another important source has been *Harold Adams Innis: Portrait of a Scholar*; a biography written by his close friend, the historian Donald Creighton (University of Toronto Press, 1962). I have drawn also from *The Idea File of Harold Adams Innis*, introduced and edited by William Christian (University of Toronto Press, 1983); from *Harold Innis As I Remember Him*, an essay by another close friend, Arthur Lower, published in the *Journal of Canadian Studies* (Vol. 20, No. 4, winter 1985–86); and from *Harold A. Innis*, a memoir by Eric A. Havelock with a preface by Marshall McLuhan, published by the Harold Innis Foundation at the University of Toronto in 1982. (The substance of Havelock's monograph was delivered in two lectures given at Innis College at the University of Toronto in October 1978.) As noted earlier, the poem by W. D. Woodhead quoted in the prologue of this book was found in Havelock's monograph. I am also indebted to Elspeth Chisholm and to Paul Kennedy for excerpts from their radio documentary studies of Harold Innis undertaken, respectively, for CBC Tuesday Night (1972) and CBC Ideas (1978). (The revealing quote of George V. Ferguson about Innis's attitude to the war is contained in the transcript of Elspeth Chisholm's interview with Ferguson held at the University of Toronto Archives.)

Otherwise the discussion of Harold Innis contained in these two chapters is based upon my own minings of papers relating to his childhood and young manhood, including his wartime diary and letters held at the University of Toronto Archives (B72-0003).

Notes on the battle of Vimy are taken mainly from D. J. Goodspeed, *The Road Past Vimy,* and from Pierre Berton's excellent popular history, *Vimy* (McClelland and Stewart Ltd., 1986). My own impressions of the Vimy memorial as an astonishing expression of Canadian selfhood derive from visits made there in September 1988 and October 1991.

22: *Towards a Place of No Return*

As will be evident from the text, this chapter is mainly derived from Talbot Papineau's letters to Beatrice Fox and Caroline Papineau. Indications of Talbot's fear of death and, even more, of mutilation are contained in a long letter written to him by Lieutenant-Colonel R. F. Manly-Sims shortly after his return to the regiment. A letter written to Beaverbrook by Manly-Sims on May 20, 1917, about the possibility of Papineau returning to the War Records Office to write the third volume of *Canada in Flanders* is also revealing of the pressures on him: "It appears that Papineau is even now considering returning to his battalion as a company commander, in view of the fact that until he is more experienced, there is little probability of promotion for him on the staff. Personally, I think the struggle is still going on in his mind as between his military and literary instincts. . . ." (By default, the task of completing *Canada in Flanders* went to Charles G. D. Roberts, the New Brunswick author and poet.)

Agar Adamson's letters to Mabel about Papineau are contained in Adamson's correspondence for 1917. (The letter about the difficult interview between him and Papineau was written on May 11; his letter about Papineau's resourcefulness in battle on June 15.) The letter of October 15, 1917, from Papineau to Sarah Shaughnessy was written from Hotel Jules, Jermyn Street, and is quoted in *Sarah: The Letters and Diaries of a Courtier's Wife,* edited by Alfred Shaughnessy (Peter Owen, 1989). The letter from John Archibald to Beatrice Fox – "Talbot knew he was going into a place from which he was likely enough not to return" – exists among Papineau's papers.

23: The Lost Leader

The descriptions of Passchendaele have been drawn from a number of sources, most notably D. J. Goodspeed's *The Road Past Vimy* and *Marching to Armageddon* by Granatstein and Morton. About this horrific engagement, even this long after the fact, it is difficult to be other than enraged by the military stupidity, all the more because a hero of this book, Talbot Papineau, was killed during it on October 30, 1917, a few moments after remarking to a brother officer, "You know, Hughie, this is suicide." It should be recorded, though, that in his well-researched book, *Legacy of Valour: The Canadians at Passchendaele* (Hurtig Publishers Ltd., 1986) Daniel Dancocks presents a well-argued case for the oppo-site opinion; that Haig, despite all the blood-letting, was militarily correct in pursuing the Battle of Passchendaele, for purposes of wearing down the German armies by attrition. The last word on Passchendaele as an exercise in futility, however, is provided by the British military historian, Denis Winter, in a superbly docu-mented study, *Haig's Command* (Viking, 1991). Even now, as Winter notes, "Most of Passchendaele's statistics have been with-held from the Public Record Office [in London], but the implica-tions . . . are as clear to us as they were to those in a position to know the facts at the time. Josiah Wedgewood, a radical MP . . . was one of those who did know what was happening. His memoirs describe a graphic eyewitness account of the battlefield he deliv-ered to the House of Commons. On leaving the Chamber, Bonar Law came over from the government's front bench and said to him, 'you did right to say what you did but never let any of that be known outside. The public could not bear it.'"

The description of the role played by the PPCLI at Passchendaele is drawn mainly from Hodder-Williams's regimental history. Agar Adamson's letter to Mabel – "I cannot help wondering if the position was worth the awful sacrifice of life" – is contained among his letters for 1917. Talbot Papineau's message of 11:05 PM on October 29 is contained in the narrative of operations of the PPCLI during Passchendaele, written and signed by the adjutant, and found among Adamson's papers; his last remark to Major Hugh Niven is quoted by Jeffery Williams in his 1974 short history of the regiment. The farewell letters to Beatrice Fox and to Caroline Papineau can be found among Talbot's papers, as can the programme of the memorial service at Holy Trinity Brompton and the poem, *There Is No Death*, sent to Caroline Papineau by a friend; the eulogies written about Papineau in both Canadian and British papers were reprinted in *The Brazen Nose*. Further details of Caroline's later life, and about the sale of Montebello, were also gleaned from the Papineau papers; similarly the note about Joseph Bech's meeting with Mackenzie King in San Francisco in 1945. Information about Jay Rogers's conversation with King was provided by Jacqueline DesBaillets. Notes on Montebello's incarnation as the Seigniory Club and as the hotel, Chateau Montebello, were taken from a short article that I researched and wrote for the July-August 1979 issue of *Saturday Night*. Mackenzie King's note on Papineau's death – "one of the finest and bravest of men, a great loss to Canada . . ." – appears in his diary for November 3, 1917. The words of Beatrice Fox – "If you think that as a bit of dream-stuff which has outlasted the war, it is precious" – are quoted from the covering letter accompanying her 1934 gift of Papineau's letters to the Canadian Army Historical Section. (In the early 1960s these letters, and also the letters written by Papineau to his mother, Caroline Rogers Papineau, were transferred to the National Archives, along with other family papers.) Information about Beatrice's career as a sculptor was found in *Mantle Fielding's Dictionary of American Painters, Sculptors and Engravers* (Apollo Book, 1987). Additional details were provided by Bill Lang, head of the Art Department of The Free Library of Philadelphia. Beatrice's obituary appeared in the New York *Times* on December 7, 1968. The information that her portrait bust of Sir Wilfrid Grenfell can still be seen in the chapel of the International Grenfell Association Hospital in St. Anthony, Newfoundland, was provided by Ronald Rompkey, author of the excellent biography *Grenfell of Labrador* (University of Toronto Press, 1991).

24: *The Worst of Times*

Atmospheric details providing the description of the winter of 1917–18 as the "worst of times" are drawn from a number of sources including *How We Lived Then* by Mrs. C. S. Peel, *Dear Old Blighty*, by E. S. Turner, and *Marching to Armageddon* by Granatstein and Morton. The information that cocaine-sniffing was sometimes described by Canadian soldiers by the code-expression, "hooking up the reindeers," is taken from *Gunner Ferguson's Diary* (Lancelot Press Ltd., 1985), an intriguing personal account of the war written by an artillery private from Nova Scotia, Frank Byron Ferguson, edited by Peter G. Rogers, and kindly brought to my attention by John Bell of the National Archives. Information about the Halifax explosion of December 6, 1917, is taken from the official report of the disaster, a brilliant account prepared by Archibald MacMechan, the legendary professor of English at Dalhousie University. (Curiously, MacMechan's report languished unpublished until 1978 when, along with a number of relevant documents compiled and edited by Graham Metson, it was issued by McGraw-Hill Ryerson.)

Notes on the Conscription Crisis of 1917 and the Khaki Election and its aftermath are also drawn from a variety of sources, including *Ordeal by Fire* by Ralph Allen, *The French Canadians* by Mason Wade, and *Borden: His Life and World,* a lively short biography by John English (McGraw-Hill Ryerson, 1977). (This work is also the source of the anti-Quebec quotes from the *Manitoba Free Press* and the *Toronto News.*) A short biographical appreciation of the pacifist-feminist Francis Marion Beynon by Anne Hicks introduces a recent edition of Beynon's novel, *Aleta Dey* (Virago Press, 1988). A dramatized account of the conflict between Nellie McClung and Francis Beynon is provided by Wendy Lill's 1984 play, *The Fighting Days*. General Arthur Currie's refusal to obey Haig's order to dismantle the Canadian Corps is noted by Granatstein and Morton in *Marching to Armageddon*. A more detailed account of this affair is contained in *General Sir Arthur Currie: A Military Biography,* by A. M. J. Hyatt (University of Toronto Press, 1987).

The account of Sir Robert Borden as a nascent Canadian nationalist is drawn from the definitive biography by Robert Craig Brown, also from John English's, *Borden: His Life and World*, and from Borden's own private diary. The gist of Borden's speech to the Imperial War Cabinet on June 13, 1918, has frequently been quoted; the fact that "he spoke with mounting anger and concluded his denunciation by striding up to Lloyd George, seizing his lapels and shaking him," is noted by Denis Winter in *Haig's Command*. (Winter cites as his source, "severely pruned Cabinet minutes.")

25: Casualty of War

This chapter is drawn almost entirely from Agar Adamson's letters and from *Wasps in the Attic*. The letters describing the sexual exploits of a Canadian officer on leave were provided to me by a private source.

26: The Education of Grace MacPherson

The diaries of Grace MacPherson, upon which this chapter is based, were kindly lent to me by her daughter, Diana Filer. A copy of the diaries, along with a number of relevant newspaper clippings and a copy of the speech describing her wartime experiences, made by MacPherson to a gathering of Vancouver women after the war, is available at the Canadian War Museum in Ottawa. Diana Filer also provided information about her mother's postwar life.

Notes on the participation of Canadian army nurses in the Great War were taken from *Canada's Nursing Sisters* by G. W. L. Nicholson, a comprehensive account published by the National Museums of Canada in 1975. Information about munitions workers (including the recollections of "Elaine Nelson") was found in *The Great War and Canadian Society*, that most useful oral history originating in an Opportunities for Youth project edited by Daphne Read and published in Toronto by New Hogtown Press in 1978. The figure of 35,000 female munitions workers in Quebec and Ontario is contained in *Canadian Women: A History* by Alison Prentice and others (Harcourt, Brace, Jovanovich, 1988). The comment of an army chaplain about medical services comes from *My Grandfather's War: Canadians Remember the First World War* by William D. Mathieson (Macmillan of Canada, 1981). Useful background information about Red Cross ambulance drivers during the Great War is contained in *The Roses of No Man's Land*, by Lyn Macdonald (Michael Joseph, 1980). F. Tennyson Jesse's article about the convoy at Etaples in British *Vogue* was found in *The Vogue Bedside Book*, edited by Josephine Ross (Hutchinson, 1984). Vera Brittain's impressions of the hospital complex at Etaples are contained in *Testament of Youth*, her brilliant and anguished account of the war, first published in 1931 and reissued in 1978 by Virago Press. An interesting sociological novel documenting the changing role of women during the war is *We That Were Young*, by Irene Rathbone, originally published in 1932 and reissued by Virago in 1988. (Rathbone was writing about the experiences of Englishwomen, but those of many Canadian women, including Grace MacPherson, were comparable.) A moving personal account of the effects of the war on a young Canadian woman and her family is contained in *But This Is Our War*, by Grace Morris Craig (University of Toronto Press, 1981).

27: The Hundred Days

This chapter is derived mainly from an unpublished memoir written by Brooke Claxton, contained among Claxton's papers at the National Archives (MG32 B5 Vol. 220-224). Background information about Canadian participation in this last stage of the war has been provided by Granatstein and Morton in *Marching to Armageddon* and by D. J. Goodspeed in *The Road Past Vimy*. The biographical sketch of General Sir Arthur Currie and the account of his quarrel with Sam Hughes and Garnet Hughes is drawn from information provided by A. M. J. Hyatt in his comprehensive study *General Sir Arthur Currie: A Military Biography* (University of Toronto Press, 1987). Additional information about the feud between Currie and the Hughes *père et fils*, including the fact that Beaverbrook, as a close friend of Hughes, was probably involved in it, was found in *Amid the Guns Below*, a short history of the Canadian Corps by Larry Worthington (McClelland and Stewart Ltd., 1965).

The information that twenty-five Canadian soldiers were executed by firing squad during the Great War is taken from *The Supreme Penalty*, an article by the military historian Desmond Morton, that appeared in the Autumn 1972 issue of the *Queen's Quarterly*. An extraordinary account of the last hours of one of these condemned Canadians was written by the Canadian army chaplain, Canon F. G. Scott, in his memoir, *The Great War As I Saw It* (Clarke & Stuart, 1934) and is quoted by Heather Robertson in *A Terrible Beauty* (James Lorimer and Company Ltd., 1977).

28: Ave Atque Vale

Notes on Armistice celebrations in London and Paris are taken from *A Stillness Heard Round the World: The End of the Great War* by Stanley Weintraub (George Allen & Unwin, 1986). Information on celebrations in Ottawa comes from clippings from the *Citizen* and the *Journal* contained in the scrapbooks of Ethel Chadwick. Information about Brooke Claxton's post-war career and his involvement with the "Canadian Movement" is taken mainly from his unpublished memoir. A clipping of his short essay, "The Unreturning Army That Was Youth," is contained in a photo album cum scrapbook of Claxton's, held at the Photo Division of the National Archives. The role played by Claxton in the establishment of the Massey Commission and of the Canada Council is described in an article that I wrote in 1977 to mark the twentieth anniversary of the council's founding. This was published in *Saturday Night*, in June 1977. The key information was provided by interviews with the Right Honourable J. W. Pickersgill and Père Georges-Henri Lévesque.

Princess Patricia's farewell to her regiment in February 1919 and the ceremonies that surrounded its demobilization in Ottawa the following month were described by Agar Adamson in post-war letters to Mabel. The princess's letter to Adamson is contained among his papers. Ethel Chadwick's account of the Patricias return and of Adamson's tea party are taken from her diary for 1919.

Adamson's letter about the finding of Talbot Papineau's body was written to Mabel on November 20, 1917, three weeks after Papineau's death at Passchendaele. Charlie Stewart's letter to Adamson describing this gruesome discovery was written on November 16, 1917, and is contained among Adamson's papers. "We found Talbot's body and are having a service and putting up a cross tomorrow."

Just over ten months later, on September 26, 1918, Stewart himself, now Commanding Officer of the PPCLI, was killed at Bourlon Wood on the eve of the great Canadian victory at Canal du Nord. In his memoir, *My Grandfather's House*, Stewart's nephew and namesake, Charles Ritchie, describes how in 1919 he and his mother and younger brother made a pilgrimage to Charlie Stewart's grave.

Index

An "ill" after a page number indicates an illustration.
An "n" after a page number indicates a footnote.

A